THE GRAND MINOR LEAGUE

AN ORAL HISTORY
OF THE OLD PACIFIC
COAST LEAGUE

Jacob Ruppert, owner of the New York Yankees, came to Oakland in October, 1935, to see his star acquisition, Joe DiMaggio, play in the Alameda Elks Major-Minor League game.

THE
GRAND
MINOR LEAGUE

AN ORAL HISTORY OF THE
OLD PACIFIC COAST LEAGUE

DICK DOBBINS

WOODFORD PRESS

In Loving Memory of Dick Dobbins

Woodford Press
5900 Hollis Street, Emeryville, CA 94608
Visit our website at www.woodfordpub.com

Book design: Jim Santore
Cover design: Pat O'Connell

ISBN: 0-942627-51-2 (softcover), 0-942627-53-9 (hardcover)
Library of Congress Catalog Card Number: 99-61467

Printed and bound in Canada
Distributed to the trade by Andrews McMeel Universal, Kansas City, MO

To order additional copies of this book or for a Woodford Press catalog, please call toll-free 1-888-USA-BOOK or (510) 250-3006.

CONTENTS

ACKNOWLEDGMENTS

*I*f you ask longtime baseball fans to name their favorite book in baseball literature, many will recommend *The Glory Of Their Times*, by Lawrence Ritter (MacMillan, 1966).

Ritter made the most of a simple concept. He interviewed 22 players from the first few decades of the century and let their comments speak for themselves. Apart from cleaning up grammar and eliminating redundancies, he did little editing and editorializing. The result is one of the most revealing and nostalgically appealing baseball books ever published.

I kept Ritter's book in mind whenever I discussed baseball with friends, students and colleagues during my career as an educator. Ritter's approach also inspired much of what appears in this book.

In 1990, I retired from thirty-two years as a high school teacher and administrator. I had many ardent baseball fans in my classes, but I consistently refused to allow them to nudge me off of the day's topic to talk about baseball. I must admit this was a ploy I attempted in my youth. As a teacher, I was more than willing to talk baseball during the breaks between classes, but let me earn my keep during class time.

Later, as an administrator, I was in charge of the school's attendance, and I admit to allowing students to "legally" cut school on opening day of the baseball season. After all, I had to be consistent. When I was a high school student, somehow I managed to catch the openers each year, the only times I ever cut school.

After college, my passion for the game included research, and I soon found myself writing, and being asked to write, articles on some facet of California's marvelous baseball tradition. By the time I retired, I figure I had written almost 100 baseball articles.

Once I retired, people started saying, "Now you can write your book." My response was, "No, that's hard work." But four years later, in collaboration with my good friend Jon Twichell, I completed *Nuggets on the Diamond*, a history book about the development of baseball in the San Francisco-Oakland Bay Area.

As I began the project, I asked myself how I could possibly write 200 pages on the subject.

Well, after spending hundreds of hours bent over newspaper microfilms and Pacific Coast League record books, my concern shifted to how I could squeeze all the information into 300 pages. In fact, almost forty pages were cut to bring the count down to 300.

The research also included interviews of the players. Like Ritter, I found out these men were intelligent, positive and very willing to share their memories of the PCL. These men are the treasures. All I tried to do was to immortalize them through the written word.

Artistically, *Nuggets* was a huge success. Financially and tactically, I can't say the same. Although it was backed by a good promotional campaign, sales were hurt by a truckers' strike as the book was being delivered, and by a baseball players' walkout, the Strike of '94.

Well, I finally made it into the black, but only after restarting our promotional campaign after the strike was over.

Why would I ever want to do a second book after all the problems with the first one? My wife kept asking me that question. The bottom line is, it was fun! The people I met and the encouragement I got made it worthwhile. And I already had a topic. Since the first book was about the Bay Area, book number two could be on the rest of the West Coast teams. My focus would be on the old Pacific Coast League, the league that dominated West Coast baseball before the New York Giants and Brooklyn Dodgers moved west.

Book two had to be different from book one. This is where Ritter's concept came into play. I could let the players speak for themselves. Speakers are identified with tag lines after their quotes, with the pertinent team affiliation added to each tag.

While this book includes a fair amount of factual and background information (espcially in the photo captions), it is not a comprehensive history of the PCL. Rather, it is a collection of observations about the Coast League and its lore that highlight the cunning, playing skills, humor and emotion that made the league special.

I also wanted to examine the differences between the game today and the way it was played forty years ago. In order to sell the beauty of the Pacific Coast League of the 1940s or 1950s, I had to show there *is* a difference.

One way to illustrate the differences is to discuss what we have witnessed at the ballpark recently. I remember the ball bouncing off Jose Canseco's noggin and going over the fence for an unorthodox home run. And how many times have I witnessed Raul Mondesi of the hated Dodgers picking up a one-bounce single to right field and throwing a one-bouncer to third base, missing the cutoff man, the third baseman and the pitcher backing him up?

How many times have we seen the batter miss a perfect bunt pitch? That's OK, though, because the catcher promptly threw the ball into center field, allowing the runner to advance anyway.

We could go on.

Did misplays like this happen forty and fifty years ago? Of course they did. Did they happen as frequently? No, they did not. Virtually every player I talked to made an important point: When they reached the PCL, they had to know how to play the game and not make those types of errors, because if they did, they were gone quickly. Today's style of baseball would not have been tolerated then by the fans, the manager or the players.

Research and interviews for *The Grand Minor League* required me to travel to cities outside the Bay Area. But that too was fun. So for Book Two, the format is the same, it just includes a different cast of characters.

During a trip to San Diego, for example, I was able to interview Johnny Ritchey and his charming wife Lidya. This was a key interview because Johnny was the first black player in the league. I also met with and/or talked to former players such as Pete Coscarart, George McDonald, Tony Criscola, Frank Kerr, John "Swede" Jensen, Jack Graham, Ed "Bud" Stewart, Jack Harshman, plus Bob Kerrigan and Eddie Erautt, teammates on the famous 1954 Padres.

During a trip to the Sacramento area, I interviewed players Jim Westlake, Carl "Buddy" Peterson, Ferris Fain, Dwight "Red" Adams and Bud Watkins. Follow-up interviews included those with Bud Beasley, John Pintar, Hershel Lyons and Lou Vezilich.

I did Seattle interviews mostly by phone, talking with George Archie, Len Gabrielson, Paul Gregory and Edo Vanni about Civic Stadium and the Jack Lelivelt era, and with Claude Christie and Marv Grissom, teammates on the 1951 team.

Having often spent time in Portland and Los Angeles, I found it relatively easy to land interviews in those cities. From the Portland Beavers, I talked with Ad Liska, Steve Coscarart, Nino "Bongy" Bongiovanni, Charlie Silvera, Eddie Basinski and Bill Fleming. From Los Angeles/Hollywood, Bob Usher, Bernie "Frenchy" Uhalt, Gene Freese, Bobby Loane (the last available member of the 1934 Los Angeles Angels), George "Bee" Mandish, Gene Handley and Chuck Stevens of the 1940-54 Hollywood Stars, Bob Talbot, Paul Pettit and Stars bat boy George Grant.

Helping out with insights into the exploits of the Vancouver Mounties were Martin Johnson, a fan and bat boy, Mounties radio announcer Jim Robson, and Lennie Neal from Scio, Oregon.

Any way you look at it, though, the Bay Area was still the greatest place for my interviews. I was able to speak with Ernie Broglio, Dino Restelli, Duane Pillette, Bill Renna, Bill Laws (son of Brick, the owner of the Oakland Oaks), Bill Rigney, Dario Lodigiani, and Don Rode, a San Francisco Seals clubhouse boy.

Then you pick up interviews along the way that are meaningful. I was lucky enough to talk with both Joe DiMaggio and Ted Williams, plus Tommy Lasorda, George "Sparky" Anderson, Spook Jacobs and Cece Carlucci — "Mr. Ump."

And there are interesting comments overheard at banquets and other gatherings. I picked up gems from Hal Saltzman, Roger Osenbaugh, Eddie Bockman and Bob Stevens, emeritus sportswriter of the *San Francisco Chronicle*.

I also have some fifty interviews from the first book. To avoid repeating myself, I didn't do much with them in *The Grand Minor League*. But there were a few players whom I went back to for a second round: Rugger Ardizoia, Con Dempsey, Billy Raimondi, Emil Mailho and Seals broadcaster Don Klein. They were able to add a broader perspective on the whole league.

For photographs, I was once again able to dip into my own collection for the bulk of the images, but I needed and received help from others. Of big assistance were Bill Swank, Chuck Christiansen, Andy Strasberg, Bob Reiss, Robb Wocknick, Dave Eskanazi, Baseball America, the San Diego Historical Society and the San Francisco Public Library, all of whom helped by providing good images of ballparks and other tidbits.

Larry Zuckerman, renowned ballpark researcher, also was of invaluable help in providing some of the elusive details about some of the more obscure ballparks. Bill Weiss, league statistician and historian, was always there to help round up information. Jack Lantermann and Peter Sheldon provided additional technical help. Thanks to you all.

Helping on player or action photos were some of the above, plus players Charles "Red" Adams, Frank Kerr, Charlie Silvera, Dino Restelli and Cece Carlucci.

Doug McWilliams, a longtime personal friend and fellow camera-wielding gate-crasher, was of great assistance in the production of the book. We traveled up and down the coast together, sneaking into the parks and capturing our heroes on film. Doug gave us many great memories, and helped enormously with editing and technical insights for the book.

Dick Beverage, secretary-treasurer of the Association of Professional Ball Players of America, also worked wonders with the text.

Another close friend, Sanjay Tiburon, was always there with helpful suggestions and expert proofreading. Others who helped proofread my copy include Jon Twichell and Dr. Paul Hirsch.

Tony Khing and Richard Defendorf at Woodford Press further polished the text, Woodford's Jim Santore produced a terrific book design and Pat O'Connell created a wonderful cover.

Finally, my thanks and love to my wife Judy for her patience and support on this lengthy project. Our daughter-in-law Anne, her husband Pete and our daughter Annette all helped in their special ways, assisting me through some serious medical problems as the project neared conclusion.

✳✳✳

The Grand Minor League is an oral history of the Pacific Coast League. It is, by design, an incomplete story. It is not filled with averages and other statistics, nor is it a systematic, chronological account of Coast League events. Rather, it is a collection of observations by people who took their roles in the PCL seriously, and enjoyed them enormously. The players played, the fans cheered, the bat boys fetched. All of them put their hearts into it, and each had his own impression of how it all came out.

The Grand Minor League is about winners and losers. Better yet, it is about people with winning and losing records, for any player who had the skill to play in the Pacific Coast League was a winner.

Because so much time has passed since the PCL was launched, *The Grand Minor League* does not include voices from its very early days. In fact, we couldn't find anyone who was around when the league began, or anyone who could speak with authority about its first thirty years.

But we found many who remembered the Depression, the war that followed, the ensuing peace and prosperity, and the PCL's demise as the major leagues usurped PCL turf.

Of the fifty players who were interviewed for *Nuggets on the Diamond*, and of the additional sixty or so we interviewed for *The Grand Minor League*, all spoke with enthusiasm and reverence, although not always with accuracy. Many hours were spent checking the facts behind their statements. From their interviews, we have attempted to weave a nostalgically appealing tapestry of what was indeed a grand minor league.

Some license has been taken to organize and clarify these players' recollections. Because each chapter focuses on a different topic, segments of each player's reflections may have been sprinkled throughout the book. Great care was taken where these comments were edited for clarity.

The old Pacific Coast League was "major league" in so many ways, those of us who experienced it have indelible memories of its pleasures. We were very lucky.

PUBLISHER'S NOTE

Dick Dobbins lost a long battle with cancer on January 3, 1999. But his spirit survives in these pages. In spite of their grief, Dick's family and friends rallied to help the editors at Woodford Press get this project into print quickly and smoothly. It is powerful evidence that Dick's love of baseball and his enthusiasm for its history and personalities were contagious. This book is dedicated to him.

In 1939, Joyner "JoJo" White of the Seattle Rainers hit a fly ball for an out on his first trip to the plate in the Hollywood Stars' new ballpark, Gilmore Field.

I IT WAS A GRAND MINOR LEAGUE

THE OLD PACIFIC COAST LEAGUE WAS A GRAND MINOR LEAGUE. ALAS, IT WAS STILL A MINOR LEAGUE.

IT WAS NOT UNTIL 1958, WHEN THE BROOKLYN DODGERS AND THE NEW YORK GIANTS MOVED WEST, THAT PACIFIC COAST RESIDENTS COULD TRUTHFULLY SAY ANYTHING DIFFER-ENT. WHILE AN EXCELLENT BRAND OF BASEBALL HAD BEEN PLAYED ON THE WEST COAST FOR ALMOST A CENTURY, IT WAS STILL NOT MAJOR LEAGUE BASEBALL. BUT PCL FANS KNEW IN THEIR HEARTS THAT THE LEAGUE HAD BEEN "MAJOR LEAGUE" FOR YEARS.

THE GRAND OLD GAME

The origins of baseball in the United States can be traced to the late 1830s in New York state. The Knickerbocker Baseball Club was organized in 1845, and the game's popularity spread rapidly along the Eastern seaboard.

In 1846, gold was discovered in California, and after the first wave of prospectors arrived, hundreds of settlers began migrating westward. In their pouches were, among other things, baseballs. In their hearts was a love of the game.

But the game didn't catch on in California until the late 1850s. Why did it take so long? California was a rough territory and times were hard in 1850, when the population west of the Mississippi consisted mainly of cowboys and Indians. Actually, in California, it was vaque-ros and Indians.

America's — and baseball's — entry into the Pacific Northwest lagged the settlement of Northern California by roughly ten years. The Oregon Territory was a fishing and trapping frontier until the early 1850s, when westward migration expanded. Both Oregon and Washington obtained statehood in 1859, nine years after California.

Through the remainder of the century, teams and leagues formed along the West Coast, and the game of "base ball" became a weekend passion for players and spectators alike. But the game did struggle in the early going.

Many of the diamonds were but green pastures. Team managers stiffed players of their pay cuts, players regularly changed teams for better pay. And the sport became fertile ground for gambling, with all its negative consequences. But despite these shortcomings, baseball grew in popularity on the West Coast.

By 1885, the sport had taken on a regional look as teams from the Pacific Northwest played teams from Northern California. Groups from Los Angeles also traveled to the Bay Area for competition. Professional leagues developed, flourished for a time, then fell back, only to rise again. These leagues proved there was a large enough fan base to organize a league that would play all week, not just on weekends.

ORGANIZING THE PACIFIC COAST LEAGUE

In 1903, the directors of the California League, representing the cities of Los Angeles, Sacramento, Oakland and San Francisco, took the ambitious step of organizing a league that truly represented the Pacific Coast by inviting team owners from Portland and Seattle to join them. Because the rival California State League was already operating in California and the Pacific Northwest League existed in Oregon and Washington, this action was illegal, according to the bylaws of the National Association, an organization of baseball clubs and leagues formed to bring sanity and order to the game.

Harry Heilmann was one West Coast player whose Coast League tenure was very short. After one season with San Francisco, in 1915, where he batted .364, he went on to a Hall of Fame career in Detroit, with a lifetime .342 batting average.

Because the formation of this new league — the Pacific Coast League — was counter to the National Association's bylaws, the PCL simply dropped its NA membership and became an "outlaw" league.

The two aggrieved leagues, the CSL and the PNL, attempted to do battle with the interloper. The PNL placed teams in San Francisco and Los Angeles, but both folded before the first season concluded, and the CSL lacked the power or the popularity of the new PCL. With its territory now secured, the Pacific Coast League rejoined the National Association in 1904.

During its first decade of operation, the Pacific Coast League enjoyed only limited commercial success. Franchises left cities, then returned. Others dropped out altogether, reducing the league to four teams at one point before new franchises were established. And, of course, the league had to withstand the tremors created by the 1906 San Francisco earthquake.

In the early stages of the PCL, San Francisco was the keystone franchise. Pacific Coast League headquarters were located in San Francisco, and the franchise in that city boasted the best attendance. The earthquake destroyed Recreation Park, San Francisco's home diamond, and league headquarters, throwing the league into chaos. But league pioneers J. Cal Ewing of Oakland and Walter McCredie of Portland helped stabilize and rebuild the league just before it collapsed from the blow.

On the field, the PCL quickly became known for its exciting and wide-open style of play, and for developing its stars ... and its characters.

Eustace "Doc" Newton of Los Angeles pitched the league's first no-hitter in 1903, one of his thirty-five wins. The next season, he had thirty-nine victories and set a record for errors by a pitcher, with twenty-eight. Charles "Truck" Eagan of Tacoma hit an unheard-of twenty-five home runs in 1904, only to be topped by Frank "Ping" Bodie's "world record" thirty homers in 1910 for the San Francisco Seals.

The Vernon Tigers' Happy Hogan was the earliest of the league's true characters. Hogan was a thorn in the sides of the umpires, and a delight to fans of both the Tigers and the opposition. In later years, players such as Carl "Buzz" Sawyer, Bill Schuster, Bud Beasley and "Chesty" Johnson carried on Hogan's tradition of zaniness.

DEVELOPMENT OF GREAT TEAMS

The early Los Angeles Angels, featuring Frank Dillon, dominated the league before teams to the north began to show some strength. The Angels were anchored by Dillon on first, "Gavvy" Cravath in the outfield, and "Spider" Baum on the pitcher's mound. Walter McCredie's Portland Beavers won four pennants between 1910 and 1914. Roger Peckinpaugh and future Hall of Famer Dave Bancroft were shortstops for McCredie during this period.

Later in the decade, the Vernon Tigers, managed by Bill Essick, won three consecutive pennants behind a squad of major-league and Pacific Coast League veterans. The Tigers fell from favor in 1920, though, when the PCL was rocked by a gambling scandal.

THE 1919 VERNON TIGERS — PCL CHAMPIONS
Rumors about fixed games plagued the Vernon Tigers. Sadly, the rumors proved to be true. Standing, left to right: Sam Ross, Jan Finneran, Irish Muesel, Rex Dawson, Tom Long, John Mitchell, Willie Mitchell, owner Roscoe "Fatty" Arbuckle (also in inset), Wheezer Dell, Frank Edgington, Hugh High, Forbes Alcock. Front Row: Al DeVormer, Art Fromme, Chet Chadbourne, Clarence Brooks, Byron Houck, manager Bill Essick, Tom Fisher.

Bill "Babe" Borton was at the center of the 1920 gambling scandal. He was acquired from Portland in 1918. At left is his 1919 Zeenut baseball card and the championship medal awarded to his teammates in 1920.

The scandal starred Tigers first baseman Bill "Babe" Borton, who effectively bribed Salt Lake City Bees outfielders Harl Maggert and Bill Rumler, and pitcher Jean Dale. Several Tigers players, as well as local gamblers, contributed money that Borton rather clumsily distributed to select opponents. Bill McCarthy, the league president, investigated and punished several players, banishing some for life.

The Tigers also featured oversized mascot-owner and silent-screen star Roscoe "Fatty" Arbuckle, who purchased the club in 1919. While the popular actor was a welcomed attraction at the ballpark, he quickly fell into disrepute when a call girl was murdered in a San Francisco hotel room registered in his name.

American League President Ban Johnson was particularly critical of the Pacific Coast League for its inability to handle its "gambling problem." It seemed that each Coast League ballpark had its own gambling section, and the fans in that section made no attempt to be discrete about their actions. And the fact that several Chicago Black Sox players had West Coast backgrounds did little to assuage Johnson's ire.

THE GOLDEN TWENTIES

World War I was a setback for the league and all of baseball. With players being inducted into the service or being forced to perform war-industry work, the Pacific Coast League terminated the 1918 season in July, leaving more than three months on the schedule unplayed.

Demobilization from World War I and the shock waves created by the gambling scandals were quickly forgotten as the Coast League forged ahead into the 1920s, a golden era for Pacific Coast League baseball. It was also when the competitive edge shifted to the Bay Area. San Francisco won four pennants, Oakland one, and both the Missions and the Seals won additional divided-season championships during the decade.

It was an era of 200-game schedules, bloated statistics, superstars and future Hall of Famers. Between 1925 and 1929, three players — Paul Waner, Smead Jolley and "Ike" Boone — won batting championships with marks above .400, and, in 1930, Earl Sheely batted .403!

Tony Lazzeri hit sixty home runs in 1925, many in the rarified air of Salt Lake City.

And while "Jakie" May's 35-9 record for Vernon in 1922 was the only thrity-win season during the '20s, it was not unusual to find as many as three twenty-game winners on the same team in a season. In fact, the superb 1925 San Francisco Seals boasted four.

The PCL was playing like a major league, and it was sending its share of players east to prove it.

THE DEPRESSION AND WAR "DOWNSIZE" BASEBALL

The 1930s were serious times for all Americans. The decade-long Depression displaced hundreds of thousands of American workers and threatened the economic stability of households across the country. While many baseball leagues folded, the Pacific Coast League was able to hang on. Roster sizes were cut, and so were salaries. Teams couldn't afford high-priced players, so they recruited veterans trying to hang on and raw youngsters in their teens. Ted Williams and Joe DiMaggio were two of the latter.

Night baseball was inaugurated on the West Coast in 1930 to attract tired and stressed workers who were looking for an inexpensive form of entertainment. Sacramento was the first club to offer a night game in the PCL, and by 1932 each Pacific Coast League team offered night baseball.

Amazingly, four new diamonds were constructed during the Depression. San Francisco opened play at Seals Stadium in 1931. The Seals' ownership had already committed its resources to the project before the Depression. In 1936, the Hollywood Stars moved to San Diego, where they sought financial relief after performing in the shadow of the Los Angeles Angels. The transfer prompted the construction of Lane Field, the new home of the team renamed the San Diego Padres.

Two years later, the bankrupt Mission Reds of San Francisco moved to Hollywood, looking for greener pastures themselves. After playing one season at Los Angeles' Wrigley Field, in 1938, and one week at the race track called Gilmore Stadium, in 1939, the new Hollywood Stars moved into their permanent home across the lot — Gilmore Field.

Finally, wealthy beer magnate Emil G. Sick purchased the Seattle Rainiers franchise in 1938 and built a beautiful new stadium, which opened in 1939. The attraction of these new stadiums undoubtedly helped boost attendance throughout the league during hard times.

As the Depression ended, another problem arose — World War II. The Japanese attack on Pearl Harbor sent shock waves along the West Coast. The threat of attack on West Coast cities prompted some team owners to advocate shutting down for the duration, but President Franklin Delano Roosevelt, convinced the sport was good for the nation's morale, encouraged organized baseball to continue to play ball.

Baseball's problems shifted from the financial to the strategic. The war effort put a strain on both human and material resources, which left the teams struggling to fill their rosters with able-bodied men and forced them to impose strictures on the use of equipment, including baseballs. The game survived. Owners robbed the high schools of their senior (and in some cases, junior) stars and some older players came out of retirement.

A RETURN TO PEACE — ARE WE "MAJOR LEAGUE"?

During World War II, the West Coast population grew. Many Americans migrated from the heartland to work in the war industries that emerged at Pacific debarcation points. And when peace returned, most of these workers stayed on the coast.

Walter McCredie was the first dominant manager in the Coast League. In the first twelve years of the PCL, his Portland Beavers won five pennants.

People also were ready for entertainment, and a sports renaissance spread along the West Coast. Competition was intense in the Pacific Coast League and record crowds cheered its teams.

The 1946 San Francisco Seals, the 1947 Los Angeles Angels, the 1948 Oakland Oaks and the 1949 Hollywood Stars fielded excellent veteran teams that would have been competitive anywhere in the system. This "grand minor league" was producing a "major league" product.

And the moguls of baseball had noticed.

WHY NOT US?

It seems the only thing that stopped the St. Louis Browns from claiming the Los Angeles territory for the American League in 1942 was Japan's attack on Pearl Harbor. The Browns' bid to move west was rejected by the American League two days after the attack on the Hawaiian Islands.

In 1945, at the conclusion of hostilities, the clamor to bring major league baseball to the west got louder, but this time it came from a unified, albeit cautious, group of Pacific Coast League owners.

Clarence Rowland, Pacific Coast League president, led the assault, and A.B. "Happy" Chandler, Commissioner of Baseball, had to deflect it. There was no way major league owners, the power structure of organized baseball, were going to share their wealth with anyone, especially a bunch

Above: Ray Rohwer was one of the sluggers during the Renaissance period of the 1920s. The league was unbelievably strong at that time.
Opposite page: Paul Strand was the premier slugger in the early 1920s. In 1923, he set a professional record of 325 base hits in a season. Strand finished with a Coast League career average of .359.

of upstart owners from the West Coast.

But the Pacific Coast League wouldn't go away. Veiled threats of congressional investigations, backed by anti-trust protections and the possibility that the league might withdraw from organized baseball — and form an "outlaw" major league — got everyone's attention.

WE ARE MAJOR LEAGUE — ALMOST

Major league team owners eventually agreed to "throw them a carrot." After half a decade of agitation, the Pacific Coast League, in 1951, was granted "Open Classification" status. This unusual classification elevated the PCL above the AAA league and featured a plan and timetable for the PCL's ascension to full major league status.

The plan gave Coast League players the option of waiving their right to be drafted by a major league team, and it set goals for upgrading the PCL's stadiums to a major league standard. It appeased the PCL and gave it hope.

But time was running out. America was changing, and the minor leagues faced new pressures. Television and more efficient radio technology allowed East Coast sports broadcasts to find West Coast listeners, and American interests were becoming more diverse. New professional sports franchises were being established, guaranteeing that

baseball would never again have the field to itself.

Equally devastating to all minor leagues was the major league teams' growing practice of signing amateur players. Originally, major league teams had been content to purchase budding stars developed by independent minor league teams. But this process was costly and produced inconsistent results.

By establishing farm systems and searching for talent themselves, the major league teams felt they had better control over their own destiny. Pay the top prospects a bonus to join your organization and train them "your way." Then place these players within your own system, and train them with your own coaches.

This trend was a form of slow death for independent minor leagues such as the PCL.

By the mid-1950s, the worst fears of the Coast League directors were coming true. Their scouts were getting outbid by the major league teams for a decreasing number of talented amateurs, and PCL general managers found themselves asking for assistance from the major leagues to fill their rosters.

San Francisco, once the jewel of the PCL, was forced to relinquish its franchise to the league because of declining revenue. A community-generated campaign to sell stock through a public offering gave the Seals a two-year reprieve before their financial woes returned. As a final indignity, the league sold the franchise to the Boston Red Sox, the major league team whose owners hoped to claim San Francisco as American League territory.

Across the Bay in Oakland, Oaks owner "Brick" Laws watched his attendance plummet by 350,000 in four years, and moved the team to Vancouver, B.C.

In Southern California, the Pittsburgh Pirates became a minority stockholder in the Hollywood Stars, and the Chicago Cubs, among the strongest supporters of Pacific Coast League baseball, traded ownership of the Los Angeles Angels to the Brooklyn Dodgers for their Fort Worth, Texas, franchise. The great Angels tradition was doomed.

By 1957, speculation was rampant about the intentions of the Brooklyn Dodgers and the

New York Giants. Metropolitan newspapers, several of which openly advocated bringing major league baseball to the West Coast, helped ruin an exciting PCL pennant race by refusing to give it decent coverage. It was just a matter of time before the PCL was completely undermined.

Speculation became reality when the Brooklyn Dodgers and New York Giants filed papers with the National League to move their franchises to the Pacific Coast for the 1958 season. With the announcement that they would claim Los Angeles and San Francisco as their new homes, major league baseball finally became a truly national entity, and all hope that the Pacific Coast League would one day attain major league status disappeared.

Major league expansion created a diaspora among PCL teams that mocked the name Pacific Coast League. The transfer of the major-league Dodgers and Giants to the West Coast uprooted the PCL's Los Angeles Angels, Hollywood Stars and San Francisco Seals, three of the strongest PCL franchises. Those teams then moved to Spokane, Washington, Salt Lake City, Utah, and Phoenix, Arizona, respectively.

Although two of its franchises stayed in California, the Pacific Coast League had become so geographically diffuse it lost cohesion. Sacramento lost its natural Bay Area rivalries and had to compete with the Giants for fan support. Isolated from the rest of the PCL teams, San Diego had greater travel expenses.

The PCL's days were numbered. The Sacramento franchise was forced to relocate in 1961, and San Diego, a growing city, was presented with a National League expansion franchise in 1969. For the first time since the league was organized, in 1903, no Pacific Coast League team represented a California city.

Vernon "Lefty" Gomez played only one year in the Pacific Coast League, 1929, with the San Francisco Seals (18-1, 3.43 ERA, 267 IP). He then was sold to the New York Yankees.

THE "UN-PACIFIC" COAST LEAGUE

As major league expansion continued along the West Coast, the redistribution of PCL teams prompted other changes. The league's size ranged from eight franchises immediately after the Dodgers and Giants arrived on the West Coast to a dozen in the mid-'60s.

At its largest, the PCL had little connection to its former "Pacific Coast" identity, as franchises could be found in Indianapolis, Indiana, Little Rock, Arkansas, Dallas, Texas, Tulsa, Oklahoma, and Denver, Colorado.

The PCL later shrank to more reasonable geographical dimensions, extending east only as far as Salt Lake City, Utah, Albuquerque, New Mexico, and Edmonton and Calgary, Alberta. To the west, the Hawaiian Islands were blessed with a franchise until the economics of long-distance travel made fielding a team on "the Garden Isle" impractical.

The arrival of major league baseball on the West Coast made these changes inevitable. An American League franchise was presented to Los Angeles in 1961, and Seattle was rewarded with an American League franchise in 1969. And the American League's Kansas City A's relocated to Oakland in 1968, striking a balance between the National League and American League on the West Coast in towns that formerly had been home to PCL teams.

Although the Pacific Coast League is operational today, most fans are careful to distinguish between the "old" Pacific Coast League of pre-major league days and the current Pacific Coast League. The changes that have marked organized baseball over the last fifty years further underscore the differences between the old and new versions of the PCL. The emphasis of this book is on the old league, the version we call the grand minor league.

Just to prove it could be done, Hollywood Stars chairman of the board George Young, left, poured gasoline on a beam of the Stars' new ball-park, Gilmore Field, while team vice president Bob Cobb supplied the blowtorch. The wood had been treated with fireproof chemicals that prevented it from scorching while the gasoline burned.

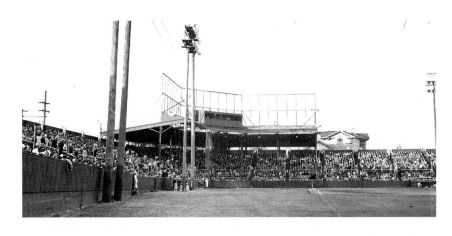

Oaks Ball Park in Emeryville, California during World War II. After the war, the park's bleachers were expanded onto the field.

2
THE BALLPARKS

Pacific Coast League ballparks helped give the game personality. Hardly state-of-the-art, these ballparks had characteristics that favored some players, tormented others.

In 1951, when the Pacific Coast League accepted "Open Classification" status as a step toward gaining recognition as a major league, each PCL city was asked to provide a modern park for its team. Each was required to have a minimum seating capacity of 25,000. At the time the pact was signed, ballparks in only three PCL cities — Los Angeles, San Francisco and Seattle — came close to meeting that requirement.

Conditions at other ballparks ranged from adequate (Hollywood and Sacramento) to aging (Oakland) to downright embarrassing (San Diego and Portland). Each of the cities with substandard parks already had drawn up plans for new venues, but the economic insecurities surrounding the minors at the time made the owners cautious about building new facilities.

Today, only Portland's Civic Stadium and Vancouver's Nat Bailey Stadium remain from the days before the Open Classification agreement was ratified. All the other ballparks have been razed. But memories of these parks live on in the following comments by PCL participants and in the accompanying photographs.

GILMORE STADIUM - Hollywood

Gilmore Stadium was used for one week at the start of the 1939 season while workers put the final touches on Gilmore Field, the new home of the Hollywood Stars. Otherwise, Gilmore Stadium served as a venue for football, auto racing and boxing matches.

In 1939, we started the season at Gilmore Stadium. I pitched an exhibition game there against the White Sox.. We trained in Whittier and played at Gilmore Stadium. The other ballpark wasn't ready yet.

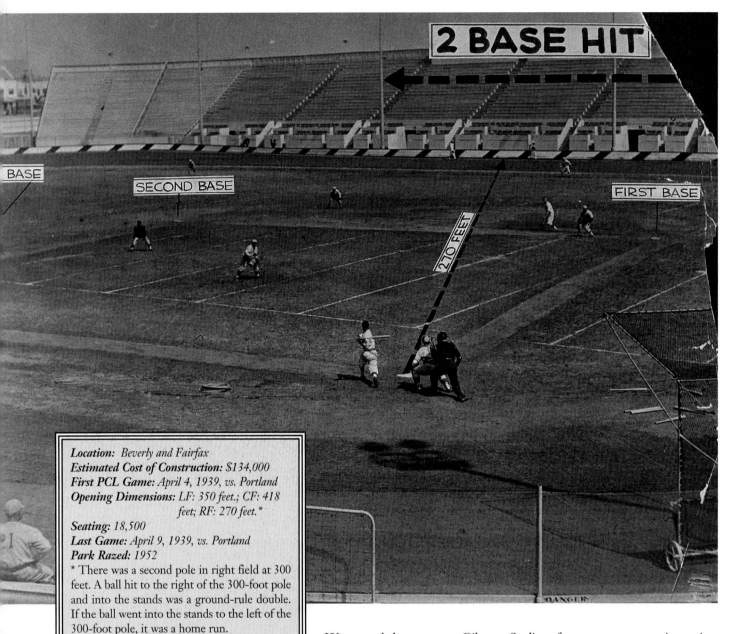

2 BASE HIT

BASE

SECOND BASE

FIRST BASE

270 FEET

Location: *Beverly and Fairfax*
Estimated Cost of Construction: *$134,000*
First PCL Game: *April 4, 1939, vs. Portland*
Opening Dimensions: *LF: 350 feet.; CF: 418 feet; RF: 270 feet.* *
Seating: *18,500*
Last Game: *April 9, 1939, vs. Portland*
Park Razed: *1952*
* There was a second pole in right field at 300 feet. A ball hit to the right of the 300-foot pole and into the stands was a ground-rule double. If the ball went into the stands to the left of the 300-foot pole, it was a home run.

The Stars played at Gilmore Stadium for only one week before going on the road, then came back to their new stadium, located just feet away from the old field. The picture above shows Gilmore Stadium marked for football. A track where midget autos raced on Saturday nights is visible in the foreground.

We opened the season at Gilmore Stadium for a seven-game series against Portland, then went on the road, up north against Portland and Seattle, for two weeks. When we came back, the new stadium (Gilmore Field) was ready for us.

Gilmore Stadium was an auto-race track and football field. Right field was only 270 feet. At about 300 feet, there was another pole. It was a ground-rule double to the right of the pole and a home run to the left. It was up to the umpire to decide.

The outfielders in right and center field had to go back across the race track. It was all dirt. The left-fielder had a lot of room.

There was no backstop. The batting practice cage was used as a backstop. We were on the third base line, an open dugout, and Portland was on the first.

They had a cut infield, but they didn't do it like they would today. They just left the football lines on the field. The field had lights, but they weren't good. They weren't high enough. They were for auto racing, not baseball.

After we moved to Gilmore Field they'd have the big auto races behind right field, and all the dust and fumes would come over to our ballpark.

RUGGER ARDIZOIA - Hollywood Stars

I pitched four innings in the first exhibition game at Gilmore Stadium. We beat the Chicago White Sox. I also got the win in the league opener against Portland. I pitched the ninth, and we scored four runs to win, 9-5.

We only played there that one week and then we went on the road. We only played day games there. There were lights, but they were low and not focused on the diamond. They had put in an elevated mound, but it was sort of flat. You couldn't come down off of it with any power. If you're a fastball pitcher and you come off a high mound, it will give you more momentum.

When we moved into Gilmore Field, we drew well.

BILL FLEMING - Hollywood Stars

GILMORE FIELD - Hollywood

After the 1937 season, the Mission Reds, near bankruptcy, moved their franchise from San Francisco to Hollywood, California. The owners of the Los Angeles Angels grudgingly allowed the Stars to play one season in Wrigley Field, but a new ballpark had to be ready for the Stars in 1939. Cozy Gilmore Field opened on May 2, 1939, one month after the season started.

We went on a road trip after the first week at Gilmore Stadium, and when we returned we moved into the new park just behind the stadium. At the opener there were lots of movie personalities. We got to know many of them. Gail Patrick sat in the first box seat next to the dugout. She was married to Bob Cobb, who owned the ball club. It was a festive atmosphere there, and they were true fans.

BERNIE "FRENCHY" UHALT - Hollywood Stars

When we moved to Gilmore Field, they only had the grandstand. There were no bleachers down the left field or right field lines. At the end of the year, they completed the stands.

A scorecard touting the Hollywood Stars' first week at Gilmore Field.

Location: *Beverly and Fairfax and Genessee*
Estimated Cost of Construction: *$200,000*
First Game: *May 2, 1939, vs. Seattle*
Opening Dimensions: *LF: 335 feet; CF: 400 feet;*
RF: 335 feet.
Seating: *12,000*
Last Game: *September 5, 1957, vs. San Francisco*
Park Razed: *1958*

The Hollywood Stars' Gilmore Field celebrated its grand opening in filmland style on May 2, 1939. However, the home nine fell to the Seattle Rainiers 8-5.

The Gilmore Field front entrance. Construction was underway even after the park opened. But the finishing touches created a cozy, fan-friendly facility.

The gambling section was high behind third base.

We didn't get big crowds at [old] stadium, but when we came to Gilmore Field, we doubled and tripled the crowds.

The first year, *we* were the celebrities, not the actors. They had the boxes, and they put their names on the boxes. People would come early and they'd spot the names, then when the stars came they knew exactly who they were.

Gilmore Field was a good park to pitch in. I enjoyed it. Right field was tough to hit out of, but left field wasn't too hard. The wind blew that way.

It was a clean park. The stands were close to the field.

RUGGER ARDIZOIA - Hollywood Stars

Gilmore Field was a great ballpark to play in, but it couldn't have been ten to twelve feet between the foul lines and the people. You could read their minds, you were so close. And a wooden ballpark at that.

The infield was good, but as a first baseman I dreaded the lights during a night game. The lights were all right at the plate, but they weren't high enough defensively. I lived in constant fear defensively. Line drives didn't bother you. But high hops — you would lose the ball in them. I remember one year I kicked a ball because I lost it. It hit me in the shoulder. Chuck Connors bounced one off home plate, and that ball went up, and there wasn't an infielder on the right side who knew where the ball was. We had to wait for it to hit the ground.

One thing that disturbed line-drive hitters was the tall grass at Gilmore Field. They let it grow tall, and taking away those extra base hits. But it sure protected those 2-1 ball games. It was not unheard-of for your groundskeepers to enhance your ball club through the way they maintained the field. And they did ours.

CHUCK STEVENS - Hollywood Stars

Gilmore Field was a small stadium, so you were very close to everything. For example, a foul ball hit behind the catcher at Dodger Stadium, you'd run a mile. But at Gilmore, it was right on the screen.

The clubhouse was under the stands, right behind the dugout. There was a tunnel beside the dugout, on a line from first base to second base, that we'd go through to the clubhouse. It was a short trip.

GEORGE GRANT - Hollywood Stars Bat Boy

The last game at Gilmore Field, I believe Hugh Pepper had a no-hitter going for eight-and-two-thirds innings. It was nostalgic, and a couple of days after, they started demolishing it. (Hollywood beat San Francisco in the final game, 6-0, before 6,354 vocal fans. Eddie Sadowski singled to center field to break up a no-hitter.)

I enjoyed playing at Gilmore Field. It was a much better-balanced park than Wrigley. Wrigley Field had that short porch. The lights never bothered me at Gilmore Field.

Of course, we knew the stars. George Raft, Frank Lovejoy, Humphrey Bogart and Lauren Bacall ... she brought their boy down and wanted to see some players, so we took him into the clubhouse and showed him around.

FORREST "SPOOK" JACOBS - Hollywood Stars

I remember one time at Hollywood they had to call the game on account of fog. That was unheard-of, but that fog came in and you couldn't see fifty feet. They had to call it.

BILL FLEMING - Hollywood Stars

WRIGLEY FIELD - Los Angeles

Wrigley Field was the queen of minor league ballparks in the 1920s and 1930s. Patterned after Wrigley Field in Chicago, it was major league in every way except size.

When the Brooklyn Dodgers moved west in 1958, they set up headquarters in the Wrigley Field Tower, but played at the Los Angeles Coliseum until Dodger Stadium was built. When the American League Los Angeles Angels started in 1961, they played their inaugural season at Wrigley Field before moving to Dodger Stadium, or "Chavez Ravine," as Angels management preferred to call it.

Wrigley Field was used for other activities, including the famous "Home Run Derby" television series, before it was torn down.

Wrigley was my favorite minor league ballpark of all time. You always felt the major-league feeling playing there. A great, great hitter's ballpark. Short fences.

CHUCK STEVENS - Hollywood Stars

Wrigley Field was the spitting image of Chicago's Wrigley Field, and one of the most popular parks in minor league baseball. Here, a standing-room-only crowd enjoys Sunday baseball in the sun.

Location: *435 East 42nd Place, at Avalon*
Estimated Cost of Construction: *$1.1 million*
First Game: *Sept. 29, 1925*
Opening Dimensions: *LF: 340 feet.; CF: 421 feet.; RF 339 feet. Power Alleys in left- and right-center field: 345 ft.*
Seating: *25,000 (stated), 21,500 (realistic)*
Last PCL Game: *Sept. 15, 1957, vs. San Diego*
Park Razed: *1966*

I liked to play in Wrigley Field. The fence to right field wasn't too far away. I think I hit two homers in a game there, the only time I did that in my career. Left field all the way to center had a high brick wall. I bumped my head against it once chasing down a long fly. I saw stars for awhile after that. It didn't move when you ran into it.

NINO BONGIOVANNI
- Seattle Indians, Portland Beavers

I loved pitching in Wrigley Field. When I went to L.A., I was just a kid, and Wrigley Field was by far the nicest park I had ever seen. And the weather in Southern California, before smog, was so nice. Although it was a hitter's park — if I hadn't been so young and naive, I would have thought about that. Lots of players who go into a park that favors a hitter try to change their pitching, and try to pitch a different type of ball game.

As I grew up, I did appreciate it was a hitter's park. There was an advantage to that: runs are cheaper, and if you're on a pretty good-hitting club, you win games 5-4, rather than 1-0. I did learn that if someone hit a pitch out of the ballpark, don't let it destroy you because you'll get it back. But try not to have the bases loaded when they hit it.

CHARLES "RED" ADAMS - Los Angeles Angels

I thought Wrigley Field [in Los Angeles] was a great park to play in ... I never was in Wrigley Field in Chicago, but they say they were identical, except for the wind. But it was pretty easy to hit 'em out of Los Angeles. It was pretty easy for right-handers to hit the ball out of right field and right center, the off-field. I can even remember one day our little lefty pitcher Al Olsen hit one way up in the stands in right field.

JOHN "SWEDE" JENSEN - San Diego Padres

Los Angeles was a big-league stadium. It was a great park to play in, but the clubhouse was kind of screwy. To get to it, you had to go down through the dugout, then they had a wire cage with steps leading to the clubhouse, which hung up under the grandstands ... this cage was built around these rather steep stairs that you had to go up to the clubhouse.

CLAUDE CHRISTIE - Seattle Rainiers

Wrigley Field was a hitters' park, but it was all right to pitch there. Center field had a lot of room. At night ball games, the air was deader. The balls didn't go out there like they did in the daytime.

BILL FLEMING - Los Angeles Angels

OAKS BALL PARK - Emeryville

*T*he Oakland Oaks played in several ballparks between 1903 and 1912. Cozy Freeman's Park, at Fifth Street and San Pablo Avenue, was considered home in 1912, the year the Oaks won their first PCL pennant. But Oakland's continued success would require a larger, permanent home.

The Oaks also called Recreation Park in San Francisco home during this period, playing many weekday games at "Old Rec" to stimulate attendance.

Construction of Oaks Ball Park began December 15, 1912, and the park was ready, with time to spare, for the season opener in April, 1913. Located on San Pablo Avenue in Emeryville, the park offered easy access to the train lines that served the East Bay and San Francisco.

Oaks Ball Park was "viewer friendly," although as time went on its wooden structure became more susceptible to small fires. Luckily, the Emeryville Fire Department was located a short distance behind home plate.

After the team relocated to Vancouver, British Columbia, for the 1956 season, the park lay vacant until it was razed in the spring of 1957. The stadium lights are still in use at several local high school football fields.

The new Oaks Ball Park, 1946: the man in the third-base coach's box is Casey Stengel. Two photographers position themselves nearby as the overflow crowd watches the action.

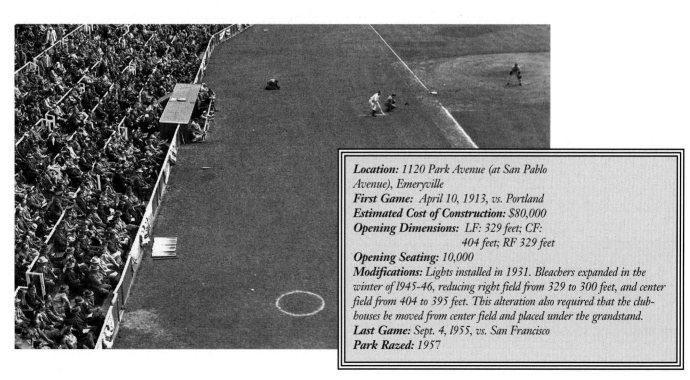

Location: 1120 Park Avenue (at San Pablo Avenue), Emeryville
First Game: April 10, 1913, vs. Portland
Estimated Cost of Construction: $80,000
Opening Dimensions: LF: 329 feet; CF: 404 feet; RF 329 feet
Opening Seating: 10,000
Modifications: Lights installed in 1931. Bleachers expanded in the winter of 1945-46, reducing right field from 329 to 300 feet, and center field from 404 to 395 feet. This alteration also required that the clubhouses be moved from center field and placed under the grandstand.
Last Game: Sept. 4, 1955, vs. San Francisco
Park Razed: 1957

This is how the Oaks Ball Park looked during World War II. After the 1945 season, the bleachers would be expanded onto the field, and the front lights would be replaced by standards behind the bleachers.

Before the war, Oaks Ball Park was a nightmare for left-handed batters. The wind blew in from right field. The lights weren't good. They were low on [Oaks owner Vic Devencenzi's] priorities.

The clubhouse was out in center field, and there was a high fence in front of it. That was before they put the bleachers in center and right field. The gamblers used to sit right at the end of the bleachers down the right-field line.

BILL RIGNEY - Oakland Oaks

Before they remodeled Emeryville, it was a tough park for left-handers. It was a long way out to right field, and there was always a breeze coming in off the Bay. The clubhouse out in center field wasn't too good. We had showers and hot water, but you had to get your shower early.

Out in center field, directly over the pitcher's mound, was the old scoreboard. When a guy would throw, the ball would come right out of the lights on the scoreboard, and when it was 2-2 or 3-2 on the batter, you had to bear down. You had to make sure you could see the ball because of the lights.

BILLY RAIMONDI - Oakland Oaks

The clubhouses at Oakland were in center field before they modernized the stadium. They accused Shine Scott, the Hollywood [Stars] trainer, of using binoculars out there. He could see the catcher's signs, and would give a sign for a fastball, or curve. The Oaks figured it out quickly and they said, 'No more of that!' And the lights at Oakland, they were just giant buckets. Shadows all around, especially in the outfield.

EMIL MAILHO - Oakland Oaks

I wasn't around when they remodeled the ballpark, but I was simply amazed at what a terrific job they did to add all those seats in center field and from the right-field foul line out to center field. And since the club was going so well, those seats were always filled up, and so they still had to put the fans out in standing-room-only in left field.

The park got to be real old, but the beauty of it was that you were so close to the game. You were part of the action.

BILL LAWS - Oaks Radio Announcer

Emeryville park was a great park. The wind would blow off the Bay all the time. You'd come in and look at that right field wall and say, 'Oh, boy!' Then you'd hit a fly ball out there and the wind would blow it back. The second baseman could almost catch the ball. You could hit a home run there if you could hit a line drive.

JACK GRAHAM - San Diego Padres

VAUGHN STREET BALL PARK
– Portland *(Lucky Beaver Stadium)*

Vaughn Street was the oldest Coast League park and a real fire trap. But players loved to play there. Vaughn Street had its challenges, but players were well received by its fans. Possibly more baseball lore comes from Vaughn Street than from any other park in the league.

Vaughn Street was a grand old ballpark. I first saw it when I came down from Brooklyn. I said, 'Oh, my god.' Vaughn Street, built in 1902! Can you imagine?

And that park had great tradition. Many great players came through that ballpark. And the people loved it. They were so close to the field they could hear the arguments and the swearing. They could even hear the spitting. We packed them in.

I loved playing there and I loved the fans. Opposing players would come to me and tell me that they loved to play in Portland because the fans were so neutral and appreciative of baseball. When a player made a good play, the fans didn't give a damn what uniform he was wearing. They'd give him a hand.

Just like Gilmore Field, there were cracks in the seats where you would look through ... players took advantage of that, but you could also get peanut shells in your eyes.

Rocky Benevento was our groundskeeper for forty years. He brought a chip of paint in from the outfield after [Joe] Brovia knocked it off, and you could see forty coats of paint on that fence. That's what was holding it up! This park was old!

Location: N.W. 24th and Vaughn streets
Estimated Cost of Construction:
   Unknown
First PCL Game: *April 16, 1912,*
   vs. San Francisco
Opening Dimensions: *LF: 331 feet;*
   CF: 368 feet; RF 315 feet.
Seating: *Opening Day - 12,000; 1955 -*
   9,000
Modifications: *Slightly reduced first-base*
and center-field bleacher size. Right field
eventually reduced to 301 feet.
Last Game: *Sept. 11, 1955, vs. Oakland*

Opening Day at Vaugh Street, 1951. Day-night double-headers would attract twice the usual crowd — about 23,568.

I remember one time when people started stomping for a rally, and I looked at the light poles. They were waving around like there was an earthquake. I told Frankie [Austin], 'You know, one day the whole place is going to go down like dominoes.'

And the lights were bad, terrible, permeated with the smoke from the foundry in right field. You could smell it — orange smoke.

Rocky said he never saw a Sunday double-header. He would have to put out about six fires on the average each Sunday. There were peanut shells six inches deep, and Rocky was running around with fire extinguishers all afternoon.

EDDIE BASINSKI - Portland Beavers

I loved playing at Vaughn Street. It was a small park with lots of base hits. The fans were great too. One time when the field was wet and muddy I hit a home run to win the game and the fans started throwing coins — half dollars, quarters and the like — and they were falling into the mud. The players were helping me pick them up, and they were handing me clumps of mud with coins stuck in it. I spent quite a bit of time in the clubhouse digging the coins out. The fans didn't do that often, only when there was a key homer.

Vaughn Street was only about 301 feet down the right-field line. There was a wooden fence about twenty feet high, then a ten-foot screen, and beyond that was the foundry. They had fifty-gallon barrels of water spaced up on the roof for fire, I suppose. And if you hit one to the first, it's a one-barrel homer, the second was a two-barrel homer.

I remember outfielder Ralph Graves when he played for the Seals. He was running for a ball hit to left field, up against the fence, and he ran right through it. Never slowed down. It was like the cartoons when somebody runs through a fence and leaves a silhouette of his body. The fence at Vaughn Street wasn't too strong.

There was a six-by-six-inch hole through the backstop behind home plate with a pipe that they used to return foul balls. One night a black-and-white cat came out of that hole, walked to the plate and, of course, the game stopped. The cat went over to where a right-handed batter would put his back foot, dug a little hole and did his business, covered it up and sauntered back and went through the hole again. The fans went crazy.

NINO BONGIOVANNI - Portland Beavers

Sundays at Vaughn Street were always huge crowds. You'd come to the park and fans would be waiting to encourage you.

It was a small, smelly clubhouse. You entered the dugout through a door in the clubhouse. Our dugout was on the third-base side. You had to walk around half-humpbacked so you wouldn't knock your head off.

It was an old ballpark, and they kept talking about condemning it. Rocky Benevento used to say, 'Condemn it? Hell, let the son of a bitch burn.' One Sunday (September 21, 1948), we came out for a double-header, and the bleachers out in left-center had burned. We still played the game.

The lights weren't the greatest in the world. Del Ballinger used to pinch hit for us quite a bit. When he knew he was going to pinch hit the next inning, he'd go into the little groundskeeper's room and turn out the light and swing the bat. Then when he'd come out to pinch hit, he'd say, 'Boy, those lights look bright now!'

Rocky Benevento had a little shed on the first-base side, and Del Ballinger would go over there and drill our bats. We had corked bats then. In fact, we left them hollow, and he'd put a cork back and sandpaper it down. After a while, the bats would crack — split down the middle — and we'd tell the bat boy that if he saw that cork fly, go get it. But they really didn't care.

Vaughn Street was built on fill. We used to call it Benevento's Brick Yard. Balls would be hit through the outfield walls. It was decrepit, but it had character.

CHARLIE SILVERA - Portland Beavers

One thing about Portland — the ballpark was up this canyon, and if you're at the hotel and you look up the canyon and it was dark up there, you didn't have to leave the hotel.

Vaughn Street was a bit uneven. You ran uphill to first, downhill to second, downhill to third and uphill to home.

BILLY RIGNEY - Oakland Oaks

At Portland on Sundays, you'd see bucket brigades. Rocky had a crew that just went around putting out fires.

BILL FLEMING - Portland Beavers

I pitched the last ball game there, in 1955, with Oakland. Vaughn Street was the oldest ballpark in the world, but I liked it. Sinker pitchers had the grass. Rocky used to always leave the grass a little longer when I pitched.

DUANE PILLETTE - Portland Beavers

MULTNOMAH STADIUM (CIVIC STADIUM) - Portland

The Beavers finally moved from Vaughn Street in 1956. The homey atmosphere of Vaughn was replaced by a rectangular field — death for left-handed hitters. Owned by the Multnomah Athletic Club (located behind the right-field wall), Multnomah stadium could hold twice the crowd Vaughn Street could. But any way you approached it, it was still a football field.

Multnomah had real grass when I went there. The left field had a short porch. It was high, but a lot of 'em went out of there. It was a real hazard. You are always setting up on the outside of the plate at Multnomah, shading the outside all the time for right-handed hitters.

The pitchers had to adjust more than anybody. We had some veterans who knew how to pitch — Larry Jansen, Vic Lombardi, Duane Pillette, Howie Judson. We had plenty of experience to work with. They all knew how to thread the needle on the outside corner.

Converting Multnomah to baseball was a hurry-up job. Dugouts and clubhouses needed to be constructed. Our clubhouse wasn't anything famous, nothing like what we had in San Francisco or Oakland.

LEN NEAL - Portland Beavers

As far as the fans were concerned, moving into Multnomah Stadium was a big mistake. The stadium used to be a big [running] track and a football stadium, and it separated the players from the fans. The distance became too great. The wall around the dugouts was about eight feet tall. It was a bad idea.

EDDIE BASINSKI - Portland Beavers

Location: *S.W. 18th & Morrison streets**
Estimated Cost of Construction: *$502,000*
   (1926)
First Game: *April 27, 1956, vs.*
   Sacramento
Opening Dimensions: *LF: 305 feet; CF:*
   389 feet; RF: 335 feet.
Seating: *28,870*
   Modified for baseball use in the
   winter of 1955-6
Status: *Still in use.*
* Original field acquired in early 1890s by
the Multnomah Athletic Club and sold to the
City of Portland in 1967. Flood and fire
prompted several major renovations to the
structures before the current plant was built,
in 1926. AstroTurf was installed after the
1981 season.

An aerial view of Portland's Multnomah Stadium, owned by the Multnomah Athletic Club. Multnomah was a multi-sport complex, which meant it didn't work well for baseball. Left field was a long putt away, and the fans felt they were too removed from the action of the game.

Multnomah Stadium was a terrible place. I hit two home runs there one day, and I'm not a home-run hitter. You could drop-kick the ball over the left field fence. Now you hit it to center field or right field and it was about 9,000 yards. And the lights were poor. The field was poor. It was still grass.

BUDDY PETERSON - Vancouver Mounties

MOREING FIELD - Sacramento
(a.k.a. Doubleday Park, Cardinal Field, Edmonds Field)

*I*n 1922, Senators owner Lew Moreing began refurbishing his dilapidated Buffalo Park into a larger, more modern facility. The diamond was shifted slightly to provide a symmetrical field, and the seating capacity was expanded by roughly 4,000.
   Twenty-six years later, the park was ready for modernization again. Fire facilitated the process.

Cardinal Field was an old ballpark. The lights were bad, but the field was pretty good. The stands were rickety. The clubhouse was well below average, but we had hot water ... if you got there early.

EDDIE STEWART - San Diego Padres

It was a wood park with high fences around. Right field wasn't too far away. It was a good field for a left-handed hitter. There was a large scoreboard in center field, and that was a long way out there. You couldn't hit one over center field.

The clubhouse was all wood. The floor in the clubhouse was old-time, ancient wood, worn on many a year. With any team, not everybody wants to shower at the same time after a game. Some players lounge around for a while. We didn't have beer in the clubhouse, but players would relax with a Coke.

HERSHEL LYONS - Sacramento Solons

I started going to baseball games in Sacramento when I was five. Most of those years it was a St. Louis Cardinal farm. Sacramento fans were intense. If fans came up from San Francisco and cheered, there would be fights in the stands. You couldn't root against the Solons.

ROGER OSENBAUGH - Sacramento Solons

The ballpark was right on top of the players, and you got to know the fans. The same ones came out every night.

I played in the minor leagues where they had lights, and I come out here where the lights were so much better than in the minor leagues. At least you could see the outfielders.

Seals Stadium and Seattle had real lights, but Portland didn't have good lights. Cardinal Field was somewhere in the middle. At that time, they were better than average.

JOHN PINTAR - Sacramento Solons

There were fires at Edmonds Field every Sunday double-header, but they'd go around and put them out. I pitched in the double-header for Seattle the day the park burned. In fact, we were at the train depot, waiting for our train to take us back to Seattle when we saw the smoke and red glow coming from the fire. It was a good ballpark, but it was a real fire trap.

BUD BEASLEY - Seattle Rainiers.

Sacramento's Moreing Field in 1924. Note the style of dress of the men, who greatly out-number the women in attendance.

Location: *Riverside Boulevard and Broadway*
Estimated Cost of Construction: *$100,000*
First Game: *April 4, 1922*
Opening Dimensions: *LF: 320 feet;*
CF: 452 feet; RF: 330 feet
Seating: *10,000*
Modifications: *Concrete box seats and dugouts added in 1946.*
Last Game: *July 11, 1948 (The park was destroyed by fire after a Sunday double-header, making the Solons a road team for the remainder of the season.)*

One of the first night games in PCL history was played at Moreing Field in Sacramento, on June 10, 1930, at the start of the Depression. This photo was taken a couple nights earlier, when the players tried out the new (marginally adequate) lighting system.

I pitched one of the last games the Sunday before the ballpark burned down. We had the Monday off before San Diego came to town, so I had gone home to my family in Red Bluff.

The next day I got up early and went up in the mountains for trout fishing. I got back in the afternoon, and my mother-in-law met me and said the ballpark just burned down. I called Jim Tabor ... to ask what had happened.

He said that the team was going to get together and get on the train and go to San Diego to play the series. We were now a road team ... the team was going to go to the United Sporting Goods store (in Los Angeles) to get outfitted — gloves, shoes, whatever we needed. We played a double-header to make up the games.

The Sacramento road uniforms were at the laundry when the fire hit, so we had uniforms. There was only one glove that was saved, and it was in a repair shop. That was Joe Grace's glove. Everything else — shoes, gloves — were all burnt.

We were on the road all the time, but we were the home team when we were supposed to be home. It was great, the people in the ballparks would always give us a hand when we came on the field. That's just the way that it was; it was a two month's road trip.

When we got to San Diego, all the gamblers were betting everything on San Diego, but we only lost four out of seven that week. With brand new gloves and shoes, and all that, you know, I don't think anybody suffered any massive blisters from the new shoes or made any more errors than we did with the other gloves. It didn't make that much difference.

MARV GRISSOM - Sacramento Solons

EDMONDS FIELD - Sacramento

*F**ire swept through Moreing Field on the evening of July 11, 1948, after a double-header with Seattle. A new ballpark was built on the same site with the same dimensions. The new park,* *dubbed Edmonds Field, was concrete block and cement, and had no roof. It was a comfortable venue for Solons baseball.*

Edmonds was a really nice ballpark. We weren't supposed to have any wind in Sacramento, but I can remember Joe Brovia hitting the most prodigious fly balls out to right field. I mean huge! He'd start his home run trot. The ball would get out to about the right field fence, would start to quiver and fall straight down and the right fielder would catch the ball. Brovia would run down to first base, hollering and looking up to the skies, 'You're not with me up there! You're not with me!' Right field was the only place that the wind had any effect at Edmonds Field.

BUD WATKINS - Sacramento Solons

Edmonds Field was an open park — no roof on it. It was well maintained. The clubhouse was big enough. It was located under the grandstand, not far from the dugout. It could get pretty warm inside during the summer.

FRANK KERR - Sacramento Solons

I always liked pitching at Edmonds Field very much. I grew up around Fresno, where the weather was hot. I liked warm weather.

I liked coming into Sacramento because the Solons were usually loaded up with right-handed hitters because they had that left field fence. They had a few guys who hit a lot of home runs over there through the years. So that was to my favorite because I was a little more effective against right-handed hitters than I was against left.

CHARLES "RED" ADAMS - Los Angeles Angels

Sacramento was a nice place for baseball. It was hot. At 5 o'clock it could be 100 degrees, but by 7:30 it was down to seventy-two. The breeze came off the river. When I came in here with the Padres, I used to feel it was the best infield in the league. They had a groundskeeper,

Edmonds Field in Sacramento replaced the rickety Moreing Park, which was destroyed by fire in 1948. The breeze off the Sacramento River cooled the new park. This photograph is dated 1955.

Location: *Riverside Boulevard and Broadway*
Estimated Cost of Construction: *$290,000*
First Game: *March 20, 1949, vs. Oakland*
Seating: *9,000*
Last Game: *April 12, 1964*
Park Razed: *May, 1964*

Shorty Smith, a Scotsman. But when I came here, they had let him go, and it wasn't the best infield around anymore. The lights were fair, not as good as Vancouver.

BUDDY PETERSON - Sacramento Solons

LANE FIELD - San Diego

On January 22, 1936, William Lane, owner of the Hollywood Stars, announced the team's relocation to San Diego. On January 28, modification of a waterfront sports field began. On March 31, the San Diego Padres played the first game at Lane Field, the team's home for the next twenty-two years. It also was home to tens of thousands of voracious termites. But everyone — humans and insects alike — enjoyed this ballpark.

I was a left-handed batter, but I wasn't a home-run hitter — lots of singles and doubles. I think I hit two home runs out of Lane Field. The groundskeepers kept it up well. The lights were adequate, not too shabby. It was a nice place to play, and the fans were great.

The clubhouse was a typical clubhouse. It was rectangular, with stalls on both sides and a trainer's table in the back, right in the open. Some parks had separate rooms for the manager, but there wasn't a separate room in Lane Field.

A tunnel ran from the clubhouse to the dugout. The dugout was recessed with brick walls and an entrance to the field on the home-plate side. There was a screen above the wall to protect the players from foul balls.

TONY CRISCOLA - San Diego Padres

When you played in Lane Field, you had a helluva wind blowing to right. Right field was only 325 feet. Jack Graham, Luke Easter, Max West — they all hit to right field. They had fences out there with ads on them: 'Hit me and win a suit of clothes,' or something like that to give away. Left-handers had a benefit in San Diego because of the wind.

RUGGER ARDIZOIA - Hollywood Stars

I always liked San Diego. The fans were right on top of you, but it was a good infield and a good hitter's ballpark, particularly for left-handed hitters. There was something intimate about that ballpark. The seats were recessed. You could sometimes lose a pitched ball in the shadows during an afternoon game.

CHUCK STEVENS - Hollywood Stars

We used to have our high school championships at Lane Field. I liked the atmosphere because the stands were close. It was fan-friendly. The field was pretty honest as far as size was concerned. It didn't give anybody an advantage, left-handed or right-handed. It was a good-sized ballpark. I hit a home run there when I was in high school. Almost hit another. I think that impressed Pepper Martin, who was there that night.

It could get very foggy on occasion. I have seen the fog so thick there, as a spectator, that you couldn't see the outfielders. They had to delay the game until it cleared up.

JACK HARSHMAN - San Diego Padres

Lane Field was a great place to play. The wind blew out to right field all the time, and if you were a pull hitter, it was just great. That park was just made for me because I pulled everything. Max West was also a pull hitter.

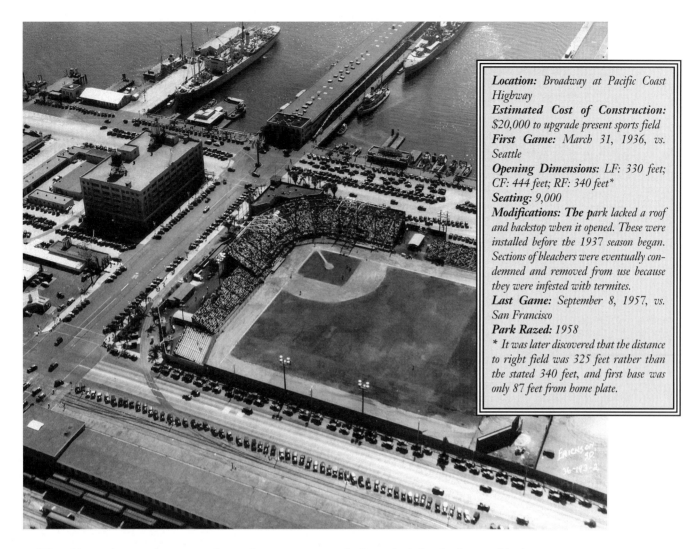

Location: *Broadway at Pacific Coast Highway*
Estimated Cost of Construction: *$20,000 to upgrade present sports field*
First Game: *March 31, 1936, vs. Seattle*
Opening Dimensions: *LF: 330 feet; CF: 444 feet; RF: 340 feet**
Seating: *9,000*
Modifications: The *park lacked a roof and backstop when it opened. These were installed before the 1937 season began. Sections of bleachers were eventually condemned and removed from use because they were infested with termites.*
Last Game: *September 8, 1957, vs. San Francisco*
Park Razed: *1958*
* *It was later discovered that the distance to right field was 325 feet rather than the stated 340 feet, and first base was only 87 feet from home plate.*

The old wooden stands were so close, when you were in the batter's circle, the fans could almost reach out and touch you.

JACK GRAHAM - San Diego Padres

Lane Field was fine to play in until a ball was hit up into the air. The lights were low. A ball would be hit up in the infield, and you'd look up and say, 'Where the hell is the baseball?'

BUDDY PETERSON - San Diego Padres

Lane Field was something else. The clubhouse was small and stunk like sweat all the time. The wood was all rotten. The city was going to kill the termites. No! No! Kill the termites and the walls fall down! It was a city-owned park, and they never took care of it. They finally had to condemn it.

The Navy helped the old Padres. Lots of sailors would come off the ship and say, 'Hey, there's a ball game down there. Let's go see the ball game.' They'd get in for fifty cents, but they'd drink five-dollars worth of beer.

FRANK KERR - San Diego Padres

We had a lot of fans who would take the streetcar and get off at the old train station and come to the ballpark.

Lane Field lasted only twenty-two years (1936-1957) before it was replaced by a new park in San Diego's Mission Valley. This photograph shows the park before the roof was completed, in early 1937. Foul balls presented interesting problems for unwary fans.

Of course, the ballpark was pretty rickety. But it was a good field, well maintained.

San Diego was a great place for a left-handed hitter. The wind blew out towards right field. It seems to me that one year, when Johnny Barrett was with us, he hit four high flies in one game and they all went out. The wind really blew out at old Lane Field.

I was pretty much a pull hitter, and hit a lot of balls to left field. If I had hit them to right field they would have been long gone. It was pretty tough to hit them out of the park to the left field side.

They had to call three or four games because the fog came in. I can recall one game when [Hal] Patchett was playing center field and I was playing left field, and somebody hit a high fly. Patchett and I ran together, and I said, 'Do you see it, Pat?' He said, 'No, I don't see it.' All of a sudden, that ball hit between us. It wasn't four feet away.

There was a low fence in left field, about three-and-a-half feet high, and above it was a wire fence, and somebody hit one and I went over the whole thing. I landed in the first row of seats. I was shaken up a bit, but didn't get hurt. After that they rebuilt it.

JOHN "SWEDE" JENSEN - San Diego Padres

Lane Field was a good field to play on — kind of a small ballpark. The lights were bad, but you only played the one night game, on Thursday night. All the other games were during the daytime.

There was a concentration of lights on the home plate area so nobody would get killed, but in the field there wasn't much light.

I had trouble at night picking up the ball when I first joined the Padres. It took me about two weeks to be able to judge a fly ball under the lights. I don't know if it was me or the lights.

EDDIE STEWART - San Diego Padres

WESTGATE PARK - San Diego

For years, people had acknowledged the need for a new ballpark in San Diego. Building a new ballpark in the Mission Valley was more difficult than anticipated. Bureaucratic entanglements delayed the start of construction to the extent that, on October 17, 1957, the San Diego Union ran a story headlined: "Lane Field for Padres in '58 Opener?"

While the grass was maturing at another site, work started at Friars Road and reached a feverish pace. By mid-March there was hope. By late April, San Diego partisans were watching baseball in one of America's finest minor league ballparks.

Westgate Park was absolutely one of the top minor league ballparks I ever played in. And it was another well-located ballpark, like Lane Field was. It was easy to get to from any place in San Diego.

The lights at Westgate were designed for a modern park, and they were really excellent.

Westgate Park was designed for expansion, and could have been expanded almost limitlessly. There's no question it could have been converted into a major league ballpark. None of the area in the outfield had any seating to it, and it could have been expanded into a 40,000-, 50,000-seat stadium. But they had to build a multipurpose stadium for football anyway.

JACK HARSHMAN - San Diego Padres

Location: 7227 Friars Road, in Mission Valley
Estimated Cost of Construction: $1 million
First Game: April 29, 1958, vs. Phoenix
Opening Dimensions: LF: 320 feet; CF: 410 feet; RF: 320 feet
Seating: 8,268
Last Game: September 8, 1968, vs. Phoenix
Razed: 1969

Westgate was a nice park. A funny thing about that park was, you'd go into the dugout and there would be water in there, on the floor. It wasn't raining. Beyond the outfield fence, there was a little creek, and both dugouts would always have some water in them. They couldn't keep it out.

BUDDY PETERSON - Sacramento Solons

I remember Willie McCovey hitting one over me in right field. He hit that ball so hard it hit one of the light standards dead-on. You could hear the ring all the way to L.A., I'm sure.

BILL RENNA - San Diego Padres

The San Diego Padres moved from Lane Field to attractive Westgate Park, in Mission Valley.

RECREATION PARK -
San Francisco

*R*ecreation Park was constructed out of the ashes of the Great Earthquake of 1906. This quaint *park, along with Ewing Field, San Francisco's "other" PCL park, is discussed in depth in Nuggets on the Diamond. Charlie Silvera, a fine Pacific Coast League catcher, had the unique privilege of playing at all three San Francisco parks — Recreation, Ewing and Seals Stadium.*

I graduated from St. Ignatius High, in the shadow of "Old Rec" (Recreation Park, home of the San Francisco Seals from 1907 through 1930). They had torn it down, but the grounds were still there, and we practiced there. While I was in high school, SF State took it over and had a ball field and we played a couple of games there — us versus the SF State freshmen. That was in 1937 or '38, before the war started.

I actually played at old Ewing Field (the Seals' park for part of the 1914 season, before the fog encouraged them to return to Recreation Park), but it wasn't baseball. They had a soccer league at that time with the CYO, and they played at Ewing Field. The stands were still there, but it was a bleak looking place by then.

Seals Stadium was like a second home to me. I remember seeing Joe DiMaggio play. there. In fact, I was there for his sixty-first [consecutive-hit] game.

CHARLIE SILVERA - Portland Beavers

A full house watches the Oakland Oaks (dark uniforms) play the San Francisco Seals, circa 1927. The ground-level seats were known as the "Booze Cage," where San Francisco's rowdiest fans congregated.

Location: *16th & Bryant streets*
Estimated Cost to Construct: *$1.25 million*
First Game: *March 13, 1931, vs. Detroit*
Opening Dimensions: *LF: 365 feet; CF: 404-424 feet; RF: 385 feet*
Seating: *25,000 (stated); 21,500 (realistic)*
Modifications: *2,000 bleacher seats in right field, bringing distance to 350 feet (1945-6)*
Last Game: *September 15, 1957, vs. Sacramento*

SEALS STADIUM - San Francisco

Seals Stadium was built at the start of the Depression, almost causing financial ruin for the team's owners. This all-concrete stadium sported high-quality lighting and a public address system, advanced technology for the time. Its spacious lines guaranteed the Seals would be perennial league leaders in triples and last place in home runs. Seals Stadium embodied the "class" that Pacific Coast League owners hoped would advance them to major league status.

You always felt you were in the major leagues playing at Seals Stadium, even with the adverse climactic conditions — the fog, the wind and the cold.

You could drill a ball in Seals Stadium and get nothing for it. I've jumped on pitches in San Francisco, given it my best shot, and if the wind was blowing in from right field, that's the biggest out you ever saw. And you figured that one's out in the parking lot someplace.

We had some strong guys on the teams I was on, but you could shut them down in San Francisco.

CHUCK STEVENS - Hollywood, San Francisco, Sacramento

Hitters had to battle San Francisco's ocean winds and Seals Stadium's generous dimensions to belt one out of the park.

Seals Stadium was probably the best stadium in the league. Its clubhouses were spacious and comfortable.

It could get damp at night. I often played at Seals Stadium at night. I played in the first Esquire Magazine All American Boys baseball game, and it was quite an experience. This guy hit a swinging bunt, and I went out and got the ball and threw it in about the twelfth row, it was so wet and slippery.

I can remember freezing there. If I wasn't catching, I'd put Capsolin on my arm and bundle up.

CLAUDE CHRISTIE - Seattle Rainiers

When we played in the afternoons at Seals Stadium, these big beer suds would come floating over the field. It made you want to have a beer.

NINO BONGIOVANNI - Seattle Indians, Portland Beavers

In 1957, we went into San Francisco for a seven-game series during the season. We were in the race, and by winning all seven games we could take over first place.

We won five out of seven, and the other games we lost on close plays. In one game, our pitcher, Chuck Churn, had the bases loaded, and Clyde King pulled us in to go for the double play, going to home, then first.

Sal Taormina hit a come-backer off the grass, and Churn threw that damn ball two-thirds the way up the screen. It had picked up so much moisture he couldn't hold on to it. So we lost that ball game.

In the other game, if the ball was hit fifteen rows into the stands, you'd better stay with it,

cause it's going to come back on the field. They had a runner on third base, the winning run, and a fly ball goes up like that.

Jim Baumer is at third base, and the wind's blowing in. The ball drops back of him, about four feet behind third base and one foot inside the line, and we lost that game.

Seals Stadium was a hard place to play.

FORREST "SPOOK" JACOBS - Hollywood Stars

Lane Field and Wrigley Field were made for left-handed pull hitters. Seals Stadium was just the opposite. You could hit the fly balls, and they'd hit that wind, and that was just it. You had to be a line-drive hitter up there or be an opposite-field hitter. In 1948, the first Sunday we were in there, I hit one over the back wall and one into the top row off of Jack Brewer. I think those were the only ones I hit there. We were playing in the daytime, and it just happened the wind was blowing out, which didn't happen very often.

JACK GRAHAM - San Diego Padres

I loved San Francisco. I thought it was the finest park to umpire in. Everything was solid green. There were no signs out there. The only thing that was white were the lines and bases. You could pick up a lot there, and there was a lot of foul territory.

CECE CARLUCCI - Umpire

Seals Stadium was a great place to play, although the fences were awfully high. The outfield was great, sometimes maybe too soft, but it was just a great surface to play on. Very good lights.

I didn't enjoy the fog. Sometimes with night games it could get pretty damp out there. You

Seals Stadium offered all of the beauty — and the windy, foggy dampness — typical of San Francisco.

hit a ball and it would go out of there. It wouldn't jump out, but it would go out. If you got it up in the [airstream], you'd be all right.

BILL RENNA - San Francisco Seals

Teddy Beard used to say, 'You know, they complain about the cold weather here in San Francisco, but you're going to play three or four years longer than the guys who are faced with 100- or 105-degree weather.'

JIM WESTLAKE - San Francisco Seals

DUGDALE PARK - Seattle

I used to go to Dugdale as a fan, but was not involved with the organization under [owner] Bill Klepper. It was an old wooden-frame structure. It was a nice ballpark. It was like old Emeryville and Vaughn Street in Portland. That's how they were constructed in those days. It had poor lighting.

EDO VANNI - Seattle Indians

Fly balls soared skyward, then out of sight, during night games at Dugdale Park in Seattle.

Location: *McClellan Street, at Rainier Street*
First season of use: *1913*
Seating: *15,000*
Dimensions (est.): *LF: 390 feet; CF: 460 feet; RF: 245 feet.*
Burned: *July 4, 1932*
Note: *When Sicks Seattle Stadium was built, in 1938, it slightly overlapped the former Dugdale Park site.*

CIVIC STADIUM — Seattle

I grew up in Seattle. I remember the Seattle Indians playing in Dugdale Stadium before it burned down, and for six years they played at the old Civic Stadium, at the Civic Auditorium, before Emil Sick built the new Sicks Seattle Stadium.

I don't know why they would have allowed games to be played in that stadium. There was a big left-field wall and a big balcony of the Civic Auditorium right behind it. But sometimes .... a line drive deep in right field would get up toward a bank of gooseberry bushes.

I can remember Leo Lassen broadcasting a line-drive triple — to me the most exciting play in baseball. He would broadcast, 'The ball is going to right field, and there it goes, and the ball is rolling for the gooseberry bushes!' And once it got in there, it was a ground-rule triple or something.

DON KLEIN - Seals Radio Broadcaster

The Seattle Rainiers were forced to use Civic Stadium after Dugdale Park burned down, in 1932. Civic's hard field was blamed for many bizarre misplays.

I was a clubhouse boy out at Civic Stadium. The clubhouses were side-by-side out behind left field. There wasn't a blade of grass on the whole field — it was all dirt. They had telephone poles for the lights alongside third base, and [Seattle Rainiers outfielder] Joe Coscarart became famous for running around, dodging those light poles.

It was 260 to 270 feet to left field. They lied about it, and it was about 360 feet to right field. There was a big concrete wall, and there used to be gooseberry bushes out there.

[Announcer] Leo Lassen used to say, 'There goes another ball into the gooseberry bushes.' In other words, if you hit a line drive over first base on that hard pad, it would roll for an hour.

And center field used to be huge. That's where [Seattle outfielder] Bill Lawrence used to roam. He used to cover all those fields. He was one of the best.

EDO VANNI - Seattle Indians

I think it was one of the worst ballparks I ever played in. Civic had a pretty short left field and a short fence. Pop flies were often hit for home runs. It was hard and gravelly. It would wear out a pair of cleats real quick. There was no grass at all.

Right field was a mile out there. I learned to shade things to right field to cut off balls hit to the gap. When a ball was hit to the outfield, pebbles would fly up. When a ball was hit to you, you'd say your prayers it wouldn't take a bad hop. You wouldn't dive for a ball there. It would tear your hands apart.

The lights were terrible. I don't remember any lights in center field. It seems they were behind the plate and down the sidelines. I think there was one in left field, but they seemed like they were a mile away.

NINO BONGIOVANNI - Seattle Indians

In 1936, [San Francisco Missions manager] Gabby Street took me on a trip to Seattle. We were in old Civic Field. It was built like a football field, but it was all sandstone. The only grass was on the infield.

They had a big broad jump pit off first base, and Herm Michael — quite a prospect — used to play first. He ran for a foul ball, fell in the pit and broke his leg. It about killed him.

RUGGER ARDIZOIA - Hollywood Stars

Playing at Civic was like playing out in the street. We used to call it Hogan's Brick Yard.

There were light standards that were outside the playing field, but with open space behind them that was still in play. The right field had a gradual upward slope to it. The lights were terrible. It was like playing in their closet. And it was really dark in center field. Thank God we were only there for the first couple of months of the season before we moved into the new ballpark.

One time we were playing the Seals, Dominic DiMaggio was playing center field. I hit a hard shot through the box, and it hit that hard pavement and bounced nine miles high, and I was on third base before the ball came down.

LEN GABRIELSON - Seattle Indians

Location: 2700 Rainier Avenue and McClellan Street
Estimated Cost of Construction: $350,000
First Game: June 15, 1938, vs. Portland
Opening Dimensions: LF: 335 feet; CF: 415 feet; RF: 335 feet
Seating: 14,200
Modifications: With the arrival of major league baseball, in 1969, grandstands were expanded down the left-field and right-field lines, and were placed behind the outfield walls.
Last PCL Game: September 2, 1968, vs. Spokane
Date Razed: 1977

SICKS SEATTLE STADIUM - Seattle

Sicks Stadium — now that was class. Huge lockers, big cubicles in the clubhouse and large dugouts. The park was built large enough for long outs. It was a good pitcher's park.

The wind wasn't a major factor, but it could be cold at nights. You never saw so much coffee sold up there and so many whiskey bottles cleaned up in the morning — Coffee Royale.

I lived in west Seattle over by the railroad station, fifteen minutes from the park. When I first got there, it felt like San Francisco — steep hills, cable cars, waterfront, wharf, fishing boats and ferry boats — almost like home.

RUGGER ARDIZOIA - Seattle Rainiers

I loved Sicks Stadium. It was symmetrical, not the odd-shaped park, and you were close to the fans.

They must have had terrific groundskeepers, too. The ballpark was always beautiful.

CLAUDE CHRISTIE - Seattle Rainiers

We were all happy to get out of Civic Stadium. Sicks Stadium had grass and good lights, and good crowds. Our crowds came out into the rain, even.

There was a garden behind left field at Sicks Stadium. A produce man grew vegetables back there. They called it Tightwad Hill. We kept driving balls into his vegetable garden.

LEN GABRIELSON - Seattle Rainiers

Compared to Civic Stadium, just about any other park would have seemed like heaven. But Sicks Seattle Stadium was indeed wonderful — a player's and fan's paradise.

Location: *4601 Ontario Street*
Estimated Cost of Construction: *unknown*
First PCL Game: *April 27, 1956, vs. San Francisco*
Opening Dimensions: *LF: 335 feet; CF: 415 feet;*
RF: 335 feet

Seating: *9,200*
Status: *Currently in use*

Even damp coastal weather didn't keep fans from filling the seats in Vancouver's Capilano Stadium.

CAPILANO STADIUM - Vancouver

Capilano Stadium, aka Nat Bailey Field, was upgraded to greet the transfer of the Oakland franchise to Vancouver in 1956. It is a clean stadium in a delightful neighborhood. Because of its northerly location, night games are played in perpetual twilight. Somehow, the atmosphere at baseball games played in Canada was different — and more refreshing.

Vancouver was sore-arm time. It was a nice place to pitch, but it was too damp. I tore a muscle there. I told Charlie [Metro, the Vancouver Mounties manager] you might as well let me go. But he kept me. I pitched in spot relief, but I was done and I knew it.

They had the best mound I ever saw in baseball. I asked the groundskeeper, 'Where do you get this dirt?' He told me he got it on the backside of the hill, behind the cemetery.

It was a beautiful park with good fan support. You didn't play on Sundays. Double-header on Saturday, and everything was closed on Sunday. The only things open were the movies and restaurants.

EDDIE ERAUTT - Vancouver Mounties

It was a fairly new ballpark in a beautiful setting. There was a lot of enthusiasm from the city. The stands were packed every night. I had played at Capilano Stadium when I was in the Western International League.

It was a difficult stadium to play in at night. You're so far north, the games would start at 8 o'clock, and about 9 o'clock somebody would hit a pop fly and the outfielders couldn't see it.

I know [team manager] Lefty O'Doul would always say to us, 'Pop it up! Pop it up!' About 9 o'clock, you'd see the outfielders holding their hands and gloves over their head. They didn't know where the ball was.

They took good care of the field, and the ballpark was neat and clean. The lights were average. The clubhouse was a good one.

LEN NEAL - Vancouver Mounties

Capilano Stadium was a great park. They kept the grass long. That helped us infielders. It was tiled underneath. It could rain up until 5 o'clock, and if it stopped raining, you could play. It was a nice ballpark, with good lights. We drew well.

BUDDY PETERSON - Vancouver Mounties

Capilano Stadium was a clean park, in an attractive section of town. The main entrance was behind home plate, and to get to the home clubhouse, you'd make a left turn. There was a players' side entrance outside, along the third-base side.

There was a screen in front of the dugout, and you could enter the field from either side of the dugout, a few steps up to the field. We had a bat rack by the entrance to the dugout on the home-plate side.

They had all those billboards around the outfield fences advertising all types of things. They go with old ballparks. I remember there was a target area: You hit this ad and you would win some money. As I recall, the ad was at the bottom of the fence, and any reasonable right fielder was not going to let that ball hit the sign.

They would turn the lights on for night games, but you could still see the blue skies to the north. Even when the game was over, it wasn't terribly dark. It's dark enough that you need lights, but when you leave the park, you didn't need lights. It was like it was dusk.

I've been by the old stadium in the last few years. My memories of Capilano Stadium as a kid were of this majestic place. I look at it now, after having been to major league parks and some of the new minor league parks, and I look at it and say, 'Holy cow.' It was nothing fancy.

MARTIN JOHNSON - Mounties Fan

With good players, a great manager and devoted fans, the Oakland Oaks had the ingredients for a financially secure franchise. Note the standing-room-only crowd in left field. Chuck Stevens of the Hollywood Stars tried to break up a double play as shortstop Ray Hamrick jumped over him. Second baseman Dario Lodigiani made the toss to Hamrick, who threw on to first baseman Nick Etten.

3 GREAT TEAMS

Ted Williams signed with his home team, the San Diego Padres, in 1936. He was assigned a regular spot on the team in 1937, the year the Padres won the PCL championship.

MANY CHAMPIONSHIP TEAMS DISTINGUISHED THEMSELVES AS SPECIAL. THE 1927 NEW YORK YANKEES AND THE 1930 PHILADELPHIA ATHLETICS COME TO MIND. SIMILARLY, THERE HAVE BEEN TEAMS THAT HAVE SHOWN GREATNESS OVER SEVERAL SEASONS. THE GIANTS OF JOHN J. MCGRAW, THE YANKEES OF CASEY STENGEL AND CINCINNATI'S "BIG RED MACHINE" FIT IN THIS CATEGORY.

BUILDING A DYNASTY IN THE MINOR LEAGUES WAS MORE DIFFICULT. THE MAJOR LEAGUE PLAYER DRAFT COMPELLED MINOR LEAGUE TEAM OWNERS TO SELL OFF THEIR PRIZED PLAYERS TO AVOID ECONOMIC HARDSHIP AT SEASON'S END.

STILL, SOME DOMINANT MINOR LEAGUE REGIMES FLOURISHED ON THE WEST COAST — THE SAN FRANCISCO SEALS OF THE GOLDEN '20S, THE LOS ANGELES ANGELS OF THE '30S AND THE PREWAR SEATTLE RAINIERS. OTHER TEAMS EMERGED, CINDERELLA-LIKE, INTO CHAMPIONS FOR A SEASON.

GREAT TEAMS INCLUDE GREAT PLAYERS, BUT GREAT PLAYERS ARE NO GUARANTEE OF GREAT TEAMS. SO MANY INTANGIBLES AFFECT A TEAM'S ABILITY TO PERFORM LIKE A CHAMPION: LEADERSHIP, GOOD HEALTH, BAD BOUNCES AT GOOD TIMES, TEAM CHEMISTRY, WEATHER AND EVEN LUCK.

MOST FRANCHISES HAD MORE THAN ONE TEAM THAT MIGHT HAVE BEEN CONSIDERED THE CITY'S BEST. THEY ARE USUALLY FROM DIFFERENT DECADES, WHICH MAKES COMPARISONS DIFFICULT. FOR OUR PURPOSES HERE, THESE TEAMS' OUTSTANDING ERAS ARE PRESENTED CHRONOLOGICALLY. READERS MAY DRAW THEIR OWN CONCLUSIONS ABOUT WHO WAS BEST.

EACH OF THESE TEAMS POSSESSED THE INGREDIENTS FOR GREATNESS, POSSIBLY FOR AN ERA, OR FOR JUST A SINGLE SEASON.

THE SAN FRANCISCO SEALS

1 9 4 6   S E A L S

*O*rganized baseball at all levels benefited when World War II soldiers came home. The Seals assembled a veteran club strong in all facets of the game. And they had a charismatic leader in Lefty O'Doul. The Seals outlasted their cross-Bay rivals, the Oakland Oaks, establishing a minor league attendance record that stood for three decades.*

One of the PCL's all-around best ball clubs, the 1946 Seals attracted solid, experienced players returning from military service after World War II, and earned the league championship behind Frank "Lefty" O'Doul (second row, far left).

The 1946 Seals was the best minor league ball club I ever saw. The Philadelphia A's came out and played us four games in spring training, and we beat them in all four. We had a better ball club than they did. We had a bunch of veterans. Hugh Luby had just returned from the military. He was owned by the Giants. Larry Jansen was back, and we had other players back from the war. The club could do everything.

Frenchy Uhalt was our leadoff hitter. He brought experience, speed — he could run like hell. He was a great outfielder. He didn't throw all that great, but he stabilized our younger outfielders. He was a good hitter and was always on base. He did the little things that great players have to do to be great.

Roy Nicely was simply one great fielder. It's just a shame he couldn't hit just a little. He couldn't buy a base hit. He had no power, but what an arm he had. He could throw like hell and catch anything that was hit. He was kind of an Ozzie Smith.

He and Luby formed a great double-play combination. Luby was steady. He always seemed to be in the right spot. Those two worked well together. The ball was always right here (chest high).

Luby was the guy who would go in to calm the pitcher down. I didn't do any of that, and we know [Ted] Jennings didn't. Jennings was an adequate third baseman. Jennings couldn't even get a sign. O'Doul would stand down there in the third-base coaching box and say, 'You're bunting, Ted. Ted, you're bunting.' Poor Ted. But he could hit that ball!

I led the league in RBI and runs scored, and I think I hit twelve home runs, the most I ever hit. I actually hit the first home run into the bleachers in right field. 'Who's going to hit the first home run? [Joe] Brovia? [Ted] Jennings? [Sal] Taormina?' But not Ferris Fain. I was the last guy they were betting on.

Larry Jansen — you really don't know how good this guy was until you play with him. I used to stand out there and marvel that he wasn't overpowering with a fastball and he didn't have a great curve. But who did you want out there with a key game on the line? Larry Jansen.

He had uncanny control. The toughest thing to hit is a ball that moves. It doesn't make any difference if he throws 100 miles per hour if there's no motion. If there's motion, you've got a weapon.

Jansen had that good, hard slider, but he wasn't overpowering. Everything he threw had movement. And he was always around the plate, never walked anybody. Later, when I batted against him in spring training, I realized how good his slider was. I couldn't see it!

Cliff Melton was another who didn't overpower anybody. He just stood out there and gave you a lot of motion. Billy Werle was tough on left-handers. He'd throw from that side ... and he could hit too. He and Jansen were good hitters.

The only guy on our squad who really threw hard was that big kid, Bob Jensen. But he had trouble controlling it. He'd walk as many as he'd strike out.

The mainstays of the staff were Jansen, Melton, Werle, Frank Seward and Ray Harrell. Lefty had a lot of veterans back from the war, and he used them all. He let them stay in to finish their own work. Most of them had pretty good control and didn't walk many.

The Oaks had a good team with good pitchers — Rugger Ardizoia, Gene Bearden, Frank Shea, The Cheater (Ralph Buxton). Manager Casey Stengel had a lot of veterans too, and when we'd play the Oaks, Stengel and Lefty would really put on a show, and we had great crowds.

After 1946 season, the Giants were going to draft me and send me back to San Francisco. They had already agreed to that with Mr. [Charlie] Graham. But the Coast League was wanting to go big league. After losing Larry Jansen to the Giants that left me to be available for the draft.

But at the last minute, they took Jack Lohrke instead of me. San Diego had some deal to sell him to the major leagues, but it fell through, so Jack was available and the Giants took him instead of me. So Philadelphia drafted me.

FERRIS FAIN - Seals First Baseman

At the time and when I was in the majors, I knew Roy Nicely could play big league ball with anybody. He was the best at getting the ball. Of course, hitting kept him out of (the major leagues), but in this day and age, he probably would have been a major leaguer.

We had a very good defensive ball club and, of course, a big ballpark. That made it easy for me. I wasn't much of a strikeout man. I had to have a good ball club behind me.

Our pitching was balanced. We had lots of guys who could start — lefties or right-handers.

Lefty [O'Doul]'s thinking was to develop a pitcher. Let him work out of a jam, if he could. He wanted to see you grow. I think if he came out and got us [off the mound] all the time, we would have been a different type of ballplayer.

One thing I always appreciated was his giving you a chance to get out of it, to see if you had the courage, what kind of battler you were.

Known for his coolheaded pitching, Larry Jansen signed with the San Francisco Seals in 1941. The war kept him out of baseball in 1943 and '44, but he re-signed with the Seals in '46, the team's championship season.

Some of the San Francisco Seals, above, on their way to spring training in Hana, Hawaii, where club owner Paul Fagan owned a ranch. Below: Bruce "Oggie" Ogrodowski's fashion statement didn't pass muster with league officials, but it was a hit in Hawaii.

Spring Training in Hawaii was fun. We played all the military teams in 1946. In 1947, they made an arrangement for the Giants to come over for eight or nine days. I think that was part of the working agreement. That year we had real good competition.

That was also the year they had the great tidal wave over in Hawaii, and we couldn't get out. I was one of the first to return (to the mainland) because I had pitched the last game and wasn't going to pitch anymore. So me and Joe Sprinz and someone else got on the old Pan Am Clipper and came back to San Francisco. By the time the season was ready to start, we still had four or five players stranded in Hawaii.

The weather was great. You'd have periodic rain showers. It would rain ten minutes, but the field was on volcanic rock, so the water would just drain right down. We did our basic drills at Hana, Maui. Fagan was trying to build it up as a tourist attraction. So we worked out for two weeks at Hana, then went to Honolulu when the Giants arrived and played the exhibition games there.

BILL WERLE -
Seals Pitcher

I had trouble with the Oaks in 1946. I think they were just a bunch of good low-ball hitting players. [Les] Scarsella was a good left-handed hitter. And [Brooks] Holder. I was a low-ball pitcher, and they had some good low-ball hitters. They had a small right field and good left-handed hitters, and I wasn't a strikeout type of pitcher.

I'll never forget Easter Sunday morning against the Oaks, when they split the double-header. I'm going to start the morning game. O'Doul says to me, 'You're going to pitch at 10 o'clock. We'll probably have 2,000 in the stands, and that'll put an end to all this junk.'

We didn't have to get to the park too early. We didn't hit or run, just took infield, warmed up and then played. So I go out to warm up about twenty minutes before the game, and there are over 10,000 people in the stands already. I think, Sure, this is going to end these (split double-headers). And we played that way the rest of the year.

In the playoffs, we played Hollywood and swept them in four. I think I pitched the first game against Hollywood and won. Then I relieved in game four. We had a lead, but Lefty told me to go down and get ready, so I finished up at Hollywood and also hit a home run.

Against the Oaks, we went with lefties — [Al] Lien and [Cliff] Melton. I started game three at Oakland, but didn't last, and Bill Werle replaced me. Al Lien shut them out in game six to win the series. I wasn't a factor.

I was sold to the Giants with about a month to go in the 1946 season. Melton, [Frank] Seward and [Francis] Rosso were on loan for the opportunity to collect the first player off our roster.

LARRY JANSEN - Seals Pitcher

Lefty was a good guy to pitch for because he stayed with his pitchers real well. You look at the complete games that we had. I think [Larry] Jansen had thirty-one. I can't recall him pitching a bad game that year. I can remember sitting next to Lefty in the dugout one game that Jansen was pitching, and Frank ['Lefty' O'Doul] says, 'I know I can just sit back and enjoy the game with Jansen out there.' He didn't have to worry about the bullpen or anything. I don't recall any team ever getting more than three runs off of him. It was the best season I ever saw at any level. And Larry never walked anybody.

If I had a favorite catcher, it was Bruce 'Oggie' Ogrodowski. I feel he was a better receiver than Joe Sprinz and had more 'inside baseball' than Joe. I think he called a better game than

Joe. But it was right after the war, and we had a lot of catchers who came through San Francisco — Ray Orteig, and Dixie Howell. Jimmie Gladd was outstanding. With all the catchers from the Giants and later the Pirates, there was always a difference, so you couldn't build up a favorite.

Our infield was outstanding. Luby was finishing out his career, and he wasn't that fast, but he knew how to position himself to take best advantage. Nicely had outstanding range. Ted [Jennings] was very erratic. But he could hit like hell.

Ted was in a world of his own. I remember one inning with Sam Gibson on the mound. Ted made two straight errors, then goes over to Sam [Gibson, the pitcher] and says, 'C'mon, Sam. Let's bear down.' I thought Gibson was going to tear him apart. Of course, Sam had a short fuse anyway.

[Ferris] Fain was a great player, but more than that, he kept order on the club. If somebody dogged it, he'd be waiting on the top step, 'Hey, you're fooling with my money. You either shift it into gear or we're going to have more to say about it.'

Don Trower was a good backup. He didn't play a lot, and he didn't hit much, but he was a good fill-in and did his job when he was called upon.

BILL WERLE - Seals Pitcher

I got home in the middle of May of 1946, and was back in time to play half a season in 1946 with the championship Seals.

We had a bunch of young outfielders with the 1946 Seals. Frenchy Uhalt was a real veteran, and he helped me more than you can imagine. I hung out in his back pocket. When they were taking batting practice, I would go out to center field and just talk baseball with him. I picked up things from him that I had never seen before.

I never saw any outfielder come in and slide under a ball like he did. I questioned him on what he was looking for. When I went to Pittsburgh, Billy Meyer put me in center field, and I took that as a huge compliment. Then I realized that Ralph Kiner was playing left field and

Above: Cliff Melton tries out his "Aloha" windup.
Left, from left to right: Wil Leonard, Joe Sprinz, Bruce Ogrodowski, Doug Loane and Jack Holt discuss catching strategy at Paul Fagan's ranch in Hawaii.

Wally Westlake was in right field. Westlake had good speed and had a good arm. Kiner had flat feet. Jackie Tobin had flat feet, but he could fly. He got a great jump on the ball. He was one of the quickest — his mind was always ahead of the game. He also leaned forward as he ran.

Don White was a kind of outfielder that you liked to have on your ball club because he was always there. He had the right instincts and fundamentals. He is the guy who moved to center field when Frenchy took a day off. He had a good arm, threw to the right base.

Neill Sheridan played mostly in right field. He had a great arm and had no qualms about throwing all the way to third. He'd throw the ball so hard some times, it would skip right by Ted Jennings, and O'Doul would go bananas. 'Neill, aim for the second baseman, and if you overthrow him, the third baseman has a nice hop to the base.' He was the type of guy that if he got to the ball, he caught it.

Neill had great potential. In 1948, Babe Ruth came by the clubhouse. We all got to meet him, and he gave Lefty one of his bats: forty-two ounces and thirty-six inches. We used to use it to swing with another bat to loosen up. Sheridan was the only player who could use it [to hit]. He used it in batting practice and he'd hit some shots out of the ballpark.

Neill would try to fake out the pitcher after a walk. He'd jog three-quarters of the way to first, then he'd take off for second. He was able to catch the pitcher asleep. But after he did it a couple of times, the word got around the league, and he's still trying to do it. O'Doul would say, 'Why? They're used to it now.'

Jennings knew how to play his position, and was such a talent, but he didn't learn different techniques. He wouldn't get down on the ball, waiting for the big hop, and balls would get under him. Lefty would get so frustrated because he wouldn't knock the ball down first.

He had a great, compact swing, much like what O'Doul's swing was like. He didn't have a big swing, but always made contact.

BILL WERLE - Seals Pitcher

1 9 4 7 - 4 9   S E A L S

The Seals had a working agreement with the Giants that soured when they sold Larry Jansen. [The Seals] got money and three players, but we never got the third player. Finally, Charlie [Graham, the Seals owner] went back at the All-Star Break and had it out with Horace [Stoneham, of the Giants], and they gave us a kid, Dick Lajeskie. But they broke off the working agreement, and the Seals affiliated with Pittsburgh.

BILL WERLE - Seals Pitcher

In 1947, we came down to a one-game playoff with the Angels. They beat us 5-0. Clarence Maddern hit a grand slam home run, and then Larry Barton hit a solo home run. But we should have won the pennant at San Diego on a Sunday (September 28). We had the bases loaded against Bob Kerrigan, I was on third base with the bases loaded and Roy Nicely at bat. Kerrigan was taking such a big windup.

Lefty said, 'Just kind of creep down the third base line, and if you get a good jump, go!' I got a good jump, and I slid in, across home plate, and as I'm coming up, the catcher tags me. [Umpire] Phil Mazzeo calls me out. O'Doul comes flying down the line, screaming bloody murder. That would have been the fourth run in the [top of the seventh inning]. The count was 3-1 on Nicely, and the ball was up here (chest high), and Mazzeo calls it a strike.

Jack Graham comes up later and hits a home run to win it. If we had won that game, we would have won the pennant.

With the 1948 club we had an offensive machine. At the top of the lineup we had Jackie Tobin and Hugh Luby. Both of them could run. Then you come up with Gene Woodling and Mickey Rocco to drive them in.

After Woodling and Rocco, there was Brovia and me. Dixie Howell, our catcher, was a good contact hitter, as were Frank Shofner or Ray Orteig at third. Then Nicely and the pitcher.

The Seals always used to get good players from their working agreements. In 1946 they had a working agreement with the Giants; in 1948, it was with the Pirates. And we always seemed to get good pitching from these teams. Frank Rosso, Frank Seward, Dale Mathewson came from the Giants in 1946.

In 1948, Tommy Fine and Mickey Rocco came in the transaction that sent Neill Sheridan to the Red Sox. We got Kenny Gables from Pittsburgh for Con Dempsey. For someone who couldn't see home plate, he was a pretty good pitcher. He would get out there, and someone would get out there with a pair of glasses, and he'd put them on and he still couldn't see the catcher's signs. But he was a helluva pitcher.

And Manny Perez and Dewey Soriano. Of course, we got [Gene] Woodling and [Dixie] Howell from Pittsburgh. [Seals owner] Charlie Graham had a good sense about players. He was a shrewd trader. He could get more ballplayers for his dollar. And it was always the right mix. There wasn't a guy on the ball club that you didn't enjoy playing with.

Charlie Graham died in August, and we had our share of injuries. Of course, we lost

The top of the 1948 Seals lineup, left to right: second baseman Hugh Luby, left-fielder Dino Restelli, center-fielder Gene Woodling, first baseman Mickey Rocco and right-fielder Joe Brovia.

Woodling for six weeks. And Rocco was like Bernie Uhalt — he was always on the rubbing table. He had a bad back, and it was questionable whether he was going to play. They would adjust him and heat him and put all kinds of stuff on him.

He'd step off the table and Leo Hughes would ask him, 'Are you going to be able to make it tonight?' 'Oh, yeah, I can make it.' But there were many nights when he couldn't make it.

DINO RESTELLI - Seals Third Baseman

The 1957 San Francisco Seals struck a winning balance with young players and veterans.

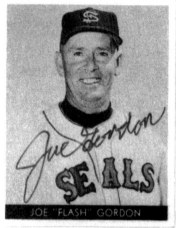
JOE "FLASH" GORDON

GRADY HATTON, JR.

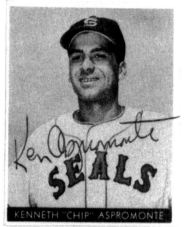
KENNETH "CHIP" ASPROMONTE

LEO "BLACK CAT" KIELY

JOHN McCALL

HARRY WILLIAM MALMBERG

FRANK KELLERT

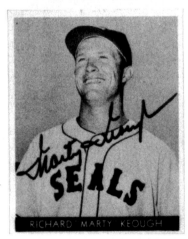
RICHARD "MARTY" KEOUGH

ALBERT "ALBIE" PEARSON

1957 SEALS

*N*o one realized it at the start of the season, but 1957 would be the last year of the "normalized" Pacific Coast League. The Brooklyn Dodgers and New York Giants were formalizing plans to move their operations to Los Angeles and San Francisco, respectively.

The Boston Red Sox had purchased the San Francisco territory two years earlier with the intention of "locking it up" for the American League. Their boasts that the 1956 San Francisco team would be "second to none" turned out to be empty, as the Seals finished a dismal sixth. Seals president Jerry Donovan vowed that would not happen again.

Jerry Donovan went out and acquired a bunch of veterans — Grady Hatton, Jack Phillips and Frank Kellert. We had a helluva club in 1957. It was a well balanced team with the older guys. Then they had Albie Pearson, Marty Keough, Ed Sadowski and Haywood Sullivan. The Seals owned a lot of veterans and the Red Sox sent the youngsters out on option.

Thank God I got out there. And I had a fair enough year to go up to Boston the next season.

Joe Gordon was a just real nice guy. He'd say, 'Play the game hard and loosen that top button on your jersey, and swing that bat!' He kept the team loose. He had a lot of fun playing and he wanted everyone else to have fun.

Our pitching was average. That's where [Leo] Kiely made a big name for himself, because we'd come back strong in the late innings. We'd start pounding the ball around and get runs in chunks. Leo would come in and relieve. He'd come out of the bullpen with that sinker, and he was effective as hell.

I think he won twenty games (21-6, 2.22 ERA.). I don't think he started a game, maybe one. (Three, actually, and pitched relief in fifty-six.) He was too valuable coming out of the bullpen. We had Bill Abernathie (13-2) and Bert Thiel (5-4) down there too. It was a good relief corps, I can tell you that.

Riverboat [Smith], a left-hander, could throw the ball pretty hard. Jack Spring, another left-hander, was a Boston guy. As I recall, the rest of the staff was a little gray.

I don't know what Leo had done before — whether he was a starter or not — but it seemed like Leo pitched every night. I guess Joe must have found something. It probably worked a couple of times, so he said, 'That's a pretty good idea.'

I'd bat fourth or fifth. Frank Kellert often batted cleanup. We both batted in over 100 runs. Kellert was a consistent hitter. He just kept banging out hits. I felt he could have played more in the majors. He impressed me as a real good hitter. He could hit the ball sharply and he had a good idea of where the strike zone was. The only problem was that he couldn't run too well.

It was a good infield — [Ken] Aspromonte and [Harry] Malmberg up the middle. Aspromonte was a really good hitter. He had a good year (leading the league in hitting, at .334). Malmberg could hurt you. You think he'd walk up there like a little splinter, but he was very aggressive.

We had [Grady] Hatton and Jack Phillips at third. Phillips was so tall and lanky, he didn't look like a third baseman. More like a first baseman, but we had [Frank] Kellert there. Jack was a pretty good hitter, but he wasn't a Frank Kellert.

I liked to see Grady Hatton out there rather than Jack. Grady was a better fielder, and he had a pretty good year out there too (.317). We had a pretty good ball club, but thank god for good relief.

I was out in left, and Sal Taormina alternated with me. Albie Pearson was in right and Marty Keough was in center. We were doing pretty good until Marty threw one low between innings.

Vancouver was our big opposition. There were other teams that weren't as strong, and there were excellent players on weaker teams, but Vancouver was really heavy.

BILL RENNA - Seals Outfielder

COMING TO SAN FRANCISCO

IN 1956, THE KANSAS CITY ATHLETICS TRADED ME BACK TO THE YANKEES, WHO SENT ME TO RICHMOND IN THE INTERNATIONAL LEAGUE. IN THE LATTER PART OF THE SEASON, I WAS TALKING WITH LEE MACPHAIL OF THE YANKEES. I TOLD HIM, 'IF I AM PLAYING MINOR LEAGUE BALL NEXT YEAR, I'M NOT GOING TO BE PLAYING IT HERE. I'M GOING TO BE PLAYING IT OUT ON THE WEST COAST.'

HE SAID, 'IF YOU'RE NOT PLAYING IN THE BIG LEAGUES, WE'LL DO EVERYTHING WE CAN TO GET YOU BACK TO THE COAST.' WELL IT DIDN'T HAPPEN THAT WAY.

TO PROTECT THEMSELVES FROM THE DRAFT, THE YANKEES MOVED SEVERAL OF THEIR PROSPECTS ON THE RICHMOND ROSTER TO DENVER. SO I WAS ON THE DENVER ROSTER WITH FOUR OR FIVE OTHERS. ONE WAS CAL NEEMAN, A YOUNG CATCHER.

THE CHICAGO CUBS WERE LAST IN THE WORLD, SO THEY GOT TO DRAFT FIRST, AND THEY TOOK NEEMAN. YOU COULD DRAFT ONE PERSON OFF A AAA CLUB, SO THAT FROZE THE REST OF US ON THE DENVER ROSTER. CHARLIE SILVERA WAS PURCHASED BY THE CUBS FROM THE YANKEES BEFORE THE DRAFT AND THEN THEY DRAFTED CAL NEEMAN. HE WAS A NICE KID BUT HE WASN'T NEARLY READY. CHARLIE WAS MORE OF A HELP THAN CAL. SO IT WAS OBVIOUS WHAT THEY WERE DOING.

SO AFTER THE DRAFT, I CALLED MACPHAIL AND I TOLD HIM THAT I SMELLED THAT DEAL ALL THE WAY OUT HERE ON THE COAST.

THAT'S WHEN HE SAID, 'I DON'T KNOW WHAT YOU MEAN.' I SAID, 'YOU KNOW WHAT I MEAN. I WANT TO PLAY OUT ON THE COAST.'

HE SAID, 'NOBODY OUT THERE WANTS YOU.' I SAID 'OK, FINE,' AND HUNG UP. THAT'S WHEN I CALLED JERRY DONOVAN [PRESIDENT OF THE SAN FRANCISCO SEALS]. JERRY SAID, 'DON'T SAY ANYTHING TO ANYBODY. JUST SIT TIGHT.' SO I DID. TWO WEEKS LATER I GET A TELEGRAM FROM THE YANKEES THAT MY CONTRACT HAD BEEN ASSIGNED OUTRIGHT TO SAN FRANCISCO IN THE COAST LEAGUE. I ALREADY HAD MY BAGS PACKED.

BILL RENNA - San Francisco Seals

LEAVING SAN FRANCISCO

IN 1956, I WAS RECOVERING FROM A SORE ARM AND WAS STUCK IN THE PHILADELPHIA PHILLIES BULLPEN, SO I REQUESTED A CHANCE TO PITCH IN SAN FRANCISCO AND THEY SOLD MY CONTRACT THERE. WITH THE SEALS, I HAD AN INCENTIVE CONTRACT. WE WERE ABOUT FIVE WEEKS INTO THE SEASON, AND I HAD FOUR WINS AND WAS LEADING THE CLUB IN ERA, AND JOE GORDON CAME UP TO ME AND SAID, 'DEE, WE HAVE TO LET YOU GO.'

I THOUGHT JOE WAS KIDDING. WE HAD A LOT OF OLDER GUYS ON THE CLUB — [WALTER] MASTERSON, [JIM] KONSTANTY, GUYS THAT WERE MY AGE OR OLDER — AND I WONDERED WHAT THE HELL WAS THE DEAL. HE SAID, 'I'LL BE HONEST WITH YOU. YOU HAVE A CLAUSE IN YOUR CONTRACT THAT YOU'RE GOING TO MAKE A PRETTY GOOD CHUNK OF MONEY ONCE YOU PROVE YOUR ARM ISN'T BOTHERING YOU. WE'VE ALSO GOT A COUPLE OF YOUNG KIDS THAT BOSTON WANTS TO SEND DOWN.' SO THAT WAS THE DECISION.

I CALLED LEFTY O'DOUL IN SEATTLE. I SAID, 'CAN YOU USE A RIGHT-HAND PITCHER?' HE SAYS, 'WE CAN USE ALL THE HELP WE CAN GET. WE'RE NOT DOING TOO WELL.' I SAID, 'WILL YOU PAY HIM $2,500 TO SIGN?' HE SAYS, 'WE DON'T PAY MONEY FOR THAT.'

I SAY, 'HEY, LEFTY, IT'S ME.' I TOLD HIM WHY AND HE SAYS, 'THEY'RE CRAZY. THEY CAN'T LET YOU GO.' HE SAYS, 'COME ON UP. I'LL GIVE YOU $2,500.' SO I WENT UP. I WON 12 AND LOST 7 UP THERE. I NEVER GOT A SHOT BACK IN THE MAJORS, THOUGH. I WAS GETTING UP THERE IN AGE, AND THEY DON'T TAKE CHANCES WITH SORE-ARMED PITCHERS.

DUANE PILLETTE - on his move from San Francisco to Seattle

The Oakland Oaks, managed by Casey Stengel (second row, fifth from left), were bound for championship glory in 1948.

1948 OAKLAND OAKS

*I*n 1946, C.L. "Brick" Laws hired Casey Stengel to manage the Oakland Oaks. Stengel promised to
transform his ragtag team into a championship outfit within three years. Acquiring seasoned minor
league veterans from all corners, Stengel molded and remolded the Oaks, presenting the league with his
"Nine Old Men," the 1948 Pacific Coast League champions.

Casey had been a good friend of Cookie Devencenzi's. My dad said, 'Casey and Cookie, go
ahead and put the team together. We're going to draw a whole lot of people this year. The war
is over and everybody's coming home and they're going to want some entertainment.' This was
before television. All we had was radio, and these were the years we wanted to get going.

He acquired veterans from the American Association and the International League. One of
the best examples of that was Maurice Van Robays, a longtime minor leaguer who could still
play infield and defense, but whose specialty was hitting. Casey had that knack of figuring out
where they belonged, in what spot, and how to platoon.

I guess he was really the first one to really platoon and, of course, he used that when he went
to the Yankees. About the only person who really objected to Casey's platooning in New York
was Gene Woodling, the old Seal. He wanted to play every day, and was good enough to. Boy
was he a hitter.

The reporters, Clyde Giraldo (of the *San Francisco Chronicle*) and Emmons Byrne (*The*

Oakland Oaks manager Casey Stengel, left, knew how to get the most out of the brash, volatile Billy Martin.

Oakland Tribune) and the rest said Casey had one team playing, one team coming and one team going. He was always trading and acquiring veterans to fill holes. And Brick gave him and Cookie free rein.

And Casey had a knack with the pitchers. Of course he had some great relievers with Ralph Buxton and Floyd Speer. I think he relied on Johnny Babich a lot. Johnny was quite a pitcher in his day, and he was Casey's coach. I think Babich could sense it, along with Casey. They just had an instinct about it.

I was doing the broadcasting for the last game of the season. Bud Foster was off doing the 49ers. After Jimmy Tobin made the last out, it was just mayhem in that clubhouse. That was quite a deal. They hadn't won a pennant in Oakland in twenty-one years.

I remember the parade in Oakland and I remember Casey just dominating the parade. The fans just loved it. I never thought there could be that many people who would show up for a parade for a baseball team in a minor league town!

BILL LAWS - Oaks Radio Announcer

In 1948, I was one of the 'Nine Old Men' of the 1948 Oaks. Casey was as good a manager as I ever played for, and that's including Connie Mack and Jimmie Dykes. Stengel was the kind of guy that you had to get to the clubhouse really early to beat him.

The last day of the season, we're playing Sacramento at home. We're two games ahead of the Seals. Now if we win one game, we win the pennant. If we lose both ends of the double-header and the Seals win a double-header, then we're tied. So Casey says, 'Go out and win the first game, I'll buy you a twenty-dollar dinner.' Oh gosh, Casey's going to go big time! But before that, Jack Salveson was pitching the ball game for us, and he got to the eighth inning and he told Casey, 'Casey, I don't think I'm going to make it. You'd better get somebody else in there.'

So he tells Jim Tobin to get ready. Tobin goes out to the mound, throws a few balls. Tobin had a rubber arm, throwing a knuckleball. And Casey says, 'You get 'em out one-two-three, I'll give you a $1,000.'

I'm playing third base, and I'm listening to this! Sure enough, Steve Mesner is the first hitter and he hits a ground ball to me and I throw him out. Well, I figured that was worth a couple of hundred bucks to me.

The next guy up is Joe Marty. Marty really screams one at me. I knocked it down and threw him out. Joe Grace is the next guy, and he hits a ground ball back to Tobin who runs to first base for the last out.

We win the first game, 5-2, and go to the clubhouse. Casey comes in and he's jumping around. So he walks over to his locker and he pulls out a big roll. He peels off some hundreds — one, two, three ... up to ten, and he hands them to Tobin. A thousand dollars!

I say, 'Tob, he hit two ground balls to me and I threw 'em both out.' Tobin said, 'He didn't say anything about giving you any money. See ya later.' And that was it.

The 1948 season was the happiest I had in twenty years. I enjoyed it so much. We started the season, and before you knew it it was over. We won the pennant, we won the playoff. It was great!

DARIO LODIGIANI - Oaks Infielder

We heard [a lot of negative things] about Stengel when he signed to come to Oakland, but he was nothing like that. He was great. That was one of my best years. He told me not to try to hit home runs.

Casey didn't teach. He was too old. He just wanted players who could play. He moved players in and out of the lineup. There were many old players and he had to protect them from breaking down. He had a lot of left-handers for the short right-field fence at Oakland. He was a shrewd old man. He was great to play for.

In my career, I batted first, second, third, fourth, fifth, sixth, seventh and eighth. I hit ninth with Casey. He had Will Hafey pitch, and Will was a great hitter and he'd bat Hafey fourth or fifth. He called me over and told me I was hitting ninth. He said that if he hit Billy Martin ninth, he'd moan and wouldn't play.

Casey told me when [Maurice] Van Robays was playing first base to catch everything I could reach, and generally I did. Once there was a high pop foul that came down close to first base. I could have caught it, but I let Van Robays catch it, and sure enough, he dropped it.

Casey used his staff well. We had so many good pitchers that they ended up only pitching one ball game a week. Charlie Gassaway led the staff with fifteen wins, and pitched less than 200 innings!

BILLY RAIMONDI - Oaks Catcher

Casey was a popular and an active man. When he came to the Oaks in 1946, I was twelve years old. He would ask me a baseball rule about once a week, and if I didn't know the answer, I'd have to run laps in the outfield with the pitchers.

In 1948, he insisted I got a championship gold watch like the rest of the team. It was engraved with my name by the City of Oakland. I still wear it. Casey was much like a father to me. In fact, I had twenty-five fathers.

CHUCK SYMONDS - Oaks Bat Boy

In the heat of the 1948 pennant race, Seals manager Lefty O'Doul had the umpires inspect Oaks pitcher Ralph Buxton's glove for a foreign substance. Pine tar was found, and league president Clarence Rowland decreed that the ninth inning be replayed.

On an Oaks day off, the team had to travel to San Francisco to replay the one inning as a preliminary to a Seals-Seattle Rainiers game. There was no change in the outcome.

Ralph Buxton — he used so much pine tar. He stuck it on his pants along the crease. All he'd do is rub his hands on his pants. He never used resin. He always used pine tar. He had it in his hip pocket all the time, which was a good deal because he used to throw the sinker, and that's the only way he could do it. Oh, what a relief pitcher he was. You could always count on old Buck.

O'Doul got him that time, and they postponed the game. We took a trip over to San Francisco for one inning. We won the game on something like four pitches. That gave us the pennant.

JOHNNY BABICH - Oaks Coach

Even at age forty, Ernie Lombardi was a threat at the plate. He's shown here batting against the San Francisco Seals.

THE HOLLYWOOD STARS

1 9 4 9   S T A R S

*O*ut of the rubble of the 1948 season came Fred Haney, play-by-play broadcaster turned manager, and a new-look roster. Haney built his team on pitching and defense, with an abundance of dangerous hitters. This was the start of a Pacific Coast League dynasty.

I came to Hollywood in the last month of '48. It was a bad ball club. Mule Haas took over for a while, then Lou Stringer took over for a couple of weeks. Jimmie Dykes and Haas were great managers. They just had lousy ball clubs — old guys and a bunch who didn't have a hell of a lot of talent.

Fred Haney was broadcasting for the Stars, but he had managed the St. Louis Browns. He recommended me to Oscar Reichow, who called me and wanted to know if I would sign a two-year contract.

Frankly, I wanted to get as close to my home in Long Beach as I could. I signed and joined the Stars in San Francisco, and a few days later Dykes was fired.

During the winter Haney became manager. I think Haney knew something. He had the nucleus of a pretty good ball club coming up in '49. He had a chance to get a working agreement with the Dodgers, and he decided to manage in '49. It was the right decision for him — he won a couple of pennants.

The majority of the club was home-owned. I believe Mike Sandlock was on option, but only two to four were. The Stars owned the nucleus of the pitching staff — Jack Salveson, Gordy Maltzberger and Johnny Lindell — plus second baseman Gene Handley, shortstop Johnny O'Neil, and Frankie Kelleher.

At this time the Stars had a working agreement with Brooklyn. They had two AA and three

A struggling team in 1948, the Hollywood Stars redeemed themselves under the guidance of Fred Haney, who left the broadcast booth to manage the Stars to a PCL pennant in 1949.

AAA ball clubs. We had the nucleus and got the privilege if we needed a player quickly.

I don't think we got Irv Noren until not more than three or four days before the season started. Then we got Jim Baxes and Mike Sandlock. Herb Gorman came west. He was a helluva hitter, one of the better left-handed fastball hitters I've ever seen.

We met Noren the first time on the train to San Diego. We had a good series down there and realized we were going to have the nucleus of a good ball club. We had guys who could run, and they could beat you. And spectacular pitching, spectacular defense from almost every position. We'd go out there and beat your brains out 2-1. I was batting third in the lineup, and led the league in sacrifices. Haney sensed what kind of a ball club it was.

In the following series against Sacramento, Haney said to me, 'Have you ever led off?' I said no and he said, 'Well, you are now.' So I led off that year. Got a lot of hits and scored a zillion runs (actually 121) because Noren was batting third and Kelleher fourth.

CHUCK STEVENS - Stars First Baseman

I grew up in Los Angeles and was bat boy for the Hollywood Stars in 1949. It was a veteran club, except for Jim Baxes, and I think it was one of the better clubs of the time.

They had Irv Noren, Herb Gorman, Frankie Kelleher, [Johnny] O'Neil at shortstop and George Genovese and Baxes at third, [Chuck] Stevens at first, and [Mike] Sandlock and [Al] Unser catching, and Artie Schallock, Pinky Woods, Willie Ramsdell all pitching. I remember most of them.

My favorite was Gorman and Baxes. Herb taught me a lot of things about the game. I was fifteen and Jimmie was twenty, so we were really close. We used to talk a lot about things. And Herb used to look after me a lot. So did Noren.

Irv led the league and was Most Valuable Player. I felt Jimmie was just going to be a dominant player in the major leagues.

GEORGE "SPARKY" ANDERSON - Stars Bat Boy

A youthful Irv Noren joined the Hollywood Stars in 1949 and helped lead them to a PCL pennant with his .330 batting average, 130 RBI, 29 homers and spectacular outfield play. Voted Most Valuable Player, he was traded to the Washington Senators in 1950.

I came to Hollywood in 1948. It was a pretty good ball club, but we didn't have any pitching. Fred was fair and was a good manager. He played for one run, all the time. We had some fellas who could fly, so we'd bunt a lot in the first inning. He was pretty conservative.

The best thing about Fred was he was also the general manager. Of the ballplayers that he got, he wouldn't tolerate a player who wouldn't hustle. If you wouldn't hustle for Fred, he'd get rid of you. With the working agreement, you'd be off [to Mobile, Alabama].

He was a good judge of talent, and he surrounded himself with ballplayers who hustled. With Chuck [Stevens] and [Johnny] O'Neil, [Jim] Baxes and [Irv] Noren — they all hustled. These were players who were twenty-eight, twenty-nine or thirty years old. This meant they had proved themselves already, and Fred had plenty of opportunity to scout them.

To me, the 1949 team was a big thrill because Hollywood had never won a pennant. The backing was great. [Owner] Bob Cobb took an active part in the season. If you were the most valuable player of the game, you'd have a complimentary dinner at his Brown Derby restaurant.

The Hollywood ballpark was conducive to the fans being close to the players. When we won the pennant that year, they gave us nice rings with real diamonds in the middle of it. It was a first-class operation. The second time, the rings weren't as good.

Our rotation was [Pinky] Woods, [Willie] Ramsdell, [Jack] Salveson and [Gordy] Maltzberger, who was the closest thing to a relief pitcher. He would come in and relieve once in a while against right-handers.

Pinky was a sidearm, three-quarters pitcher, and had a rubber arm. He threw hard. He was very competitive and was willing to take the ball all the time.

Willie Ramsdell had an outstanding year for us. He threw the knuckle ball and had outstanding control with it. He was our best pitcher. He wasn't always always in the best graces with management, however, and that might have hurt him a bit.

Jack Salveson was a great pitcher. He had control like you couldn't believe, and he worked fast. It was fun to play behind him. He threw strikes, so we were on our toes all the time.

Salveson wanted to pitch his own ball game, and Haney sometimes got on him for his selection of pitches. I recall one game where he was two strikes and no balls on a hitter, and he grooved one that the batter hit out of the park.

I can remember Haney after the game, coming into the clubhouse and saying, 'If anybody allows a home run with a two-strike, no-ball count, you're going to be fined.' Later on in a game, Salveson had an 0-2 count on a batter, and he threw the ball over the back of the grandstand.

Above: At a 1954 Seals game in San Francisco, Hollywood Stars manager Bobby Bragan argued too vigorously with umpire Frank Walsh, who ejected Bragan moments later.
Right: This telegram, sent to Bragan in June, 1953, indicates his dispute with Walsh was by no means his first with an ump. League President Clarence Rowland fined Bragan fifty dollars for "use of foul language audible to the stands" during a faceoff with an umpire over a play at first base.

Gordy Maltzberger could thread the needle. He was a three-quarters-to-sidearm pitcher. He had outstanding control. Not a lot of speed but good know-how.

Artie Schallock could throw hard and had a good curve ball. He had good stuff with us, but he didn't seem to meet his potential. Glen Moulder was just another pitcher for us. He was on the down side of his career.

Mike Sandlock was a good catcher and could throw well. He was a real good AAA catcher, and would be a good type to have in the wings at the major league level. He took charge and called a good game. He handled the pitchers well and had a quick release.

Chuck Stevens was a real good glove man. His arm was weak, but he could come up with the ball, and he was a pretty good hitter. Both Chuck and I were the oldest, so we were the ones who would calm down the pitcher.

My shortstop was Johnny O'Neil. He was a good fielder but didn't hit much. He made the routine plays, which is what you want from a shortstop. He made very few errors and had an accurate arm. His range was average, but he played the hitters well. He was very good in turning the double play. You got the ball right where you wanted it. He was the best shortstop I ever played with, an intelligent player.

George Genovese was a better hitter. He was a left-handed hitter, and later went up to Washington.

Jim Baxes had a lot of raw talent. He had a strong throwing arm, but you didn't know where he was going to throw it. He could hit a ball a long way, but his contact was not good. He struck out a fair amount. He had a world of natural ability, but it didn't come to fruition.

We had a lot of offense out in the outfield. Herb Gorman was an outstanding hitter. He was with us in 1949. He was adequate in the outfield — not a great runner or thrower, but he could *hit*.

We were playing San Diego when he collapsed on the field — he was with San Diego then. I didn't know anything was wrong with him. He made it into the dugout and collapsed there. (Gorman died in the clubhouse after suffering a heart attack on the field.)

Irv Noren was the best player we had on the club. He could run, he could throw, he could hit and he could field, and was an intelligent ballplayer. He was only an average runner but he got a good jump on the ball. He was the league's Most Valuable Player in '49.

Kelleher was a good outfielder. Limited range, but he threw well, and he had a good sense of getting a jump on the ball. He was easy to pitch to, but if you made a mistake, he'd hurt you.

I generally led off or batted second. Chuck was usually second. Neither Chuck nor I were power hitters, but we got on base a fair amount. Irv Noren would normally bat third and Kelleher fourth. The top of the lineup scored a lot of runs that year.

GENE HANDLEY - Hollywood Stars

1950-1955 STARS (the Hollywood dynasty continues)

*B*etween 1950 and 1955, the Hollywood Stars were the most dominant franchise in the league. Although not always winning the pennant, they were always in the race. The Stars won in 1952 under Fred Haney and, after Haney moved to the National League, under Bobby Bragan in 1953. They lost a pennant in 1954 in a one-game playoff.

Although Bragan's managing style differed from Haney's, his teams continued to scratch for runs, just as Haney's had done.

Slugging Hollywood Stars first baseman Dale Long, right, and manager Bobby Bragan.

Bobby Bragan came in 1953. Bragan inherited Haney's players, but his managerial style was different. He was a showboat. He was a Branch Rickey man (Rickey had been general manager of the Brooklyn Dodgers in the 1950s) and always got along well with management. All his antics were planned before. He was just an average catcher.

We continued to have very good pitching. I was with [pitcher] Red Munger again in Hollywood after Sacramento in '42. He was an outstanding athlete. He could field his position well and was a good hitter. He could throw fast and had a good curve ball. He had some good years with the Cardinals.

Ben Wade came in 1950, and could throw hard. He'd be in the high nineties. A very intelligent man. He never did make the most of his ability, but he was a much better pitcher at the end of his career than at the beginning. He learned he had to throw strikes. He had good stuff.

Johnny Lindell joined the Stars in 1951. He was huge. He must have learned to throw the knuckleball from Ramsdell. He was very effective and a good competitor. He was a strong hitter but didn't make good contact, or he would have been in the big leagues. He was well liked by Fred Haney, but if you win twenty games, you should be liked. He was Most Valuable Player in 1952.

Paul Pettit loved to play. He was signed as a pitcher but had to end up as an outfielder. I'm sure he hurt his arm, but he had the drive, desire and everything. He had some success as a pitcher but undoubtedly his career was cut short.

George O'Donnell was a young sidearm, sinker pitcher. We didn't have many young pitchers at Hollywood. He won twenty games for us that year (1951).

Dale Long — you talk about a good ballplayer. He was a good athlete, a complete ballplayer. He was no speedster but he was agile around first base. He was an excellent hitter.

I moved over to third in 1952 so Monty Basgall could take over at second. He was a good fielder, made all the routine plays. He could turn the double play. He wasn't much with the bat. He was one of the younger players that year.

Jack Phillips was just a great big good old boy. His level of intensity wasn't as great. Here I'm thirty-nine, playing double-headers, and he's sitting in the dugout. The year after I left, 1954, he had a real good year, but that was at third base. Jack was not a good runner. Dick Smith came in to play shortstop, and Jack moved over to third.

Tommy Saffell could run well. He'd always get a piece of the ball at bat, and could bunt well. He was a little man and was a good competitor. He was there with Teddy Beard and Lee Walls.

Beard was a quiet man but had good power for a little man. He was an outstanding runner, and had more talent than Saffell. Walls had a lot of ability — run, throw and power — but he didn't put it all together that year. He was young.

GENE HANDLEY - Hollywood Stars

I loved Fred Haney. He could talk with the players. Haney's style was to play for the single run. He had a real good sense for the game. With Chuck Stevens leading off, Gene Handley was excellent at advancing the runner. I often batted third, and if I didn't drive him in, Francis Kelleher behind me would. It wasn't unusual to start the game off with at least one run in the first inning.

In the outfield we had Kelleher in left and George Schmees in right. Schmees was quiet, but as the season progressed he started to loosen up. It was a good ball club and everybody fit in.

DINO RESTELLI - Hollywood Stars

THE SACRAMENTO SOLONS

1937 SOLONS

*S*acramento had a horrible baseball team in 1936. The St. Louis Cardinals had purchased the *franchise during the previous winter, adding it to its controversial farm system. It appears General Manager Branch Rickey underestimated the quality of the other teams in the Pacific Coast League, or overestimated the talents of his farmhands. In any case, he vowed not to repeat the mistake in 1937.*

Detroit had a lot of its players under contract declared free agents by Baseball Commissioner Kenesaw Mountain Landis for contract irregularities, so I ended up a free agent. So I signed with St. Joe and went to Omaha. That's where Rickey stepped in at the end of '35 and bought ten of us for the Sacramento Solons. He bought the Sacramento franchise and needed bodies for the roster.

Rickey came out to Sacramento and was both surprised and pleased with the team's success, from last place to first place. Nineteen-thirty-six was our first season with the Solons, and we were all 'at-work riggers.' In other words, inexperienced players from lower leagues. But in '37, he balanced it with veterans who had experience in the big leagues. It was a very good ball club.

Bill Killefer — 'Reindeer' — was our manager in '36 and '37. He was an old-time catcher, and had a brother, Red, who managed in the league. Reindeer didn't say too much. He'd leave you alone. He was an easy manager to play for.

Red Worthington was our utility player. He was older and served as our pinch hitter and first-base coach. But there really wasn't any individual instruction on hitting or fielding that went on. If they carried four outfielders that would be it. It was nothing like today.

Of our pitchers, Tony Freitas was our ace. He was a crafty screwball pitcher. He wasn't fast but had a tantalizing screwball. He had good control and liked to work fast. He could also get his curve over.

Any time you played behind Freitas, the game was over before you knew it. Players liked that kind of pitcher. When a pitcher pitches fast, you're ready.

Bob Klinger was a hard-working pitcher who threw hard. He won nineteen for us and threw a lot of innings.

Cotton Pippen pitched 'scientifically.' He had a curve ball and he knew how to pitch. But slow. When you played behind Pippen, you looked for a three-hour game. Slow every pitch. When a pitcher pitches like that, it takes you off your toes, puts you back on your heels.

Bill Schmidt from Berkeley won fifteen and pitched a lot of innings, and Dick Newsome was a hard thrower. Tom Seats was a good curve-ball pitcher. He had big hands.

Walker Cooper was a good young catcher with a lot of power. He went up to the Cardinals in '38. Cooper and Herman Franks were the catchers. It was a good, balanced club.

Around the infield, Dib Williams was steady, not flashy, at second base. He wasn't very fast, and was just an average hitter. He always had a chaw of tobacco in his jaw. It was [shortstop] Joe Orengo working with Williams. They were a good double-play combo. I didn't see any weakness there. We had a guy named Murl Prather at first base with Bill Prout backing him up. Johnny Vergez and Art Garibaldi would play third. It was a steady infield.

Garibaldi was a quiet person, but a good hitter. He had a quiet personality. He was a good player to have on a team. Garibaldi would be the cleanup hitter.

Johnny Vergez came in the middle of the '36 season. He could play second, third and short. He was a great guy, and provided versatility for the infield.

Buster Adams could hit the long ball. He had power and was a pretty good outfielder with good speed. He was probably the fastest guy on our club. He usually played center field with Nick Cullop in right and me in left. In '36 I hit fourth and in '37 I hit third.

Cullop was our home-run slugger. He was mean. They called him the Babe Ruth of the

Backup catcher Walker Cooper, left, and coach-outfielder Robert "Red" Worthington shoulder some lumber at the Sacramento Solons' 1937 spring training camp.

minor league. In 1937, Seattle had an Indian playing for them, Levi McCormack. Buster was supposed to have a 100-yard dash race against him, but he got sick, so I substituted for him and beat him. I had a long stride. They used to kid me that it only took me four or five steps to get from second to third.

We were dead last in 1936, and in '37 we finished in first place. In those days we had the Shaugnessy Playoffs, and San Diego beat us in four straight. Ted Williams hit everything, left and right. Just a skinny kid. He played his first game against us when he got out of high school a year earlier.

Over the years, we became good friends. Ted always said to me, 'I like your style of hitting.' A lot of people didn't get along with him, but we got along well.

It was frustrating to lose four straight to San Diego, and it cost us some money, so San Diego earned more money even though we finished first in the regular season.

LOU VEZILICH - Solons Outfielder

1942 SOLONS

John "Pepper" Martin, manager of the 1942 PCL-champion Sacramento Solons.

*P*ossibly no team in PCL history finished with as much of a flourish as the 1942 Sacramento Solons. After losing fourteen of its first twenty games, the team clawed its way into first place on June 15, only to lose the slot to the Los Angeles Angels a month later. As luck would have it, the season closed with the Angels in Sacramento for a seven-game series.

The Angels entered with a two-game lead and won the first two, opening up a four-game lead with five to go. But yes, the Solons won the pennant.

Pepper Martin was the 'Wild Horse of the Osage.' The name fit. He was part Indian. Probably of all the players I played with, Pepper Martin had the best build of any of them. He was the most muscular man I saw.

As a manager, he went all out. We did a lot of stealing, not too much hit-and-run. He was adventuresome. He was a character.

Ken Penner was Pepper's coach. He did much of the running of the ball club when Pepper was playing. Pepper was the boss, but Penner would make up the lineup and work the pitchers.

Pepper was not a good ballplayer. He had the drive and makeup and the will to win. He'd do anything to win. He was not a good fielder, and his arm was just adequate. But he could run.

In 1941, we started out well and went into a slump. Our pitching — Tony Freitas, Bill Schmidt, Red Munger and Al Hollingsworth — was good, but not with a lot of depth. Buddy Blattner and Don Gutteridge were in the infield for us.

We started strong and had a big lead by mid-season, but we struggled in the second half, and Seattle played excellent ball. They had Hal Turpin and Dick "Kewpie" Barrett. They seemed to win twenty games every year.

In 1942, we only had about eighteen players, and players had to double up in positions. We only had eight pitchers, so everybody had to carry his weight. Freitas was back. We also had Blix Donnelly. He had a good curve ball. Also the left-hander Kemp Wicker. And Clarence Beers was a good starter for us.

Our pitchers were expected to throw every four days. Pitchers used to pitch a ball game, then take the next day off, pitch batting practice on the second day, have the third day off, then take your start on the fourth day.

We didn't have specializing or relief with Sacramento. We'd use four starters, and if one of them got in trouble, Johnny Pintar or Hershel Lyons or Big Bill Schmidt would relieve. If a

SACRAMENTO
1942 · Pacific Coast League
PENNANT WINNER

pitcher wasn't going well, someone else would take his start and he'd have to earn it back.

Ray Mueller was our catcher. He caught almost every game. He was an intelligent fella with a good release. Mueller was strong defensively and worked the staff well. Charlie Marshall was his backup, and he played some second base after I was injured.

I worked with Steve Mesner and Eddie Lake as our shortstops. Mesner shifted to third when Lake arrived. He could play. Lake had a strong arm and some good power for a little man.

In 1942, I jumped up in the air for a line drive and when I came down, I hurt my knee. I made a comeback by riding my bicycle a lot. That was the only real injury I had playing ball.

I stayed with the club and returned to the lineup the last week against the Angels. We had a seven-game series at home, and they came in with a two-game lead and beat us the first two games to give them a four-game lead. We won the four games leading up to the Sunday double-header, and we won the first game on Sunday. So we were playing the second game for the championship, with Freitas pitching, and we won easily.

Los Angeles had champagne ready on Tuesday, expecting to win at least one of the next five games. I don't know if we had champagne or not. I don't think we could afford it. The club wouldn't go for it.

Those were lean times. That was the Cardinal affiliation with Branch Rickey. They ran a tight ship.

GENE HANDLEY - Solons Infielder

Decent pitching and tenacious hitters kept the Sacramento Solons in the running for a championship during most of the 1942 season. The team's title-winning finish, in seven games against the Los Angeles Angels, was one of the most exciting in PCL history.

*Sacramento Solons
pitcher John Pintar in
1942.*

I went to spring training a couple of years with St. Louis, then I was optioned out to Sacramento for 1942. They brought me in as a reliever. I had been a starter before, but I think what happened was they had some younger guys that they wanted to bring along. I'd pitch well in relief and ask, 'When am I going to start?' But I never did.

They had sent down some pretty good pitchers — Kemp Wicker, Blix Donnelly, Clarence Beers, Hersh Lyons. I think they were grooming them, thinking they had more big-league potential than me.

Tony Freitas was a veteran on our club. A little left-hander, very cagey. He was a very intelligent pitcher. He had pinpoint control and he had a real good screwball for the right-hand hitters.

Kemp Wicker was another left-hander. He impressed me mostly with his fastball. I used to warm up the pitchers, and I was impressed at how much harder he threw than the other pitchers.

Blix Donnelly was more of a curve-ball pitcher. He could throw fairly hard, but he couldn't throw as hard as Kemp Wicker. He had good control.

Big Bill Schmidt and Hersh Lyons would get spot starts when we had extra games or double-headers.

Our infield was very dependable. Gene Handley was a real good ballplayer at second base, and was a leader. Then we had Jack Sturdy at first.

Debs Garms was our right-fielder. I think he led the National League in hitting a couple of years earlier. Then we had Buster Adams in center field. He had a lot of power. Averett Thompson was in left. He was young but had good speed.

All of the Cardinal clubs emphasized speed, so when I got to Sacramento, we had quite a few fellas who could run pretty good.

The people the Cardinals sent down to Pepper Martin gave him a great ball club. They were almost big leaguers, some with experience and some on the way up.

JOHN PINTAR - Solons Pitcher

My contract was transferred to Sacramento in 1942 and we went to spring training in Fullerton. I made the team and went north with them and played the season in Sacramento

Pepper Martin was our manager. What a fiery guy he was! I was 10-10, and we had an excellent staff of pitchers.

Jack Sturdy was a fixture at first. I think he got hurt late in the season. [Gene] Handley was at second base, but broke a bone, and Steve Mesner moved over from third. Eddie Lake played shortstop and Mel Serafini and Gene Lillard filled in at third.

Buster Adams was our center fielder. He was a power hitter and had pretty good speed. [Debs] Garms was more of a singles hitter, as I recall. He had some good speed. I think he was down from Pittsburgh. Tommy Thompson was an excellent young prospect.

I don't recall Pepper calling any pitches from the bench, except managers have a habit of calling pitchouts when they think they are going to steal. I think Pepper must have done a pretty good job with our pitchers to get us there.

I don't think any players had as many injuries in those days. When you were a pitcher and you were in there, you were expected to pitch nine innings, not five or four innings. Very few players were weight lifters. We all had pretty similar musculature. In those days, the word was around that you don't want those big muscles for hitting.

That last week, the Angels came in and won the first two games. That put them four games ahead. The crowds were bigger. We never drew well, but more people came out. I remember vividly the excitement of that first game in Sunday's double-header. The park was filled.

We were down, and along around the eighth inning, we rallied, and they came back, but we held the lead going into the ninth. Pepper used a couple of relief pitchers. I was one of them, and Clarence Beers. I don't remember all that I did, but I do remember I struck out pinch hitter [Jigger] Statz. He was a boyhood idol of mine.

Tony [Freitas] entered in the ninth and shut them down. Tony was a master. They talk about John Smoltz and Greg Maddux of the Atlanta Braves. I honestly believe that Tony was every bit as good with his stuff and his control. And he was a workhorse. He was no spring chicken. (Freitas was thrity-four, and in his fifteenth season at the time.)

He was crafty and would make those left-handed hitters cry for mercy. Tony came back in the second game — he was already warm — and pitched a complete game for the victory.

HERSHEL LYONS - Solons Pitcher

FROM FIRST TO WORST

*I*n the winter of *1942, Branch Rickey left the Cardinals for Brooklyn, having had philosophical differences with owner Sam Breadon. The more conservative Breadon reduced the Cardinals' farm club operations, cutting the Sacramento Solons adrift. With the war cutting into rosters at all levels, Sacramento had difficulty finding players. A few good players were surrounded by inexperienced high schoolers and lower minor leaguers. The result, in 1943, was the Pacific Coast League's worst team ever!*

Three good pitchers — Bud Byerly, Clem Dreiswerd and John Pintar — lost twenty games or more. Only Al Brazle sported winning statistics, and his contract was purchased by the Cardinals in July. In all, the Solons managed to win a paltry forty games out of 155. Attendance paralleled the team's level of success, topping out at 31,694.

NINETEEN-FORTY-THREE WAS A SAD YEAR. THEY EVEN BROUGHT HIGH SCHOOL KIDS IN TO PITCH. IT WAS A FRUSTRATING YEAR FOR ME. NOBODY CAME OUT TO THE PARK — LOUSY BALL CLUB, NO FANS. IF YOU DON'T HAVE THE PLAYERS, YOU CAN'T COMPETE.

THE LEAGUE WAS GOING TO PULL THE FRANCHISE. [*Sacramento Union* SPORTS EDITOR] DICK EDMONDS

STARTED A CAMPAIGN TO KEEP THE BALL CLUB HERE. HE WAS A VERY INTELLIGENT MAN AND HE WORKED HARD TO SAVE THE TEAM. IT WAS UNFORTUNATE WHAT HAPPENED TO HIM. (EDMONDS DIED OF VIRAL PNEUMONIA A COUPLE OF YEARS LATER, PROMPTING A SUCCESSFUL CAMPAIGN TO RENAME DOUBLEDAY PARK IN HIS HONOR.)

JOHN PINTAR - Solons Pitcher

But it wasn't all bad for the Sacramento Solons. Clem Dreiswerd, a left-handed pitcher who had escaped the St. Louis Cardinal "web," went 9-20 for a Solons team that won only forty games, making it the worst team in PCL history.

Miraculously, in 1944, Dreisewerd, pictured here, reversed his won-lost record, winning twenty and losing nine, with a 1.51 ERA in 252 innings. He walked only 21. This was for a much-improved Solons team that was 76-93 under Earl Sheely, in his first year as Solons manager.

Dreisewerd went to the Boston Red Sox in the last few weeks of the 1944 season. But he was already a twenty-eight-year-old rookie. He had spent some time in the military and too much time on the Cardinal "chain gang." He was just too old to have a chance.

1937
Pacific Coast League

Chaplin - Thompson - Walters - Berkowitz - Williams - Tobin
Shellenbach (Mgr) Detore - Cook (Trainer) - Tuttle - Craghead - Skelly
Durst - Hebert - Pillette - Ward - Mulligan - Starr
Holman - Patchett - Salvo - Lane - McDonald - Reese - Myatt.

THE SAN DIEGO PADRES

1937 PADRES

*I*n their second year in the league, the Padres finished third during the regular season to qualify for the
Shaughnessy Playoffs, a controversial winner-take-all series. The Padres took four in a row from reg-
ular-season winner Sacramento, then repeated the feat against 1936 Pacific Coast League champion
Portland.

This once-in-a-lifetime schedule gave San Diego its first PCL championship.

The 1937 Padres were a solid team of veterans. It was a good ball club. It had good pitching
and solid defense. Frank Shellenback, our manager, got a set lineup of veterans and he played
them every day. Shellenback never liked to experiment.

The pitchers were expected to go the whole way. There was no closer in those days. Herm
Pillette never started, so if there was a relief pitcher, he was it.

George Detore was a good catcher with a fairly good arm. And he was an excellent hitter.
(He edged Harlan Pool of Seattle for the batting championship, .3341 to .3340.)

Everybody on the team looked up to Tommy Thompson, the right-fielder. He was a loner,
very quiet, but he was a hard worker and sort of led by example. He had a great arm and tried
to show me how he threw the ball. He had a great spin on the ball, a backspin that kept the ball

in the air longer. He tried to show me, but I threw the ball differently and couldn't get the backspin that he did.

Hal Patchett was a great fella. Never said a word, just went out and played. He was a good leadoff man, good outfielder.

Ted Williams was on the club. He was a great hitter then, and he was all right as a fielder, but his hitting was his real interest. He was just a kid at that time. He hadn't grown up yet. So with Tommy Thompson, Cedric Durst, Hal Patchett on the club, he was a reserve outfielder.

I was a raw rookie, but it was kind of the tradition of the day that nobody helped you. Even Shellenback did very little. The closest I got to Shellenback — he lived in North Hollywood and I lived the south part of the city. Monday was an off day, of course, and every time I was going home, he'd bum a ride with me, and that was the closest we got. We didn't do much talking on the trip.

Cedric Durst was the only guy on the club who sidled up to me and tried to take care of me when I was breaking in. He made me feel good. When he became manager, in 1939, I was his boy.

[Team owner Bill] Lane just offered me one deal, $150 a month, the day I reported, and I accepted it. No bonus. That was more money than I had ever seen in my life before.

I wasn't ready for the Coast League at that time. I knew I wasn't ready, and I was just hoping to play some in games that were out of hand. I'd play the exhibition games, if they had any.

Mr. Lane was a penny-pincher. It was the Depression, and I didn't travel with the club, in order to save him money. I only went on one road trip, to the playoffs in Sacramento. I was really in awe. It was a great trip for me, although I didn't play.

Ted Williams was playing left field in the second game of the championship playoffs at Sacramento. We had two runners on base with two outs when he took a third strike. He took his bat and threw it up against the grandstand. It spun, and the barrel of the bat went right on through the grandstand wall. It was an old rickety wooden structure, and it went on through. Nobody was hurt. He went over to the bench and sat in the corner all by himself. That was the third out.

Everybody runs out on the field, changing sides, and there's old Ted still sitting in the dugout. Shellenback says, 'Ted, get out to left field.' He says, 'No, he threw me out.'

And Frank says, 'I don't think he did. I haven't seen anything about it. Go on out there and play so we can get the game going.' 'No, he threw me out,' he says again.

So Frank turned to two of his pitchers and he said, 'Boys, take him out there by the arm. Get him out to left field. Put his glove on and turn him around and get him in position so we can get the game going.' And that's what they did. He was just a kid.

Although I was part of the team I really didn't feel a part of it. As far as I was concerned, it was a year lost. It would have been wiser for me to be shipped out.

EDDIE STEWART - Padres Outfielder

I signed up when I was seventeen years old. I was pitching batting practice most of the time. I was starting to pinch hit a little bit and starting to play a little bit. I had been on one trip, to Seattle, and then into Oakland.

Frank Shellenback was a wonderful man, highly respected. He won more minor league games than any other minor league pitchers. He influenced me only as a man, not as a manager. Ced Durst and Eddie Mulligan were on the club too, but they really didn't have any influence on me. Durst was a good little ballplayer, but that was it. He didn't help me when we were

San Diego Padres first baseman George McDonald, in about 1938.

with the Padres. None are talking to me about hitting.

In 1937 we had Hal Patchett, Ruppert Thompson and Durst in the outfield. Thompson was a wonderful person, and he gave me a lot of encouragement, but he could never hit as well as I could. He didn't have the power, and he was making more money than everyone else on the club and drove a nice car.

I hit good during the playoffs up in Sacramento, but I don't remember the incident with the bat in Sacramento.

Bobby Doerr was one of my greatest friends. I was always trying to tell him how to hit. And I never played with Dominic [DiMaggio] in the minor leagues, but he was one helluva outfielder with Frisco as I was leaving for the East.

George McDonald was a real nice guy. He was a little looser than the rest of the younger guys. He liked to gamble, go around with the girls, but he was a damn good little player. But he never got any better. He couldn't hit with power. He was a slappy-type hitter.

TED WILLIAMS - San Diego Padres

Frank Shellenback was kind of partial to older players and Catholics. He brought religion into the game.

Our pitchers were great. We didn't have a large staff, but they stayed healthy. Five pitchers (Howard Craghead, Manny Salvo, Wally Hebert, 'Tiny' Chaplin and Dick Ward) who threw a lot of innings.

I was on first base, and Jimmie Reese and George Myatt were our double-play combination. Ernie Holman played third. Holman didn't have a great year. He was also sick some, but Joe Berkowitz got a lot of time at third and had a good season. Myatt threw a heavy ball. He'd throw it down by my knees, and make it hard to catch.

Eddie Mulligan was a true gentleman. He didn't play too much, but was helpful as a coach. Not many got through on that group.

Tommy Thompson was a real hustler. He'd give you 110 percent. A good hitter. Hal Patchett was a class act. He could run pretty good.

Ted hit most of the home runs late in the season. I hit in back of Ted Williams, and every time he hit one nine miles, they'd cave my back in.

GEORGE McDONALD - Padres First Baseman

1954 PADRES

The 1954 Padres finished the season in a deadlock with the Hollywood Stars. A one-game play-off determined the league champion. This was a team of destiny.

It's pretty hard to be on a championship team. That was the highlight of my career. That was the first team the Padres had win a pennant in close to twenty years. So it made headlines.

And to end the season after 168 games in a dead tie with Hollywood — a one-game playoff was scheduled for Lane Field and was played before an overflow crowd.

Going into the playoff our pitching staff was decimated. Eddie [Erautt] was out, and we played a double-header the day before to earn the tie. I had two days' rest. Lefty O'Doul had a team meeting in the clubhouse to decide who would pitch the playoff game.

So O'Doul said, 'You've brought us this far and now we've got to decide who's going to pitch this game.' Theolic Smith was rested, but he hadn't been too effective all year. Nobody was rested.

I said, 'Well, my stomach isn't in it, but I think my arm's all right.' Lefty tossed me the ball and said. 'Go get 'em.' That was right before the game.

Of course, Bobby Bragan was the manager for Hollywood, and he didn't know who was going to pitch either. He couldn't make up his lineup until he saw who went out to the bullpen to warm up. The Stars selected George Munger and Bragan caught that game.

Dick Smith, the Stars' first hitter, laid down a perfect bunt with two strikes on him. Smith ended up scoring, and they scored again in the third. But we came back to lead 3-2.

There was one guy on the Stars who I never could get out, and that was Frank Kelleher. Whether he'd hit a broken-bat blooper or a well-hit ball, I couldn't get him out, and he drove in the Stars' two runs that night.

Harry Elliott, who had hit well for us all season, drove in our go-ahead run, and Bob Elliott hit two home runs to clear everything. The next time Elliott came up, Mel Queen hit him on the backside. Bob said it broke a pack of cigarettes in his back pocket. O'Doul replaced him with Milt Smith.

Milt had played more at third during the season, and was a better defensive player. Bob was at the end of the line and often seemed reluctant to play an awful lot. In fact, up in Portland,

The San Diego Padres celebrate their 1954 playoff win over the Hollywood Stars. Manager Lefty O'Doul is flanked by winning pitcher Bob Kerrigan, left, and third baseman Bob Elliott.

San Diego Padres manager Lefty O'Doul and umpire Frank Walsh argued a ball-and-strike call on second baseman Al Federoff during a 1954 game in San Diego. Buddy Peterson tried to keep Federoff out of the fray, but both he and O'Doul were ejected.

we were short a right-fielder in a game, and O'Doul asked [Bob] Elliott to fill in.

If you're familiar with right field in Vaughn Street, either you catch the ball or it's up against the fence. Bob said, 'No way!' Towards the end of the season, he got stronger. We inserted him more at third base to see if his bat would do any good, and it did. He hit pretty good during the last part of the season.

I pitched a complete game for the win. Later I asked Lloyd Dickey if the bullpen ever got to warm up, and he said they hadn't the whole game.

When the playoff was announced, people started lining up to buy tickets on Sunday night — for a Monday night game! When we played, fans roped off all around the outfield. In fact, Kelleher's two hits were into the crowd.

The game was also the first televised game in San Diego. There was no backup tape for that one. One shot was all you got.

Winning the pennant was a shot in the arm for the city of San Diego. We had a parade down Broadway. They said 35,000 fans attended.

Our pitching staff was pretty thin. Lefty had to move us around. [Pitcher Eddie] Erautt and I started regularly, and Lloyd Dickey was used basically as a starter, but as the season went on he was used in middle relief as well. Cliff Chambers had gone home with a bad arm. Dick Smith and Bill Thomasson were used primarily in relief.

When we acquired Bill Wight from Cleveland and Al Lyons (released by San Francisco), our pitching staff got a shot in the arm. Wight started regularly, and Lyons was exceptional. Lyons would be playing center field, and they'd pull him in to relieve late in the game. He'd take his required number of tosses. He threw hard and was not wild. He had a great arm as an outfielder and was in great shape. He was only asked to throw an inning or two.

Thomasson wasn't overly effective. He had idiosyncrasies when he pitched. The mound had to be a certain way for him. I remember up in Sacramento when he was pitching, he would get in trouble, be a little wild. When he'd finish throwing a pitch, he'd look back at the mound and walk all the way around it. He didn't want to get back up on it. He hated that mound.

Our catching staff had included Red Mathis and Dick Aylward. Mathis had his arm broken in a fight, and Aylward had left the club because his wife was having a baby. Walt Pocekay filled in catching, and Mike Sandlock was acquired from the Phillies in May. Mike was an old-timer, thirty-seven, with bad knees.

With my pitching he didn't have to move around a lot because I had good control. Mike did a workman-like job for us, but you knew he was in pain.

Dick Aylward was not a great hitter, but he was a wonderful catcher with a tremendous arm. I remember one time I was frustrated with a pitch I had thrown, and when Dick threw the ball back to me, I caught it barehanded. I said, 'Uh-oh.' Boy, when he got the next pitch, he fired it back as to say, 'Don't catch my throws barehanded!'

Our infield was good defensively. Defensively [Dick] Sisler, our first baseman, was average. He had a strange way of hitting — off his front foot — but he was so strong. He was a real nice guy.

Al Federoff and Buddy Peterson formed a marvelous double-play combination. Al was a fiery player and very agile around the base. Buddy was a workhorse and always had the dirtiest uniform on the team. He always looked like he had gone through the Battle of the Bulge.

Buddy wasn't afraid of a pick-off play at second. We used it effectively. We had a prearranged signal. I'd signal by tugging at my belt, and he'd signal back. Then I'd come down to my belt, count a bit, and I'd turn and throw. I picked Carlos Bernier off a couple of times, and he got real mad.

Milt Smith shared the position with Bob Elliott. Smith was young and the better fielder but Elliott was the better hitter. Luke Easter was also on the Padres as a first baseman, but he was not effective at all. He was not the Easter he was before.

We had some pretty good outfielders. Harry Elliott led the league in hitting. [Dick] Faber and Earl Rapp also started. Faber was a speedy defensive center fielder. Later, Lyons played a lot of center field. Rapp was a free-swinger and a good hitter, and he could hit for power and average.

BOB KERRIGAN - Padres Pitcher

With the '54 team, we had six pitchers the last two months of the season. We worked every third day — [Bob] Kerrigan, [Bill] Wight and myself. [Lloyd] Dickey was a starter at first, then went to being a middle man later on. Theolic [Smith] was a long man.

Al Lyons was strong. We picked him upon mid-season from San Francisco. He was a great reliever. He'd be playing center field and Lefty would come out to the mound and call him in to relieve. Occasionally, he'd warm up in the bullpen late in the game, but other times, he'd take his eight pitches and be ready to go. He was thrity-seven, but he was our stopper.

Lefty kept everybody loose. He'd be the last guy to the ballpark, but he got in a lot of golf. Jimmie Reese didn't like it when Lefty was gone. Lefty was a good hitting instructor, but he never bothered the pitchers. He'd tell you, 'If you're a fastball pitcher, throw fastballs.' He'd say, 'You got yourself into this jam, you get yourself out of it. Show me something. It's all yours.'

My arm went dead in Oakland with about two weeks before the end of the season. I was supposed to pitch the second game of a double-header. I was in the outfield shagging flies, and I got a ball and went to throw it back to the infield, and the ball dropped right in front of me. I said, 'What is this?' I got Tommy Herrera to throw me another ball, and it just dropped again when I tried to throw.

I went and told Lefty, 'My arm's had it. It just went dead.' Of course I was pitching every third day and volunteering for the second game of double-headers. So I was basically through.

We were hurting at pitcher and catcher. Our catcher, Dick Aylward, went home too. We missed him badly. Aylward could have gone to the big leagues as a defensive catcher. He was one of the best defensive catchers I've ever seen. What an arm! You'd better duck when a guy was stealing.

Our other catcher, Red Mathis, punched out Jerry Priddy in Seattle. Priddy was at bat, and they started jawing at each other, really going at it. That's when where Mathis hurt himself.

Lane Field before the September 13, 1954, playoff game between the Hollywood Stars and the San Diego Padres.

Mike Sandlock worked with me most of the time. When he'd come out to the mound, he'd say, 'Hey, did you see that blond sitting in the first row over there?' He'd get your mind off the game. He'd get you completely relaxed.

We went into the last series with Hollywood and beat them five out of seven to catch them. Kerrigan was about the only guy who could pitch the playoff. I was supposed to get it, but no way!

Kerrigan pitched a gutty ball game. And Harry Elliott's two home runs off Red Munger put the game away. He played against him in the majors and knew what to expect from him.

The Governors Cup followed, and we were dead. The Stars and us were all beat up. Neither of us won a game.

EDDIE ERAUTT - Padres Pitcher

The 1954 Padres had good pitching and we had good players. It was a veteran club, and we didn't need to be motivated.

With our club, we didn't have to take a lot of chances because we had [Earl] Rapp and [Bob] Elliott and [Dick] Sisler behind us. We'd get on base, bunt 'em over to second, then drive them in. We didn't steal a lot of bases that year because we had a lot of power down the lineup. We had guys who could hit. Lefty didn't want guys thrown out. He wanted them on base.

Al Federoff was just great, and we were good friends. He was just a superb infielder. I can't ever recall him giving me a bad throw at second base. I thought he was very underrated because he wasn't very flashy, but he made all the plays. He always made the double play. He was the best I ever played with. We had some sinker-ball pitchers, so we got a lot of ground balls. Al was predictable.

Luke Easter didn't help the ball club outside of attendance. Most of the time, he didn't play. It got to the point that Luke struck out so much that when we came to a new city, they would announce Luke Easter was going to put on a pregame hitting exhibition.

He'd hit some huge balls out of the park in batting practice, but in the game, he'd strike out two or three times. He couldn't move at all. And he was making great money. They remembered him from Cleveland and from his first time through San Diego, but he didn't help the ball club at all. I always felt he was a lot older than the roster stated.

It was a veteran club. Dick Faber in center field was younger and Ed Kazak and Earl Rapp were older. Rapp carried that ball club all the time. He only weighed about 175 pounds, but could he hit. He had power and drove in a lot of runs, and he hit for average too. Federoff and I would get on, and he'd be the guy to drive us in. A good clutch hitter.

Then we picked up Al Lyons. He was a great man to have on that club. He played center field and did some relief pitching.

Harry Elliott could hit. He was our left fielder. He had been a football player, and he'd fight at the drop of a hat. He was the only guy I ever knew who hit .350 all year. He'd go two for two, then line out, and he'd be mad. It was a feisty group.

When you had the pitching staff that we had, you knew they weren't going to give up a lot of runs, and with the artillery we had, we knew we were going to score. That gave us the confidence that we could win any game. With Federoff and me on base all the time, you knew you were going to score some runs. If you beat us, it was a tough job. It was easy to manage this club. And everybody had good years.

We collapsed for the playoffs. We couldn't go another week longer. Both us and Hollywood: We beat each other up and couldn't go further. We were really hurting.

BUDDY PETERSON - Padres Shortstop

THE LOS ANGELES ANGELS

1934 ANGELS

For many, this is the best PCL team of all time. For others, the 1956 Angels were the best. Which again raises the question: is it possible to compare teams from different eras?

As a manager, Jack Lelivelt was aloof. He never was very demonstrative. If he had had a computer, Lelivelt could have just pushed a button. When I look back at that team, it was a helluva ball club. Everybody on the '34 Angels was a star. Everybody was very professional, but not necessarily close.

Truck Hannah was our coach, and he was a backup catcher to Gilly Campbell. He didn't really help the youngsters — Bobby Mattick or Kenny Richardson or me. He felt we should have known it if we had reached this level. He kind of left me alone. But he could get down on a player. I was nineteen when I joined the Angels. I felt more like I should have been a clubhouse boy than a player. Everyone was competitive. They didn't go out of their way to help anybody. Mike Gazella tried to help some.

I stepped out of high school, and here I am in the Coast League. I did it too quick. If I had a few bus rides, it might have been better. They kept telling me I was one of the greatest fielding outfielders in baseball. I was too young and couldn't handle that.

While we were unified on the field, most of the players went their own way off the field. You take guys like Marv Gudat, who was very quiet, Carl Dittmar, who stayed to himself, Frank Demaree, who was aloof, Lou Garland, who thought he was pretty tough, and I think he was.

I respected Dick Ward. He was a hard guy, but I respected him and got along with him. And Fay Thomas was a real sweetheart. Emmett Nelson, Jimmie Reese and Marv Gudat — all nice guys.

Mike Meola was a pretty nice guy. He challenged me a couple of times. He'd say, 'Goddamit, Bobby, with all your talent, why do you have to be that way?' I wasn't smart enough to pick that up. I thought about it later. If I had done right I could have done very well, but I was young.

The only ones who hung around together were Bobby Mattick, myself and Kenny Richardson. We were all reserves.

All of our pitchers could fire that ball — Thomas, Emmett Nelson and Lou Garland. Emmett Nelson didn't always start, but he was a helluva tough guy to face. Nelson, Garland, Thomas and Mike Meola, they seldom ever needed help.

Los Angeles Angels outfielder Arnold "Jigger" Statz played eighteen years for the team before taking over as its manager, from 1940 through '42. Note Statz's glove, with the center cut out, a feature he said gave him a better "touch" with the ball.

Meola would poop out a little in the eighth or ninth inning, but if the other ball club was not a fastball-hitting club, then Lelivelt would bring in somebody like Nelson or some other hard thrower. Everybody was confident they could handle anything. If someone pooped out, there was someone who could pick it up.

Whitey Campbell could throw the slowest curve ball you ever saw in your life. And he was a helluva a nice guy too. Dick Ward, another hard thrower, would get himself in trouble, and Whitey would come in for him.

Whitey could come in with men on first and second, one out, game on the line, and throw that wet fish with a break to it, and they'd ground into a double play. We had the people who could execute it. It was just a methodical ball club.

For a left-hander, we'd have Artie McDougall or Roy Henshaw, two very different pitchers. Gilly Campbell, our catcher, was a red-ass, a pop-off, but he was a good hitter with some power and some speed.

Jim Oglesby, our first baseman, was a journeyman ballplayer. He wasn't quick. You could bunt on him. He and Jimmie Reese left the right side wide open. They would play deep. They couldn't do that in the big leagues. I used to be bat boy at Oakland. I knew Jimmie real well. It was a real thrill for me to play on the same team with him.

Dittmar was our shortstop and Gene Lillard was at third. Lillard and I were pretty good friends. We used to stand on the side, in front of the crowd, sixty feet apart, and play 'burnout' — throwing the ball as hard as we could to the other. We both had good arms, and we'd try to see who would holler uncle first.

Our outfield was excellent. Frank Demaree, Jigger Statz and Marv Gudat were all great hitters. Demaree had lots of power, and defensively they weren't a bad threesome. I was the fourth outfielder. They used me for insurance, and I could run for somebody. I did go in and play some, but most of the time I'd go in and run for somebody like Reese or Walt Gobel. This was easily the best team I ever played on, major or minor. The only minor league team I saw that could compare to it was Oscar Vitt's Newark Bears of 1937. I played against them.

It's a coin toss between the Angels and the Newark Bears. If you'd take a seven-game series between the two clubs, a break would win the series, but if you were a major league owner and had your choice between the Angels and the Bears, there would be a lot of Bears in there. Bears went up and stayed.

If the '34 Angels were put into the major leagues, we would have had to have more help. The difference between the Coast League and the majors was the pitching. A team like the Angels would beat the St. Louis Browns, Washington Senators and Philadelphia Athletics, but the rest of the teams had too much depth.

BOBBY LOANE - Angels Outfielder

1947 ANGELS

T   *he 1947 Angels, managed by Bill Kelly, were a solid veteran club. The team ended in a dead-even tie with the San Francisco Seals, but won a one-game playoff for the championship. This team epitomized the strength of the Coast League after the war — solid in every phase of the game, and owned outright by the Angels.*

The 1947 Angels were an outstanding club. Bill Kelly, in his first year, was our manager. He had actually been an umpire for several years. It was a veteran team with many players returning from 1946, but several new players made the difference, especially in the outfield. Clarence Maddern was a great ballplayer. He was a quiet leader and a great clutch player. He and Cecil Garriott were new outfielders to the club. And Tuck Stainback was down from the majors. He was finishing up, a little older than the rest of us.

Eddie Sauer was a good outfielder and a real hustler. He was also a good hitter. He was with the Angels in 1946.

Cliff Chambers was our ace. He had a great year. It just seemed like all he had to do against San Francisco was throw his glove on the mound. Our pitching rotation was Chambers, me, Red Lynn and Red Adams, with Russ Bauers spot starting. [Oren] Baker, [Don] Osborn and [Jess] Dobernic were our relief. The others were long relief.

Dobernic had good control and would pitch the last two innings. Dobernic actually put us in. They gave him a night at Wrigley Field and gave him lots of presents. He had a helluva year. Osborn was another veteran.

Eddie Malone was a very good caller behind the plate. He knew his pitchers. No need to shake him off much.

We picked up [first baseman] Larry Barton, [second baseman] Lou Stringer and [third baseman] Johnny Ostrowski for the infield. They were all good hitters, and Ostrowski had over 100 RBI (actually 110). Billy Schuster, our shortstop, was our pop-off. We all agitated some.

[Bill] Kelly used to coach at third and Jackie Warner was our coach at first base. Warner was a good guy and did his job. You became friendly with the coaches, but not with the manager. Of course, he'd tell the coach what he wanted the players to do. We were a solid veteran team. We could win in the big leagues.

On the final day of the season, we split the doubleheader. I won the final game 2-1, guaranteeing us a tie for the pennant. We could have won the first game, but Red Lynn didn't slide into home plate on a close play and was tagged out. We wouldn't have had to play that one-game playoff.

It seemed like L.A. and the Seals were battling all season long. They brought in the big crowds. In the playoffs, Chambers won the playoff game against the Seals. Kelly debated who to start. Cliff always had good luck against San Francisco, and Kelly picked the right one. Cliff didn't want to pitch at first because he only had a couple of days rest. But they talked him into it.

We had the Governors Cup after the playoff game with San Francisco. The top four teams met. We beat Portland, then Oakland in five games. It gave us some extra money, but not a lot.

We were honored by a couple of dinners and were presented with championship rings. I forget what our cut was — $500 or $600, something like that.

BILL FLEMING - Angeles Pitcher

Los Angeles Angels shortstop Billy Schuster was known as a clown — and a clutch performer.

Bill Kelly was a real conscientious, sincere, nervous guy. People liked him. We worried more about his stomach ... he drank a lot of milk.

Jackie Warner was a fine man. He was a helluva ballplayer himself. He was in the majors a long time, and he came to the Seals (in 1939) when he was thirty-four or thirty-five and he hit .306. I remember Brooks Holder telling me how Jackie had helped him. Brooks was just breaking in, and Jackie helped him with his running the bases and cutoffs.

Jackie could run like hell. I remember him telling the story how he went to Detroit after he had a good season with Vernon. He had a race up there and outran Ty Cobb. Cobb never liked him after that. Jackie was never a guy who did any boasting. He was a good guy and a good coach, and I think he was a real help to Bill Kelly. Bill was a new guy, and Jackie knew the league.

We had a club that year that had good chemistry. It was guys who didn't necessarily have good years numbers-wise, but you put them all together and it made a good team. That's what we know baseball is. It was just a good, solid team.

We had good defense. We had good pitching. It was just good balance. No big stars, other than Cliff Chambers. A helluva ball club.

Chambers was probably our best pitcher that year. The Seals were our nemesis that year, and he just outright owned them. He killed them. Cliff had a good live fastball, and he was just coming into his own. He was a big, strong guy. He'd improved his curve ball. He would come right at you.

Red Lynn — I'll tell you that little son-of-a-gun had the damnedest arm of anyone I ever met in my life. You could take him out in the middle of winter and he could cut loose and do it again tomorrow. I remember the first day of spring training, he hadn't been working out and he's out there pumping. Everybody was remarking about how hard Red was throwing.

Someone said, 'He'll have his arm in a sling tomorrow.' Well, the next day, he's doing the same thing! He was an amazing guy. One year in the East Texas League he was 35-13! (He pitched 340 innings, not including playoff innings.)

Bill Fleming was a right-hander with a good fastball. Sometimes he was off on his control, but he was a quality spot-starter for us.

Russ Bauers was a phenom. Went to the majors early but hurt his arm. He had a great curve ball. It broke straight down. He was a big man, a gentle giant.

Once I hurt my arm and got my body tied up, I never should have continued doing what I was doing. I never felt I was throwing with the freedom I had prior to hurting my arm. I was continually fighting to keep my back loose. My wife was continually digging her elbow into my back to loosen the knots. My stuff was pretty inconsistent.

Jess Dobernic had a helluva arm. He was our stopper guy. That was the first year I remember having a guy designated to come in the last inning or so. He had a great year and went up to the Cubs next year.

Oren Baker was kind of a jack-of-all-trades. He was a good middleman. He'd get hot sometimes and they'd use him anywhere, or as a spot-starter. He was a side-wheeler, a durable, journeyman type.

I liked to pitch to Eddie Malone. Malone was a scrappy guy and he wasn't an out man himself. I don't know what he hit (.260), but he was a battler.

Larry Barton, our first baseman, came over from Oakland and had a good season. Lou Stringer was our second baseman. He had some power for a second baseman, and he could run. Billy Schuster played short, and [Johnny] Ostrowski was our third baseman. He had the best power for a guy his size I ever saw.

Clarence Maddern was a good hitter and knocked in over a hundred runs. He teamed up with Eddie Sauer and Cece Garriott. Sauer and Garriott were both fast and good defensive outfielders. Maddern led the team in hitting (with a .332 average), but all the outfielders hit in the clutch and drove in a lot of runs.

Albie Glossop, a switch-hitter, had a helluva year pinch hitting for us. And Loyd Christopher was off the bench. Paul Gillespie was our backup catcher.

Everyone contributed. We had an excellent bench.

CHARLES "RED" ADAMS - Pitcher

1956 ANGELS

*T*he 1956 Angels were Los Angeles' last Pacific Coast League champions, and some say they were the best. The team, anchored by triple-crown champion Steve Bilko, was overpowering offensively, and it had a youthful and talented pitching staff. Is it even possible to fairly compare three different teams from three different decades? Or do we conclude they were all great?

I played on the 1947 Angels team. I was also on the 1956 club, and it was different. The 1956 team's numbers were much more impressive. The Angels played two or three day games a week in Wrigley Field. They had a whole different format (from the one they used in 1947). They were televising day games, and the ball jumped out more during the daytime. Look at the ERA of the staff. You could add a run to their averages.

We did have some good arms on that staff. It was a young staff. Dave Hillman won twenty-one games. Gene Fodge and Bob Thorpe and Dick Drott were all just kids and big-league prospects. But they didn't throw as many innings.

Mo Bauer was a left-handed reliever for us. That son of a gun was a big, tall, skinny, real nice guy with a sharp breaking ball. He had a great season. And Bob Anderson was a reliever as a rookie. Neither started a game all season.

I think manager Bob Scheffing did a great job of juggling things. And Bob always liked to have some veterans around. That was his thinking. He had Chick

Los Angeles Angels manager Bob Scheffing, above, and infielder Gene Mauch, in 1956.

Los Angeles Angels pitcher Charles "Red" Adams, in 1956.

Pieretti, Harry Perkowski and me as veterans on the staff.

When I got there, quite frankly, I didn't think I could help them. Bob contacted me and told me they had a chance to get me. He asked me if I thought I'd be able to pitch any before the season was over. I was on crutches at the time. I had hurt my foot. I told him that my foot would be OK, but I said my arm was bothering me. I told him, 'If I were you, I wouldn't get me.'

He said, 'Hell, you've pitched with a sore arm all your life. I'd just kind of like to have you around. If you can pitch once a week, spot start, I'd like to have you on this club.' Adams went 6-4 and pitched 100 innings.

There were some of the neatest guys on that team, a bunch of Midwesterners. It was like a great big family. I felt privileged to join them. They had by far the best team in the league, so I felt pretty lucky just to be on it.

Then there was a guy everybody liked. Piper [Davis] was a great guy to have around. He didn't play a lot, but just the influence of some guys — just their being around and the things they say — it's important to have that type of person around.

The other thing about that team, I can remember there was a lot of comparing going on between the 1934 and 1947 teams. It was Gene Mauch and those guys.

They were very proud about that team, and rightfully so. For me, it was difficult to say which was best because there was a different setting. I don't think you can do that.

Gene was a very intense player, a great competitor. He had a big influence on the success of that team. He was the type of guy that, if there was anyone around that wasn't with it, focused or whatever, they're going to hear from Gene. That took an enormous pressure off Bob Scheffing.

Bob was an easygoing guy. Gene wasn't trying to manage or take over the club, but he was a big help to Scheffing. Gene was into the game all the time, all the way. You knew you had his backing when you were on the mound.

Casey Wise was a helluva guy. He was our shortstop. He was always ready to laugh at the humor you can find in baseball. He had been around baseball all his life. His dad was a scout, and Casey grew up playing ball. He was sharp, and got a kick out of everything going on. He later became an orthodontist.

He and Gene were a good team because Casey was young and a bright guy, and he was willing to learn from Gene. I think Gene made him a better player.

Elvin Tappe might have been as good a defensive catcher as there was around. He didn't have a great arm, but he could throw you out. He was quick and smart.

Bobby Coats could hit that ball and run pretty good. He was just happy to be there. And there was Bob Speake, a quiet guy and a gentleman. He batted in over 100 runs (111).

Gale Wade, old 'Windy,' was our maverick. Every team needs one of those. He played center field. I remember him running through the fence in San Diego, going like hell. He caught a ball over his head and hit that gate in center field head-on. The gate swung open, then closed. We were waiting for him to get up. Pretty soon he came back through there. He was a real hustling, bear-down type.

You don't see a club like that that doesn't have good chemistry. A good mix of personalities. It was one of my most enjoyable years in baseball.

CHARLES "RED" ADAMS - Pitcher

Bob Scheffing was a quiet type of manager. I think he knew in his mind that we had one helluva ball club. He didn't press anybody. I started out going something like 1 for 25, and he didn't say anything, and he kept me in the lineup. One time in L.A., I came up with the bases loaded, and he didn't pinch hit for me. I got a base hit. It seemed to just mushroom from there.

Jackie Warner was quiet also. He just seemed to be happy that he was there. He never forced himself on anybody. He'd do anything for you.

We were a club with great field players, a good bench, but suspect on the mound. Bob Anderson set some kind of record for relief pitches, so it tells you something when you have so many relief appearances. We had Ray Bauer early, and he probably helped Bob Anderson to adjust. And we had Hy Cohen, who went 5-0, and was sent out.

When Hy Cohen leaves, he was replaced by veterans. We picked up Red Adams, Chick Pieretti and Harry Perkowski. That gave some experience to go along with Gene Fodge, Bob Thorpe, Dave Hillman and Dick Drott. I just think he wanted some older pitchers around — spot-starting, relief and everything. The Coast League was an old player's league, so these youngsters could learn from the veterans.

Steve Bilko and Gene Mauch brought everything to that team. Steve was a loner. If he didn't like you, he'd never have anything to do with you. He and I used to sit in the clubhouse for an hour or more after a game, waiting for the traffic to disburse. We'd have Joe Liscio bring us a beer or two, and we'd just sit in the hot tub.

He was quiet, and everybody just looked up to him. He had that confidence that we're going to score the runs to win the game.

Gene Mauch was like a firecracker. When I played against him with Hollywood the previous season, I'd slide into him as hard as I could. I wanted to kill him. He just wanted to win so badly. But when I got on the team with him, I really respected what he brought to that team. And he knew baseball.

When he'd get on base, he used to give Steve the signs from first base - what the pitcher was about to throw to him. He did that to me once, signaled a curve, and the guy decked me with a fastball. I looked down to him and said, 'No more!'

[Shortstop] Casey Wise and I were in constant contact with each other. He was the general of that side. I'd look over to him, and he'd make a motion to help position me.

Piper Davis was a quiet, unassuming fella, and his teammates knew they could rely on him at any position. And Scheffing knew he could rely on Piper at any time.

We had some good catchers back there. [Elvin] Tappe went wherever Scheffing went. He was a good receiver, knew how to handle the pitchers. He was only an average hitter. Joe Hannah was equally as good as El's backup.

Our outfield was excellent — each of them was a center-fielder. They could all get under a ball at the same time, and then we had Bob Coats and Eddie Haas as backups.

Everyone jelled. Each person knew what his role was and they did it. This was a better club than any major league team I played on. Mauch has said it many times that this club could have been competitive in the major leagues.

GEORGE FREESE - Angels Pitcher

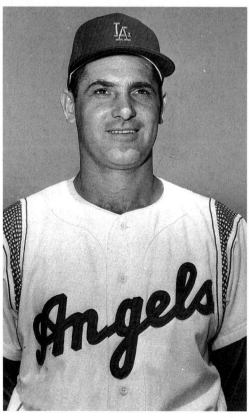

Infielder George Freese, in 1956.

I am not a big enthusiast of the '56 Angels. I thought they were an ordinary ball club. I thought they were overrated in a bad league, and I can name five ball clubs in my history that could have beaten them hands down any day of the week.

I can think of a couple of other Angel ball clubs that could have beat that ball club's brains out when I was a kid — the 1934 Angels, with Frank Demaree, Jigger Statz and a guy named Jim Oglesby at first base. That ball club could have beat Steve Bilko's group. And some of the better Hollywood clubs — it would have been touch-and-go in L.A., but we would have gotten 'em in Hollywood

Another was the '48 Oakland Oaks — they scared the hell out of you — and the club that finished second that year, the San Francisco Seals. They were good ball clubs.

CHUCK STEVENS - Hollywood Stars

You know, in 1956, the Vancouver Mounties went 12-12 against the Angels. During the last half of the season we were hot. They beat us the first six games, so we went 12-6 against them during the second half. They talk about how that team was so good. I was thinking about that. We handled them pretty good.

They were battling Seattle for first place, so they'd battle them for a week, then come up to Vancouver. They'd think, 'OK, they're in last place. We'll kick their ass.' Well, it didn't happen that way.

Steve Bilko didn't do anything against us. We'd take the left fielder and right fielder and push them toward center. Steve was a left-center, right-center hitter. He'd hit one out occasionally, but he didn't do anything if he kept the ball in the park. We were the only team to beat the Angels in a double-header that year — *in* Los Angeles.

You jammed Bilko. Just let him hit the ball to left-center, right-center. The Mounties, when they started the season, were a bad ball club. When I joined them they were 3-27 or something, but we picked up some good players and were tough during the second half.

JIM WESTLAKE - Vancouver Mounties

That 1956 Angels club was awesome, and playing in Wrigley made it even worse. I can remember Bilko hitting balls out of deep center field. Of course, that park was optimal for him. He was not a pull hitter.

They had great personnel. Their field team was outstanding, but their pitching was just average. The best pitcher on that squad was Bob Anderson, their reliever.

BILL WERLE - Portland Beavers

THE PORTLAND BEAVERS

1936 BEAVERS

*U*nder the control of the Philadelphia Athletics, the Portland Beavers of the 1930s were a good team. They won in 1932 and finished second in 1933. They were a 'Cinderella' team in 1936, when their expectations for success were low. But the Beavers' combination of veterans and youngsters outlasted Oakland and San Diego, and brought an emotional victory to the City of Roses.

Tom Turner was the president and Roy Mack was the general manager. In 1935, Steve and

I asked for more money from Mr. Mack, and they sent us to St. Joseph so they wouldn't have to pay us. We had a great team there, and we all came back to Portland in 1936.

Max Bishop was our manager and second baseman, but he wasn't there very long, and they brought in Bill Sweeney. Max was a sweet guy.

We had a good pitching staff — George Caster, Ad Liska, Bill Posedel. Posedel went to Brooklyn with me after our season at Portland. Also Hobo Carson. These guys did it all. I don't remember any relief pitchers. They threw a lot of innings for us.

Earle Brucker had a great season for us. He was a good catcher. Not an outstanding arm, but good enough to get rid of it. His strong point was working with the pitchers.

Dudley Lee was a good shortstop. He didn't hit much, but he helped me a lot. He showed me how to play the hitters and how to make the throw to the shortstop to make it easy for the double play. I remember when I started, I used to throw the ball when I was fairly close. He told me, 'Don't ever throw — do this (he demonstrates an underhand lob). You gain much more time by [lobbing] and I can see it better.' He used to talk with me and give me confidence. He was at the end of his career too.

Fred Bedore — didn't he hit. And he could field, and he had a snake for an arm. He could whip it from any position. He was a good third baseman.

Nino Bongiovanni had Moose Clabaugh and Johnny Frederick in the outfield. They were a little slow, but they had good wood. That Frederick, what a beautiful hitter he was. He was at the end of his career. Clabaugh too. Steve played infield and outfield, a lot of at-bats, but he didn't have a position.

We didn't have too many fast guys. Bongiovanni was as fast as anybody. I was just an average runner — quick in the field, but not fast. I had a quickness and quick release right from the start.

It was an exciting season. It was very close all season long. Seattle was tough on us. We beat them in the last game of the season to win the championship. I remember I got the hit to win the game. It was extra innings, and I got a hit off Don Osborn. He sent me a curve ball and I hit it to right field. I know we won the playoffs, but I don't remember the details. (Portland defeated Seattle 4-0, then Oakland 4-1 to win both series.)

PETE COSCARART - Beavers Second Baseman

The most noteworthy thing about the 1936 Beavers was we didn't have any cliques. Everybody was welcomed. That year we were just lucky. It was breaking for us real good, and everybody worked hard. And there were no smart guys, just a happy bunch working together.

They got Max Bishop here to manage, but they also wanted him to play second base. But we had a guy, a kid by the name of Pete Coscarart. Bishop went to the office and tried to tell them, 'You've got to play him. You've got a young guy that you'll be able to sell to the majors.'

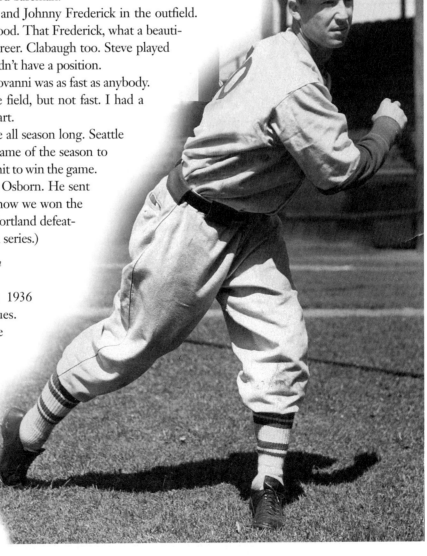

Crafty submarine pitcher Adolph "Ad" Liska was the cornerstone of the Portland Beavers' pitching staff for more than fourteen years, including the team's pennant-winning seasons, 1936 and 1945.

And Bishop had some intestinal problems, so he didn't play much on account of that. But they figured they were paying him to play, that he was from the big leagues and they expected him to be a gate attraction.

He had Pete playing, and we were in second place, one game out. We were to catch the train going south, and Max came over to me and said, 'I'm not going with you.' I said, 'What's the matter, are you sick?' He said, 'No, I'm not sick. [Bill] Sweeney's your next manager.'

And boy, that was a shock to me. I had liked Bishop as a manager. He was fired because he wasn't playing. They thought he should play, but he wanted the kid to play. Then they sold the kid, but they wouldn't replace him with anybody good.

That was a year they had the playoffs: First vs. fourth and second vs. third, then the winners would play for the championship. We beat Seattle four straight, then go to Oakland and down them four games to one. So we won eight out of nine games in the playoffs. We had a good team.

Our starters were Bill Posedel and George Caster. I relieved for the first few games then became a starter. Then we added Hal Carson. If you had four guys that were going good, they would be the ones to start.

Sweeney was our first baseman. As a manager he was all right. He had ulcers and he drank. He had beer all the time, even in the clubhouse.

Johnny Frederick was a pretty good player in the majors. He played left field and subbed at first. Along with Coscarart, shortstop Dudley Lee and Fred Bedore, it gave us a good infield.

AD LISKA - Beavers Pitcher

On opening day, I went five for five. I think that was my greatest thrill in baseball. I got three doubles and two singles, and I didn't sleep all night. I was so excited. That was a great way to start the season.

Moose Clabaugh and Johnny Frederick were in the outfield. Those two guys were on their last legs, and any time a ball was hit to the outfield they'd yell, 'Come on, Bongy! Come on, Bongy!' I had to go catch the ball even if it was way over in left or in right.

I remember Bill Sweeney spitting in an ump's face. We were playing in Civic Stadium and the ump missed the call. Bill was face-to-face with him, then he leaned back and let it go. I didn't like that. I think he was fined, but I don't think he missed any games.

NINO BONGIOVANNI - Beavers Center-fielder

The 1936 Beavers had a good pitching staff. We had George Caster, Ad Liska, Bill Posedel and Hobo Carson. Caster had just come back from the big leagues. He had been with the Athletics and had a good year (twenty-five wins) and Posedel won twenty. Liska had a submarine ball. He had a good year.

We had some also-rans that helped. They won six to eight games — Bill Radonits, Tom Flynn and Don French. They didn't win as much as the other guys, but they helped in between. They were always good for a couple of innings. Pitching was the reason we won it.

Bill Sweeney was a real strict manager. Sweeney told you to do everything. I just couldn't play for him.

Early in the season, when Max Bishop was managing, Sweeney got hurt and he went back up to Portland. When the team came back to Portland, Sweeney was the manager. Bishop was near the end of the line as a player and they were paying him a lot to both manage and play second.

But Bishop just played in spots, so Pete Coscarart would play at second, and [Fred] Bedore was at third. Bedore was an older guy coming to the end of his career, but he was a good hitter.

So sometimes when he wasn't playing I'd fill in there too. Dudley Lee was one of the best [at shortstop]. Lee taught both Pete and me a lot — the double play and things like that.

With Moose Clabaugh and Johnny Frederick in the outfield, Nino Bongiovanni had to play center field. [Clabaugh and Frederick] were both good hitters but didn't run too good. Bongiovanni was fast. He could bunt and beat them out. He had good legs and was a consistent hitter, a .300 hitter. He wasn't a bad outfielder, but he didn't have a real good arm.

STEVE COSCARART - Beavers Outfielder, Utility Player

THE SEATTLE RAINIERS

THE JACK LELIVELT YEARS, 1938-40

*T*he Seattle Rainiers began building a dynasty after the arrival of Jack Lelivelt in 1938. Lelivelt, who had had great success in Los Angeles a few years before, joined Rainiers owner Emil Sick to open a new ballpark, Sick's Seattle Stadium. The team placed second in 1938, a decided improvement over the previous season, when the team finished sixth.

The Rainiers won in 1939 and 1940. They were primed to repeat in 1941, but Lelivelt died unexpectedly in January of that year. Nonetheless, the team persevered, hired longtime Yankee farm-club manager Bill Skiff, and went on to make 1941 another championship year for the Rainiers.

World War II, however, took away many of the team's stars, and thoughts of further developing a Rainier dynasty were put aside for the duration.

I played for twelve managers during my baseball career, and I would have to put Jack Lelivelt at the head of the list. He was fair to all his players. We got the same treatment with Lelivelt. He made a lot of calls.

Jack looked out for the welfare of his players. One spring my second child was expected, and Jack allowed me to remain in Seattle until her arrival, missing spring training entirely. While I was there I was attending the University of Washington, working on a master's degree which allowed me to enter college work after my baseball career ended.

Jack and I were close friends. I recall he used to ask me to go to the races with him in L.A. when we had an off day. He knew all the owners.

Respected for his fairness and visionary ideas, Seattle Rainiers manager Jack Lelivelt led the team to championships in 1939 and 1940. His death in January, 1941, shocked and saddened the baseball world. This picture was taken in 1939.

To show how he reacted as a sentimental manager, one summer my parents were visiting me in Seattle, and on one of my days to pitch, we were one run behind in the ninth, with runners on first and third with two outs. Rather than using a pinch hitter, he allowed me to hit. I always thought it was because my parents were at the game. Fortunately, I hit a double to win the game. My dad was seen standing in the box, saying, 'That's my boy!'

Mrs. Lelivelt was a charming lady, quite often giving tea parties for the players' wives — anything to keep harmony on the team.

Kewpie Barrett was a character. He had a remarkable physique, considering he abused his body with alcohol. But he was a fan-pleaser. When I was traded to Seattle along with Louie Koupal in 1936, Kewpie won twenty-two games. Louie won twenty-three and I won fifteen.

Fred Hutchinson brought more people into the park. He was a rookie for us in 1938. I remember Freddie as an interesting youngster. He wanted to learn everything he could from everybody with any experience. In fact,

Billy Schuster was a sparkplug for Jack Lelivelt's Seattle Rainiers in 1940. But after Lelivelt's death, new manager Bill Skiff balked at Schuster's comic antics and traded him to the Los Angeles Angels in mid-1941.

he asked me to work with him on his curve ball. He was an exceptional boy and a terrible loser. He just couldn't take it — knocked down doors, picked up water coolers and carried on.

I was surprised when they named him manager, but he apparently was a good one.

Hal Turpin was always an amazement to me. I couldn't understand how he could get people out until they decided that he was one of the original slider pitchers. He had an excellent slider and could throw it in a knot hole. His control and his movement on the ball without remarkable speed gave him the winning edge.

Our catcher, Gilly Campbell was a free-wheeler, an easygoing guy, a lot of fun. He mixed up the pitches pretty well, and he could throw well.

We had excellent infielders. Lennie Gabrielson and George Archie at first, [third baseman] Dick Gyselman and [shortstop] Alan Strange. George Archie was a fine fella. He and catcher Buddy Hancken were good friends. We had a club that could have finished pretty well in either of the major leagues.

Alan Strange and I roomed together on road trips and we talked about baseball constantly. He was helpful to me, making suggestions regarding batters or helping to hold them on. He was a very capable fielder.

Billy Schuster joined us in 1940. He was a wild man. As long as Schuster performed and behaved himself otherwise, there was no problem. He was just entertaining the public. He was a performer, but he wasn't so much of a clown away from the public. He was a clutch player. I wouldn't mind having him on my club.

Bill Lawrence and I were very close. All you had to do was keep the ball in the ballpark and Bill would get it. Can you imagine pitching to a ball club with Edo Vanni, JoJo White and Bill Lawrence in the outfield? It was just a question of how far the fences were back.

Mike Hunt was also there, and he could use the bat better than any of them. Jerry Donovan was also there. He was also from San Francisco, very pleasant to be around. He was a good outfielder, but never reached his potential.

Frank Kelleher was a good hitter and a good outfielder. He couldn't break into the Seattle outfield but he could hit that ball a long way. And Spencer Harris was another good hitter. He wasn't a long-ball hitter but he was a consistent hitter. When he was with Portland, I had a couple of no-hitters going late in the ball game, and he broke them both up. I was happy to see him with us, but he was getting up there in age and was at the end of the line.

[The pitchers] always said, 'If we could keep the ball in the ballpark, we could win.' We didn't hit many home runs, but we put the ball into play very well. Vanni and White could steal most any time they wanted.

Jack Lelivelt's death from a heart attack was a real shock, coming right before spring training. It shocked the whole city. I can remember one time we were pushing along and [new manager] Bill Skiff was struggling, and on a train trip to the South a bunch of us got him and sat him down.

We just said to him, 'If you'll just sit still and enjoy the game, we'll win the pennant for you.' That's pretty rough, telling the manager. But we were a group of veterans and most anyone on the club could have operated the team. He acquiesced and came along pretty well.

That was the year Sacramento, with Pepper Martin, got a big lead early in the season and we all had to catch them. That's why Skiff was so down and why we talked with him.

PAUL GREGORY - Rainiers Pitcher

I had signed with the Yankees and was sent to Oakland in '37, but I had a bad case of sinuses, so they sent me to Binghamton in the New York-Penn League. That helped correct the sinuses. The next year they sent me back out to the coast, to Seattle, on option. Jack Lelivelt was my manager. He knew the game real well and was easygoing.

Our infield in l938 was outstanding. Alan Strange and Freddy Muller were the double-play combination. They turned it very well. And Dick Gyselman was our third baseman, a great third baseman. Not a bad hitter, too.

Bill Lawrence was one of the greatest center fielders I ever saw. He could go back on the ball, come in on the ball. I saw him go behind the left fielder one day to catch the ball. Bill was a quiet guy. He minded his own business and was pretty much a loner.

We had Mike Hunt in left field and Levi MacCormack, the Indian, in right field. And along came Edo Vanni. Edo played against right-handers and Levi played against left-handers. They were adequate in the field. Hunt was a power hitter.

Edo was raised in Seattle — Queen Anne High School. He could hit the right-hand hitting, but didn't like the left-handers, so it worked out well with Levi.

The Seattle Rainiers in 1940, their second consecutive championship year.

We had Hal Turpin and Paul Gregory, 'Kewpie' Dick Barrett, Les Webber and Freddie Hutchinson. Walter 'Boom-Boom' Beck joined us halfway through the season. He used to get bombed pretty good.

Hal Turpin was a real veteran. He used to pitch for the San Francisco Seals, a twenty-game winner all the time. He was a right-handed pitcher but a left-hand hitter, and was used as a pinch-hitter. He was such a good hitter, very quiet and unassuming. You couldn't get him to smile. But when he went up there to pinch hit, you could be sure that he was going to get a base hit. He hit the ball hard, a line-drive hitter.

Freddie [Hutchinson] was a real gruff guy. He was a tough kid. His father and brother were doctors. He was already ready for a beef. He often chewed out his infielders if they made an error behind him. He never did that to me. I'd have gone right after him. I was in good shape in those days, and was probably 210. He was a cocky guy and a great pitcher. That cockiness motivated him. Both he and Kewpie Barrett pitched over 300 innings that year.

Kewpie was another cocky guy, but he was roly-poly. One evening in Sacramento, Nick Cullop, a pretty good hitter himself, was trying on glasses for the first time. He made the statement, 'I hope I can get used to wearing these new glasses.' Barrett responded, 'Don't worry, I'm going to knock you on your ass.' The second time Cullop came up, Barrett knocked him down and Cullop went right after him. I didn't even move.

He knocked Kewpie right off the mound. Cullop was a big guy with thick arms. The only guy who went to help him was [third baseman Dick] Gyselman. We used to call Dick 'Needle,' he was so skinny. If guys wanted to fight, OK. The umpires and players would gather around and let them fight.

Because [team owner] Emil Sick was a beer magnate, after every game they'd roll in fifteen or twenty cases of beer, ice cold. We'd have everyone in there — sports writers and everyone. Sick was a generous man.

LEN GABRIELSON - Seattle Rainiers

Jack Lelivelt had been the manager at Los Angeles, and he had some great ball clubs down there. He had guys like Jigger Statz, Marv Gudat, Jim Oglesby and Frank Demaree — I'd say one of the great ball clubs of all time in the Pacific Coast League.

Lelivelt would give you an opportunity to perform the way you should perform. He let you use your own initiative.

If you gave your best and your best wasn't good enough, he didn't downgrade you. He'd find a place for you to play ball without knocking you. His ballplayers realized that, and it gave our team strength and spirit, and that's what held our ball club together.

There wasn't one guy on that ball club who wasn't helpful or who wouldn't cooperate with each other. That's the way Jack handled his ballplayers. That's the way they played for him in Los Angeles, and I'd say our 1940 ball club was just as good as any.

His wife was just a beautiful person too. When we were rookies, she took Freddie Hutchinson and myself to Bullocks department store in Los Angeles and bought us two suits of clothes, a sport outfit, slacks and shoes. That showed me all kinds of class.

How could you not play your heart out for him and, for that matter, her too. He felt that he could help us. It was things like that that got us together as a team and held us. He was like a father to me.

In 1938, my rookie year, we were down in Los Angeles. Out of the seven games played down there, I lost five ball games for the Rainiers — missing second base, missing third base, getting caught off a base.

I think I had about fifteen hits that week. In the last game of the Sunday double-header, I tried to make a shoestring catch and I hit the glove on my knee and I dropped the ball and we lost the game. Kewpie Barrett lost two games that week.

You come up the ramp to the clubhouse at Wrigley Field, and Barrett's yelling, 'If we don't get that kid off the field, we'll never win another ball game out there.' But as I came in from the outfield, there was only one guy sitting on the bench and that was Jack Lelivelt.

He says, 'Sit down,' and he puts his arms around my shoulder. 'You had a tough week, didn't you?' I says, 'Yeah. Everything I did was wrong.' I thought maybe I was heading for Vancouver.

So we start heading up the ramp together, and Barrett is still spouting off up there, and Lelivelt brought a halt to everything. He said, 'You know something? He may have cost us five games, but he was the only guy getting on base to make mistakes.' That took care of that.

We went to San Diego next series, and I won three games out of four for them. So that just goes to show you, he could have made or broken me right there. I played my heart out for that guy.

Lelivelt seldom had signals. He'd turn the game over to us. JoJo White would get on and I'd fake a bunt to third, then lay one down the first base line and he'd go from first to third. They'd try to nail him and I'd go to second. This way you upset the defense. That's the way we liked to play the game. We'd lose a ball game, and he wouldn't come in ranting and raving. He'd just say, 'Tough luck. We'll get 'em tomorrow.'

Freddie Hutchinson and I were rookies on a veteran ball club in 1938, and we roomed together that first year. If we were on the road and he lost a ball game, he'd go back to the hotel and tear the room apart. I finally said, 'I hope you lose your games in Seattle so your mother can take care of you. I've got to sleep on the floor tonight.'

When Hutch was sold to Detroit after the 1938 season, we got George Archie, Buddy Hancken, Ed Selway and JoJo White. Hancken replaced Tony Piet, who didn't report. Archie and White were regulars immediately for us.

JoJo White was an inspiration to the ball club. He was just great. We'd get in the clubhouse, and he'd say, 'OK, this is how we're going to do it tonight against these guys.' He'd set up the plays. 'If I'm on second base, lay a ball down third base, but lay it foul. Bring that guy in. On the next pitch, if I get a chance, I'm going to steal third base. Then with a ground ball or fly ball, we've got to run.'

George Archie was soft-spoken. If he said a swear word, it would be, 'Dag nabit.' He was a quiet guy, and defensively he was very good. He would bat number three because he could line the ball.

Alan Strange was a great incentive too. He'd take me aside and say, 'What the hell did you do that for?' He'd say, 'When you've got a man on second base and no one out, pull the ball and get the man to third.' I was going through college all over again, the fundamentals of how to play the game right.

Bill Lawrence helped me, too. I used to say that Lawrence used to tell me to catch the foul balls — over by the foul line. But basically he spent a lot of time with me. While we were playing, he'd say, 'Now look, in the late innings, if they have a man on second base and we have a two-run lead, if the guy singles, throw the ball to second base. Keep the guy on first.' Stuff like that. It was very helpful. He was just a beautiful person.

Seattle Rainiers manager Bill Skiff, center, reviewed batting strategy with first baseman Earl Torgeson, left, and shortstop Ned Stickle in 1942.

During those years, we won with pitching and great defense. We had Hal Turpin, 'Kewpie' Dick Barrett, Paul Gregory and Bill Walker as our nucleus.

Turpin was fantastic. Gilly Campbell was our catcher. Lelivelt had brought him up from Los Angeles. Gilly would dress next to me in the clubhouse, and he'd come in after the game and say, 'Turpin was wild today. He walked one guy. Let's get two runs. That's enough.'

Kewpie would go 3-2 on everybody, load the bases, then strike the side out. That was Kewpie. He was a showman, but he was also a helluva competitor. He had two kinds of curve balls. I'd like to see today's players hit Barrett's curves. He'd have them sitting one foot in the dugout.

The Seattle Rainiers' holiday greeting card from 1941, manager Bill Skiff's first season.

And Paul Gregory was another curve-ball pitcher. He was good. Les Webber and Bill Walker, down from the Cardinals, also were good. [Walker] threw a curve ball and sinker ball. He was the well-dresser on the ball club, the fashion plate.

Bill Lawrence used to say, 'You guys have got two runs. For crying out loud, hold em!' That kind of spirit. Lelivelt used to say, don't walk anyone and we'll win the game. And the outfield — I could have been the defensive weakness.

In 1940, almost the whole team returned. Alan Strange was drafted by the St. Louis Browns and Al Niemic replaced Joe Morrissey. We had Bill Schuster at shortstop. Don't ever underestimate that guy. He was a very knowledgeable shortstop, and a clutch ballplayer.

A lot of guys used to say, 'That guy is goofy, and he's going to drive Lelivelt crazy.' He didn't drive Lelivelt crazy because he played outstanding ball. Let Schuster be Schuster. If that's the way Bill wants to be, let him be. He shows up every day to play. That's part of the game.

We picked up Aldon Wilkie after San Francisco had released him. Hell, with that ball club we had he won nine straight. We just told him to get the ball over the plate. Let 'em hit the ball, someone will catch it. That was the attitude we had.

I couldn't say there was one bad guy on the ball club. I never saw such camaraderie on a ball club, and that's what wins championships. We all cooperated and played beautifully. Nobody did anything in detriment to hurt any individual ballplayer. Our club in 1940 couldn't hit a home run out of a phone booth, but I don't think we ever lost more than three games in a row.

Everybody on the club was a manager. Jack would just stand out there on the third base line and say, 'Come on. Let's see you hit one.' He knew how to handle personnel and he knew how to get the best out of you. The guy should have been a psychologist at a university.

I cried when Jack died. He was down at a basketball game not far from where I lived. I was just shocked. He was like a father to me. The whole club was shocked. We felt so sorry for his wife, Ethel. She was just a gracious lady.

Bill Skiff inherited a good ball club, and he won again in 1941. He was more like a Yankee. He wanted to bring in the guys who hit home runs. He brought in Bill on and Les Scarsella. But he was a good manager.

That was the year I broke my leg. I came up to hit and somebody knocked me flat on my ass. I got on first base, and I was thinking, 'One of those S.O.B.s has got to cover out there, and it was [Eddie] Pellagrini. I slid into him and I knocked him [several] feet away and broke my leg. I said, 'Well, if they're going to get me, I'm going to get them.' That's the way we played.

Skiff didn't care for Schuster's antics. He came from the Yankee organization, and they didn't tolerate that kind of stuff. They sold him to Los Angeles. Skiff didn't care for Gilly, so he got traded to Los Angeles. That was nothing against Skiff's managing; that was just the way he handled the ball club.

But what this meant was the slow breakup of a great team. Then the war came along and I went in. After the war ended, I returned to the Rainiers. Dewey Soriano and I were all that remained of the great teams of the Lelivelt era.

EDO VANNI - Rainiers Outfielder

I signed with the Detroit organization after high school in Nashville, in 1933, and went to Seattle as part of the trade for Fred Hutchinson. Jo Jo White and I slipped right into the Seattle lineup, and we managed to play some pretty good ball for them.

Seattle was a fine place to play. The weather was right, although some of the boys didn't think it was warm enough. The fans were great. The same group seemed to be there every night. They were from all walks of life, and they knew what was going on. They were good to us. To me, that was the greatest fun I had in baseball. Of course, we were winning. I enjoyed playing at Seattle. It was a good park and Jack Lelivelt was a good manager.

We had no problems at all. He just made up the lineup out and we went out and played. We had a bunch of fellas who knew how to play the game, and we had pretty good success.

We ran a lot; we could fly. We had JoJo White and Edo Vanni and myself and, in 1939, Alan Strange and, in 1940, Bill Schuster. We could all run. He just turned us loose, more or less. I don't want to say he let us go altogether, he just oversaw it. The first three or four hitters in the lineup did a lot of hit-and-run.

Our infield was a good defensive infield. The infielders were true on their throws to me. They had the good arms and got rid of the ball quickly to give you time to get over to the bag and away from it before the runner came down.

We had most of the same players in 1939 and 1940. Dick Gyselman played third and I was on first. Joe Morrissey was our second baseman in 1939, and Al Strange was the shortstop. But Morrissey got injured at the end of the season, and Strange was drafted by the Browns.

In 1940, Al Niemiec was our second baseman and Bill Schuster was new at shortstop. Schuster was different. We called him one of the loosey-screws guys, but he was in the ball game day in and day out. He was a good clutch player.

Bill Lawrence was the 'Daddy-dog' of the outfielders. He caught everything between the foul lines. He was a great fellow, too, the nicest man. Edo Vanni was a youngster coming on at the time, and he had good years for us. He was to get on base, and we would hit-and-run. He was a good addition to the ball club.

Gilly Campbell was as steady as a rock behind home plate. I won't say he was a quiet man, but if you happen to know him, he was all right. He did his job, and the pitchers had confidence in him.

The Rainiers in 1951, another of Seattle's pennant-winning teams.

In 1939, we had to fight an uphill battle because Los Angeles got off to a fast start. We finally caught them by mid-July. The 1940 team was probably better because we were more mature. We had gotten used to playing with each other.

Sick's Stadium wasn't suitable for home-run hitters. In 1940, JoJo White and I hit eight apiece to lead the club. We went for the hit-and-run, the steal. We all had enough experience to put the thing together. If something was wrong, we'd have a little conversation among ourselves to see how we could do better.

In 1940, everybody said I was the most valuable player. We had the pitching to go with it. You had to have the pitching to give the infielders something to do, and we did.

GEORGE ARCHIE - Rainiers First Baseman

1951 RAINIERS

I went to spring training with Seattle in 1951. They had bought me from Detroit, and when I get there, I find six other catchers. I'd say, 'Why the heck did they get me?' I do remember in spring training, [manager Rogers] Hornsby, he didn't really speak to anybody.

Bennie Huffman, Hornsby's coach, brought Joe Montalvo with him from the Venezuelan winter league. Montalvo got most of the playing time during the season. He was a big, powerful guy.

And we had Bud Sheely, the son of Earl Sheely, who was the Rainiers' general manager. Bud was slower than heck but a good receiver, and he was a left-handed batter.

Bill Salkeld, a major league veteran, was in camp but didn't make it. That's why I was surprised that I made the club.

I wasn't even supposed to be there. One morning in Palm Springs, Hornsby called me over to the dugout. He asked me if Earl Sheely had contacted me the evening before. I said he had not. Earl wanted to send me to Tacoma.

I was having a good spring, and here I am, holding this bat and talking to him. I happened to use Hornsby's style bat. I have a contract with Louisville Slugger, and I use a H117 model, his model. And the 'H' stands for Hornsby. I told him, 'Mr. Hornsby, I wanted to come here and play for the greatest right-handed hitter of all time.'

I was really pumping him up. I had nothing to lose. And I'm waving this bat in front him, and I said, 'I'm leading the team in hitting.' And he said, 'Yes, but it's only spring training.' He said, 'I'll tell you what I'll do. I'll keep you until the cut-down.' He did, and in the meantime I had some success at the plate.

Hornsby started pinch-hitting me, and I got lucky and hit a few home runs. And he started playing me regularly, and the big honor there was that he batted me fourth. But all three catchers started the season hitting well. He actually put Montalvo on first for a while because he was hitting good. But we had George Vico and Gordon Goldsberry there. So they kept three catchers — Sheely, Montalvo and me.

Marv Grissom was the ace of our staff. He won twenty games that year. With Grissom that year and Al Widmar the next, neither of them had any great form as a pitcher, and neither one had a fastball, but both of them had that great, great control. They could throw the ball just where you wanted them. As a catcher, it was kind of like you were on the same page with them. Both went on to have great careers as pitching coaches.

We also had Paul Calvert. I roomed with him on the road. He was called The Little Professor. He had those thick glasses, and he took two suitcases with him on the road, one filled with books. It must have weighed 100 pounds. On the plane he'd be studying Italian. He was always busy studying something.

He was a spot-starter for us, and he had a heck of a slider. He snapped the ball because he held it so tight. He developed callouses on his hand, and was always putting Tufskin on it to prevent getting blisters. If he developed a blister, then he couldn't throw. When he was right, he was unhittable.

Al Lyons pitched some games for us too. He was normally our center-fielder, but he'd pitch the second game of the Sunday double-header. Jim Davis did a lot of relieving, but our main reliever was Steve Nagy.

I hated catching Jim Davis. The first few games I caught Jim, I'd try to call fastballs and he'd shake me off. Finally I came to the conclusion he wanted to throw the knuckle ball. We didn't have those big catchers gloves like they came out with later. All you tried to do was box that pitch in. I was a good defensive catcher, but Davis gave me fits.

Jim's knuckleball was hard to catch because he threw it up hard. It didn't float. You never knew which way it was going to go. It could sail on you, or it could come up to the plate, explode and break down.

It didn't make any difference where we were playing because he threw it so hard. The guy that throws the floater might be affected by wind currents, but Jim's broke so many ways every time he threw it.

Earl Johnson did some relieving for us. Earlier in my career, I pinch-hit and got a base hit off of him. That was the first game of a double-header. In the second game, he hit me. As I went to first base, I was giving him holy hell, and I can remember him responding, 'We don't throw at piss-hitters.' Not much I could say.

I was catching Marv Grissom down in the bullpen one afternoon. Mr. Hornsby used to like to come down and take his stance in the batters box. Marv was throwing sliders and Mr. Hornsby turned back and asked me, 'What's he throwing?' I responded, 'He's throwing sliders, Mr. Hornsby.' He looked back and said, 'Hell, it looks like a cheap curve to me.'

It wasn't until years later that I got thinking about that. As great a hitter as he was, he probably didn't know what a pitcher threw. He probably just saw the ball and hit.

In 1951, we opened in Los Angeles, and in the clubhouse before the first game, Mr. Hornsby's total speech that I heard for the whole year was before that game. And he said, 'If you hustle and you make errors, they're all part of the game, and I won't count 'em against you.' That was the end of the only meeting for the whole year!

Kay Chorlton was out playing left field one night, and he dropped an easy fly ball. Mr. Hornsby, instead of waiting until the end of the inning to take him out, sent Walt Judnich out right then. Kay Chorlton came right in, and the next morning he was on a bus to Vancouver. That's how he managed.

One night, Charlie Schanz, with the big glasses, was pitching for us. Billy Raimondi, at the end of his career, was catching for Los Angeles. Charlie was batting, and the ball came close to him. Charlie turned to Billy, threw his glasses off, Billy threw his glasses off and here are the two twenty-year veterans out there, wrestling around on the field, and here's Jim Rivera out there in the middle of this thing.

Charlie and Billy were the two most unlikely players in the league to be fighting. But 'Jungle Jim,' that was a different matter.

We were picked to finish in the second division that season, but we had a lot of talent there.

We never lost over three ball games in a row. Hornsby had the fear of God over us. He didn't talk to you. In one visit to the manager's room, you could be gone. You just never knew where you stood.

Hornsby used to substitute liberally. You could be playing regularly, then all of a sudden you're not playing. Whether he got hunches or what ...

We had good chemistry on the club, and the spiritual leader was our second baseman, Wes Hamner, Granny Hamner's brother. Wes would get in the dugout before the game and we'd have a little cheer. He started about a month into the season when we were going real good. We'd all do it, every single night. and it went like this:

Seattle Rainiers catchers, left to right: Don Lundberg, Claude Christie and Joe Erautt.

'Strawberry shortcake. Huckleberry pie. V-I-C-T-O-R-Y!'

Every night we did that in the dugout! Here's a bunch of grown men. But by god, it put us all in good spirits. It was funny, and Hornsby never said anything. He just sat in his damn corner.

George Vico and Gordy Goldsberry were our first basemen. Wes Hamner was on second with Alex Grabowski and Jack Albright at short and Rocky Krsnich at third.

Jim Rivera, our right-fielder, was always in trouble. The club attorneys were always bailing him out of some situation. But the guy could play ball. He was one solid muscle.

He could run and he could field. He had that head-first slide where he'd take off and run down the line and slide head-first into the base. He was one of the few hitters who could hit home runs to the opposite field.

You could also count on the other outfielders, Walt Judnich and Al Lyons, in almost the same way. Judnich played left and Lyons was in center. I played with a lot of outfielders in my career, and Al Lyons had the best arm of any outfielder I have ever seen. He almost stood flat-footed, and he threw that ball, and it came in like a shot. He knew how to play the batter, too. He knew how to go back on the ball or come in.

When we won the pennant that night in Seattle, the guys wanted to know if they could have champagne or something in the clubhouse, and Hornsby said, 'Not until I'm out of here.' You could understand why the press didn't like him. No press in the clubhouse.

It was a great thing for the ballplayers because they knew they would never read anything bad about them in the newspapers, and if you did, the reporter made it up, because Hornsby never went to those social hours held at each ballpark after the game. The press was not allowed in our clubhouse, period. Even the night that we won the pennant!

Then we had the Governor's Cup after the end of the season. We went through the whole season and won the league, and the amount of money that we got — if the fourth-place team had won the Governor's Cup they would have gotten as much money as we did. We went down to the wire and finally beat Hollywood. So we won both championships.

CLAUDE CHRISTIE - Rainiers Catcher

The club we had in Seattle would have been able to compete favorably with many of the lesser teams in the major leagues. We maybe wouldn't have been able to sustain it over the long season, but we were a competitive bunch.

We had a veteran staff, and we got information from those pitchers who had been in the league for two or three years. My nephew was on the team, Jim Davis. In fact, we roomed together.

Charlie Schanz, Skinny Brown and myself, we all took our regular turns. Jim Davis was a spot starter. Paul Calvert was a reliever. He was a game finisher more than anybody else. But there were a lot of us who finished our own ball games. And Steve Nagy and Earl Johnson both relieved, but they started games too. Hornsby would use anybody if he thought he might win. Rogers Hornsby didn't communicate a lot with his players, but he was a fair man. I was 20-10, and Charlie Schanz had just pitched the game to win the pennant and, of course, we all celebrated. Hornsby comes to me and asks me if I wanted to make it twenty-one, which would have passed Bill Ayers of Oakland for the lead in victories. Or did I want to open the playoffs. I said, 'I'd like to go for twenty-one.' He said, 'OK, You're the pitcher.' We proceeded to lose, and I went to 20-11. I did win two in the playoffs. But that's the way he was. He was completely fair.

I think Joe Montalvo caught me the most. One time in a tied game with two outs in the last inning, we had Jim Rivera on third base. Joe's got two strikes on him, and I don't know what Jim was thinking about, but he was going to steal home.

He did. He came in, and the pitch was about belt high and Montalvo swung and missed! Here's Jim sliding in. If he'd made contact, it would have torn the top of his head off. We laughed at it later, but it could have been disastrous.

Jim Rivera was a catalyst to that team. He was a Willie Mays on the field. His timing always seemed to be perfect. When he did those things it would mean something. He could hit with power, he could steal a base. It would have been a very different team without him.

Then we had Al Lyons and Walt Judnich. They provided a lot of power, and Al would pitch the second game of a double-header a lot of times, too. In the infield we had lots of versatility. Earl Sheely, the general manager, called me in and gave me a raise in the middle of the year. That's the kind of organization it was. They respected guys who were doing the job for them. I appreciated that. But we never saw Emil Sick.

Hornsby wouldn't allow beer in the clubhouse. I generally would get the first game of the Sunday double-header, and so after the game, I'd dress. Earl Sheely would often come down to the clubhouse between games and he'd say to me, 'Come on. Let's go into my office and have a beer.' Earl understood all those things and handled them pretty well.

I remember Skinny Brown, my nephew and I would get up early in the morning and go trout fishing at Ellensburg (southeast of Seattle). We'd catch our limit and come back in the early afternoon, take an hour-and-a-half nap and then go out to the ballpark.

I can remember we took Lew Burdette and Eddie Lake of the San Francisco Seals with us. We'd had it set up to take them fishing when they came in. Well, we had played a night game and left right after the game, had something to eat, and arrived at Ellensburg just at daylight. We started fishing, got our limit and headed back about 10:30.

We go to the ballpark that afternoon, and the guy who was supposed to start couldn't start. I'm put in the lineup against Lew Burdette! We hadn't had any sleep all night except what we got that afternoon. We went out there against each other and I beat him 1-0.

Hornsby and Lefty O'Doul — they put on a batting exhibition in Seattle. That was an awesome sight. It was a rather misty night, but they put on quite an exhibition. Hornsby, a right-handed hitter, kept hitting line drive after line drive to right field, the opposite field. And O'Doul, a left-handed hitter did the same to left field. Everything was just a line drive. As old as they were, they could still make contact with power. It was great.

MARV GRISSOM - Rainiers Pitcher

THE VANCOUVER MOUNTIES

THE LATE 1950s

*W*hen the Oakland Oaks moved to Vancouver after the 1956 season, they weren't very good. Vancouver was led by Cedric Tallis, of the Baltimore Orioles of the American League. The Orioles sent some of their finest young talent to Vancouver, where a combination of veteran pitching and youthful bats and arms made the Mounties competitive, but not champions, for several years.

The city of Vancouver really accepted Coast League ball in the beginning. For years, we had been a farm club of Seattle and there would be a few players with Vancouver connections —

Although the Phoenix Giants won the pennant that year, the 1959 Vancouver Mounties offered a highly competitive mix of youth and experience.

A hustling infielder, Carl "Buddy" Peterson broke in with the Portland Beavers and went on to play with the San Diego Padres, Vancouver Mounties and Sacramento Solons.

Kay Chorlton, Bud Sheely. The big games were when the Seals or Angels would come to town, especially the Angels. But then the majors came west in 1958 and removed those two teams, and the league became sort of a patchwork with other teams — Salt Lake City, Hawaii, and then expansion to Tulsa and Indianapolis. It wasn't like it used to be when it was an established, eight-team league.

The Mounties had Erv Palica and George Bamberger as the mainstays of the pitching staff. Palica had just come down from the Dodgers, and he always seemed to have something wrong with him. He was a good hitter, and that's when pitchers had to hit. He had some key home runs in this park. But he was always complaining, 'I'll be OK, if my elbow holds out.'

But George was the real strength on the staff. He was here longer and was very popular among the fans.

Charlie White, a black catcher who stayed in Vancouver for many years, and Bamberger were the most popular with the fans. Capilano Stadium was an intimate ballpark. You could sit in the box seats and talk to the on-deck batter.

In 1958 and 1959 we had very competitive teams. Palica and Bamberger anchored the pitching. George actually pitched 68 ²/₃ innings with no walks. And we had Charlie Beamon, Joe Hatten and Russ Heman. Along with Buddy Peterson we had Owen Friend, Jim Dykes, Joe Durham and Barry Shetrone in the field.

In 1959, we had basically the same team, but with an infield that included Ray Barker, Ronnie Hansen, Marv Breeding, Eddie Basinski and Brooks Robinson. Robbie was only there for forty-one games, but everyone knew he was going to be a star.

Eddie Basinski joined us at the start of the season. He was a skinny infielder who

Vancouver Mounties manager Charlie Metro ran a tight ship. Many players appreciated his managerial skills, but he also was disliked by several players who caused dissension on the team.

had better years at Portland. He was unathletic-looking, but the kind of guy you want on your team. He undoubtedly helped the young infielders develop.

The Mounties were always competitive during that time, but there seemed to be another team just a little better. It was a great league.

JIM ROBSON - Mounties Radio Announcer

San Francisco Seals owner Paul Fagan, shown here cracking into a peanut shell, once banned peanuts from Seals Stadium because, according to his calculations, it cost more to clean up peanut shells than could be made on peanut sales. Under pressure from fans and peanut suppliers, he lifted the ban.

4

Vancouver Mounties business manager Nat Bailey was among those front-office executives who truly cared about team stewardship.

THE OWNERS

BEFORE THE MINOR LEAGUES WERE ABSORBED BY THE MAJOR LEAGUE FARM SYSTEM, MOST MINOR LEAGUE CLUBS WERE PRIVATELY OWNED. SOME WERE OWNED BY ENTREPRENEURS WHO HAD MADE THEIR FORTUNES ELSEWHERE, SUCH AS EMIL SICK OF SEATTLE'S RAINIER BREWING COMPANY AND ROBERT COBB OF HOLLYWOOD'S FAMOUS BROWN DERBY RESTAURANT. OTHER OWNERS, SUCH AS BILL STARR OF SAN DIEGO AND CHARLES GRAHAM OF SAN FRANCISCO, WERE FORMER PLAYERS WHO ACQUIRED AND RAN THEIR TEAMS AS THEIR ONLY BUSINESS. AND SOME OWNERS JUST LOVED THE GAME AND WANTED TO BE A PART OF IT.

THE RESOURCES OF SOME TEAMS WERE ENORMOUS. THE LOS ANGELES ANGELES, FOR EXAMPLE, WERE AMONG MANY ASSETS IN THE WRIGLEY FAMILY'S IMPRESSIVE FINANCIAL EMPIRE. OTHER OWNERS FACED FINANCIAL CONSTRAINTS THAT LIMITED THEIR ABILITY TO COMPETE. THAT LED TO INTERESTING SITUATIONS FOR THEM, THEIR PLAYERS AND THE FANS.

NAT BAILEY - Vancouver Mounties

Nat Bailey had a box seat at Capilano Stadium, and sat behind third base. He loved baseball, and whenever there was a problem with ownership, Nat would always be there to bail them out. He was a sponsor of a lot of philanthropic things around town.

When the PCL came back into Vancouver in 1966, they named the ballpark after him. He was the type of guy who would have just as soon left it the way it was. He was not a seeker of publicity.

I think he took over after Brick Laws sold the team to the city. Through the '50s and the '60s, he was the savior of the team.

I sat with him once when we were going down to a series in Seattle, and he told me about his good friend Colonel Sanders (founder of the Kentucky-Fried Chicken restaurant chain). He had met him at some restaurateurs' convention, and the Colonel wanted Nat to go in with him as a partner. Nat told him, 'Naw, I've got my own chicken farms and a couple of drive-ins. I don't need any more ventures.'

But they still had an association, and when KFC fast-food franchises came to Vancouver, Nat Bailey owned them.

JIM ROBSON - Mounties Radio Announcer

BOB COBB - Hollywood Stars

Probably one of the great guys in the world was Bob Cobb. He used to tell us daily that we were going to win the pennant in '49. He was sure we were going to win the pennant, but he'd say he was still nervous about it. I'd say to him, 'Bob, there's no sense in both of us being nervous. I'll worry for both of us.' It was not uncommon for Cobb to go around the league with us.

CHUCK STEVENS - Hollywood Stars

VIC DEVINCENZI - Oakland Oaks

Vic Devincenzi threw dollars around like they were manhole covers.

DARIO LODIGIANI - Oakland Oaks

San Francisco Seals owner Paul Fagan, seated left, discussed a 1951 working agreement between the Seals and the New York Yankees with Yankee scout Joe Devine, seated right, Seals manager Lefty O'Doul, standing left, and general manager Joe Orengo.

PAUL I. FAGAN - San Francisco Seals

P aul Fagan was kind of a strange duck. He always reminded me of the guy who used to play Charlie Chan in the old movies, Warner Oland. He dressed like him — hat and rain jacket. But he had some good ideas, and he had more money than anyone else. A lot of the things he wanted, the other owners couldn't go along with because they were working on a shoestring [budget].

BILL WERLE - San Francisco Seals

I didn't know Paul Fagan well. I got to see him when we went to spring training on Maui in 1947. He was always around. He had built this beautiful complex for us. We had motel rooms that were beautiful, a big dining area, a fountain where we could get ice cream. He owned much of the island.

He was very nice to us. As a matter of fact, when we won the pennant, his wife had a beautiful diamond necklace, and she gave it to him, and they went out and had diamond rings made for all the players. He was very generous.

The players didn't have much contact with him because Charlie Graham took care of all the contracts. Later, when [Graham] died, Fagan took a more active role. He wanted to make the league into a third major league, but everything fell apart with the Seals after he fired Lefty O'Doul.

DINO RESTELLI - San Francisco Seals

When I came to San Francisco in 1949, I was the publicity director as well as the broadcaster. It was my job to tell Harry Borba, Bucky Walter, Harry Jupiter and Bob Stevens, our local beat writers, of any breaking stories about the Seals. So I had the 'pleasure' one morning of telling them that Paul Fagan, owner of the Seals, had banned the peanut from Seals Stadium. 'He's what?' That was their response.

Fagan had figured out that by the time he had sold the peanut for about ten cents a bag and got that revenue, that by the time the stadium clean-up crew went through the stadium the next day in getting ready for the next day's game, they were paying them more than he was getting for the peanuts.

So he decided to ban the peanut, setting off an international crisis. The Dominican attaché and the Colombian minister were up in arms because it would ruin their trade, and they were afraid it would spread across the country. Fagan was on to something. Everyone was pinching pennies, and they thought they could save some money this way. (Note: The backlash was severe, and Fagan rescinded the ban.)

DON KLEIN - Seals Radio Broadcaster

Mr. Fagan was one of the nicest people around. One of the biggest raps he got was the peanut incident. What the papers didn't write was the bad rap he got. When he joined the Seals, he told Mr. [Charles] Graham, 'I know only two baseball names — Bob Feller and Joe DiMaggio. I don't know what they will cost. I want 'em.'

He was told, 'You can get 'em. They will probably cost about one million apiece. But the next year you're going to lose them for $25,000 each.' At that point, the major league draft was explained to Fagan. His only comment was, 'That's not right.'

Obviously, he was trying to form a third major league. When he found that wouldn't work,

Mission Reds owner "Red" Killefer, San Francisco Seals owner Charlie Graham and PCL secretary A.C. Baum conferred before one of the league's winter meetings.

he put a million dollars into the ladies' lounge. It was one of the most beautiful places. The rugs — you would sink way down.

People don't realize it, but the concession stands at Seals Stadium were the first such in major sports. That was 1947.

That was also the first year they had the Plexiglas window backstops. They didn't work the first year, but they made some changes and they did work the second year. When Feller threw against them in the first year, he broke one. They retooled them and then they worked.

DON RODE - Seals Clubhouse Man

CHARLES H. GRAHAM - San Francisco Seals

Charlie Graham — it was always Mr. Graham. I used to be up in the front office with Charlie Graham and he was constantly worried about having enough money to get the players paid. When he brought Paul Fagan in he had better security but, of course, he lost a little control.

DON RODE - Seals Clubhouse Man

I made $6,500 with the Seals in 1946. I had come back from the service and I'm home one day when I got a call from Charlie Graham. 'Ferris, how would you like to be the first Seal to sign for the 1946 season?' I said, 'Sure. Why not?' He says, 'Come on over.'

I knew I was going to be obstinate. I knew I was going to get what I wanted. We didn't have agents in those days, but I felt confident that I could demand my price. You see, nobody knew what the other guy was making, but I was ready to hold out for my price.

So I went over to see the old man and after all the little niceties, he asked, 'What do you want to play for this year?' 'Well, Mr. Graham,' I said, 'I've got to have $700 (a month).'

He says, 'Well, OK.' He goes out of the room and he comes back and hands me a contract. He wasn't gone but two seconds. I look at it. One thousand dollars a month! I did a helluva negotiating job. He had already decided I was going to get $1,000 a month.

At the end of the year I was drafted for $10,000, and a couple of days before Christmas, here comes a check for $1,000. When the season was over Lefty O'Doul said, 'I want you to come on over. Come drop by the bar. I've got something for you.'

So I go down to Lefty's, and he's got this beautiful shotgun, an Ithaca 16-gauge. He says, 'You son of a bitch, you did a great job. I'm sure going to miss you.'

The next year I get my contract from the Philadelphia Athletics. It's for $6,000. I write back that I got more money out here in the Coast League in 1946. I get the same contract back, and I write that I'm not going back there to take a cut. Well, I finally got my raise. I don't remember if I got $6,500 or $7,000. They finally opened up the purse strings.

A couple of years later I was holding out and said I wasn't coming back unless I got my money. Earl Mack finally pleaded over the phone, 'All right, all right, we'll give you your money. But,' he says, 'please don't tell dad.'

FERRIS FAIN - San Francisco Seals

I didn't receive a bonus when I signed, but in 1948, when I was having a good year, I got the courage to visit Mr. Graham up in the ivory tower (the Seals' offices out in right field). I told him, 'I never got a chance to sign for a bonus, and now I'm hearing that I'm going to be sold to a major league club. All I ever gotten is a salary, and I've earned that.'

Well, he flustered a little, but promised that he'd take care of me if I was sold. Mr. Graham died about a month before the season ended, while the team was negotiating my sale. I talked to Lefty, expressing my concern, and he went up to young Charlie Graham about it. When I was sold, they ended up giving me $4,000.

There was lots of talk about Lefty going back to manage the Giants, but Lefty had such a great agreement in San Francisco that it didn't make much sense for him to go East. He had a great relationship with Mr. Graham — never a contract, just a handshake. And his roots were here.

Mr. Graham didn't want to let go of any of his players. If he did lose anybody, he got two or three in return. That was his plan. He had visions of the whole league advancing to major league status, so he didn't want to let go of anybody.

BILL WERLE - San Francisco Seals

BILL KLEPPER - Seattle Indians, Portland Beavers

In 1937 'Kewpie' Dick Barrett won nineteen games, and if he won twenty he'd have gotten a bonus, but Bill Klepper, the owner, went down and told Johnny Bassler, the Seattle manager, not to pitch him. Bassler said, 'Get out of here. I'm the manager and I'll do what I want.' And Kewpie got his twenty games. I don't know if he got his bonus or not, but shortly thereafter, Johnny Bassler was fired. You didn't cross Klepper.

Klepper later went on to Portland, but he had a reputation of not paying his guys, paying them late. We were in Seattle one time at the hotel, and we heard a bunch of yelling, 'He's going to kill me! He's going to kill me!' A guy named Bill Thomas, who pitched for Portland, was carrying a bat, trying to hit Klepper because he didn't pay him.

RUGGER ARDIZOIA - Oakland Oaks

I had a verbal contract with Klepper that was interesting. When I signed with him — trying to get more money, of course — I finally got him to agree to give me transportation back to Mississippi after the season. He said, 'OK, that will be fine.' I asked him to write it into the contract, and he said, 'Well, that's most unusual.' But he did.

After the season was over, I went into the office to collect my money and he said, 'I've never heard of such a thing.' I reached over to pick up the telephone, and he said, 'What are you doing?' I said, 'I'm calling the president's office in Los Angeles and get him to look in the contract.'

He said, 'No. That won't be necessary. I seem to remember we did have some kind agreement.' He said, 'How much was it?'

I raised the ante about $500, and he said, 'No it wasn't. It was ... ,' and he quoted the exact amount.

He pulled another one on us. We had gone about a month and a half without a pay day, and we had a big day on Sunday with a big crowd. They were giving away an automobile, which they often did. We went out and took infield practice, then we all went back into the clubhouse and put on our 'sit clothes' and went up and sat in the stands.

Well, of course, Klepper came rumbling down, wondering what was the matter. We explained to him that we hadn't been paid and weren't going to play unless we were. So he sent us on back to the clubhouse and brought two or three sacks of money down and paid us off. I often said that was the shortest, first strike in baseball.

PAUL GREGORY - Seattle Indians

Oakland Oaks owner C.L. "Brick" Laws, left, met in 1951 with manager Mel Ott, center, and coach George L. Kelly at the start of spring training.

BILL LANE - San Diego Padres

We trained up to Seattle, then came down for our second week to Oakland. The owner of the club, 'Hard Rock' Lane, he was a typical, old business-looking guy, but tough. He beckoned me over one day in the Oakland lobby.

I went over to him, and he said to me, 'You're leading the league. You're leading the league in eaters.' I was leading the team in eaters! We had a $2.50-a-day limit, and I was eating like a son of a bitch and going over my limit, so Lane was castigating me for eating so much.

TED WILLIAMS - San Diego Padres

Old Bill Lane called me in after the 1937 season and says, 'The New York Giants want to buy you, but I think you can have a better year.' I say, 'But, gee, I had a pretty good year. I want to go now.' He said, 'No, I think you can do better. I'll give you part of the sale price next time.' That never happened.

GEORGE McDONALD - San Diego Padres

CLARENCE "BRICK" LAWS - Oakland, Vancouver

Brick Laws was the best owner I ever worked for. I can recall my wife had a miscarriage when I was on the road, and she

insisted they not call me and tell me. Brick's own personal doctor took care of her and everything was first-cabin. He treated me and my family real good, and he paid well.

LEN NEAL - Oakland Oaks

Dad and Joe Blumenfeld were great fans, and they knew [team owner] Cookie Devincenzi. They used to go to the ballpark a lot. During the war, they decided that Cookie might need some help, so they asked if he wanted to sell the club and he agreed. They met the price. Now they're in the baseball business.

Dad and Joe were in the theater business, and they believed in promoting to get people into the theaters. They went through the Depression, when you had to have 'Bag Night' and give-aways at the theater. They knew what you had to do to get people out, and when they bought the Oaks ball club, that's the first thing they did.

They went out and promoted the Oakland Oaks as one of the best teams in the Pacific Coast League, having a manager like Dolph Camilli. They brought in bright new faces and had a line of great managers — Casey Stengel, Charlie Dressen, Mel Ott, Augie Galan. Everybody knew those men.

BILL LAWS - Brick's Son and Oaks Broadcaster

MAJ. CHARLES LOTT - San Diego Padres

I can still remember Major Lott washing baseballs in the main office.

JOHN "SWEDE" JENSEN - San Diego Padres

In attendance on opening night in Oakland in 1950, left to right: Oakland Oaks owner C.L. "Brick" Laws, California Governor Earl Warren, New York Yankees owner Del Webb, Baseball Commissioner A.B. "Happy" Chandler; PCL president Clarence "Pants" Rowland (standing behind Chandler), Oaks manager Charlie Dressen and Chicago White Sox general manager Frank Lane.

Portland Beavers manager Bill Skiff, left, and general manager Bill Mulligan.

BILL MULLIGAN - General Manager, Seattle, Portland

When Portland sold me to Denver, I was walking by the office and I had taken three bats. The door was open, and I hear, 'Hey! Where are you going with those bats? You can't take those. They belong to the ball club.' That was Bill Mulligan. That's the way owners were brought up. People were tough in those days. Those guys never smiled, you know.

BUDDY PETERSON - Portland Beavers

In 1943, Bill Skiff, the manager of Seattle, contacted me. Because of shortages, he needed a first baseman. I said, 'You don't need me. I've been out of baseball for three years.' I had been playing semi-pro, so my batting eye was still there. I also felt I was going to get drafted into the service, but I said, 'If I hit .300 for Seattle, you have to give me so much money.'

So I went to spring training and sat down with Bill Skiff and Bill Mulligan, the general manager. We agreed on terms, and Mulligan said, 'That's fine. This will just be verbal.' I said, 'No, I'd like it in writing.'

'Don't you trust me?' I said, 'I don't really know you. I trust Skiff.' Well, it didn't get in the contract, but I did hit .306. After the season, we were getting ready to go down to Los Angeles for the playoffs and I dropped into the front office to collect my bonus for hitting over .300.

Mulligan said, 'I don't know what you're talking about.' Oh, Geez. I was about to tear him apart. I went back to Skiff and told him I wasn't going to Los Angeles. I was going home. Skiff said, 'Aw, you don't want to do that. Let's go down to the office. I'll take care of this.' We get down to the office and Skiff says to me, 'You're too mad. You stay outside.'

I heard them beefing back and forth in there. Skiff said, 'I'll let [owner] Emil Sick know about this. We made a promise to this man. You write him a check right now. I should have you double the amount for all this crap.' I got my check.

LEN GABRIELSON - Seattle Rainiers

BRANCH RICKEY -
Sacramento, Hollywood

While Branch Rickey qualifies more as a general manager than as an owner, his influence was greater than that of most owners, and it was felt throughout all of baseball for several decades.

When I signed with the Cardinals, I was living in Reno. I was newly married, with a baby, and Branch Rickey sent me out a contract and said to meet him in St. Louis. So we packed up and drove across country to St. Louis.

I went into his office there and when we started talking I said, 'Well, Mr. Rickey, I think I'm worth more than the contract is offering me. I'm married and have a youngster. The price of food is going up. The price of transportation is going up.' So I got through with my speech, and he said, 'Well, I'll tell you, John. We've got a lot of "C" leagues and "D" leagues, and down at such-and-such a town we broke so many bats there, and each one of those bats costs a buck apiece.'

Then he says, 'Now in the big leagues, if you hit a foul ball into the stands, they don't throw the balls back anymore, and it's costing us so much.' And he goes on giving me all these details. I'm there by myself, and I'm just a raw rookie. Here is this guy, the owner of the ball club, and he's got all these facts and figures.

Finally I say, 'You know, Mr. Rickey, maybe what you ought to do, maybe you should give me a cut in salary.'

JOHN PINTAR - Sacramento Solons

Fred Haney, right, who had just led the Hollywood Stars to the 1952 PCL pennant, played chess with Pittsburgh Pirates/Stars general manager Branch Rickey. Haney's mission: manage Rickey's Pirates out of the National League cellar.

In 1938, Mr. Rickey had a baseball school in Winter Haven, Florida. The purpose was to invite their new players, and they had all their coaches and managers, scouts and even the major league coaches there. The purpose was to teach and observe and give an opportunity to play. They put us up in boarding houses. Baseball up and early in the morning, baseball all day. Then in the evening he would give speeches on morals and manners and sex and all the other stuff that he wanted to talk about. That school was designed to have all Cardinal farmhands trained in the same techniques of the game. I saw those skills in action when I was with Sacramento.

HERSHEL LYONS - Sacramento Solons

EMIL SICK - Seattle Rainiers

Emil Sick was a fine addition to baseball. He was new at the game and brought wealth to it. He built a new stadium and promoted the team well. We had excellent crowds. He would have made an excellent big-league owner.

I understand that [New York Yankees owner] Colonel Ruppert encouraged Mr. Sick to get into baseball, telling him that it would be good for his business.

PAUL GREGORY - Seattle Rainiers

Mr. Sick was really good with the ballplayers. He turned baseball operations over to Torchy Torrance, but [manager Jack] Lelivelt handled most of the dealings with the players. Torchy was a baseball man himself.

When he first purchased the ball club, the team was called Indians. The liquor board wouldn't let Mr. Sick change the name to Rainiers because it identified with liquor. They finally got it through the liquor board in July, and the club changed its name to Rainiers. But they wouldn't let him use the special signature that was on the bottles for the uniforms. They said, 'No. We'll let you use block letters only.'

They had a blue law in Seattle at that time, and you couldn't sell beer on Sundays. So we never pitched Hal Turpin on Saturday night, because he'd pitch a ball game in one hour, twenty minutes. They'd pitch Dickie Barrett, and he'd pitch a three-hour game and that would be their best beer night. Turpin would pitch the Sunday afternoon game when we were going on the road because he'd pitch the game in one hour, twenty minutes, and we'd catch the train in time.

EDO VANNI - Seattle Indians

You never spoke to Emil Sick. He wasn't involved in it at all. Torchy Torrance ran the front office for him.

Emil Sick — his chauffeur used to drive him out to the ball game. He had a box right behind home plate. He would come out to the ball game and he would bring a newspaper. He would sit there, reading the newspaper, and when he was finished, he would fold it up and leave. That was the extent of Emil Sick at the ballpark. No matter what the score or the inning, once he finished the newspaper, he would leave.

CLAUDE CHRISTIE - Seattle Rainiers

DEWEY SORIANO - Seattle Rainiers

I had a couple of good years with Seattle, and after the '58 season I got into it with Dewey Soriano. Before I signed my contract for the '58 year, I said, 'Dewey, I'd like to have a $1,000 bonus in there if I have an outstanding year.' He says, 'Fine. I'll take care of it.'

I say, 'I'd like to have it in writing.' He said, 'Don't you trust me?' I just said, 'Look. I've been through this before. People have short memories,' and he got real mad at me. He says, 'My word is as good as gold.'

Well anyway, I hit .301 and had a helluva year. I came into the office at the end of the season, and I got into it with Dewey. He practically bodily threw me out of the office. But I never yelled at him or anything. He practically shoved me out of the door. 'Get the hell out of here!'

Vancouver bought me for $10,000, and that was great, because that was one of the finest teams I ever played on.

Lefty O'Doul and Soriano didn't get along. That's the only reason he didn't come back [to manage in 1958]. Lefty would not bow down to him. He was just a so-so right-hand pitcher. So Lefty had his fill of Soriano and went back to San Francisco after the '57 season was over.

EDDIE BASINSKI - Seattle Rainiers

BILL STARR - San Diego Padres

Bill Starr was a good owner. He understood the business end of baseball, and he was very fortunate that, when he took the club over, he had some good players. He worked a couple of years with Cleveland and a couple with the White Sox, and they send him players who were real AAA players and good prospects. He was very fortunate. I'm sure he made a lot of money there.

But he was tough. I think it was in 1952, I came back and he'd offered me a contract, and I wanted a little raise, and finally said, 'Listen, just give me twenty-five dollars more a month and I'll sign. I'll know I got a raise, and I'll feel good about it.' He wouldn't do it. That was Bill Starr. I guess that was one of the reasons he was so successful.

But I'll tell you another thing — we traveled first class. I never rode the train in the four years I was there. We flew every place. When we flew into Sacramento, we flew PSA charter, and when we traveled elsewhere, even L.A., we flew Western Airlines. Going into the Northwest, we'd fly out Tuesday morning and play that night. We'd get there about noon, and you could catch a nap or whatever, then eat about 4 p.m. and head out to the ballpark. Three or four of us would catch a cab. They didn't have buses like they do today.

Les Cook was the trainer. Starr turned him loose, and we had first-class equipment all the way. If you needed bats, he never ordered less than a dozen bats. With the Browns, you were lucky if you got three.

They tell me that after he got out of baseball he built a shopping mall and became a millionaire.

JACK GRAHAM - San Diego Padres

Former San Diego Padres reserve catcher Bill Starr purchased a controlling interest in the team in the late 1940s. Starr was known as a tough negotiator at salary time, but he also was respected for his ability to search out talent.

I led the league in RBI (with 110) in 1945 and played in every game, and I held out in '46 for a raise. Starr finally gave me a twenty-five dollar raise. I held out all spring training. Finally I talked to [league president Clarence] Rowland, and he said, 'Why don't you go down to spring training? He'll take care of you.' Twenty-five dollars. Starr was tough.

It just wasn't the same. I couldn't see playing for him anymore, so he sold me to Tulsa. He didn't pay his players very much. I wasn't high-priced to begin with.

When I managed Fresno, I actually got more than he paid me.

LOU VEZILICH - San Diego Padres

Frank "Lefty" O'Doul, right, moved north with the franchise when the Oakland Oaks moved to Vancouver. He's pictured here with Cedric Tallis, who was appointed general manager of the Vancouver Mounties, which affiliated with the Baltimore Orioles.

I wasn't too happy with Bill Starr in 1948. I had contract troubles with him. I really didn't care if I played for him or not. The only reason I was glad to be there was that I was close to home. I was happy they traded me. I was traded to Sacramento for Dee Moore and Whitey Wietelmann. I had a pretty good year up there.

PETE COSCARART - San Diego Padres

CEDRIC TALLIS - General Manager, Vancouver Mounties

Cedric Tallis was there in 1957 through 1959. He had access to a lot of money, and he bought a lot of good players for the franchise — Joe Taylor, Joe Frazier, Spider Jorgensen and others. We had a good working agreement with the Orioles, and we got good young players. Lennie Green was on the 1957 team, and Barry Shetrone came after him. And some young pitchers. We had Chuck Estrada here, and Mel Held and Don Ferrarese. But then Tallis would augment them with these veterans.

Tallis ran it like a big league team. He used to take the media down to spring training, at Riverside, California. He did it up right, but when he left, there was no more money left in the till.

And poor old Bob Freitas had to pick up the pieces. He and Nat Bailey sort of patched it together after Cedric left.

JIM ROBSON - Mounties Radio Announcer

Cedric Tallis was a nice fella, but you could tell he was a tough guy. You didn't want to cross him, because he'd fire you. He was a square shooter. He was paying us all the major league minimum. He told me to go to the eye doctor and get a pair of glasses, that the club would pay for them. He was great. I was treated better by Cedric Tallis than when I went to the big leagues. There was nothing cheap about him.

When I broke in, owners had a different outlook toward players. Cedric Tallis had a more humane approach. He'd talk with you on your level.

BUDDY PETERSON - Vancouver Mounties

Portland Beavers pitcher Tommy Bridges, left, and manager Jim Turner participated in a kids' clinic in Portland in 1948. Bridges could have taught the kids plenty about spitters. He was a master.

5
THE MANAGERS

Ｔhe list of men who have managed in the Pacific Coast League reads like a Hall of Fame roster. But the list is deceiving. Seldom did anyone stay long as a Coast League manager. Lefty O'Doul, Bill Sweeney and Tommy Heath were exceptions. While they might have been enticed to work with teams in the East, they enjoyed a degree of contentment in the PCL that kept them on the West Coast.

For the rest, if they produced winners or showed they were solid teachers, they became hot properties and, eventually, major league managers. Likewise, if they didn't win out on the West Coast, they probably wouldn't be rehired.

While managers' tenures often were short, coaches typically became fixtures. Journeymen players often became successful coaches with their old team. Jimmie Reese of Los Angeles and San Diego, Jackie Warner of Los Angeles, Joe Sprinz of San Francisco and Eddie Taylor of Seattle had long coaching careers in the PCL. Each helped his boss look good.

DEL BAKER - Sacramento Solons, San Diego Padres

Ｄel Baker was a tough guy. If you won 10-1, we'd come in and the door would go 'bang.' 'What's the matter with him?' Well, we didn't win 15-l. You could go a whole year and he wouldn't say five words to you. In 1950, the season started and every time I'd get on first, I'd get the steal sign. I stole eight bases in a row. I stole them because nobody expected me to run.

The ninth time I get thrown out, and as I walk by him at third base on the way to the dugout,

Oakland Oaks manager Casey Stengel promised to bring a pennant to Oakland. He made good on the promise in 1948.

he says, 'Don't you know the signs?' I said, 'Sure.' He said, 'Just remember, the left-hand hitters take the sign from the left side and the right-handed hitters from the right.'

He's giving me the sign from the right side to decoy the other team. So I'm taking the wrong sign. But he never said a word. Well, I never stole another base the rest of the year.

JACK GRAHAM - San Diego Padres

Del Baker was a very quiet man. He was the manager at the time we were playing at Hollywood. A new player came to the Stars and none of us knew how to pitch to him. We decided to pitch him high and he hit it out of the park to end the game. Baker came over and said, 'I told you to pitch him high.' I responded, 'I did. Go over and ask the catcher,' which he did. So he came back and said, 'You didn't have enough on it.' All I could say was, 'I can't put enough on any of my pitches.' With that he walked away.

BOB KERRIGAN - San Diego Padres

BOBBY BRAGAN - Hollywood Stars

Hollywood Stars manager Bobby Bragan shared catching duties with Jim Mangan and Eddie Malone.

Bobby Bragan replaced Fred Haney in Hollywood for 1953. Haney was mature. Bragan was a young manager and a young ballplayer, and he was managing absolute veterans who were capable on the field and capable enough to manage. He was quick with the hook as a manager with the pitching staff. It was a strange turnover for us.

When he came to Hollywood, he wasn't fully accepted. The old-timers figured he was a 'Rickey guy' (a reference to owner Branch Rickey). But we matured Bragan. We got the sophomoric attitude out of him, and I think we probably planted the seed where he could now manage in the major leagues. He had matured enough to do it.

By now we had a working agreement with Pittsburgh. Then we start getting the Tom Saffells, the Ted Beards and the Lee Walls. We could have beaten Pittsburgh. We knew in spring training we were going to win it by six or seven or ten games. And we did!

So Bragan was an entirely different kind of guy. I think everybody liked him, but there were exaggerated stories. I remember one time it was all over the West Coast that Bragan and I had gone to it. I got a phone call asking about the fight, and I said, 'What fight?' I go to Bob and ask him if he has any bruises and he says, 'What are you talking about?'

We were supposed to have had a big fight the previous night. Neither of us knew how it started, so that kind of made us good friends from the start.

CHUCK STEVENS - Hollywood Stars

Bobby Bragan was pretty sharp. He'd pull a lot of stuff that a lot of guys wouldn't like. I remember working one night in a game and he's catching. About the seventh or eighth inning he says, 'You know, a lot of my players are coming back saying that [umpire Cece Carlucci] is calling those strikes on the corners, but I haven't said anything to you. Do you know why?' I said, 'I sure do.' He was catching those pitches to the other batters, and he knew I was calling them the same to the other team.

He would look away as he would talk to me. He wasn't trying to show me up.

A couple of times he got me a little angry with what he did to some of my partners. We were in Spokane, and they brought in a new man, Bob Motley, a black guy. Motley was afraid to call strikes. So one night when Motley was behind the plate, Bragan was just going crazy in the dugout. Finally Bragan got up and hollered, 'I'll take any bets that he's not going to call anybody out on a third strike,' at the top of his lungs.

I figured, 'Holy cow!' So I got over there and I told him, 'Hey, Bobby, you've got to cut that out.' 'Well goddamn, Cece, he's not doing it!' Well, I knew he wasn't doing it. That's the first time I saw Bobby holler something like that, real loud.

One night he started getting on me, and I went over and said, 'You've got every goddarn umpire on your butt. If you go against me, you're up to 100 percent.' He kind of smiled and let it go.

CECE CARLUCCI - Umpire

DOLPH CAMILLI -
Oakland Oaks

We got Dolph Camilli in 1944 to manage the Oaks by trading Billy Rigney for him. Billy was still in the service, and may not be out for another year or year-and-a-half. But the Giants were satisfied to make that trade because they wanted Rigney.

In 1945, Dolph did a heck of a job, but he was dealing with wartime players and wartime problems. There was no classier guy in the world than Dolph Camilli. But about the middle of the 1945 season, my dad was upset because Camilli didn't want to play first base. He just wanted to manage. My dad wanted him to play first base because he was a draw.

Dolph was about thirty-seven, and while that wasn't old, he didn't want to play anymore. We had also signed Vic Picetti out of Mission High in San Francisco. But the old man felt Picetti could wait. All I know is one day Dolph was gone and Billy Raimondi was the manager.

BILL LAWS - Oaks Radio Announcer and Son of Oaks Owner Brick Laws

Dolph Camilli was a great National League first baseman who came to Oakland to manage the Oaks in 1944 and part of 1945. Camilli was a draw as a player, but he took himself off first base to give the young phenom Vic Picetti playing time. The move displeased team owner Brick Laws, and led to Camilli's dismissal as manager.

JAMES "RIPPER" COLLINS -
San Diego Padres

Ripper Collins was a great guy. He was an old-time manager. He came out and said hello in the spring, and, 'Goodbye, have a good winter,' at the end. And if you were hustling, you might not talk to the guy the whole season. That's the way managers used to be.

Collins was surprising because he was from the old Gas House Gang. He was so mild-mannered. He never had a meeting where he raised his voice or anything.

We had Jimmie Reese as a coach. Most of your talking was with the coach, and if he felt it was worth mentioning, then he'd go to the manager and tell him what was the matter. It was that kind of club.

Most managers were that way. If you came out and hustled, you might never say anything to him. If he wanted you to play left field that day, Jimmie Reese would tell you.

JACK GRAHAM - San Diego Padres

Ripper Collins was fair to me. I didn't feel any discrimination from him, but he didn't talk to me about any things on race.

JOHNNY RITCHEY - San Diego Padres

GEORGE DETORE - San Diego Padres

George Detore was a good guy to play for. I was with him in '44. He was smart and a good hitter. It's tough to be a player-manager. You coach, have to handle pitchers and keep the bench, then bat and play yourself.

LOU VEZILICH - San Diego Padres

Sacramento Solons manager Del Baker and Oakland Oaks skipper Charlie Dressen chat before the 1949 season opener, which also inaugurated the new Edmonds Field.

CHARLIE DRESSEN - Oakland Oaks

I thought Dressen was a great manager, a real smart baseball man. Dressen tried to call the pitches. He'd call them until it came down to the pitch that meant the ball game, then he'd be looking someplace else.

Charlie was a little fella, and he didn't like big men. Don Padgett was our other catcher, and he took a terrible beating from him. Padgett could hit, but he couldn't catch anymore. His legs had taken a beating. I don't think Don could remember pitches as well from one batter to the next.

I hated him. Hated him with a passion. Whatever Don or I did, it was wrong. George Metkovich and Earl Rapp — those fellas could do no wrong.

Artie Wilson was on Dressen's 1949 Oaks team, and Charlie wanted Artie to pull the ball. Well, Artie *couldn't* pull the ball. So Charlie said, 'I'll give you twenty-five every time you pull the ball.' Well, Artie was batting .350 or so, hitting the ball to left, and he drops close to .300 when the ballplayers say to Charlie, 'Let's stop this stuff.'

He tried to get Billy Martin to hit the ball to right field, be a hit-and-run man. Billy said, 'You give me twenty-five and I'll break you!' There was agitation between those two all the time because Billy was a hard nose and Charlie was an agitator.

Charlie agitated Billy into picking a fight with Walt Dropo of Sacramento. Dropo just looked at him, shook his head and walked away. Charlie was that way. He did stuff like that all the time.

Dressen's signs were more sophisticated. Most managers would give signs, but just a few. I would watch them in the third-base coach's box, especially on steal situations, and figure what their steal sign was. I'd remember it and not tell anyone. Then the next series, I'd check to see if they were using the same signal and pitchout to nail the runner. I never played for a manager who ever called a pitchout for me, or called pitches, except Dressen.

Charlie was a teacher, and he knew baseball — the intricacies of baseball — but it was sometimes hard for him to teach them. Of course, Cookie Lavagetto, Dario Lodigiani and others, they understood what he was talking about.

I liked him and hated him at the same time.

FRANK KERR - Oakland Oaks

Charlie Dressen had a Napoleon complex. Charlie was just that way. He was the manager, and he was going to make the decisions. With Charlie it was 'I this' and 'I that.' It was never 'we.'

Billy Martin has told the story many times. The Oaks were behind by three runs late in the game in about the sixth inning, and Dressen said to the gang, 'Don't worry, fellas. Just stay close. I'll think of something.'

Dressen knew as much about baseball as anyone in the game, including Casey Stengel, but he was not able to verbalize it to the players the way that Casey could so that they could understand and appreciate the manager for what he was trying to do.

There was animosity that developed, and we knew about it. It all started, unfortunately, when he wanted to get Billy Raimondi out. He thought that Billy was not the kind of catcher that he wanted, so we traded for Frank Kerr.

I'll say this for Dressen. He continued to coach at third base, and boy, those fans really let him have it. There was nobody more popular in Oakland than Billy Raimondi. But Dressen took it. He was tough.

BILL LAWS - Oaks Radio Announcer

CEDRIC DURST - San Diego Padres

Ced Durst was great. He really took Al Olsen and me under his wing. We were the real rookies on the club. When we played at L.A., a lot of the guys drove up, and he'd always take us along.

We had some pretty good clubs with some pretty good pitching staffs there from '39 to '43, with Byron Humphreys and Wally Hebert and Al Olsen, and we had 'Old Folks' Pillette.

JOHN "SWEDE" JENSEN - San Diego Padres

JIMMIE DYKES - Hollywood Stars

Taskmaster Jimmie Dykes, who managed the Hollywood Stars from 1946 through '48, jokes with the Portland Beavers' legendary groundskeeper, Rocky Benevento, before a game in Portland.

Jimmie Dykes was another typical old-school baseball man. He always had that cigar in his mouth, but there was an aura about him: 'You screw around and I'm going to have your ass.'

He was a short little guy, big chest. The players respected him. They knew who the boss was. The game was becoming more sophisticated. New signals. Dykes was more of a student of the game. He knew his baseball. Babe Herman fit the same mold, but Herman would have more difficulty imparting it. Babe would have been more rough.

GEORGE GRANT - Hollywood Stars Bat Boy

Jimmy Dykes was a good guy. He loved his cigars. Anytime you did something wrong, you'd have to buy him cigars. That was your fine.

We had both Gus Zernial and Frank Kelleher with Hollywood in '47. Boy, could Gus hit the ball. But he was young. Frank was the guy, when you needed a win, he was there. Kelleher was very good in the pinch. In the outfield, not too fast, but he was there all the time.

Dykes would hide his eyes when Zernial was up in a pinch and say, 'Let me know if he strikes out or pops up.' That was the difference between Zernial and Kelleher.

RUGGER ARDIZOIA - Hollywood Stars

Jimmie Dykes was a great manager. I'll never forget when he took the club over from Buck Fausett in 1946 up in Portland. The pitchers took the second infield in pregame. When he looked out there and saw the pitchers out there — Newt Kimball, Art Cuccurullo, Xavier Rescigno and all — he said, 'Who the hell are those guys?'

Someone responded, 'Pitchers.' When they came in, he said, 'Come here, you guys. If I catch you out there once more, I'm fining the whole lot of you. Stay off the infield!' He didn't want them there. He was really hot.

EDDIE ERAUTT - Hollywood Stars

JOE GORDON -
Sacramento Solons,
San Francisco Seals

I played with Joe Gordon in his first year of managing, and I was really impressed and honored to have him sit behind the batting cage. He would discuss things with me about what I was doing that would help him. He was a playing manager at the time, and for a guy that came down after playing ten, twelve years with the Yankees and Cleveland — that he should ask *me* what I could contribute to *his* batting — I mean, this guy was a helluva ballplayer.

The thing that I really appreciated about Joe Gordon was that he was a player's manager. He loved talking baseball and he had rules and regulations on the ball club — the things I never had on other ball clubs. To play for a guy like Gordon — there was an incentive.

If you didn't get a runner in from third base it cost you five dollars. If you missed a bunt, it cost you five. If you struck out with men on base, it cost you five. So at the end of the year, we had a banquet that you couldn't believe. It could have served a regiment. It was all in the clubhouse.

DINO RESTELLI - Sacramento Solons

Joe Gordon was a total man's man. He was in and out of bars. He was a good man. He told me, 'When I got out of baseball, I thought I knew all there was to know about it. Then when I got to be a manager (in Sacramento in 1951), I found out what a dumb S.O.B. I really was.' Joe had a pretty good ego, so that's quite an admission.

BOB STEVENS - San Francisco Chronicle Beat Writer

Like many PCL players, Joe Gordon went into the service during World War II. Few players-turned-soldiers saw combat. Gordon was stationed at Hamilton Field in California.

FRED HANEY - Hollywood Stars

Haney was soft-spoken but ran a very tight ship. He didn't put up with a lot of nonsense. He wouldn't say too much if you made a mistake, but don't make that same mistake twice because then he's going to give you about a fifteen-minute dissertation.

Very defense-oriented, he'd get you a run and hope that it could hold up. He had some guys who could really go get the balls, and he had a good touch with teaching.

You got to realize that during those years, a manager didn't have the time to coach. Fred's forte was base running. He knew how to teach you open-base running. But again, the only guys you're going to teach are three or four — the guys who can run. Gene Handley, Irv Noren, Herb Gorman, myself.

But Fred ran a good ball club. We had a game in Sacramento, one of those nights when

Fred Haney *manager of the Hollywood Stars.*

everything we threw was a line drive someplace. One of our relievers, Jean Pierre Roy, was ripped hard.

We were staying at the El Rancho Motel, and there was one of the name bands playing there. Haney's rule was you do not have a beer or do any drinking at the hotel bar because that's his domain. He's in there with the press, and we always showed him that courtesy.

But we were standing around early, and we agitated Jean Pierre to sing. He was trying to break into the Hollywood routine, and he went up there. I think he was singing 'Tenderly.' Haney's not around at all, and he gets about a chorus into 'Tenderly' and Haney walks in. Fred's veins are sticking out, and the next day Jean Pierre is in Oklahoma City.

When I walked into the clubhouse the next day, somebody told me. I went up to Haney and said, 'Hey Skip, I don't know whether it was his fault, because some of the guys and myself were agitating him to get up there.'

Haney says, 'Naw, Chuck. I appreciate what you said, but he's a big guy. He knew better.' But that's how he reacted.

I later heard that John Fitzpatrick, a lovable guy and our coach, questioned it too, and Haney said, `Let that son of a bitch sing "Tenderly" in Oklahoma City.' That's the kind of guy he was.

CHUCK STEVENS - Hollywood Stars

Fred Haney was a kind manager for me. In 1952, I was twenty years old. I had just signed a bonus in 1950 and I had arm trouble, but Haney went to bat for me with Mr. [Branch] Rickey and asked him to let me pitch at Hollywood. We had some rocky times, but he stuck with me through the whole year. I did finally win fifteen games that year, and was happy that he stuck with me. He showed me the most patience.

PAUL PETTIT - Hollywood Stars

I always appreciated Fred Haney. One thing about Fred was that he was always honest. If you had a good day, as you walked in, he'd say, 'You golden Greek.' The next day, you had a bad day. He'd say, 'You goddamned Greek.'

JIM BAXES - Hollywood Stars

TOMMY HEATH - San Francisco, Sacramento, Portland

I don't know of anybody who played for Tommy Heath that didn't admire the guy. The way he handled a ball club — the tone — gave you lots of latitude, but yet there was always a short leash. An ideal mixture.

I thought he was the greatest handler of pitchers that I ever saw. He was a former catcher. I think when an infielder or outfielder wants to manage, handling pitchers and knowing when to jerk, knowing when to stay with them is of prime importance. He had that touch.

Tommy charted pitchers, and when I was his player-coach, I had the responsibility of charting them. So I could see what he was doing — the long-range picture.

He was very quiet, low-key. Playing against him and looking back, I would suspect he was tough to figure out. He'd be liable to run at any time — home or road, at any time. Tom would play for one run. He liked the big inning, but seldom had the privilege of having a good ball club.

With San Francisco in 1954, we had a pretty good ball club with the 'Kiddy Car Express.' We had Jim Westlake, Mike Baxes, Reno Cheso, Nini Tornay. But the team didn't have any money. That was 'The Little Corporation.' They were on a shoestring, but they were nice people.

Sacramento Solons manager Tommy Heath, left, accepted roses from Tommy Holmes, manager of the Portland Beavers, on opening day in 1956 at the Beavers' new ballpark, Multnomah Stadium.

Bob Stevens, veteran
sportswriter for the
San Francisco Chronicle,
coined the term "The
Kiddie Car Express" for
the 1954 San Francisco
Seals. The Seals had
decided to go with
youth, and to the sur-
prise of many, the kids
kept the Seals in con-
tention for most of the
season.

This was also the first
year of public ownership
of the Seals, who were
dubbed The Little
Corporation. It was an
exciting year for San
Francisco baseball, and
even a profitable one,
although the profit was
less than a thousand
dollars.

I thought when I left Hollywood that any ball club I joined would be a disappointment, but that wasn't the case.

One of my great regrets in baseball is that Tom didn't get a chance to manage in the major leagues.

CHUCK STEVENS - San Francisco Seals

Tommy Heath knew more about pitchers than I ever saw. Of course, being an old catcher, he could think two or three innings ahead and know where he wanted his staff to be during a ball game.

You know, he never chewed anybody out. When you screwed up under Heath, he wouldn't say much, if anything, but he'd look at you, and you said, 'Now he's going to chew me out,' but he didn't. And now you're carrying a double burden around, and you want to do better for the guy.

I remember us playing a Saturday afternoon game in Los Angeles when Bilko hit his fifty-five home runs (in 1956). Strangely enough, we were two games out at the time, and we flew down for the series. It was my luck to get the assignment for the Saturday afternoon game. Heath came to me and said, 'Young fella, I don't want you to give that big bastard anything he can hit. I don't care if you walk him five times, but just don't give him anything to hit. If you throw him a strike, I kill ya.' 'OK, Tom.'

So Bilko leads off the second inning and I said, 'I've got to be careful.' Actually, I had pretty good luck with Bilko because he didn't like to be sidearmed. I used to sidearm him, cross-fire him, anything unusual to throw him off. So the first pitch, I said, 'I'm going to get the pitch outside.' So I sidearmed him, and it tailed right back and caught the corner of the plate. 'Strike one!'

I look in the dugout, and Heath had jumped off the bench. I'd gotten his attention. So I say, 'I'm going to really throw this one outside.' I threw that thing a foot outside, and I'll be damned if it didn't tail right back and catch the corner again. 'Strike two!' Now Heath's got his hat off. He's mopping his brow. I can tell he's really, really mad.

So now the next three pitches: I bounced one up there. I threw one about four feet over his head, and all this stuff. So now I've got him three and two and I say, 'I'm going to go outside so I won't be really obvious.' Well, I'll be damned if the ball didn't tail right back over the outside of the plate for strike three.

Now, I took two steps off the mound, and Heath is out there in a flash! If you remember the way Heath was built — like a barrel. I've never seen a man move so fast in my life. He's looking me right in the face, 'Young fella, either you're going to manage this club or I am.' He said, 'Either you're going to do what I tell you to, or I'm going to give you a train ticket a yard long.' Needless to say, I walked Bilko three more times.

Tom would come out to the mound. About four feet from the mound, if he spits in his hands, you're gone. You'll never talk him out of it. But if he didn't spit in his hands, you had a chance.

BUD WATKINS - Sacramento Solons

Tommy Heath had a pretty good command of the queen's language. He could barb with the best. In fact, marvelous, absolutely marvelous, a Hall of Famer. And his run-ins with [umpire] Emmett Ashford were legion.

He had a strange build, but he wasn't fat. He was a miniature Babe Ruth. He was a very muscular man. Lousy catcher, apparently.

Willie Mays played for Tommy at Minneapolis before he went to New York, and he was hitting .477 when he was called up. I hadn't seen Tommy for a while, and I was telling him how well Willie was playing. At the time he was hitting .354 or something.

Tommy shoots back, 'I told you. I knew damn well the big leagues would screw him up. He's only batting .354. I told you!'

BOB STEVENS - San Francisco Chronicle Beat Writer

Heath had a sense of humor. He'd pull little things. Not too bad, really. I never thought he got really way out. Tommy had one of the quickest tongues I ever saw. He'd come up to you with that goddamned tobacco. It was all over the front of him.

We had a few things with Emmett Ashford and a riot between Oakland and San Francisco. I had to take over. I was crew chief then. Tommy Heath was on Emmett Ashford all the time.

CECE CARLUCCI - Umpire

I went 0-24 to start the 1954 season. Tommy would work with me on my stroke, and we finally got it turned around.

We started poorly as a team, and they got rid of all the veterans — George Vico, Frank Kalin, Bill McCawley, Neill Sheridan — and [Heath] played the rookies. We went from last to first in about two months. We just hit the hell out of the ball, played before huge crowds and just turned it around. It was so much fun to go out on Sunday and see these great crowds coming to watch a Coast League ball game.

The Kiddie Car Express — we were all young. Nini Tornay and Will Tiesiera, Mike Baxes, Leo Righetti, Reno Cheso. We were fearless.

Chuck Stevens was our coach. He was a first baseman, too, and he'd walk by me and ask, 'Are you OK tonight? Can you play tonight?' I'd say, 'Yeah, I'm fine.' He didn't want to play.

'Make sure you're OK.' We still laugh about that. He was a slick first baseman, but I didn't need help there. I was pretty quick with my hands. I needed help with my hitting. He had one of the greatest years as a pinch hitter I've ever seen. He must have hit five home runs as a pinch hitter.

Leo Righetti was a good shortstop. He was a helluva nice guy. We called him Teepee Head. Leo was the first guy I ever played with who would go into the hole and throw the ball on a bounce to first base. His ball was alive. Maybe that's where his son got his great fastball.

We had a good outfield with Ted Beard, Sal Taormina, who was a character, and Bob DiPietro, who was another character. We also had Dave Melton.

Our pitchers were older, but the rest of us were young. We had a lot of fun that season.

JIM WESTLAKE - San Francisco Seals

CLAY HOPPER -
Portland, Hollywood

Clay Hopper joined Portland in 1952. He was a fine man and a good leader. We had competitive teams under him.

Clay gave me authority to run the pitchers. Working with the pitchers, you'd try to help the younger ones — Dick Waibel, Bill Bottler. With the veterans — Chick Pieretti, Bill Werle, Royce Lint — you'd leave them alone.

Southern gentleman Clay Hopper, right, managed the Portland Beavers from 1952 to '55, and the Hollywood Stars in 1956, before retiring for health reasons. He's pictured here with Bill Fleming, a Portland coach at spring training.

I went into the ninth inning 1-1, and I came into the dugout and I was hurting. I said, 'Clay, I won't go out there again. No way!' Well, Basinski came up and hit a home run to win the game, but I was hurting. I was off the active list the next day, and I wasn't back again. I was over forty!

The second year Clay Hopper was with Portland. He had colon cancer and was operated on. He couldn't come to spring training, so I ran the ball club during spring training. He finally joined the ball club about five days before the season started. He was very kind in thanking me for getting his ball club in shape for him.

But there were some times he just couldn't run the ball club, so I would take it over. I'd come check with him in the hotel after the game. He'd always say that he would have done the same thing that I had done on the field.

I remember he was a good manager. That's why Branch Rickey picked him. He was from Greenwood, Mississippi, and Rickey chose him to be Jackie Robinson's first manager.

BILL FLEMING - Portland Beavers

Clay was a Deep Southerner. I actually think he was slow to react. But he did let his players play, straight out.

Back in the 1950s, pitchers used to hit balls to the outfielders during infield practice. I remember one day I was hitting to Joe Taylor, and balls are falling left and right. I become aware of a shadow behind me and I turn around, and there's Clay. Clay says, 'You know, I think Joe's drunk.' And he was. He took him out of the lineup

He sent him down to the bullpen to sleep it off. [Eddie Basinski] sends a screecher down into the bullpen. It wakes Joe up. He reaches down and throws the ball back to the left-fielder.

Clay came out. 'Joe, get your ass out of here. Get dressed. I don't want to see you again today!' I liked Joe. He had a lot of ability, but seemed to be snakebit.

He was staying in a hotel in Seattle with the rest of the team, and he'd been drinking. He comes out and gets into this Cadillac and drives it off, and gets arrested for stealing a car. He had a key that fit exactly the same Cadillac as his, but it wasn't his car. Can you imagine the odds of that?

BILL WERLE - Portland Beavers

I hated Clay Hopper as a manager, just hated him. He was the worst manager I ever played for. Four years of Siberia with Clay Hopper. He berated his players all the time. He'd say, 'I've got absolutely nothing here to work with.'

He went on television once in Hollywood, and he didn't know we were listening. He just destroyed our whole team. He said, in his Southern drawl, 'I don't have a catcher who can throw the ball on two hops to second base. I haven't got an outfielder who can hit the cutoff man, and I don't have a pitcher who can go four innings before he's looking for help.' And he said, 'My infield is like a sieve!' He was from Mississippi. He was horrible.

We were at a Chamber of Commerce lunch in Vancouver during the season and there were three of us with him. Someone asked Dick Waibel what his favorite pitch was. Dick responded, 'I believe it was my slider.' And Hopper is sitting there, and he says, 'And every one of them goes over the fence.'

I beat him in Portland when he was with Hollywood with a grand-slam home run in the ninth inning, and I just loved it. He was very jealous of his players.

EDDIE BASINSKI - Portland Beavers

ROGERS HORNSBY - Seattle Rainiers

*R*ogers Hornsby was in the Pacific Coast League only one year, 1951. He led the Seattle Rainiers to a pennant and left an indelible impression on everyone he met. Feelings of fear, anger, respect and envy were all mentioned in discussing him. But his drive to excel very likely had something to do with his inclusion in baseball's Hall of Fame and his success with the Seattle Rainiers.

I worked the Seattle ball club in spring training several years. In 1951, Hornsby was there. If I have to pick an umpire's manager, it would be either Hornsby or Preston Gomez. Hornsby never said boo to me.

Up in Seattle, one of Hornsby's players was on my butt, and Hornsby came out and said to the player, 'If you read your contract, you'll find you're being paid to play ball, not to play umpire. Go do your job and let him do his.' With that he walked off. I nearly fell over. He wanted his players to toe the line pretty good.

One night they had a hitting contest between Mel Ott of Oakland and Hornsby. I remember Ott hit one out, but Hornsby scattered 'em. Out of the ten outs, Hornsby got about six hits. So they gave him this big trophy.

There was a retarded kid there, maybe twenty-some years old, and Hornsby gave him that trophy and had him sit in the dugout during the game. Well about the fifth inning I was told that I had to get that kid out of the dugout. He wasn't in uniform. Hornsby figured he was good luck. So what I did was make them put a jacket and a cap on him and let him stay in the dugout.

CECE CARLUCCI - Umpire

Rogers Hornsby managed in the PCL only one year, in 1951, for the Seattle Rainiers, but nonetheless brought a championship to the city. He then moved on to the St. Louis Browns, who, unfortunately, released him in mid-season.

Most of his team called him Mr. Hornsby or Skipper. He was distanced from his team. He had these steely gray eyes, and when he looked at you, you had the feeling he was looking right through you.

With Hornsby, he never spoke to us. The only time is that once in spring training when he talked about playing hard. He didn't talk to anybody. He would come in, put his uniform on and make out the lineup card. You'd go out and see if you were in the lineup that day.

We had a fairly large training room up in Seattle, and we had an osteopath for a trainer, Doc Richards. I can remember Charlie Schanz going in there and Dewey Soriano. Doc used a big oil can to put liniment on their arms.

And I can remember Hornsby. He'd never go in there, but he'd stick his head in there and he'd see them getting a rubdown, and you could hear him under his breath ... There they were lying on the table, and he just didn't like that at all. Night after night, he'd be mumbling and getting himself all upset over that. He thought they were 'putty' ballplayers. Hell, I wouldn't dare set foot in there.

He never showered after the game. I got to know his wife, a lovely person, and I got the chance to visit with her a couple of times. She told me that he didn't shower — he got dressed and came home, and he'd get in the tub and go over every play of the game. I doubt anybody ever knew that.

He never said anything to anybody. I guess that was his nature. I know if I was a great hitter, I'd want to pass it on, especially if it was the team I was managing.

I just never knew how to classify him as a manager.

CLAUDE CHRISTIE - Seattle Rainiers

The only manager I can remember who called pitches was Rogers Hornsby. He used to call a lot of pitches. You could figure that when you played against Hornsby, a lot of his hitters would be taking on 2-0 or 3-1 because Hornsby only needed one pitch to hit it. He figured everybody else could do the same.

HERSHEL LYONS - Sacramento Solons

Rogers Hornsby was like a rough, tough old codger, but he was very fair with everything he did. If he wanted you to do something that you didn't agree with, if you'd go to talk with him and proved your point to him, he say, 'OK, that's fine.' But if you didn't go to him, he'd kind of roughshod you. That's the way he was. He was tough.

His one big thing was that he'd stand on the top of the dugout and call the new pitcher in from the bullpen and wave the pitcher off the mound. To me that was an embarrassment.

The first game that I pitched, I was waved off of the mound. We were in San Diego. If he happened to change pitchers, he wanted his pitchers to go into the clubhouse, change his sweatshirt, and come back and sit on the bench. Well, I'm just taken out of a game, and if I come back on the bench, I might be teed off, and the first thing you know I'm hollering at the umpires and I might get kicked out of the game.

When he took me out of the game, I went into the clubhouse and sat there with my uniform on. I took off my sweatshirt, sat there, and listened to the rest of the game on the radio.

After the game he came in. We lost the ball game, and he took one look at me and kind of growled. A few minutes later Doc Richards, the trainer, came out and said, 'Hornsby wants to see you in his office.' I went in there, and he says, 'When I take pitchers out of a game, I want you to come back and sit on the bench.'

I explained to him why I didn't want to do that. I said, 'I will stay in the ballpark,. but as far as coming back to the dugout, I won't do it. You can fine me or whatever you want. When I'm taken out of a ball game, I will wait in the clubhouse until the game's over.' He said, 'Aw, shit,' and that was the end of it. I was the only pitcher on the club that didn't go back on the bench.

MARV GRISSOM - Seattle Rainiers

FRED HUTCHINSON -
Seattle Rainiers

*F*red Hutchinson broke in as a rookie with the Seattle Rainiers in 1938 and was voted the league's most valuable player that year. He later returned to Seattle, in 1955, as a manager, leading the Rainiers to the league championship. Few matched Hutch's level of intensity. Cancer cut his great career short.

I tangled once with Fred Hutchinson and the goddamn veins in his neck got so big I wanted to run. It seemed that all the blood ran to his face. He got excited over a play at third base — he was right there. He looked in my face, and it seems like his neck got bigger. He laid off on me on balls and strikes. I'd seen him get on some of my partners sometimes, though.

CECE CARLUCCI - Umpire

BILL KELLY - Los Angeles Angels

*B*efore taking the helm of the Los Angeles Angels in 1947, Bill Kelly's only experience with the Pacific Coast League was his one year as an umpire. He managed the Angels four years, bringing a championship to Los Angeles in his first year with the team.

When I came in to the league, I was told, 'Don't take any shit from Kelly.' He was a former umpire. I never had to knock him, but most of the other umpires would move him fast. He'd come up with a mouthful of tobacco, and he had a stutter, and you'd find tobacco stains all over your uniform.

CECE CARLUCCI - Umpire

WADE "RED" KILLEFER - San Francisco Missions, Sacramento Solons, Hollywood Stars

*W*ade Killefer was our manager with the Stars in 1938 and '39. He didn't go over too well with the younger guys. He stayed only two years, and he didn't have any speed.

RUGGER ARDIZOIA - Hollywood Stars

Red Killefer, left, and his coach, former pitcher John Miljus, guided the Hollywood Stars at Gilmore Stadium just before the team moved to Gilmore Field, in 1939. Both men had long PCL careers.

When the Missions moved to Hollywood in 1938, we played our first season at Wrigley Field. Red Killefer was our manager. When the Angels were away, we were the home team there. We didn't pay much attention [to the fact we were renters in the Angels' stadium]. So many people came from Hollywood to see us play.

There had been a Hollywood ball club before. (It moved to San Diego after the 1935 season, leaving Hollywood without a team for two seasons.) They were all good fans. It was a pleasure to play in Hollywood.

BERNIE "FRENCHY" UHALT - Hollywood Stars

JOHN "PEPPER" MARTIN - Sacramento Solons, San Diego Padres

John "Pepper" Martin was among the PCL's most volatile (some people said craziest) managers.

*P*epper Martin came to the Coast League with a reputation as a hellbent daredevil. He played and managed hard and expected nothing less from his players. His 1942 season with Sacramento is one of the league's greatest comeback stories.

Martin spent two seasons managing Sacramento and a little more than a year in San Diego.

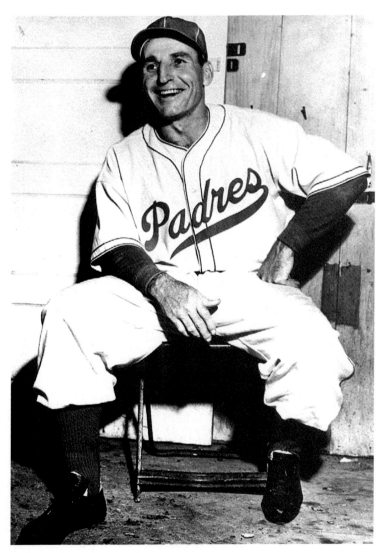

Pepper Martin was just starting out as a manager. I didn't think he was as good as other managers I had. I played under Bill McKechnie, Zack Taylor, Luke Sewell and Fred Haney. All were good managers. Martin wanted his players to play the way he did, and most of us couldn't play that way.

At Oakland in 1945, I was the batter after our leadoff man got a hit. Pepper gave me the sacrifice sign. I think to myself 'What the hell. I'll bunt for a base hit. Then we'll have two on.' Well, I dragged it too close to the pitcher who turns and throws our runner out at second. I'm on at first. I call myself a so-and-so. 'The manager told you what to do, and you didn't do it.'

So the next pitch I stole second. No sign. All right. Now the pitcher's lookin' at me, holdin' me on; then he turns away. I don't know what hits me, but I take off and I make it.

Pepper is there. He rips off his belt and hooks it around my belt and hangs on to it. Well, the umpire calls time and says, 'Pepper, you can't do that.'

Anyway, Dick Gyselman was the next hitter, and he got a base hit. I could have scored from second. That was the winning run.

In the clubhouse, Pepper comes up to me. 'Tony, when you laid down that bunt it was twenty-five bucks. When you took second base I took the fine off. When you started running towards third, I fined you fifty bucks, but when you made it, I took it off. Don't be taking those bases unless someone tells you.'

I said, 'Yes sir.' And he was right.

TONY CRISCOLA - San Diego Padres

Pepper Martin was nuts, crazy. I suppose it was mainly because he wanted to win so bad, and we had some pretty bad teams there. He would lose his cool all the time, baiting the umpires and even his own players. He fined me fifty dollars over in Oakland one time for not jumping enough on a ball that was ten feet over my head.

He did some awful strange things and got awful upset in the clubhouse, and just stormed and ranted. The fans liked it, but he kind of lost the confidence of his players.

I remember a period when we had a couple of players hurt. He went in and played a double-header and he even stole home. He must have been fifty years old. (He actually was forty-two.) For the next week, he could hardly walk. He put on quite a show, but he sure paid for it.

JOHN "SWEDE" JENSEN - San Diego Padres

Pepper Martin was a character. A lot of things he did made you laugh. He was a great hustler. He was a wild swinger. He was always chewing tobacco. You'd walk by and he'd spit on your shoes. Wild Horse — he had the right name.

Pepper Martin as a manager? Fair.

LOU VEZILICH - San Diego Padres

CHARLIE METRO - Vancouver Mounties

Charlie Metro, who played for Seattle and Oakland, also managed at Vancouver, where he was successful but controversial. He later was a major league manager.

I had troubles with Charlie Metro. We didn't get along. He used that tough approach when he managed. He was at odds with damn near the whole ball club. We didn't quit. We just went out and played. We didn't let the manager bother us. But once he took the uniform off, he was one helluva nice guy. I think it motivated us to play harder — to show him.

A couple of the kids he jumped on were bonus kids with Baltimore and one of them, Ray Barker, just picked up and left the club. He was our regular first baseman in 1958, and hitting a lot of home runs.

Charlie was constantly on him. We were in Portland, Oregon, and we went out after our half-inning, and we've got no first baseman. And I see Barker walking down the right-field line towards our clubhouse. Never saw him again. He had several good years in the majors, with the Yankees. He was kind of a lazy kid, but he could play. Charlie got all over him, and he left. Baltimore phoned up and asked, 'What the hell's going on out there?'

It was raining once in spring training, coming down hard, and guys were starting to take their clothes off, and he comes in and says, 'Hey, keep your uniforms on. Leave your cleats. We're going out and run.' We all look at each other.

So we go out, and there's water all over. Charlie's sittin' in the clubhouse and we're running around. We come in, and we're soaked. 'OK, everybody be back here at 9 a.m. tomorrow.' I think he wanted us mad at him because he thought we'd play better. Up in Vancouver, when it was raining, he'd take us under the freeway to practice.

BUDDY PETERSON - Vancouver Mounties

I loved Vancouver. It was a beautiful city with a nice ballpark. The problem was [Mounties manager] Charlie Metro. He was like a second lieutenant in the Army. He had to show his authority to everybody. Out of baseball, he's the nicest guy in the world.

On one occasion, we had lost a close night game, and Charlie calls a workout for 9 o'clock the next morning. Pitchers run. Well, you don't get to bed until after midnight on a night game, so that went over like a lead balloon.

Connie Johnson was going to pitch the next game, so he asked, 'Even me, Skip?' 'Yes, Connie. Even you.' So now we all get up and get out to the ballpark, dress and start our running. Spider Jorgensen is throwing balls for the pitchers to catch.

Connie was the last one in line. When his turn came, Metro says, 'That's all right, Connie. You can go back now.' Connie could have killed him, and Connie was the nicest guy in the world.

In 1957, he had a major league club there — Morrie Martin, Erv Palica, George Bamberger, Ronnie Hansen, Jim Marshall, Buddy Peterson. And he couldn't win a pennant.

BUD WATKINS - Vancouver Mounties

Charlie and I got along real well together. It was only that one year. He actually treated me great as a coach. He actually asked me my opinion many many times during that year. I did my thing as a coach, and he protected me.

EDDIE BASINSKI - Vancouver Mounties

FRANCIS "LEFTY" O'DOUL

San Francisco's Lefty O'Doul managed twenty-three years in the Pacific Coast League, with five teams. Seventeen of those years were with San Francisco. The dynamic O'Doul was beloved by his players, and many observers believed he was the best batting instructor in the history of the game.

O'Doul turned down offers to manage in the major leagues, and it is believed that, in the late 1940s, he was the highest paid manager in the game.

Lefty was a great teacher, but he wanted his hitters to pull everything. He got players to fit his style. 'Just get the ball down a bit and hit it in the hole.' Brooks Holder, Ted Norbert, Frankie Hawkins, Joe Sprinz: Pull the ball. I'd play shortstop halfway in left field and throw 'em all out. They couldn't run. They'd say, 'That four-eyed son of a gun ...' They hated it. I'd play thirty feet on the grass because I knew they were all going to pull the ball.

[Seals first baseman Ferris] Fain told me later, 'Lefty wanted me to be a pull hitter, and I knew I wasn't a pull hitter, so I said, 'Frank, come on. I've got to be me.'

BILLY RIGNEY - Oakland Oaks

Lefty was a great person to play for. In 1946, we trained in Hawaii. Going over to the islands, we had rough seas for a few days, then nice weather. Lefty got the team up on deck, setting down the rules and what was going to happen in training camp.

A management troika, 1947, left to right: the Los Angeles Angels' Bill Kelly, the Oakland Oaks' Casey Stengel and the San Francisco Seals' Lefty O'Doul.

I asked, 'What is going to be curfew?' He looked at me and said, 'Young man, do you want to play baseball?' I said, 'I certainly do.'

He responded, 'There's not going to be a curfew. If you want to play, you're going to take care of yourself, and if you don't, I don't want you anyway. If anybody doesn't want to play for me, they'll get rid of themselves. All you've got to do is take care of yourself.' We all got his message.

Lefty came to Seattle as manager in 1957, and I had been there a couple of years. When we were both in San Francisco in 1946, they started putting stars on the center field wall for homers. It was a real long poke.

Well, I was pitching for Seattle at Seals Stadium and Lefty was coaching the third-base box. I hit one over the center field wall, and as I'm rounding third base, O'Doul is laying flat on his back. He says, 'Stop and pick me up!' So I stop and pulled him up, and he shook my hand and patted me on the back.

To add to the story, the next day I see [Seals manager] Joe Gordon before the game and kid him. 'I don't see my star up on the wall yet.' 'I don't know about that star,' he responded, 'but I know the guy who threw you that pitch is on his way to Albuquerque!'

LARRY JANSEN - San Francisco Seals, Seattle Rainiers

Now, O'Doul was a great teacher, but his theory was to stand up there at the top and pull everything. I would ask, 'Frank, what do you do when the ball's inside?' He says, 'Turn quicker. Just turn quicker.' Well, that's no answer to me.

BERNIE "FRENCHY" UHALT - San Francisco Seals

"KNOCKING" LEFTY ON LEFTY O'DOUL NIGHT

I HAD TO RUN LEFTY O'DOUL [OUT OF THE GAME] ON HIS NIGHT! A GUY'S GOT TO BE CRAZY TO RUN LEFTY O'DOUL ON HIS NIGHT! HE WAS WITH SAN FRANCISCO FOR ALMOST TWENTY YEARS. HE WAS THE HERO OF SAN FRANCISCO, BUT THEY FIRED HIM AFTER THE '51 SEASON AND HE WENT TO SAN DIEGO.

NOW IT'S HIS FIRST VISIT TO SAN FRANCISCO AFTER THEY FIRED HIM. WE PULLED IN BILL ENGLIN, BILL ANSKE AND MYSELF. THEY HAD A BIG NIGHT FOR LEFTY, A TUESDAY NIGHT, AND I'M BEHIND THE PLATE.

THAT WAS THE YEAR THAT THEY PUT IN THE NEW RULE THAT NOBODY COULD LEAVE THE DUGOUT OR COACHING BOX TO DISPUTE A BALL OR STRIKE. NOW IT'S HIS NIGHT, AND GUY FLETCHER WAS PITCHING AND FRANK KERR WAS CATCHING.

IT'S ABOUT THE FIFTH INNING AND I CALL A BALL ON A CLOSE PITCH. THEN A COUPLE OF PITCHES LATER, I CALL ANOTHER. FLETCHER — THEY CALLED HIM 'GRUMPY' — CAME DOWN OFF THE MOUND, AND I MET HIM HALFWAY. HE STARTS MUMBLING, 'WHAT THE HELL YOU DOING BACK THERE? I'M HAVING TROUBLE, YOU'RE HAVING TROUBLE ...' HE'S MUMBLING. THE SCORE'S 0-0, SO I CAN'T BE TOO FAR OFF.

I SAY TO HIM, 'YOU GO BACK AND PITCH AND I'LL GO BACK AND UMPIRE, AND LET'S BOTH TRY TO DO A BETTER JOB.' HE SAYS, 'OK,' AND WE EACH HEAD BACK. I WAS SURPRISED.

I GO BACK AND FRANK KERR IS RAISING HELL WITH ME FOR GETTING HIS PITCHER EXCITED. SO I SAID, 'HOW IN HELL AM I GOING TO GET HIM EXCITED? HE'S FIFTY (ACTUALLY THIRTY-EIGHT), AND YOU GUYS CALL HIM GRUMPY. AND BESIDES, REMEMBER THAT NEW RULE. DON'T GET LEFTY OUT HERE.'

KERR KEPT PUTTING ON A SHOW, FACING ME, AND I LOOK OVER AND SEE LEFTY COMING OUT OF THE DUGOUT. I SAID TO MYSELF, 'OH, BOY. HERE COMES LEFTY WITH THAT BIG RED HANDKERCHIEF IN HIS BACK POCKET. IF HE COMES TO HOME PLATE AND SAYS ONE WORD TO ME, I'VE GOT TO KNOCK HIM.'

SO I FIGURED, 'I KNOW WHAT I'M GOING TO DO.' SO I GO MEET HIM, HALFWAY, BEFORE HE GETS TO HOME PLATE. NOW THIS ALL HAPPENED FAST, AND THE GUYS IN THE OTHER DUGOUT ARE WATCHING. SO I GO RIGHT UP TO HIM, IN AN EFFORT TO STOP HIM. I WANT TO TELL HIM I'LL LISTEN TO HIM, BUT DON'T GO UP TO HOME PLATE.

YOU KNOW WHAT HE DID? HE WENT RIGHT AROUND ME TO HOME PLATE! RIGHT ON AROUND AND HE'S TALKING TO FRANK KERR. I'M THIRTY-FIVE, FORTY FEET FROM HOME PLATE. THAT'S MY HOME. I'VE GOT TO GET THERE. I SAY, 'OH SHIT. I KNOW IF I GET THERE, HE'S GOING TO SAY SOMETHING, AND I'LL HAVE TO KNOCK HIM AND IT'S HIS NIGHT.'

THE CROWD IS REALLY HOOTING. SO I GO THERE. I DON'T EVEN WANT TO LOOK AT HIM. I WANT TO GET THE GAME GOING. SO HE SAYS, 'WELL, KID, SO YOU MISSED ONE IN THE CLUTCH.' ALL I COULD SAY WAS, 'AH, LEFTY, DOGGONE IT. YOU KNOW, I GAVE YOU EVERY CHANCE IN THE WORLD TO STAY IN THE GAME, AND YOU KNOW THAT NEW RULE. I TRIED TO MEET YOU SO YOU WOULDN'T COME TO HOME PLATE. I WAS GOING TO LET YOU HAVE YOUR PEACE, WHATEVER YOU WANTED TO SAY, BUT I'M SORRY, BUT YOU HAVE TO GO.'

I DIDN'T PUT ON A BIG SHOW. NO BIG SWING. I JUST PUT MY ARM OUT, UP AND AROUND AND POINTED TO THE DUGOUT. HE SAID, 'TO HELL WITH YOU,' OR SOMETHING LIKE THAT, AND WALKED OFF.

WELL! HEADLINES THE NEXT DAY: 'EVERYBODY LOVES LEFTY BUT CARLUCCI.' BOB STEVENS AND THOSE GUYS RIPPED ME FROM ONE END TO THE OTHER. I GOT WIRES AND PHONE CALLS ... THREATENING ME ... SOME WITH WORDS I HAD TO USE A DICTIONARY TO LOOK UP! THEY RIPPED ME GOOD, AND I'VE GOT TWO MORE GAMES BEHIND THE PLATE THAT WEEK!

SO NOW COMES THE NEXT NIGHT. LEFTY COMES TO HOME PLATE WITH AN OPEN BOX OF CHOCOLATE. HE GOT LOTS OF GIFTS THAT NIGHT. HERE COMES WITH THE OPEN BOX RIGHT UP TO ME. 'HERE, CECE. HAVE A PIECE OF CANDY.'

I SAYS, 'NO WAY!' HE SAYS, 'WHY?' I SAID, 'I DON'T KNOW WHAT IN HELL YOU'RE PUTTING IN THAT THING AFTER LAST NIGHT.'

HE SAYS, 'OH SHIT. YOU KNOW, YOU'RE RIGHT. I WAS JUST PUTTING ON A SHOW FOR THEM.' HE SAYS, 'HAVE ONE,' AND I SAY, 'NO!' FINALLY, I FIGURE, WELL, HE'S GOOD ENOUGH TO BRING THEM OUT HERE, SO I SAY 'OK, LEFTY, YOU EAT ONE AND I'LL HAVE ONE.' SO HE GRABS ONE AND I TAKE ONE. NOW WHILE HE'S EATING THE CANDY, HE'S WAVING HIS HANDS AND GESTURING. AND THE CROWD'S YELLING, 'ATTA BOY, LEFTY!' THEY THINK HE'S ON ME AGAIN. 'YOU SON OF A GUN,' I SAID TO HIM. BUT HE WASN'T ANGRY AT ME OR ANYTHING. THAT WAS JUST LEFTY.

CECE CARLUCCI - Umpire

Lefty and I got along beautifully because Lefty knew what I was doing and I knew what he was doing [with the unorthodox pitching style]. We became real good friends because of it. Lefty would try to break my concentration. He'd carry on a conversation with me from that third-base coaching box and he'd try to get me into a conversation to break my concentration. And I knew what he was trying to do. We played our little game with each other when he was coaching and I was pitching, but it was on a high-level basis, which was entirely different than Billy Martin and myself.

BUD BEASLEY - Sacramento Solons

I remember some of the years when the Seals went on the road, they had their golf clubs with them. It looked like a country club. But that was the way Lefty was. When you played ball for Lefty, you got to realize what kind of a man he was, it was like playing for your big brother.

I can remember playing a series in Sacramento. Lefty had a gang he used to play golf with up there. He would come to the ballpark, and as the game went on, he'd look at the scoreboard and see we were leading 6-1 or something like that, and he'd say, 'You don't need me. I'll see ya tomorrow,' and he'd be gone. He kept everybody so loose. Between Joe Sprinz and Del Young — they had to run the ball club, and they were a bundle of nerves and Lefty didn't give a goddarn. I was very fortunate to have played for San Francisco my last three years, and I couldn't have been more fortunate. I couldn't have played for a better guy than Lefty O'Doul.

DARIO LODIGIANI - Oakland Oaks, San Francisco Seals

Lefty O'Doul, left, won a championship with the San Diego Padres in 1954, then joined the Oakland Oaks and hired longtime PCL coach Eddie Taylor.

My whole relationship with the San Francisco ball club was just great. I loved playing for them, and dearly loved playing for Lefty. Anybody who didn't want to play for that man didn't want to play baseball.

He didn't bug you. He was the type of guy who said, 'Hey, if I walk into a place and you're already there, don't get up and leave. Invite me over and we'll all have a beer.'

Lefty knew his players' abilities. I remember a ball game — it's late in the game, a close ball game, and we've got a runner on. I look down at Lefty and he's giving me the bunt sign. Now Neill Sheridan is hitting behind me, and he's having a terrible time. I also see the left-fielder is shading me over in left-center field, really playing me for a pull hitter.

I step out and nod towards left field at O'Doul. He looks around and kind of nods back. Do what you want. All I do is double down the line, score the guy, and everything's cool. But how many other managers would do that?

FERRIS FAIN - San Francisco Seals

We got O'Doul the last year I was in San Diego. He was a great guy, but he'd be out playing golf and arrive fifteen minutes before game time. Then we'd have a meeting on Tuesday,

BASEBALL DIPLOMACY -
LEFTY "CONQUERS" JAPAN

*L*efty O'Doul is given much of the credit for bringing professional baseball to Japan. As a player he made several jun-
kets to that country, and returned there in 1949 as manager of the San Francisco Seals — the first athletic group from the
U.S. to visit Japan after World War II.

The second group, arriving in 1951, included O'Doul, the
DiMaggios, Ferris Fain, Bobby Shantz, Ed Lopat, Mel Parnell,
and other current and former Pacific Coast Leaguers. It was an
exciting experience for those players, who were amazed at Lefty's
popularity among the Japanese.

LEFTY WAS A GOD OVER THERE. THE PLAYERS WERE UTTER-
LY AMAZED AT THE RESPECT AND DEVOTION HE RECEIVED FROM
THE JAPANESE PEOPLE. HE INCLUDED ME ON THE 1949 TOUR. I
WAS ONLY 19 AT THE TIME. IT WAS ONE OF THE MOST FANTAS-
TIC THINGS THAT HAPPENED TO ME. WE GOT GIGANTIC RECEP-
TIONS EVERYWHERE WE WENT. IT WAS JUST UNBELIEVABLE.

I WAS GOING WITH MY WIFE AT THAT TIME, AND IN 1984
THE JAPANESE INVITED US TO A RECEPTION IN SAN FRANCISCO.
THEY WERE TRYING TO GET AS MANY PEOPLE WHO WERE
INVOLVED IN THE 1949 TRIP TO A REUNION. THEY SHOWED
THESE FILMS OF THE PARADES WHEN WE WERE THERE. I HAVE
THREE SCRAPBOOKS FROM THE TOUR, AND THE STILLS WERE
ALL MY WIFE HAD SEEN OF IT. BUT WHEN THEY SHOWED
THESE FILMS, MY WIFE COULDN'T BELIEVE IT — THE THOU-
SANDS OF PEOPLE WHO GREETED US.

WE MET WITH GENERAL DOUGLAS MACARTHUR FOR
LUNCH ONE DAY AT THE AMERICAN EMBASSY IN TOKYO. I'LL
NEVER FORGET WALKING INTO THE EMBASSY. THERE WAS
MACARTHUR'S HAT — THAT FAMOUS HAT — WITH SWEAT
MARKS ON TOP OF IT.

THAT SON OF A GUN, HE KNEW SOMETHING ABOUT EVERY-
ONE ON THAT TEAM. HE WALKED OVER TO LODIGIANI, 'OH,
WHITE SOX SECOND BASEMAN,' AND SO FORTH. HE SAID TO
ME, 'YOU'RE THE YOUNGEST ONE HERE, AREN'T YOU?' HE HAD
STUDIED.

HE KNEW SOMETHING ABOUT EVERYBODY. IT WAS FANTAS-
TIC, BUT HE NEVER CAME OUT TO THE BALL GAMES. HIS WIFE
AND ARTHUR, THE SON, CAME OUT, BUT HE NEVER DID. WHEN
I TELL PEOPLE I HAD LUNCH WITH GENERAL MACARTHUR,
THEY SAY, 'YOU'RE KIDDING!' IT WAS QUITE A DEAL.

WHAT MACARTHUR SAID TO US AT THE LUNCHEON, IN
ESSENCE, WAS, 'DON'T LOSE. YOU ARE GOING TO WIN TODAY.'
WE DIDN'T LOSE TO THE JAPANESE. WE LOST TO A SERVICE
TEAM OVER THERE. WE PLAYED CRUMMY BASEBALL, BUT WE
BEAT THE JAPANESE EVERY TIME. WE DID HAVE A COUPLE OF
CLOSE GAMES, THOUGH.

EVERYWHERE WE WENT, THEY KNEW WHO WE WERE. OF
COURSE, WE DIDN'T HAVE UNIFORMS ON. THE AMERICAN SER-
VICE PEOPLE HATED US, JUST HATED OUR GUTS. WE WERE TAK-
ING THE PLAY AWAY FROM THEM. WE'D WALK INTO A CLUB,
AND THE SPOTLIGHTS WOULD GO ON, AND WE COULDN'T BUY
ANYTHING. OUR HAIRCUTS WERE EVEN PAID FOR.

I WAS IMPRESSED WITH EVERYTHING AT THE TIME, AND AS
THE YEARS PASSED I WAS MORE IMPRESSED. THAT WAS PART OF
HISTORY. THE JAPANESE PEOPLE, WHEN [MACARTHUR] CAME
OUT OF HIS OFFICE, THEY WOULD WATCH HIM, MOTIONLESS.

JIM WESTLAKE - San Francisco Seals

WE WERE SUPPOSED TO GO TO JAPAN IN 1948, BUT THERE
WAS SO MUCH RED TAPE THAT THEY COULDN'T GET IT DONE IN
TIME. IN THE MEANTIME, I WAS SOLD TO PITTSBURGH. SO I
TALKED TO FRANK AND TOLD HIM HOW MUCH I HAD WANTED
TO GO ON THE TRIP. HE SAID, 'IF WE GO THIS NEXT YEAR, I'LL
INCLUDE YOU AS PART OF THE GROUP.' THERE WERE SEVERAL
OTHERS WHO MADE THE TRIP ALSO — CHUCK STEVENS, LOUIE
STRINGER, AL LYONS, DINO RESTELLI.

THERE WAS A DIFFERENCE BETWEEN NIGHT AND DAY —
1949 AND 1951. IN 1949, IT WAS THE ARMY OF OCCUPATION.
THEY'D PUT US IN JEEPS, AND WE GO FLYING THROUGH.
THEY'D HOLD UP ALL THE TRAFFIC, MILITARY ESCORT ANY-
WHERE WE WENT.

IT WAS REALLY AN EYE-OPENER. WE'D PLAY RAIN OR SHINE.
I PITCHED THE WHOLE GAME IN THE RAIN, CHANGED SWEAT-
SHIRTS PROBABLY FIVE TIMES. LEFTY COACHED THE GAME
FROM THE DUGOUT, STANDING ON A COKE BOX IN THE
DUGOUT. IT WAS POURING DOWN CATS AND DOGS.

WE WERE TOO MUCH FOR THEM AT THAT TIME. THEY
WEREN'T INTO HIGH-CLASS PROFESSIONALISM. ON THE SECOND
TRIP, KAWAKAMI, THEIR HOME-RUN HITTER, SAW NOTHING BUT
LEFT-HANDERS — BOBBY SHANTZ, MEL PARNELL, EDDIE
LOPAT AND MYSELF. HE WENT CRAZY SEEING ONLY LEFTY
PITCHERS.

*BILL WERLE - San Francisco Seals (the only PCL player to
make both trips to Japan)*

the first day of a new series, to go over the hitters, and we'd go over the hitters for five minutes and then he'd tell stories. And everybody would be laughing, and we'd never go over the hitters.

JACK GRAHAM - San Diego Padres, San Francisco Seals

In 1955 we had spring training down in El Centro, and our spring training revolved around golf. I never made a road trip. All we did was throw baseballs in the morning and play golf in the afternoon. Lefty couldn't wait to get to the links. Lefty himself would tell you his greatest accomplishment was winning the Crosby [Pro-Am Golf Tournament] twice.

That spring we traveled to Las Vegas to play the Seals on Saturday and Sunday. We had opened against Sacramento on Tuesday, and these two games were on the way home. [George] Metkovich, [Joe] Brovia and I got in a little trouble. I was supposed to pitch the second day, so I went to bed about 1:30, but at least I did go to bed.

Brovia passed out in the elevator at the Thunderbird Hotel, and Jean and Lefty O'Doul put Brovia to bed that night. And he's not easy to move. The average manager would have canned him or shipped him out, but Lefty started him. And Brovia, with his eyeballs in lighter fluid, hit three amazing line drives in the middle of a sandstorm the next day. I think Lefty knew something.

I can remember in 1955 when he was managing the Oaks, he'd get the itch to step into the batting cage and hit a few. I don't know how old he was. He was well up in his fifties, and he'd still hit line drives all over the park.

BOB MURPHY - Oakland Oaks

Lefty O'Doul congratulated San Diego Padres slugger Jack Graham as he rounded third during a game at Lane Field in 1952.

It was around 1957 one day that we were talking about the current state of pitching, and Lefty would say, 'By God, when they were pitching to me back in Philadelphia and New York, they were throwing spitters and knocking you down, and I still averaged .349.'

So somebody asked, 'Well OK, Frank, against these pitchers today, what do you think you'd be hitting?' Lefty thought for a moment and responded, 'Oh, .310, .315.'

The questioner said, 'Are today's pitchers that much better?' To which Lefty quickly responded, 'Well, hell, I'm sixty years old!'

DON KLEIN - San Francisco Seals Broadcaster

I had more fun and enjoyed baseball more with Lefty O'Doul. I had admired him all the years I played against him, and he was very complimentary to me. He used to say, 'That goddamn Basinski. If it wasn't for him, we would have won a lot more games.' He was good to me, and I admired him. He made it fun. His hit-and-run sign for me was playing the violin left-handed in the third-base coach's line, and they never caught that thing. They said, 'Look at that

Oakland Oaks manager Mel Ott had his say but umpire Pat Orr got his way in a dispute over a Sam Chapman pop fly down the left-field line, at Vaughn Street in 1952.

crazy clown. He's not paying attention to the game.' Like hell he wasn't. He knew what was going on.

He spent all his time between innings talking with the fans. He was great for baseball.

EDDIE BASINSKI - Seattle Rainiers

MEL OTT - Oakland Oaks

I thought Mel Ott would be a tremendous manager. He was one of the classiest men you'd ever want to meet, but it just didn't work. [He] didn't like to fly. He would take the train, and players said, 'If he can take the train, I want to take it also.'

BILL LAWS - Oaks Radio Broadcaster

PAUL RICHARDS - Seattle Rainiers

Paul Richards was tough. We're in Hollywood, the score is tied with the bases loaded, and Tod Davis, their second baseman, gets pitched tight. The ball hits the bat and goes on up into the stands.

Richards comes storming down from third base. He doesn't ask his player or anything. He claimed the ball hit him. He got on me, and I knocked him out of there. Well, the game goes extra innings and Seattle wins. I'm in the umpire's room, and while I felt I had a great game, you have an incident and you're just beat.

There's a knock at the door. It's Paul Richards, and he wants to talk to me. So I say, 'If you've got something to say, come on in.' 'I just wanted to come in and tell ya that after the game I talked to Davis and he told me the ball hit the bat.' Why didn't he ask him out there?

CECE CARLUCCI - Umpire

Paul Richards was all business. I was banged up, so I was sitting on the bench. We were playing Los Angeles, and they had those guys who could belt the baseball, and four had already gone over the fence. Richards yells over to me, 'Vanni, go in and play left field.' I say, 'Which side of the fence do you want me to play on, Paul?' That was the first laugh the team said they had in a week!

EDO VANNI - Seattle Rainiers

CHARLIE ROOT -
Hollywood Stars

Charlie Root was a crafty manager. Whether it was in deference to his greatness as a player, many of his players were in awe of him. 'Hey, this guy's been down the road. Let's listen to the man and hear what he's got to say.' He was kind of an irascible sort.

He always had that cigar in his mouth. He always had his big chest, and now he had a potbelly. He was a power figure. Most players said, 'Hey, back off.' Root wasn't going to take any shit from anybody.

GEORGE GRANT - Hollywood Stars Bat Boy

EARL SHEELY -
Sacramento Solons,
Seattle Rainiers

I liked Earl Sheely a lot. He was the type of guy you could talk with. He died in the middle of the 1952 season, and we all went to his funeral. He was a straightforward guy.

Some of my contract negotiations with him were humorous, however. It was traditional. The first one would be for the amount you got the year before, so you'd write back and say that you felt like you deserved a raise.

You'd get a letter back that would say, 'The fishing industry has not been too good in Seattle.' So you'd write back and say something like, 'I feel that I have to progress in baseball, certainly financially.' And you'd get a letter back saying, 'Also the lumber industry is not very good.'

You'd go back and forth, and finally they'd give you a token raise.

CLAUDE CHRISTIE - Seattle Rainiers

An intense manager and excellent teacher, Paul Richards worked with the Seattle Rainiers in 1950. The Chicago White Sox liked his style and offered him a contract for the 1951 season.

CASEY STENGEL - Oakland Oaks

I think Casey Stengel was one of the smartest managers I ever played for. Casey would get in a group of guys, and he'd think to himself, 'Now I can get these guys,' and he'd start in with that 'Stengelese.' He'd be talking about something, and you'd look at the peoples' expressions and they're trying to figure what he's talkin' about. Just about the time he's got 'em all going, he'd back away, and he'd come by and whisper, 'Got 'em now.'

Casey Stengel got into this victory parade by leading the Oakland Oaks to the PCL championship in 1948. Photo courtesy of the National Baseball Library.

Casey was excellent with the pitchers. He used to take a pitcher out before he got in trouble, not after he got in trouble. He figured if this guy was leaving two men on bases but getting the side out, leaving two more on but getting the side out. 'What if someone gets a hit? Now we're behind by two or three runs. I'd better get him out of there and get someone else in.'

Casey coached at first base. He'd make a few stops before he got to the ballpark. He'd have a few martinis in him. And especially at night, he couldn't see too well. So whatever happened at first base, Casey didn't get in trouble. But Johnny Babich coached at third, so he took the brunt of everything.

DARIO LODIGIANI - Oakland Oaks

Casey was a lovable guy, and I admired him immensely. I congratulated him on getting his job with the Yankees. I said, 'Hey Casey, why don't you take me back with you and I can chauffeur your car.' He said, 'I'll be damned if I want a left-hander driving my car.' He was just a sweet old guy and we had a lot of fun together.

BUD BEASLEY - Sacramento Solons

You could try to follow Casey when he was talking, but most people couldn't understand him because he would jump to different ideas and situations and then come back to what he was originally talking about. If you could remember the original topic, he'd eventually get back to it and answer the question. Then you were all right. He would bewilder a lot of people, but I don't think he bewildered the ballplayers too much. He was just a natural for that situation.

BILL LAWS - Oaks Radio Announcer

Casey was a helluva smart guy. He knew what he was doing. He joked around, laughing like an imbecile. He was always on top of the game, but he liked to sling the bull.

Every game we won, there were two cases of beer in the clubhouse, and if we won a series, five out of seven, or won a crucial game, he'd give trainer Red Adams three dollars [for each player] for steak dinners. In those days, you could get a steak for three dollars.

Then the last series we played in Southern California, his wife, Edna, would have a big barbecue there. If you drank beer, he'd give you quarts of beer, or if you wanted drinks, he'd give you a half-pint. Then you're on your own after that.

When we got through, about 8:30, he'd have a line of taxis to take us down to Glendale to pick up the train to come home. They were real, real nice people.

RUGGER ARDIZOIA - Oakland Oaks

BILL SWEENEY -
Los Angeles Angels

Bill Sweeney was a great manager. He was real close to the players. He was strict. No eating on the bench. There were rules that were a lot tougher than they are now. We had to wear suit and tie on the road. We couldn't come down to the dining room without coat and tie.

GEORGE "BEE" MANDISH - Hollywood Stars

Bill Sweeney was a ballplayer's manager. He'd talk with you and go out with the players for a nip. He was a good manager.

I didn't have a good year in 1952, and I remember the last day of the season I was in the clubhouse, packing my gear. He came up to me and said, 'Don't worry, Claudie, you'll be back next year.' I thought that was nice. I just couldn't get it going for some reason.

Incidentally, our sign to steal was Sweeney adding 'ie' to a player's first name. He'd yell out, 'Allie,' with an instruction, and that would tell him to go on the next pitch.

CLAUDE CHRISTIE - Seattle Rainiers

Sweeney was an easy guy to play for. He was a charming guy with the press, but as a player, you never really got to know him. He never really communicated much with the players. He expected you to do your job, and as long as you were bearing down and staying in shape, that was all he'd ask.

His philosophy was that it was a simple game. I'm sure he felt most people made too much out of it. They complicated it. His signs were simple. He wasn't a guy for speech-making. One-liner stuff — 'You know what we got to do, men.' He wasn't going to hold a meeting. He was a bright guy, and he assumed we were too and we knew what we had to do. That's the way he managed.

Los Angeles Angels manager Bill Sweeney, left, and coach Jackie Warner were fixtures in the PCL.

He had a mannerism the players would pick up on. If a player was in front of the mirror in the clubhouse with a bat or if he was shouting from the dugout at the pitcher, Bill would signal a 'V' with his arms and say, 'Play it between the chalk lines, boys.' In essence, 'Knock that B.S. off.' All Bill had to do was signal the 'V.'

You'd had guys mimicking him behind his back, but something like that said a lot. We'd all do it to our teammates.

CHARLES "RED" ADAMS - Portland Beavers

Sweeney took Tommy Holmes' place in 1956. They were at spring training in '57 at Casey Stengel Field in Glendale, and I'd go over at night and visit with Bill and the ball club.

We went out to dinner, and Bill was drinking grasshoppers. I went back to the motel

Oscar Vitt, a great PCL player in the 1910s, went on to manage in the league in the '50s.

room with him, and he went into the bathroom. I could hear him heaving. He comes out and says, 'Come here. I want to show you something.' The toilet bowl was full of blood. I said, 'Bill, you've got to go see a doctor. This is serious.'

He thought he had cancer of the stomach and a doctor couldn't help. He had an ulcer. That's what killed him. He could have been saved if he'd gone to a doctor. He promised me he would, but he never did, I guess.

Tip Berg called me. [Bill] was sick in San Francisco when the season opened. Then they went to San Diego. [The ulcer] perforated sometime in the morning, and that was the end of it.

He was the greatest manager I played for. I always had good years under him. He was steady, always had a job.

He drank a lot of beer. But he was a sweet guy. On the field he was tough, but off the field he was one of the nicest guys.

BILL FLEMING - Portland Beavers

I didn't like Bill Sweeney at Portland. He didn't care for me, and it was racial.

JOHNNY RITCHEY - Portland Beavers

JIM TURNER - Portland Beavers

I loved Jim. He was one of the smartest pitching coaches that I have ever run into. He was a surgeon. He and Tommy Bridges would have discussions in the dugout, and I couldn't understand what they were saying. They used abbreviated terms. But, boy, did they know pitching.

Turner knew nothing about infield play, but he was smart enough to leave us alone. He just came to me and said, 'My boy, you're doing it out there. I'm not going to bother you. Just give it your all.' I loved playing for him.

EDDIE BASINSKI - Portland Beavers

OSCAR VITT -
Oakland, Portland, Hollywood

Oscar Vitt was a good baseball man. He played with Ty Cobb, you know. Everybody who played with Cobb had to study the game just to keep up with him. He was full of tricks, but he had his shortcomings.

As much as I admired Vitt, he would say things in front of his ballplayers that didn't go very far. You can't do that. He'd see a player on the opponents and say, 'I wish I had him on my ball club.' And here's his player hearing that. You can't say that and keep morale up.

BERNIE "FRENCHY" UHALT - Oakland Oaks, Hollywood Stars

The 1939 Hollywood Stars' Lennie Gabrielson slides across the plate as Portland Beavers catcher Eddie Fernandes leaps out of the way and starts a throw to second. Bill Doran signals Gabrielson out.

6 THE PLAYERS

CHARLES "RED" ADAMS

IN 1951, THEY WERE CLAMPING DOWN ON PITCHERS TO MAKE SURE THEY CAME TO A
COMPLETE STOP IN THEIR STRETCH. WELL, I HAD DEVELOPED A HABIT OF COMING DOWN
VERY SLOWLY AND STOPPING, BUT NOT FOR VERY LONG. THE RULE, AS WE UNDERSTOOD IT,
WAS THAT YOU HAD TO COME TO A COMPLETE STOP. IT DIDN'T SAY HOW LONG YOU HAD TO
HOLD IT. IF YOU WERE STOPPING AND TOO QUICK ON IT, THEY WERE CALLING IT.

Vic Raschi, in the American League, got called for so many balks that they reviewed their
thinking and modified it. Out here in the Coast League, they were [calling them frequently]. I
don't know if I had ever balked in my life, it was just something I didn't do. Well, hell, I was
leading the league in balks. Roy Helser and I were running neck-and-neck.

I was pitching a tight game, 1-1 or thereabouts. In the fifth inning or so, the first guy got on
base. On the first pitch I balked him to second. On the next pitch I balked him to third. I think
that was my fourth balk on the game.

As soon as they called the balk, I tossed my glove into the air a few feet, in disgust. It was just
a reaction, not something I had planned. I never thought about getting thrown out of the ball
game for doing that, but they threw me out of the game.

Bill Sweeney came out. Bill was ticked off at the umpires too, and tried to explain that I was-
n't trying to show up the umpires. Be that as it may, I was out of the game. They don't reverse
a call like that. Bill puts up a big argument for me, which was a waste of time.

*San Francisco phenom
Vic Picetti signed with
the Oakland Oaks in
1944 so he could train
under Dolph Camilli.
Camilli, however, soon
left Oakland, and his
replacement, Casey
Stengel, decided to fill
the lineup with veter-
ans. Picetti was shipped
off to Spokane.*

So before I left the mound, I had to do something, so I took about a hop and skip and threw the ball out over the bleachers along the right-field line. As the ball was sailing I said to myself, 'I hope it makes it out of there.' It did. That was probably the biggest tantrum in my playing days. I get kidded a lot about that.

CHARLES "RED" ADAMS

(Note: In 1949 in the PCL there were seventeen balks during the season. In 1950 there were 406. The rule was revised again in 1951.)

Red was a real heady pitcher. He had hurt his pitching arm before he entered baseball, but he had that courage and determination, and he was a real bright guy. He had that Herb Schriner-type sense of humor. He always took good care of himself.

When he was pitching for the Angels, I came in with Portland, and I got an awful lot of ribbing because of my violin background. There was a lot of dirty stuff said. Well, Red came to me, all the way around to first base where we were, and he said, 'Hey Ed, don't ever be ashamed of that violin background. I'm proud of what you have accomplished.

Right-hander Charles "Red" Adams pitched on both the 1947 and 1956 Los Angeles Angels. He also toiled for the Portland Beavers, San Diego Padres and Sacramento Solons. This photograph shows him throwing for Portland in 1950.

'I wish I could have done something like that, and don't think these other guys wouldn't like to do something like that outside of baseball. You be proud of that. Deep down, these guys know they're wrong, but they're too stupid to realize it.' I tell ya, that's when Red and I became friends.

EDDIE BASINSKI - Portland Beavers. [These comments are in reference to his days as violinist and concertmaster of the Buffalo (New York) Symphony.]

TOM ALSTON

Tom Alston was really introverted, very quiet and kept to himself. He had power and looked like he was going to be a great ballplayer. But he had personal problems in the off-season. He was alone all the time, and during the wintertime his career ended. He wasn't ready when the Cardinals purchased him. I never saw him again.

BUDDY PETERSON - San Diego Padres

RINALDO "RUGGER" ARDIZOIA

I was a fastball pitcher, and had a curve. I'd also mix in a few changes. When I went to Oakland I developed a slider. With Billy Raimondi, he'd give me a fastball sign and it was up to me whether I'd throw a fastball or slider. The slider would break straight across. If I'd throw it across the middle, it would break inside.

There was a guy in Portland, Frank Shone, a pretty good-hitting outfielder. I would sometimes throw a pitch sidearm, and that used to give Frank fits. Raimondi would give me the signal to come in sidearm, and I'd gesture, 'Like this, Bill?' Frank would back right off. He wouldn't stay up there with the sidearm.

If someone hit a home run off of me, he'd better not dig in the next at bat, or the next batter. Both Stengel and Dykes said, 'Let 'em know you're earning a living too, not just throwing batting practice.'

I came to Oakland in 1946 along with Frank Shea and Gene Bearden. Casey didn't have a rotation. The three of us won forty-five games (out of 111). The rest of the staff won the others. Ralph Buxton and Floyd Speer were the relievers, but they had about eight complete games each.

Johnny Babich was our coach. He and Stengel had been buddies back in Boston. John knew exactly what was going on with the pitchers. He could anticipate, and John had the fungo out to run us in pregame warmup.

He'd tell Casey who was ready to start. We'd all know when we were going to start. I knew I was going to pitch every four days. In other words, today I pitched. Tomorrow I'd throw a little batting practice, just a little, to the pitchers in early batting practice. Then rest and be ready to go on the fourth day.

They believed when you start a game, you finish it. But I relieved Bearden more than anybody. He just ran out of gas. Once in Seattle, I relieved him against a left-hander.

Bearden, Shea and myself were the nucleus. On extra games or double-headers, other pitchers would fill in — Hy Vandenberg, Cotton Pippen, Bryan Stephens. Nobody on the staff was in the fours for ERA.

RUGGER ARDIZOIA

Pitcher Rinaldo "Rugger" Ardizoia.

FRANKIE AUSTIN

Little Frankie Austin, a Panamanian, joined our ball club in '49 with Luis Marquez, who was one of the outstanding-hitting outfielders in the Coast League. Frankie played shortstop with me for six years. Frankie was probably one of the nicest guys.

With Frankie and me it was mutual. I had a great time playing with him. He was one of the surest-handed shortstops that you could find in the Coast League. He did not have a great arm, and had just an ordinary release, but he was steady. When there was a ground ball and we needed a double play, he came up with it.

And he was a great lead-off hitter, good base-on-balls batter, a good high-ball batter. Frankie had to be rated as one of the finest shortstops in the league.

I had more fun with old Frankie away from the game or on the bus or the airplane or in the dugout. And we helped each other, never double-crossed each other, and stood up for one another. One time we didn't get the sign right and the guy stole second and

Shortstop Frankie Austin integrated the Portland Beavers and, with Eddie Basinski, delivered one of the PCL's best double-play combinations.

Gladd threw the ball into center field. There was nobody there, and old Clay Hopper jumped on us. He wanted to nail somebody, but we both backed up each other. We just wouldn't let him do it. We had great fun together.

EDDIE BASINSKI - Portland Beavers

We had Frankie Austin and Eddie Basinski on the infield. They were slick. Luis Marquez played center field. He was a bit of a showboat. He and Austin were very different, but both had great hands.

JOHNNY RITCHEY - Portland Beavers

GENE BAKER

Gene Baker was an excellent shortstop and a good team player and motivator. He was not individualistic at all. He would bat number one or two, and I'm batting three.

BOB USHER - Los Angeles Angels

WIN "PARD" BALLOU

I get a kick out of some of the players' complaints nowadays. Hell, we had Joe Sprinz catching when he was forty-eight (he actually was forty-five) and Win Ballou, the ol' Pard, pitching in relief when he was forty-five (actually forty-six).

Ballou loved his bourbon and after a game would take a few swigs. Every time he saved one for Sam Gibson, Sam would say, 'Pard, I owe you a pint.' And without fail, Pard would get his pint the next day.

Gene Baker, a second baseman for the Los Angeles Angels in the early 1950s, teamed up later in the decade with Ernie Banks to form the double-play combination for the Chicago Cubs.

LEO "DOC" HUGHES - San Francisco Seals Trainer

Pard Ballou and Rudy Parsons had a deal that when one would win a game or save a game, the other would buy the rounds. They were on the bench half loaded most of the time.

BOB STEVENS - San Francisco Chronicle Beat Writer

GEORGE BAMBERGER

George was more serious than most of the players, but he was a friendly guy. The fans loved him. He retired to Florida but actually came back to Vancouver a couple of times after suffering heart attacks. He came back here to scout, and people would come down and shake his hand. He was here for so long that people remembered him.

JIM ROBSON - Mounties Radio Announcer

I caught George at both Oakland and Vancouver. He was a quiet person, but very classy. He didn't throw hard, but he was always around the plate. He was easy to catch.

The fans loved him because he was always in the game and usually finished the games that he started. Not a lot of speed, but batters knew they had better come up ready to swing.

LEN NEAL - Oakland Oaks and Vancouver Mounties

DICK "KEWPIE" BARRETT

Dick Barrett was kind of a goofy guy, never said too much. He twirled around, had a particular pitching style — pivoted on his left leg, had his back to you, then came around and pitched.

We were getting on Western Airlines to go to Seattle one day and here comes Kewpie Barrett with this valise [for carrying] papers. I said to someone, 'How come Dick's got that attache case and he doesn't have any suitcase?' He said, 'The truth is he's scared of flying, and he takes a pint of Old Grand Dad and nips at it while we're flying.'

JACK GRAHAM - San Diego Padres

The only home run I hit in my life I hit off Kewpie Barrett. I used to hit him pretty good. The time before I hit the home run, he threw one inside and I hit it over the first baseman for a double. When I hit the home run, he followed me completely around the bases, swearing and cussing me, calling me everything under the sun.

The poor guy, I felt sorry for him. For as many years as he pitched and as good as he was, he died in poverty. He drank a lot. But he could pitch!

RUGGER ARDIZOIA - Hollywood Stars

Kewpie Dick Barrett used to give you a lot of hip when he pitched. He was a stocky guy, real fat. He'd take that left leg — he was right-handed — and he'd have that ass at you before he threw. He had good stuff and good control, and was a factor in the league for years.

BOB KERRIGAN - San Diego Padres

Longtime Vancouver Mounties pitcher George Bamberger was the team's most popular player after it moved from Oakland in the mid-'50s.

EDDIE BASINSKI

Eddie Basinski was one of the most popular players in Portland Beavers history. The slender second baseman played ten of his thirteen Coast League seasons in Portland, where he was known as an "iron man" for his steady play.

I'm the only player in professional ball who never played high school or college to go right to the major leagues. It was in *Ripley's Believe It or Not*. I played in the city leagues in Buffalo. They were real fast. We had guys like Buddy Rosar and Danny Ozark and Sibbi Sisti. Warren Spahn lived only a block away from me. We used to practice together.

When I went to high school, I practiced the violin. That didn't help either. They had a concert orchestra. It was the best in the city of Buffalo, and I became the concertmaster.

I played with the Buffalo Symphony for two seasons. This was in the off-seasons, 1944 and 1945. But don't play now. I'm a perfectionist, and if I can't play well then I prefer not to do it.

Dick "Kewpie" Barrett, a crafty Seattle Rainiers pitcher during the Jack Lelivelt era, in the late 1930s and 1940, won twenty games seven times for the team. His 27-13 record, with 330 innings pitched and a 1.72 ERA, earned him his return to the National League in 1943.

A talented second baseman for the Portland Beavers, Eddie Basinski also played violin during the winter for the Buffalo Symphony in Buffalo, New York.

The war had started, and the University of Buffalo was offering an engineers program for honor students to replace the engineers who had gone off to war. So I entered that program and graduated in two-and-a-half years. I went to work for Curtiss-Wright Corporation. We made P-40s and P-47 Thunderbolts and P-46s. In the meantime, I was playing in the city leagues, having real good years. I had no real aspirations. I just enjoyed what I was doing.

One day, Boston Red Sox and Brooklyn scouts approached me, and I was shocked. I said, 'You mean you men are willing to pay me to wear that wonderful uniform to play ball?'

Branch Rickey actually flew down to Buffalo after the 1944 season had started. I got a $5,000 bonus for signing, and he asked me what level I thought I could play at, and I told him I thought I could start at the International League, which would have been Montreal.

He said, 'No. I think I'll have you travel with the Dodgers for two weeks, have Leo Durocher and Charlie Dressen look at you, then we'll decide where you will play. I was a shortstop at that time. Those were the happiest two weeks of my life. No pressure. I had the best seat in the house, sitting in the dugout, listening to these gnarly old veterans, chewing tobacco and cussing. It was great.

And of course, I saw some of the great ballplayers, even at that time. After two weeks, Rickey called me in and said, 'My boy, we're going to sign you to a Brooklyn Dodgers contract. Charlie Dressen and Leo Durocher say that you could help them out.' They put me in as a second baseman.

In my first game — it was against Cincinnati — I had a great day. Hit a triple the first time up. We made five double plays and won 6-1. But the pressure finally got to me and they sent me to Montreal for the rest of the 1944 season.

In 1945 I went back up, and Durocher put me in at shortstop. That was my great year. I made the National League All Star team. We finished third but almost won the thing. I had an 18-game hitting streak and made a lot of double plays

It was my decision to go to St. Paul in '46. Pee Wee Reese came out of the service, and you could see he was going to be a great player. But he was rusty. There was no way he was going to take my job in 1946. But, of course, Leo was looking at the long range. In exhibition games in spring training, he'd play the first four or five innings and I'd finish up.

Finally, after about a week, I went to Leo and said, 'What about me?' He said, 'Eddie, you're a major league ballplayer, but we want you in case something happens to Reese.' I said, 'No way. I want to play. Why don't you send me to St. Paul? Ray Blades is dying for infielders.' He says, 'Oh no! I won't do it.'

I asked a teammate, Art Herring, what I should do. He said, 'Why don't you send a telegram to Ray Blades telling him how much you want to play for him? After that year you had, he'll kill to get you over there.'

Blades went to Branch Rickey the next day and worked out a deal. Rickey called me in the next day and said, 'My boy, we're sending you to St. Paul.' To this day he doesn't know that I rigged that thing.

So I went to St. Paul on my own. I had a great year there, and Billy Cox and I were sold to Pittsburgh and almost immediately traded to the Yankees. They shipped me to Newark, which was a horrible experience. They shipped me to Portland, which was one of the greatest things that could have happened to me.

I don't look like a big strong guy, but I was an iron man with Portland. My looks were always against my ability. I looked like a damn doctor or a preacher, and the glasses didn't help. But man, I had the fire, and I wanted to be a perfectionist.

When I left Newark, it was August 12. When Jim Turner saw me, he later was disappointed, again, because of my looks. He called me an escaped divinity student. But he worked me out at second base, and I took over at second.

We won fourteen straight games, lost one, then won eight more in a row, and finished third. We set a Portland record for attendance. It seemed every time I came up, I had an opportunity to do something. I enjoyed that year. We pulled together, there were no cliques. Just a wonderful season. And I fell in love with Portland.

EDDIE BASINSKI

JIM BAXES

Iwas proud to play for both the Angels and the Stars. When you're twenty-one years old, you run to the ballpark. You don't care if it's eight or nine in the morning. That's how you love the game. I look back on 1949 with the Stars —184 ball games. I missed three of them — $350 a month. That's great money. If it wasn't for the great Greek restaurants up and down the coast, I'd have starved!

Chuck Stevens always rags me about my throws from third. I guess I gained a reputation. Once in pregame infield practice, I was going to play a joke on the catcher. When we are about finished, the coach hits short to the third baseman, and he fires the ball home to the catcher. Well, I had a tennis ball in my hand and I got in real close and threw the hell out of that ball. He freaked out as the ball came out at him.

Johnny Ostrowski of the Angels and I, we hated each other. I don't know whether I tagged him hard one time or he tagged me, but he ended up in the Dodger organization after '53 and he was still riding my butt after all those years. We still yelled at each other wherever we played.

JIM BAXES

Sharp-hitting Jim Baxes played third base for the Hollywood Stars during their dynasty years (1949-1955). His somewhat erratic throwing arm slowed his advancement to the major leagues, but he was an all-star in the PCL.

BUD LEWIS BEASLEY

Bud Lewis Beasley, a zany relief pitcher for the Sacramento Solons and Seattle Rainiers, would try to throw batters off guard with unusual pitching gestures. He seriously distracted some batters with his contortions.

Bud Beasley was an unorthodox left-handed pitcher who toiled with Sacramento and Seattle in the 1940s. A school teacher from Reno, he joined the team late and left it early. But while he played he drove opposing batters crazy with a delivery that included windmill arms and multiple pumps before he ever threw the pitch. Beasley was a Pacific Coast League original.

When I first broke into the Coast League, I was a fastball pitcher. I was an orthodox pitcher — first a starter, then a reliever. I developed an arm problem, so I think I started the awkward windup in my third year in the Coast League, probably 1945.

It took me a while, but I learned two things. A batter, when he comes to the plate, you can almost tell ... first, he's looking for his pitch and, second, he's concentrating on hitting, particularly if he's a good hitter. He's all concentration.

Lefty O'Doul said that hitting was ninety percent concentration. If that's the case then you've got to destroy that ninty percent that's in the head. You've got to get them thinking about something other than hitting. They either think you're crazy or they're laughing at you or they're mad at you, but they're thinking of anything but hitting. Break their concentration.

Whatever you do, don't give him his pitch. And this led me to make a fantastic study of the hitters in the league. I had a little black book that showed me every ball that every batter in the league hit, where he hit it and what the pitch was to it. When I wasn't pitching, I had my book out and I was writing like crazy about every batter. I knew those batters backwards and forwards. Now, that doesn't mean that it always works, but still, I made a study of the hitters and I had good enough control to put the ball over.

Chet Johnson told me that I gave him the idea [for the windmill windup] and he capitalized on it. One time, Cliff Melton of the Seals used it on me when I came to bat, but I was the only one he used it on, and the crowd really cracked up. If you remember Cliff Melton, with the huge ears, he looked like a big stork about to fly when he started his windup. He was laughing and he got a whale of a kick out of it.

[Broadcaster] Tony Koester enjoyed it immensely because it gave him something to talk about. He made the most of it. Incidentally, I owe a lot to Tony because his description of it on the air was a big selling point for me. He gave me a lot of real good publicity, and it helped get people to the park.

In spite of the clowning, there was a lot of seriousness that was there. Behind the clowning, I did have good control, and two years in a row I had fewer home runs hit off of me than any other pitcher in the league.

One time, in 1946, I used the multiple windup against Ned Harris of Portland. He was a good hitter and I had the bases loaded in the last inning. I knew that I had to turn it on him, which I did. I don't remember how many times that I threw to first, threw to second, threw to third, rather than pitch to him.

And it worked. I got him. I didn't strike him out, but he popped up to the infield. He could have ended the ball game right there. Someone timed that at-bat, and I pitched the length of a normal inning to that one batter.

I pitched during a period when there was freedom to perform. No way could I get away with that today. In fact, I am responsible for one rule that is in the rule book, the double pump. They put that rule in to stop me.

BUD BEASLEY

I saw Bud Beasley a couple of years ago. We talked about the home run I knocked off of him. He gave me all that motion. I didn't pay no attention. You don't hit the motion. He's got to throw the ball into the zone. He threw one into the zone and I knocked it over the fence .

I made the turn around third, and the first person to greet me at home was him. He said, 'Nice hit, Lou.' He then asked the umpire if he could have a smaller ball.

He was a screwball, a clown. It was an act. The fans loved it, but he was doing it to throw off the hitters.

LOU VEZILICH - San Diego Padres

TED BEARD

*T*ed Beard was a diminutive, soft-spoken outfielder who joined the Hollywood Stars in the *middle of their "dynasty," in the early 1950s, and helped the team win two pennants. In what probably was a mistake, he was sold to San Francisco at the start of the 1954 season, where he helped provide stability for the Seals' "Kiddie Car Express." The Stars, meanwhile, lost their third consecutive pennant, by a playoff game to San Diego. With Beard still around, that game probably wouldn't have been necessary.*

Ted Beard? That little shit. I remember he had a streak of twelve straight hits. I think we helped him on that. He had six of them already when we went into Hollywood. He had good power for a little guy, and was very intense. He was the kind of guy who could beat you several different ways. He was very quiet, though.

EDDIE BASINSKI - Portland Beavers

(On April 24, 1953, Beard began a streak that lasted for twelve hits and a walk before Lyman Linde of the Beavers forced him to fly out. The out came in Beard's first at-bat in the fifth game of the streak. This tied Mickey Heath's record set in 1930.)

Ted Beard was a real quiet guy. The Seals used to have real attractive usherettes, and he doesn't say a word, but all of a sudden, he takes off and marries one of them. Nobody knows a thing until he marries one of them.

JIM WESTLAKE - San Francisco Seals

Ted Beard — he was a fourth outfielder. He was a little guy but had great power and a good arm. I don't think he was the type who got into the intellectual part of the game.

BILL WERLE - San Francisco Seals

GENE BEARDEN

Gene Bearden broke into the Coast League with Casey Stengel's 1946 Oakland Oaks, going 15-4. After winning twenty games as a rookie for the Cleveland Indians, in 1948, Bearden gained immortality by defeating Boston in a winner-take-all playoff game.

Bearden returned to the Coast League in 1954, playing four more seasons, now a more crafty veteran.

Gene Bearden did more with less. He was done when he was with us, but he had a knuckle ball still, and a breaking ball and he'd waste a fastball and change speeds. He had a pretty good season with us in 1956. (Bearden went 15-14, with a 3.48 ERA in 207 innings.)

When we went to spring training in 1957, I never saw anyone work harder than he. He would put on one of those rubber jackets and run until he dropped. He'd pitch batting practice. He'd do everything. I was impressed. Here's this guy, thirty-six years old and he's just working his butt off. He wanted to have a great year.

We came back to Sacramento and opened with Vancouver. He lost the opener on a three hitter, 1-0. Bearden was disconsolate. He said, 'I believe that's the last old Gene is going to pitch in Sacramento.' It wasn't two weeks after that that he and Tobin were sent to Minneapolis together, and that was his last year.

I liked him because he came out in the newspaper saying that out of all the young pitchers with the Solons, the best pitcher of the group was Bud Watkins. He knows how to pitch changing speeds, he had good location and doesn't walk anyone. He gave me a helluva boost. So I've always liked Gene Bearden.

BUD WATKINS - Sacramento Solons

ROCKY BENEVENTO -
Portland Beavers Groundskeeper

He lived right behind Vaughn Street baseball park and had a gate from his back yard to it. He took care of the field when the Beavers went [there for] spring training. Later they hired him to look after Vaughn Street.

When I was traded to Portland he was glad to see me. I stayed at his home for a while. The rent was cheap.

Rocky used to have a little sideline. When a player broke a bat, he'd take it and make a lamp out of it. He'd take the upper portion and shape it, run a wire through it and put a shade on it. He'd sell it back to us for maybe a dollar-and-a-half.

He used to take the players' sweat socks home and his wife would launder them and we'd give him money for the service. The uniforms went out to be laundered. Johnny Pesky was the clubhouse boy at the time. He used to shine the shoes. I was surprised when I found out he made the major leagues.

NINO BONGIOVANNI - Portland Beavers

Rocky Benevento — he was a good guy. He was there when I got there, in '36. I kept close with him and his family. He was a great ambassador for the Portland Beavers. He opened up a spaghetti restaurant close to the ball park. He knew everybody. He did a wonderful job keeping the ballpark up, and a fine job on the infield.

Portland Beavers groundskeeper Rocky Benevento, pictured here with his son, Dickie, was one of the most popular figures at Lucky Beaver Stadium. He often bore the brunt of players' jokes, and kept busy putting out fires at the rickety stadium.

B aseball cards and players' uniforms anchored the identities of the teams in the Pacific Coast League. The cards and uniforms pictured on the following pages not only enhanced fan loyalties, they quite often were as colorful as the players who drew the crowds to the ballparks.

Seattle Indians and Seattle Rainiers trading cards and souvenirs.

Sacramento Solons baseball cards and souvenirs.

In the 1940s and '50s just about all teams produced free decals for the fans.

Above and right: The home uniform worn by the 1956 PCL-champion Los Angeles Angels.

The home uniform worn by Rogers Hornsby, manager in Seattle of the 1951 PCL champions.

A Sacramento jersey from 1946.

Manager Dick Bartell's uniform from 1947.

*Caps old and older worn by the Sacramento Solons, Vancouver Mounties,
Seattle Rainiers, Los Angeles Angels and Oakland Oaks.*

1923 Oakland Oaks.

The 1948 Oakland Oaks uniform worn by pitcher Earl Jones.

The 1953 road uniform of pitcher Con Dempsey.

The 1957 San Francisco Seals' home uniform worn by Jack Phillips.

A vintage jersey, from the 1920s.

Home uniforms worn by two top pitchers: Larry Jansen, 1946 (30 wins), and Bob Joyce, 1945 (31 wins).

The Hollywood Stars' controversial "hot weather" home uniform of 1950.
This specimen was worn by first baseman Chuck Stevens.

Right: The Stars' 1940 road uniform, featuring heavy material and unique chenille lettering.
Below: The Stars' 1940 home uniform.

The San Diego Padres began wearing pinstripes in the mid-1950s. This was one of the team's home uniforms.

A Portland Beavers road jersey from the 1930s.

A San Francisco Missions jersey from the 1930s.

A Mounties road uniform from the late 1950s.

Los Angeles Angels baseball cards and souvenirs.

One guy who had a lot of fun was Lindsay Brown, our shortstop in 1940. He pulled a good one on Rocky. We kept Rocky busy underneath the stands, and in the meantime, someone got a spade and Lindsay got a huge rock and buried it with the tip barely sticking out, on the infield by shortstop.

We were taking infield, and we call Rocky over. 'Hey, Rocky, come on over. Lindsay wants to talk with you.' Lindsay says, 'You see this hump here? I can't get that hump out of there.' So Rocky digs and finds this huge rock. We're all laughing. From then on we called it Rocky's Rock Pile.

There was a steel foundry behind right field. Sometimes on Saturday or during the week, they would clean it out. Boy, I'm telling ya, there was some dark, black smoke coming over that ballpark, and it was all full of soot. Those little ladies that were dressed in white, they didn't have a white dress when they walked out of there. It was really funny, but it was expensive to the people. When they did that, the wind was blowing in the direction of the ballpark. 'Here it comes,' and we'd all start laughing. Watch the women scatter.

I enjoyed pitching there very much. That's why I'm thankful for Rocky Benevento. I said, 'Rocky, my best success is when the mound isn't high. It's low now, so let's just keep it that way.' Somebody is going to come in here and squawk, but I said I can get a better sinker off a lower mound, and he was very good about it until Tommy Bridges came in from the big leagues (in 1947).

Well, Tommy got him over, and Rocky jacked it up about six inches. And he thought I wouldn't notice it. I says, 'Rocky, did you play with that mound? It's not the same as the last time I pitched.' I says just because Bridges comes out from the big leagues, who the hell is he? And how long did he last? Just one year. (Bridges actually lasted three years.)

AD LISKA - Portland Beavers

CARLOS BERNIER

Carlos Bernier helped revolutionize the game in the Coast League. He made the running game a more potent weapon for Fred Haney's Hollywood Stars. Bernier was a troubled man, however, and his ill-tempered behavior led to several suspensions during his eleven-year Coast League career.

I played against Carlos Bernier in Puerto Rico. He had all kinds of talent — he could run, he could throw. He could field, hit for average, but not the long ball. But he always seemed to antagonize the other team and stay in hot water all the time. He was friendly with us, but he could rile up the opposition quite a bit.

FORREST "SPOOK" JACOBS - Hollywood Stars

Carlos Bernier was an intense guy. He was a guy that when he went into a base, his cleats were always up. He was a guy that opposing players didn't like. He had a lot of fights with opposing players.

I think he bordered on being a major league player, but some things just held him back. He did some crazy things, and in those days they didn't go for crazy things. He would make little bonehead mistakes. But he could run and he could play.

BUDDY PETERSON - San Diego Padres

Hollywood Stars outfielder Carlos Bernier helped revolutionize PCL baseball by implementing the stolen base. Quick as he was on the field, though, his temper was even quicker, and it got him into trouble.

In 1961, Carlos Bernier led the league in hitting, making $825 a month, living in Hawaii — starving to death. He was a good hitter with good power to right center field. He was a great base runner. He could get under your skin. Once he got on base, he could drive you nuts.

BUD WATKINS - Sacramento Solons

STEVE BILKO

*S*teve Bilko's PCL career was brief but notable, spanning four years. With the Los Angeles Angels *from 1955 through 1957, Bilko won a triple-crown batting title, three home-run championships and three Most Valuable Player awards. Not bad! His talents were aptly suited to the confines of Wrigley Field.*

Please take this the way I say it. There's great emphasis on Bilko's success. His years with the Angels were an ideal marriage of ballplayer to ballpark. Bilko played in a lot of other ballparks and a lot of other leagues, but in L.A. it was inevitable. When I heard Steve was coming to the Angels, I said he's going to put some numbers up.

And, fortunately, they had a good ball club so you couldn't pitch around him. If you tried, other guys would sting you. So it turned out, everything worked for him. If he was on a bad ball club, they pitch around him.

Steve wouldn't have hung up those numbers if he was put in a ballpark like San Francisco or Seattle.

CHUCK STEVENS - Hollywood Stars

Steve Bilko was an easygoing guy, quiet. Everybody loved him. He was just a big old bear, a gentle giant. But that son of a gun could run for a big man.

He always called me Cholly. Our son, Dwight, idolized Steve, and somewhere during the season, Steve told me he was going to give Dwight his glove when we clinched the pennant. I can't remember whether I told Dwight or not. I figured Steve would forget. But we clinched the pennant up in Seattle, and old Steve came over and said, 'Give this to Dwight.' Nothing had been said about it for a month or two, and he comes over and tosses me that glove. It was his gamer!

CHARLES "RED" ADAMS - Los Angeles Angels

We tried to pitch Steve Bilko inside, either a curve ball or fastball, across the letters. Anything outside and he'd hit a ton.

JOHNNY RITCHEY - San Diego Padres

Steve was kind to young players. He was a gentle, gentle person, yet had tremendous power. I think I will always remember Steve for the gentleness he showed to me as a youngster.

GEORGE "SPARKY" ANDERSON - Los Angeles Angels

NINO BONGIOVANNI

I'll never forget L.H. Gregory of *The Oregonian* robbing me of a hitting streak in1935. I had hit safely in forty-three straight games — no gifts. And against Hollywood in a game at Portland, the first time up, I bunted the ball. A perfect bunt. I was running, and the pitcher threw the ball into right field. I looked over to Gregory, and he nodded yes.

Then the next time I hit a ball to Bobby Doerr and the ball took a bad hop and hit him up on the shoulders. Nowadays they'd give him a hit, and they were doing it then too — give a hit. I was at home, and I asked him again if he gave me a hit, and he nodded his head yes.

The next day, I have the paper, with a headline in big black letters: NO GIFTS FOR BONGY. You figure that Joe DiMaggio had a few on the shady side. Mine weren't. They were good clean hits other than that one that took the bad hop.

I then hit safely in the last twelve games of the season.

So that's something I'll go to the grave with. So when I go to hell, I'm going to run into Gregory and we're going to talk about a few things.

NINO BONGIOVANNI

ROGER BOWMAN

I first saw Roger Bowman in 1953. He had already hurt his arm and he tipped off every pitch. In his windup, Roger would wiggle his glove if it was going to be a curve ball. If it's a fastball, he won't wiggle his glove. So we know every pitch he's going to throw. He beat us 3-0 and struck out ten!

The 1936 Portland Beavers' go-get-'em center fielder Nino Bongiovanni.

He couldn't blacken your eye with his best fastball. But that curve ball he had would start at your neck and end up at your shoe tops. I saw Bob Speake, our first baseman at Phoenix, hit himself in the ankle with a bat, going after that curve ball.

BUD WATKINS - Sacramento Solons

TOMMY BRIDGES

Tommy Bridges had one of the greatest overhand curve balls, with accuracy, I've ever seen. And what a smart pitcher, the way he'd set batters up, or he'd wait on 'em, then quick-pitch 'em. All this stuff.

He used pine tar an awful lot. His catcher, Jimmie Gladd, used to hide it with a little rag in his back pocket and, of course, he told the umpire, 'This is for my hitting.' Every time he'd reach back for a ball [from the umpire] his hand was loaded with pine tar. He'd just rotate that ball once and throw it back to Bridges and it was loaded. They'd go out and look at Bridges' cap, looking for water and everything, but they could never find it. Gladd was the guy who was loading it up.

I told Jimmie one time, 'Jim, you're going to load that ball up one time and you're going to throw that ball back to Bridges and it's going to stick to the palm of your hand.'

JoJo White at Seattle actually had the umpires check him once and they caught him with a wet cap. All they did was warn him, because he was such a personality and draw. So he had to go back to pine tar.

EDDIE BASINSKI - Portland Beavers

Tommy Bridges used to cross me up. He was the worst at that, but it made me a better catcher. I had to expect anything from him.

CHARLIE SILVERA - Portland Beavers

JOE BROVIA

I consider Joe Brovia the best fastball hitter I'd ever seen. When Portland came into Hollywood prior to the series, Fred Haney called a meeting and said, 'If any one of you pitchers throws Joe Brovia a fastball this week, it will be an automatic fine.'

We went Tuesday, Wednesday, Thursday — we beat them all three days. It's Friday night. Ben Wade, one of the better fast ball throwers in the Coast League at the time, was pitching. We have them down four or five runs late in the ball game, and Ben is calling me from first base.

I'm thinking, 'I hope he doesn't have a bad arm or something.' And I get out there and he says, 'I'm going to throw him a fastball,' and I said, 'You heard what the man said. If you throw him a fastball, it's going to cost you.'

'I don't give a damn. I'm going to throw him a fastball."

I get back to first base. We can tell he's going to throw his fastball right by Brovia. He reaches back ... got all he could get ...

The next time I saw the ball it was in the drive-in theater. So now I get an umpire to throw me a new ball, and I'm rubbing it up. Brovia rounds third. Ben Wade looks at me, 'You know that son of a bitch *can* hit that fastball.'

CHUCK STEVENS - Hollywood Stars

Joe Brovia hated pitchers. We were all taking the bread out of his mouth. He hated all of us. He'd absolutely call you everything in the world, standing in the batter's box. Chet Johnson used to drive Brovia crazy. Joe called him everything he could think of. I learned a lot of new words from him.

BUD WATKINS - Sacramento Solons

Old Joe — he used to cuss me out from the dugout all the time. He was strictly a low-ball, fastball hitter. I used to make him hit the curve ball. He'd get in the dugout and throw his bat and cuss me out.

EDDIE ERAUTT - San Diego Padres

Joe Brovia was playing right field in Seals Stadium, and the bleachers had a screen wire fence on top. One night, Joe goes back to catch a fly ball, runs into the screen and got his finger caught. It was in pretty bad shape. Well, he's in the bar with Doc Hughes one evening. We're going for the pennant.
He looks at Doc and says, 'This damn finger is going to cost us the pennant.' He raps it on the bar and breaks it. Now it's worse. Brovia was a nice guy, but he was obviously frustrated by the circumstances.

DON RODE - Seals Clubhouse Man

Joe Brovia expected to get a hit each time he batted. In this case, Joe hit a screecher that almost killed the first baseman, but somehow he caught it. So now Joe has got to go out to left field.
In those days, we used to leave our gloves on the field. You never brought them in with you during the game. Joe was doing a slow burn as he approached his glove, and he kicked it when he reached it. He kicked it again, and on the third kick, he kicked it over the chicken wire fence in left field. He stood there and looked at it.
Now the inning is about to start. Everybody has changed sides and the pitcher is ready. Before Joe ever said a thing, the pitcher had thrown two pitches.
Finally, he realized he'd better do something, and he called time and sent the bat boy around to retrieve the glove.

EDDIE BOCKMAN - Portland Beavers

Eddie Erautt, of Portland's Lincoln High School, was among the youngsters Portland Beavers groundskeeper Rocky Benevento nurtured toward a baseball career. Here Erautt is shown preparing baseballs for the evening's game. He went on to pitch for the Hollywood Stars.

I remember one time we opened up in San Francisco and Al Lien was pitching. In this particular game, Lien had gotten Joe Brovia out a couple of times. Now Joe was a super nice guy, but hitting was his bread and butter. He took it seriously.
After the second time, Joe comes back to the dugout, and he's shouting out to Al Lien, calling him all kinds of things, loud. It really shocked me. I didn't really know Al Lien. I respected him as a pitcher and liked him. But I thought, well, Joe, he's played with this guy. He knows him better. He's really got a dislike for him. Through the remainder of the night, Joe was on Lien's case.
The next day I went up to Joe and I said, 'Hey Joe, what kind of a guy is Al Lien?' He says, 'He's a great guy, a helluva nice guy.' I said, 'Really? No kidding?'

Joe asked why I had asked, and I told him about last night. Old Joe looked at me and smiled, 'Did I really say that? Naw. I wouldn't say that. He's a helluva nice guy.'

CHARLES "RED" ADAMS - Portland Beavers

The first time I ever saw Joe Brovia was the first game I ever started in the PCL, in Sacramento. Here's this big giant standing up there with his hands clutched in front of his belt buckle, squeezing the sawdust out of the bat handle, hat pulled over his eyes and pants down to the ground. I say to myself, 'Here's this guy with his arms down at his sides, there's no way in the world he's going to be able to get around on a fastball upstairs and outside.'

So I rev up my best number one, and he hit that thing off that left field line. You could have strung a week's worth of wash on that line drive. So he hits a double. Another inning or two, I'm gone.

I get dressed, and I'm going out into the foyer at Edmonds Field, and here's Brovia coming out of the Portland dressing room on the other side. He says, 'Kid, I don't know how I hit that ball. You threw that ball just perfect. It had movement on it and you threw it just where you wanted. I don't know how I hit it.'

So the next day I go into the locker room, and we're getting dressed. I'm telling Chet Johnson about me meeting with Brovia, and he started to laugh. I said, 'What are you laughing about?' He said, 'If he gets four for four off of you, you're the greatest pitcher he's ever faced, but if he goes 0-3 against you, he'll call you everything in the world.'

BUD WATKINS - Sacramento Solons

One Sunday double-header, Joe got a couple of home runs and a couple of doubles, but the newspaper didn't give him credit for this. The next day, in the clubhouse, Joe was really steamed.

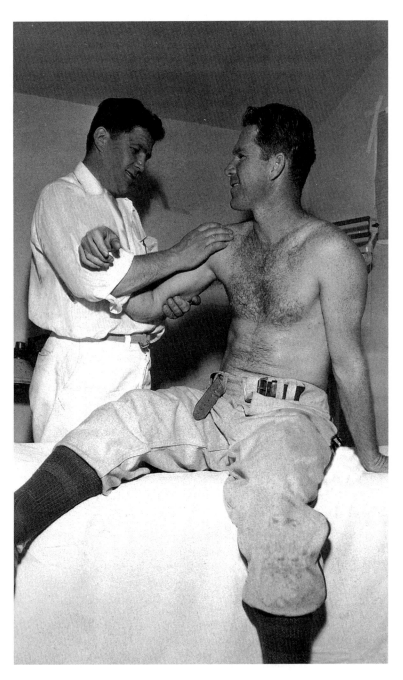

Players sought relief from aches and pains during visits to highly regarded trainers such as Portland's Tip Berg and the Bay Area's Denny Carroll. Above, Berg, Portland's trainer in the 1940s and '50s, works on pitcher Charles "Red" Adams.

He said to me, 'What's a guy got to do around here to get credit for what he's done?' 'You saw the game, Joe,' I said. 'Those were just typographical errors.'

'Hell no, they weren't,' he replied. 'They were all clean hits!'

BOB BLACKBURN - Portland Radio Broadcaster

I was called in one day to tell the press that Lefty O'Doul had traded Joe Brovia to Portland. Well, the story behind that — Lefty was called into his office one day by Paul Fagan and told that Fagan didn't like the idea that Joe Brovia wore his pants down around his shoe tops. He told O'Doul, 'Tell him to get those pants around his knees like the rest of the guys or we're going to get rid of him.'

So O'Doul went to Brovia and he told Brovia, 'You've got to get those pants up.' And Brovia wouldn't do it, so I was told that the day after this incident to tell the press that he had been traded to Portland.

O'Doul really caught hell, because Brovia was a real favorite with the fans, an all-time slugger. So Lefty went out to the third-base coaching box for the next game, and that's the incident that touched off the nickname 'Marblehead.' The fans were yelling out, 'You marblehead!' That's where it all started, that trade.

DON KLEIN - San Francisco Seals Broadcaster

DENNY CARROLL

*I*n Nuggets on the Diamond *Denny Carroll was referred to as "the Babe Ruth of trainers." Few athletic trainers had formal training in their trade. Carroll was considered the best, and players came from all over the nation to the Bay Area so that Carroll could work his magic on their injured limbs.*

Had it not been for the war, I probably wouldn't have had a sore arm. I worked on a farm for about a year and a half, waiting to be drafted, and I didn't play catch. I started throwing batting practice in 1944, and after a couple of outings, I could hardly lift my arm.

Being young and never having had a sore arm, I didn't know what was wrong. I had heard guys say they had thrown their arm out. Well, hell, I didn't throw my arm out, it was just sore.

What had happened was that it had gotten all bound up by working, and by throwing hard. I had tendinitis, like a knife in the shoulder. I was useless for a good half of that season. If it had been normal times, I would have been sent out or possibly released. From the way I was throwing, there's no way I would have stayed with the club, but it was wartime and they needed bodies.

Well, we went to Sacramento, and somebody told me about Denny Carroll. I went up to the front office and asked [team president] Don Stewart if I could visit Denny Carroll to evaluate my arm. He agreed to it.

I go over there, and Denny meets me. He gets me on the table, feels my back and says, 'I'll tell you, your back is so tied up I don't know how you can throw a baseball at all.' I say, 'Well, I'm not!'

'Ballplayers don't realize they throw the ball with their back, and you're all tied up. You've got knots all over your back. I don't know if you can stand any pain, but if you can stay a week, I can get these knots out of your back and you'll be able to throw.'

He worked on me a couple of days, real hard, then an off day, then three more days pretty hard. We did that, and I came back to the team in Sacramento and started throwing. I hadn't thrown any in that time, but I was able to throw well. I was just like a new man.

[Carroll] used to say, 'They all call me a miracle worker and all that. All I do is loosen the guys up. Very rarely will you find a pitcher who has thrown for a few years who isn't tied up in his back. Some guys have long swimmer's muscles, but most guys are going to have tied up muscles.

'You throw the ball with your entire body. The arm is just an extension of the body. Your body is like a big slingshot. Imagine you take this big elastic sling and tie a few knots into it. Now what do you have? You see how you lose your leverage? In addition to that, you're hurting because you have shortened the sling and that puts pressure on other parts of the body, and something is going to give.'

Every day, he had a system. He'd get in the back room and he'd start in rubbing you real low, in the small of your back. He had the strongest fingers. He'd work down there then start working his way up the back He'd find those knots. They were almost like marbles.

He'd work on them a bit then say, 'You know, you can't work on these knots too long in one day. It's counter-productive. They become irritated.'

They'd release a little bit at a time. And the pitching side would be tighter than the other side. After a week's time, he had worked those knots out and I headed back home. I was 0-5 before I saw him, and finished up at 21-15, and I think I had thirty-one complete games. That was Denny.

CHARLES "RED" ADAMS - Los Angeles Angels

BOB CHESNES

Bob Chesnes was a great athlete. He could do it all. He could hit, he could run. When I knew him in semi-pro ball, he was a helluva shortstop in the Golden Gate Valley League and in high school. He was used as a pinch hitter, too.

But he had a head problem. Whatever he did or how he did it, he always questioned himself. Johnny Hopp with the Pittsburgh Pirates would come in after an inning shaking his head. He'd say, 'I'm talking to him and it's like talking to a blank wall. He's just not listening.'

DINO RESTELLI - San Francisco Seals

Nobody saw Chesnes in his prime. Nobody realizes it, but he actually hurt his arm the last year he was with San Francisco before he was even sold to Pittsburgh. I saw him at Pittsburgh, and he was nowhere near the pitcher he was out here. He didn't have the stuff anymore. Bob had an outstanding fastball and a great curve ball and excellent control, and was a great competitor. He was the best-fielding pitcher I ever saw.

He played for Joe Orengo at Salt Lake, and when he wasn't pitching, he was playing shortstop. His reflexes were so great, he could actually leap for a ball hit through the box. Most pitchers would just throw their glove up.

BILL WERLE - San Francisco Seals

ROCKY COLAVITO

Rocky Colavito had a tremendous arm. When we had pregame outfield practice, I would back up third base for Johnny Merson. If you didn't get the big bounce from Rocky, you'd better get the hell out of the way!

We'd have those outfield throwing contests. He could almost hit the center field fence from home plate. As a hitter, he could also hit the long ball. He was quiet and a nice guy.

I think they might have cut down his throwing in the major leagues. You get a throw from him to second base and it could be awfully hard for the second baseman to handle.

BOB KERRIGAN - San Diego Padres

CHUCK CONNORS

Chuck Connors was on [my] club. George Goodale was the P.R. man, and Chuck gave a rendition of 'Casey at the Bat' at the Ambassador Hotel, and that catapulted him into the theatrical business.

One of the first times I ever talked with him was in 1951 with the Cubs, when

Chuck Connors, a strong-armed first baseman for the Los Angeles Angels, went on to a television acting career in the late '50s and '60s. Connors was one of the few players to hit the ball over the back right-field wall at Seals Stadium in San Francisco.

I got on first base. We were teammates in Los Angeles the next year. He was a real nice person, and a good team player. I remember seeing him hit a home run at Seals Stadium over the back right-field wall. He could really hit.

BOB USHER - Los Angeles Angels

I got to know Chuck Connors when we were in St. Paul, Minnesota. The players used to laugh at him because when we were on the road, he was always in front of the mirror, practicing his facial expressions and the like. But I found him a very interesting guy, and we were friends. He could hit the ball, but was a little clumsy around first base.

When we would come into Hollywood after he retired, he'd be at the ballpark, doing some announcing, and he always wanted to take his licks in the batting cage. I remember letting him take my turn once.

EDDIE BASINSKI - Portland Beavers

LES COOK

*L*es Cook was the longtime trainer and equipment man for the San Diego Padres. He had a checkered career as a backup catcher, breaking in with the 1917 Vernon Tigers and concluding with seven games for the 1936 Padres. As the team's trainer, he tended to the needs of hundreds of players. He died in 1968, at the age of seventy-three.

Les Cook was good to me. I knew him at [San Diego State University]. He taught a class on baseball there. He encouraged me a lot, going out of his way to speak with me and helping me to not react to anything negative. He was a good friend.

JOHNNY RITCHEY - San Diego Padres

Outfielder Rocky Colavito had one of the most powerful arms in the game, and could hit home plate on the fly from center field. He played only part of a season in the PCL, with the San Diego Padres in 1956, but still drew fans to pregame workouts.

Les Cook was there for years. A guy from the opposing team would get hurt and Cookie would yell, 'Drag him off! Drag him off!'

Swede Jensen, Al Olsen and I used to agitate Cookie, drive him nuts. I remember one time we were coming back from Portland and we had a stopover in Davis (California) to change trains. The Sacramento team also arrived to catch the same train to come down and play us.

We had to take a bus, and there was some problem, and the Solons got our bus. On the train coming back from Portland, we'd had a poker game, and I guess Cookie lost about thirty dollars, which was big in those times.

We rode him, 'Are you going to stand around here worrying about those thirty dollars while we're supposed to be getting a bus?' He got all flustered while we were breaking up at him. Poor Cookie.

When I was with Hollywood, they used to have those games with the movie stars, and one actor came in wanting a pair of sweat socks. Cookie wasn't paying much attention, so he went up and slapped Cook in the face. I thought Cook was going to kill him.

GEORGE McDONALD - San Diego Padres

THE COSCARART BROTHERS

*T*he Pacific Coast League was blessed with many brother combinations throughout its history. However, it was unusual to find three or more siblings playing in the league at the same time. The DiMaggios, Hafeys and Raimondis, featured in NUGGETS ON THE DIAMOND, were among the league's most distinguished brother combinations. But the Coscarart brothers, from Southern California, were among those rare PCL brother trios. They also had equally distinguished careers in the Pacific Northwest.

WE WERE BORN IN ESCONDIDO. JOE WAS THE OLDEST BROTHER AND STEVE WAS NEXT. STEVE AND I USED TO FOLLOW JOE ALL THE TIME. WE USED TO HAVE TOWN TEAMS THAT PLAYED ON SUNDAYS. THAT'S ABOUT ALL THERE WAS TO DO AROUND HERE. I PLAYED SECOND, STEVE PLAYED THIRD AND JOE PLAYED SHORT. BABE DAHLGREN WAS OUR FIRST BASEMAN. THAT WAS A PRETTY FAIR COUNTRY INFIELD.

JOE SIGNED WITH THE SAN FRANCISCO MISSIONS ORIGINALLY. WE WERE ALL PLAYING IN OCEANSIDE, AND THE MANAGER OF OCEANSIDE KNEW [SEATTLE RAINIERS MANAGER] RED KILLEFER AND SUGGESTED HE COME OVER AND TAKE A LOOK AT JOE. KILLEFER LIKED JOE, SO HE SIGNED HIM. WHEN JOE WAS WITH SEATTLE, THEY ASKED HIM IF HE HAD ANY BROTHERS WHO COULD PLAY. HE SAID HE DID, AND THEY BROUGHT US UP TO WORK OUT WITH THEM. WE ALSO WORKED OUT WITH PORTLAND.

PORTLAND WANTED TO SIGN US RIGHT AWAY, AS SOON AS THEY SAW US. I DON'T THINK SEATTLE OFFERED A CONTRACT STEVE AND I SIGNED TOGETHER

WITH PORTLAND. THE WAY IT HAPPENED, HE WENT TO PLAY BALL AT SIOUX CITY, A SEMIPRO TEAM. SO I WENT RIGHT INTO PRO BALL AND WAS IN THE BIG LEAGUES IN THREE YEARS.

WE GOT $150 A MONTH, NO BONUS. I CAN REMEMBER GETTING A CHECK EVERY TWO WEEKS, AND I COULDN'T BELIEVE IT — FOR PLAYING BALL! IT WAS THE DEPRESSION, AND WE WANTED A JOB.

OUR FIRST GAME WAS IN SEATTLE AT CIVIC STADIUM, AND JOE WAS IN THE LINEUP FOR SEATTLE. THAT WAS A THRILL FOR US. CIVIC STADIUM WAS JUST AN OPEN FIELD WITH A FEW SEATS. THERE WAS NOTHING IN THE OUTFIELD. NO GRASS.

STEVE WAS THE BEST HITTER. I THINK HE WOULD HAVE BEEN IN THE BIG LEAGUES IF HE HADN'T GOTTEN HIT IN THE HEAD. AFTER THAT HE NEVER WAS THE SAME. I THINK THAT WAS AROUND '36. DON OSBORN, THE RIGHT-HANDER FROM SEATTLE, WAS THE PITCHER WHO HIT HIM.

STEVE AND I BOTH PLAYED A LOT OF SECOND BASE. IN 1934 WITH PORTLAND, STEVE PLAYED SECOND BASE AND I WAS THE BACKUP INFIELDER. WHEN I PLAYED, THEY PUT ME AT SECOND AND MOVED STEVE TO SHORTSTOP OR THIRD. I DIDN'T PLAY MUCH, ONLY ABOUT SIXTY GAMES.

PETE COSCARART - Portland Beavers

I WAS THE MIDDLE OF THE THREE BOYS. JOE WAS A COUPLE OF YEARS OLDER AND PETE WAS TWO YEARS YOUNGER. I PLAYED BASEBALL ALL THE TIME AROUND ESCONDIDO AND RANCHO BERNARDO. WE ACTUALLY HAD A TOWN TEAM WITH THE THREE OF US IN THE INFIELD. WE HAD A PRETTY GOOD BALL CLUB. I ALSO PLAYED BALL IN HIGH SCHOOL. I PLAYED WITH BOTH MY BROTHERS. JOE SIGNED WITH THE SAN

Francisco Missions. After high school I went to San Francisco and stayed with a cousin. I was also playing in a semipro league there.

The Missions had a trainer, Red Adams, who was a very nice guy. This was before Little League, and he took care of the kids in the area. He'd furnish them with shoes and gloves and the like. He spent all his money on the kids.

The manager of a semipro team in Sioux City knew Adams and asked him to furnish some players for his summer team. So he picked me and Joe Chamberlain, a pitcher. He had a tryout with the White Sox, so we played for the Sioux City Stockyards, and barnstormed all over the country. Everybody had played professional ball except me. I was the rookie.

I had a real good year. The secretary of the Sioux City club knew Walter McCredie of the Portland club. McCredie had just been made manager (again), for the 1934 season, and I got a letter from him. So I went to Portland, worked out and signed.

The next spring, I went to spring training, and was having a good spring training because I had worked all winter to be in shape. I knew the older guys wouldn't be in shape so I showed to a better advantage.

They used to throw at me quite a bit. That's before they had helmets. I got hit in the head in 1936. I almost got killed. It affected me the rest of my career. I used to be able to hit that curve ball to right field, but it affected my left eye, so I couldn't hit that pitch as well. I think that had a lot to do with it.

It didn't hurt me in life, but it did hurt me playing ball. It was hard to hit that outside ball and, of course, they keep it out there anyway. I hit .311 in my first year, and they predicted I would lead the league in hitting if I went to the outfield. That's part of the reason that I did.

Pete and I were pretty quick. We could run better than Joe. After [center fielder Nino] Bongiovanni left, they moved me to center field. One season I didn't make a single error.

I used to be able to hit the good pitchers better than the poor ones. I don't know why. Willie Ludolph was real tough on me. I beat him once in Oakland, hit a ball off the wall. But that was about the only time I did anything against him. I could hit guys like George Caster better than I could those soft-tossers.

Kewpie Barrett was tough. He'd throw at you, too — he'd throw behind your ear. He was a rolypoly guy. Jack Salveson was tough also. Ray Prim was duck soup, a left-hander. I used to have a picnic off of him.

STEVE COSCARART - Portland Beavers

LORENZO "PIPER" DAVIS

Piper Davis was a heck of a nice guy to start with, and a heck of a good ballplayer. A pitcher could make him look so bad, but then he'd come back with the same pitch and Piper would hit it out of sight! He was a good example for our young ballplayers, black or white.

LEN NEAL - Oakland Oaks

Piper was a great example for the younger blacks on the Oaks. I remember one time he had pulled Dave Mann aside in the clubhouse, and he was roughing him up for something he had done that was unacceptable. Whites and blacks all looked up to him.

DON FERRARESE - Oakland Oaks

JOE DiMAGGIO

I broke in with Oakland in 1932, the same year as DiMaggio. Only he hit .340 and I hit .280. He was a great thrower, but he was wild. But he was just a kid, just 17 then. He's the best ballplayer I ever saw, and he wasn't even voted into the Hall of Fame his first year. He could run and he could throw, and he bore down. Joe did everything everybody else did. He just did it better.

BILLY RAIMONDI - Oakland Oaks

When Joe DiMaggio joined the Seals he was just a kid, but you knew he was something special. The uniform was baggy on him, and when they put him at shortstop it was a scarry sight. He had no accuracy in his throws. But with his bat and his running speed, you knew they had to find a place for him in the lineup.

When they put him in right field you knew he was a star. He was so graceful and effortless when he went after a deep fly ball.

JOHNNY BABICH - Mission Reds

BOB DiPIETRO

B ob DiPietro was a great guy to have on a ball club. He was so spontaneous about everything. The imitation he gave of a player trying to hit off of Ewell Blackwell of Seattle — you would die laughing.

BUD WATKINS - Sacramento Solons

When I first went to spring training in 1954, I didn't know who DiPietro was. And he's pulling all this crap, and Tommy Heath is falling on the ground from laughter. He really kept us loose during the season.

When Bob and I were both at Portland, the fans would treat us right, and we'd have dinners on Sunday nights. So we'd go to this restaurant and Bob would put on a show. He'd have everybody rolling on the floor. His wife would just be sitting there: 'I've heard it a thousand times before.'

JIM WESTLAKE - San Francisco Seals and Portland Beavers

DiPietro was a fourth or fifth outfielder — a little short on ability but a great guy to have on a ball club because he kept everyone loose. DiPietro busted his leg in San Francisco when he was leading the league in hitting.

BILL WERLE - San Francisco Seals

Even as he was breaking into the PCL, it was clear to newcomers and veterans that Joe DiMaggio was something special.

RYNE DUREN

When Fred Hutchinson was here in 1955, Ryne Duren was on our ball club. Hutch told him to throw the first pitch high up on the screen. The batters wondered, 'Who the hell is this guy, with his big Coke glasses?' But he could throw that ball 100 miles-per-hour. You stood loose when he came into pitch.

EDO VANNI - Seattle Rainiers

I had to face Ryne Duren. He was with Vancouver. The lights weren't too good. When he threw a fastball, you couldn't see the ball. But it balanced out because he couldn't see you either. When he threw a change-up, all the batters' eyes lit up. He was the toughest for me. (And for many others.)

JIM BAXES - Hollywood Stars, Spokane Indians

Ryne Duren was so wild he knocked Gene Baker down in the on-deck circle in Seattle.

BOB TALBOT - Los Angeles Angels

LUKE EASTER

Easter was a showboat, a good-hearted guy. He was the type of player that people wanted to see. Johnny [Ritchey] was much more reserved. Johnny and Luke were asked out to dinner once at a prominent family's home, and after dinner Luke got up and asked, 'How much do I owe you for dinner?' Johnny just kind of melted under the table.

But he didn't know he was doing anything wrong. Just a different upbringing. Luke was a

Bob DiPietro, with the San Diego Padres in 1957.

Luke Easter, who joined the San Diego Padres in 1949, drew fans to the park with his mammoth home runs. He drove in ninety-two runs while batting .363 in half a season before being recalled by the Cleveland Indians.

good player and knew how to bring attention to himself, but he didn't know any better about social things. He brought the fans out, that's for sure.

LYDIA RITCHEY - Wife of Johnny Ritchey

When Luke Easter was with us, he was a delightful fella. I went down to an old timers' game when he was still alive, and I'm not a little guy, but all the sudden, I'm two feet off the ground from someone behind. There was only one guy who could do that and that was Luke.

I used to like to pitch batting practice every once in a while, but I didn't like to throw to him because if he hit one back through the box, I'm dead meat.

When he was with us, he was hurting quite a bit, but he still carried the club. And he was a real fan favorite.

JOHN "SWEDE" JENSEN - San Diego Padres

In 1949, Luke Easter of the Padres was in Oakland, and he was killing us, just killing us! Earl Harrist asked me, 'How are we going to pitch to him?'

I say, 'We're going to throw at him. We're not going to try to hit him. We're going to throw the ball in the dirt near his feet.' He had the worst pair of feet in the whole world — corns all over his feet.

He got a couple of good swings against us and I say, 'Hey, Luke, we're going to have to knock you down, brush you back. You're hitting too good.' He says, 'That's OK.'

I said, 'No, we're going to throw at your feet.' 'Oh, my god. Don't throw at my feet! Hit me anywhere, but don't throw at my feet!'

When Harrist was pitching, we had Luke 3-2, and I didn't know what was about to happen. I threw the ball back to Earl and he got on the mound, came to the stretch and quick-pitched. It surprised the hell out of all of us, but the umpire called it a strike and Luke was out.

Luke immediately started saying, 'That's cheating. I want one more swing. I want one more swing.'

After the inning was over, I said to Earl, 'You ought to tip me off to that.' He says, 'If I tip you off, he'll know too.'

FRANK KERR - Oakland Oaks

Luke Easter hit the longest ball I ever saw. It was up in Hollywood. The center-field fence was 400 feet out with a twenty-foot fence and a flagpole another twenty to twenty-five feet above, and it went over the flagpole. Even Lefty O'Doul said, 'That's one of the longest balls I've ever seen.'

He had real bad knees. That was his downfall.

EDDIE ERAUTT - San Diego Padres

I was with the Padres along with Luke Easter. We had one of the best-hitting minor league teams ever. Al Rosen was on that team. We had a bunch of cleanup batters. Buster Adams was hitting leadoff, and he had twenty-one home runs. We had [Max] West and [Orestes] Minoso.

I always felt sorry for Easter because that guy was a lot older than his stated age. When he went up, he was supposed to be twenty-seven or something, but he was probably thirty-five, or maybe older. You knew it if you were around him. So here he is, a thirty-five-year-old rookie going up to Cleveland when he should have been at the tail end of his career.

I would have liked to see that guy play ten years earlier. I knew Satchel Paige in Miami, and he used to say, 'They talk about my age. That Luke Easter, he's as old as I am. I played against him forty years ago.' Luke might have been in his forties by then. He was a big old guy, a nice guy, a gentle man.

CHARLES "RED" ADAMS - San Diego Padres

When I was with Portland, Cliff Chambers and I had a fight. [Don] Eggert hit a home run right before me, and Chambers drilled me right in the ribs. I took my glasses off and went right out after him. We're going at it.

Now Luke Easter's playing first base. He comes over and puts his arms around me and lifts me off the ground, trying to cool the situation down. I'm so mad. Of course I can't do anything. I spiked him up and down both of his ankles.

They had to delay the game fifteen or twenty minutes while he gets his ankles repaired. He comes back out, and I'm standing on first base — they didn't throw any of us out of the game. He says, 'I'm never going to stop a fight again. If anyone starts a fight, I'm going to say go at it. I'm not stopping it.' I say, 'Thanks, Luke.' But what a monster he was.

DINO RESTELLI - Portland Beavers

OSCAR ECKHARDT

Oscar Eckhardt was the fastest man I ever saw getting to first base. I've seen a lot of 'em who could run to first base, but none were like Oscar. Two hops in the infield and he was across first base. But once he got to first base, you might as well take him out of there. He was through, he was 'Dumb Old Ox.'

But when they played him to hit, you wouldn't believe the way they played him. The third baseman was playing on the bag. Standing [two feet] from the bag, he'd still hit a line drive by him. He hit everything to left field. The left fielder played on the line, the center fielder played in left field, and the right fielder played in left-center. [He] never hit the ball to right field. He never could pull the ball. He had a crazy stance, with his foot halfway to first base. God, he was a good hitter, though.

I've seen him try to catch a ball bare-handed in the outfield. He couldn't get his glove over, so he'd catch them bare-handed.

JOHNNY BABICH - Mission Reds

Eckhardt had arms the size of tree trunks, and he hit everything in the hole to left-center. He got mad at me one time because I was playing him in the hole — right in the gap in short left-center. That's where he would hit the ball! It frustrated him. He came up to me once and asked, 'How come you're playing me over there?'

'I'm playing you there because that's where you're hitting the ball!'

NINO BONGIOVANNI - Seattle Indians, Portland Beavers

It used to be worth the price of admission just to watch Tom Flynn pitch to Oscar Eckhardt. Eckhardt was a left-handed hitter and Flynn was a left-handed pitcher. Eckhardt would try to drag, try to push, do anything to get away from the plate. It seemed he was two or three feet out of the box when he tapped the ball. I used to see him throw the bat at the ball.

PAUL GREGORY - Sacramento Solons

EDDIE ERAUTT

I was a fastball pitcher with a curve and a change-up, but I had good control. I'd challenge batters, my power against their power. My fastball didn't move too much. If I could pitch again, I'd change my grip.

My brother Joe was really helpful to me. He was a catcher and three years older than me. We played every day and night, broke every window in the house. I had a mound made outside.

He helped me to learn new pitches, and if I didn't get the ball over he'd fire it back and holler at me. Other than Joe and my dad, I didn't have any real coaching.

The Padres were playing in Vancouver, and our manager, Bob Elliott, called me in and said they were sending me to San Antonio. I said, 'No. I'll quit first.' I just walked out.

Buddy Peterson was with Vancouver and he found out and talked to [Vancouver Mounties owner] Charlie Metro. Metro contacted me and said, 'We want you over here.' The next day I was sold to Vancouver.

I think I over-trained myself. That's why the arm went. [Coach Jimmie] Reese used to tell me that between starts I go down and play pepper with the bat boys and ball boys. I never went into the clubhouse, [I was] always running and throwing. At the end of the season, my arm was usually shot. I think I cut my career short.

EDDIE ERAUTT

Young Eddie Erautt and Hollywood Stars manager Charlie Root at Gilmore Field in 1943.

I enjoyed watching Eddie Erautt because he had an excellent curve. It was a downer. He threw it overhand. I was three-quarters. His curve had a tendency to drop. When I tried throwing it, it would hang and they'd hit it. I couldn't get the spin on it.

BOB KERRIGAN - San Diego Padres

FERRIS FAIN

I was in awe of guys like Tony Lazzeri and [Frank "Lefty"} O'Doul, but I didn't look at these men as heroes. In 1941, O'Doul was injured when he was hit in the eye by a shot glass. I was struggling, and Tony Lazzeri and Larry Woodall, our coach, sat me down on the train to Portland, Oregon, and talked to me about hitting.

Occasionally, I would hit the ball to left field, and they said to me, 'We don't care how you do it, but keep hitting that ball to left field.' Lazzeri used to choke up on the bat, so I used his bat and started choking up. Well, I started hitting the ball all over. I was doing real good.

When O'Doul got back, he wasn't impressed. His theory was this: We want to sell you to the major leagues, and when those scouts come around, they want to see hitters ripping the ball, pulling it, instead of spraying it around.

I loved Frank, but his philosophy of batting was pull, pull, pull. Now, I wasn't a wrist hitter. I hit with my forearms and shoulders. Everything I hit, he wanted me to roll those wrists and pull the ball.

But still, I think the greatest thing that happened to me was when I went into the service. Early in the service, I just couldn't get untracked. I've got Lefty's teaching and my own leanings in conflict. They elected me manager. Then we were sent to Hawaii, and there we ran up against a lot of major leaguers. With the pressure on, I started reverting to my eighth- and ninth-grade training, hitting the ball the other way. Move the ball around.

When I came back from the military, I came back hitting a ton. Frank couldn't believe it. He said, 'Just keep doing what you're doing.' Well, you've got to do what you've got to do, but if it took a thousand years, I couldn't hit as well as a power hitter.

FERRIS FAIN

Ferris Fain was cocky. Was he ever. If you did anything to him, when you came down to first base he'd getcha, one way or another. Or if he was sliding into somebody, he'd slide hard. As a kid he was hot-tempered, too.

JOHNNY BABICH - Oakland Oaks coach

Ferris Fain hit me pretty good until I found something out about him. I pitched on Thursday night, and Fain hit one out of the park against me. Before my next start, Lindsay Brown, our shortstop, said, 'Are you going to let that guy beat you again? Did you ever knock anybody down? Knock him down next time.'

On Sunday, when Fain came up, I knocked him down. The bat went in one direction, the cap in another. I looked at Lindsay, and he even smiled, and all I heard was Lefty O'Doul, 'He didn't throw at you. He's not wild. The ball got away from him. Get up and hit one out.' And darned if he didn't hit one out!

'Well, Lindsay, what do I do now? I give up.' If I threw my shoe up there, he'd hit it out. So

Ferris Fain signed with the San Francisco Seals out of Oakland and became one of baseball's finest first basemen. Helped the Seals win the pennant in 1946, leading the league in RBI and runs. He also was a two-time batting leader in the American League.

Known as "Grumpy Guy" because of his disposition on the mound, Guy Fletcher threw mostly for the Sacramento Solons and Seattle Rainiers over ten seasons. He was a twenty-game winner twice.

I thought, why shouldn't I throw up a lot of crap? So I did, and I got him on three pitches. The next time: three little curves and he struck out again. That's all he got from there on. He never saw another fastball.

AD LISKA - Portland Beavers

Ferris would fight a dozen alligators. On the field, you wanted him on your side. I remember when he was coaching for Tommy Heath, one of our players missed a hit-and-run sign and Fain was all over him. When the player got back to the dugout, Fain asked him, 'Didn't you see the hit-and-run sign?' The player started making excuses, and Fain said, 'I don't want to hear any BS excuse from you. You're out here to play and to win. Is it too much to ask that you look at the signs?' The player just shut up. Don't mess with 'Burrhead.'

BUD WATKINS - Sacramento Solons

GUY FLETCHER

Guy Fletcher was a cheater. He threw the spitter. He was an intense guy. He'd deck you, and he meant it. He had those thick glasses — you didn't know whether he was serious or not.

EDO VANNI - Seattle Rainiers

Guy Fletcher was a good competitor. Every time you went against him, you knew you were in for a battle. He was like Pinky Woods and Ray Prim. We used to watch guys like Prim or Fletcher to see what they do in situations. They were pitchers with a similar style.

BILL WERLE - San Francisco Seals

Lefty pitcher Tony Freitas won 226 games in his sixteen years in the PCL. Most of his wins were for the Sacramento Solons. He is generally acknowledged as the best left-handed pitcher in minor league history.

TONY FREITAS

I remember Tony Freitas well. He struck me out three or four times one night. That was the first year I had played, and I'd never seen a screwball. After that, I hit him pretty good. Once I figured what he would throw, I changed my stance a little and just waited for it. I had some good games against him. But he was a crafty one.

JOHN "SWEDE" JENSEN - San Diego Padres

Tony Freitas was my manager in Stockton when I played there. He was forty-four years old, and I think he won twenty-four games. On and off the diamond, he was one of the finest men I ever met in my life. As a manager, he was too easy. He wasn't a take-charge kind of guy. He'd give you 100 percent himself, but when he had to deal with older players — [Joe] Brovia, [Bob] Dillinger and some of those old-time big leaguers — they ran him. He couldn't run them.

I kept in touch with Tony over the years. I'd call him every so often, and would go out to dinner with him periodically. He was a great pitcher. He knew more about pitching than anybody I knew. When we were with the Solons, I asked for his advice when I was starting. What he said actually fit life more than base-ball.

One, keep your back to the wall and don't miss nothing. Have the most fun you can possibly have. Two, be nice to everybody on the way up because you're going to meet those same people on the way down.

BUD WATKINS - Sacramento Solons

ALLEN "TWO GUN" GETTEL

Allen Gettel was a good guy and he had this thing going. He wanted to be a western movie actor. Boy, he lived the part. We'd go down to Hollywood and L.A. and he'd get on a plane wearing his six-guns and cowboy hat and the works. Everybody got a big kick out of that.

Before we'd go south, Bob Murphy would get under his skin a bit. He'd ask Allen if he was going to wear his cowboy suit. Allen wanted it called 'western clothes.'

Allen was a good, clean liver who worked to stay in shape. When he was on the mound, you knew who was in command. If a batter tried to throw his rhythm off, he'd throw at you. I remember going into Portland and talking with Joe Rossi, the Beavers catcher. Joe felt 'that damn Gettel' is creasing somebody all the time.

LEN NEAL - Oakland Oaks

JACK GRAHAM

During the winter of 1947, the Giants acquired Jack Harshman from San Diego and sent them money and four players. I was one of the players.

I wasn't too disappointed to come west. I think I was making $6,000 at New York, and when I came to the Coast League they were playing 200 games, so that made it an extra month. I ended up getting $7,000, and that year, in '48, I was the MVP, so I got an extra $1,000. That winter they sold me to the St. Louis Browns.

I didn't get any part of the sales price. I think the Browns gave Bill Starr $20,000, with the understanding that if I didn't stay with the Browns, he could buy me back for $10,000. That's eventually what happened.

At that time there was only so much money to make. Probably, I was one of the lowest paid stars in the Coast League at $7,000. I believe I got $8,000 with the Browns, but I had to hold out all spring in 1950. I had a hunch they were going to send me back to San Diego, and if I had signed for what the Browns were offering me — $6,000, I believe — then I would have been stuck with that salary at San Diego, making less than what I had made the year before.

JACK GRAHAM

Pitcher Allen "Two Gun" Gettel had talent for baseball and ambitions for movie acting.

ON CHASING HOME-RUN RECORDS

It just seems that in '48 everything that I did seemed to turn into home runs. I think every player goes through a year, if he plays 10 years, where he can't do anything wrong. Before pitchers know you they check to see if you can hit the fastball. Then they start throwing curves and changing up. I hit the fastball pretty good.

But now it's July. I'd gotten hit twice in Frisco earlier, and hadn't moved. Rip Collins came to me and said, 'I think we should give you three or four days off. You look like you're awful tired.' I said, 'Well, no, I'd better not because I've got an outside shot to break [Tony] Lazzeri's record [of sixty home runs, established in 1925].' I had forty-six at the time.

I'd hit two that week at Los Angeles, both of them on change-ups. I just wasn't getting around on the ball. It was the second game of a Sunday double-header, and the shadows were coming in. And of course, Red Adams hit me that day. He was in the sun and I was in the shade, and when the ball went from the sun into the shade, I lost it.

He came to see me that night in the hospital. We never had any problems. Adams couldn't throw hard. I saw him at the PCL get-together two years ago, and I said to him, 'Boy, am I glad you couldn't throw very hard.'

Of course, in those days, things like that happened, and people and players just accepted those things. It was part of the game. Nowadays, you come close to somebody, if you hit them in the butt, they're down for ten minutes. Formerly, if you got hit, you would bounce back up to show them they didn't hurt you. You got up and went to first base.

I was out four or five weeks, then Earl Keller with the *San Diego Evening-Tribune* told me, 'The newswriters are going to vote for the Most Valuable Player, but they don't know what to do about you. If you get back in the lineup they're pretty sure they'll vote you the MVP in the league, and there's $1,000 that goes with it.'

I got back in the lineup, and I wasn't ready to play. I got hit on the ear and on the head, and the right eye wouldn't go to the right. I had to change my complete stance and face the pitcher so I could see with both eyes. I got back in and played five days, and I hit two more home runs, but I told Rip, 'I've got to get out of the lineup.' Every time I'd look up everything blurs because the fluid in my inner ear wouldn't follow.

The only guy who raised hell was Bill Starr. He called me and raised hell with me. 'Well, you're playing.' I said, 'I know I'm playing,' and I explained to him why I was playing — for the Most Valuable Player award. I played three days and they voted, and I was the Most Valuable Player. Then I got out of the lineup again.

I wasn't really gun shy from the beaning. In fact, I moved in closer to the plate. In those days you couldn't worry about being gun shy, because if you did you'd come home and have to end up driving a bus for the rest of your life. You knew that you had to get back in and play. You never considered quitting because you got hit.

JACK GRAHAM - San Diego Padres

I was the next hitter when Jack Graham got hit in the head up in Los Angeles. I felt very sorry for Jack. I was there in the batting circle hitting behind him when he got hit by Red Adams. It was very hard to see that day.

I could tell immediately that Jack was hurt. That was no glancing blow. The ball hit him square in the temple and just dropped at his feet. I've been hit in the head before by a ball, but it was a glancing blow. That ball hit him just as square as could be and he dropped straight down. I initially worried that it might be worse than it was.

I don't think he saw the ball hardly at all. The shadows were bad, and he just didn't move much. It was a sickening thud. Everything quieted down. It was quite a while before they moved him. And he was taken off on a stretcher right to the hospital.

I don't remember who won the ball game, but I believe Red Adams stayed in. That was the second

GAME OF A SUNDAY DOUBLE-HEADER. WE RETURNED TO SAN DIEGO, AND IT WAS A QUIET RIDE BACK. I KNOW HE PLAYED A YEAR OR TWO AFTER THAT, BUT HE WASN'T THE SAME JACK THAT HE WAS BEFORE.

JOHN "SWEDE" JENSEN - San Diego Padres

JACK GRAHAM'S BEANING IN L.A. WAS TRAGIC. WE WERE PLAYING A DOUBLE-HEADER AT WRIGLEY FIELD. IN THE SECOND GAME, IT WAS DUSK AND YOU COULDN'T REALLY SEE THE BALL WELL.

I REMEMBER THE SOUND OF THE BALL HITTING HIM, WITH JUST A CAP ON, BOUNCING BACK TOWARDS THE MOUND. HE NEVER SAW THE BALL, AND HE WENT DOWN LIKE A LOG. HE TRIED TO GET UP, BUT THEY GOT HIM BACK DOWN. HE DID RETURN NEAR THE END OF HIS SEASON, BUT HIS SHOT AT THE HOME-RUN RECORD WAS LOST.

BOB KERRIGAN - San Diego Padres

IT WAS IN THE SECOND GAME OF A SUNDAY DOUBLE-HEADER AT WRIGLEY FIELD, AND THE SHADOWS WERE HALFWAY BETWEEN HOME PLATE AND THE MOUND, WHICH MADE IT VERY DIFFICULT FOR A HITTER TO SEE. IN FACT, AS PITCHERS WE LOVED TO PITCH THAT GAME. YOU COULD PITCH AN ENTIRELY DIFFERENT BALL GAME. IF YOUR STUFF WAS PRETTY GOOD, YOU COULD CHALLENGE THE HITTER A LITTLE BIT MORE.

I HAD PITCHED ONE GAME PRIOR TO THAT AGAINST SAN DIEGO THAT YEAR, AND JACK HADN'T GOTTEN ANY HITS OFF OF ME, AND HE HADN'T GOTTEN ANY HITS OFF OF ME THAT DAY. I THINK IT WAS THE THIRD INNING, AND HE HAD BEEN UP MAYBE ONCE.

I USED TO PITCH HIM TIGHT. HE CROWDED THE PLATE AND HE PULLED EVERYTHING, SO IN BALLPARKS LIKE

Max West, left, and Jack Graham supplied much of the San Diego Padres' batting power in the late 1940s and early '50s.

WRIGLEY FIELD AND LANE FIELD, A LEFT-HANDED BATTER COULD GET THE BALL UP INTO THE AIR AND GET IT OUT OF THERE PRETTY EASILY.

JACK WAS DEFINITELY A LOW-BALL HITTER. HE HAD THAT UPPERCUT THAT HELPED LOFT THAT BALL. SO I HAD PITCHED HIM UP AND IN. I HAD GOTTEN HIM OUT EARLY IN THE COUNT, USUALLY POPPING HIM UP.

THAT PARTICULAR TIME HE CAME UP AND THE SHADOWS HAD COME OUT AND IT WAS A DIFFICULT TIME TO SEE. LOOKING BACK ON IT, I FELT JACK WAS EVEN MORE CROUCHED TO GET A BETTER SIGHT OF THE PITCH. I CAN REMEMBER THINKING ABOUT STAYING UP AND IN UNTIL IT

PROVES NOT TO BE WORKING.

ONCE IN A WHILE YOU THROW A BALL THAT WILL SAIL. WHEN MY ARM WAS FAIRLY ALIVE, THE BALL WOULD TAKE OFF, ACTUALLY SAIL LIKE A SUPER-SLIDER, SAILING UP AND AWAY. AND THAT BALL DID THAT. IT JUST SAILED RIGHT INTO HIM.

I THINK IT WAS A COMBINATION OF GETTING THE BALL IN A LITTLE FURTHER THAN I WANTED IT TO, AND THE BALL SAILING A BIT, AND BEING DIFFICULT TO SEE. HE DIDN'T PICK IT UP.

I CAN'T REMEMBER THAT I FINISHED THE GAME, BUT KNOWING MY PERSONALITY, HITTING GRAHAM NO DOUBT BOTHERED ME. BUT AS FAR AS HAVING TO GO ON AND PITCH, THAT WAS SOMETHING I HAD TO DO. YOU NEVER FEEL GOOD ABOUT HITTING SOMEONE, BUT I FELT THE GUYS ON THEIR CLUB KNEW IT WAS NOT INTENTIONAL. NOBODY SAID ANYTHING FROM THEIR DUGOUT TO INDICATE THEY FELT IT WAS ANYTHING BUT UNINTENTIONAL.

I WENT DOWN TO THE HOSPITAL TO SEE HIM THAT NIGHT. I DIDN'T KNOW HIM AT ALL, AND I DIDN'T KNOW WHAT TO EXPECT. HE WAS REAL NICE ABOUT IT. HE SAID, 'I NEVER SAW THE BALL AT ALL.' HE SAID HE HAD GOTTEN HIT ON THE CHEEK ONE TIME IN THE INTERNATIONAL LEAGUE, AND HE SAID, 'I DIDN'T PICK THE BALL UP, RED. AND EVEN IF I HAD PICKED IT UP, I MAY NOT HAVE GOTTEN OUT OF THE WAY OF IT.'

HE ALSO SAID, 'I KNOW YOU WEREN'T THROWING AT ME BECAUSE I HADN'T HAD A HIT OFF OF YOU.' IF HE HAD BEEN ABLE TO SEE THE BALL HE WOULDN'T HAVE HAD A HARD TIME GETTING OUT OF THE WAY OF IT, BECAUSE I WASN'T A REAL HARD THROWER. IT WAS JUST ONE OF THOSE UNFORTUNATE THINGS, AND I FELT AS BAD ABOUT IT AS HE DID. IT WAS A SHAME NOT ONLY TO HURT THE GUY ... BUT WITH THE YEAR HE WAS HAVING IT WOULD HAVE BEEN INTERESTING TO SEE HOW MANY HOME RUNS HE WOULD HAVE HIT. I REALLY FELT TERRIBLE ABOUT THAT.

CHARLES "RED" ADAMS - Los Angeles Angels

JIM "MUDCAT" GRANT

I think Jim 'Mudcat' Grant was the best pitcher I faced in the Coast League. He threw hard and had a good curve ball. He did throw a pretty good change-up, too. He went up to the major leagues and had a good career there.

JIM BAXES - Portland Beavers

AL HEIST

Al Heist was the greatest center fielder I ever saw. Playing shortstop, you see how outfielders get jumps on the ball. By the time I would turn to watch the ball, Heist was well in motion. He was the best. When he threw, it never handcuffed you. He always gave you a good bounce. He had great accuracy and great instincts in the outfield.

He wasn't a great hitter — that was his weakness. But he got better in the big leagues. Now he'd be the fourth outfielder. He'd go in the seventh inning. I know guys who rank him with Willie Mays. He was a natural.

BUDDY PETERSON - Sacramento Solons

ROY HELSER

Roy was one of our lefties, and he was full of the dickens. He was a hard worker, so serious when he got in the ball game. For a guy who was free and easy and loose when he wasn't pitching, kidding and laughing on the bench, he was the most serious pitcher I've ever seen. Very intense.

Roy pitched his own ball game no matter who was catching, and we had a couple pretty decent catchers. Charlie Silvera was a smart catcher. He always knew how to catch the sinker ball.

But Helser pitched his own game. The few times I talked with him he helped me understand the psychology behind setting up a batter, helping to develop my style.

DUANE PILLETTE - Portland Beavers

We had a good team in '45. I won twenty and a playoff game and Roy Helser won twenty. Helser was a great competitor. On Easter, Roy pitched a great game against Oakland, winning 4-3, driving in all the runs.

Well, I pitched the second game. I had held out and was out of shape, but Marv Owen asked me to go as far as I could. So I went out and pitched a 'no-no' (no-hitter).

Roy gave me what-for the next morning: 'I hear the paper boy hit the screen with the paper, and I jump up to read about Roy Helser, and all I see is a picture of Ad Liska and the whole damn write-up of the no-hitter. And at the end it says, "Roy Helser won the first game." '

AD LISKA - Portland Beavers

Roy Helser was probably one of the greatest athletes the Northwest has ever produced. And I'm talking baseball, basketball and football. He was a Little All American as a running back in football at Linfield College.

A bright guy, but Helser had a terrible temper, as great as he was, and basically that was his undoing. If he could have settled down like Jack Salveson, he would have been great. Still, he had three twenty-game seasons in a row (1944-46). And he was one of the best hitters I've seen.

He was great in the clubhouse — easygoing. I remember [Jim] Turner had this belief about pitching — that pitchers who were going to pitch the next day should leave their wives alone. This is kind of an insult, but he went to Helser and handed him a new ball and said, 'You're our man tomorrow, Roy, and I want you to leave the little woman alone.'

Roy didn't say anything. And, of course, Roy was a battler and a pretty stocky guy. That was a helluva insult to him. Anyway, the next day Roy went out and pitched a 2-0 shutout. Turner came up to him after the game and congratulated him, repeating his charge, adding, 'You've got to listen to me. I've been through this.'

So he walked away, and I went over to Roy and asked, 'Did you let that guy interfere with your personal business?' He said, 'Oh, to hell with him. I went a couple of times extra just because of it.'

EDDIE BASINSKI - Portland Beavers

FLOYD "BABE" HERMAN

Babe Herman was an old-style baseball player. A soft nature to him, but plenty tough. He was a grizzled type of player. You knew if you stood up to him, he wasn't going to back down. He had forgotten more about baseball that I would ever know.

GEORGE GRANT - Hollywood Stars Bat Boy

Babe Herman and Billy Cissell — they were over thirty-five. Babe could hit and field, but he couldn't run too well. I remember a game at Seals Stadium. We were behind 2-1 and he pinch hit for me and hit one right over center field.

He wasn't too bad as a fielder. He couldn't move too good, but he got everything he could get to. He was a turkey farmer, and the guys would buy turkeys from him. They paid more than they would have in a store!

RUGGER ARDIZOIA - Hollywood Stars

BROOKS HOLDER

Brooks Holder took a real interest in me, something he really didn't have to do. His job on that team was to be the best hitter, best fielder, the best player he could be, sign autographs and all that stuff, and yet he went much further that that. He took an exceptional interest in me at a time when I had my own teenage problems.

I'd make a comment to somebody, and he'd look over at me — never say a word. Then a few moments later, he'd come over to me and say, 'Let's play catch, George.' We'd go out to center field and play long-catch. At that point, he'd quietly tell me, 'Hey, George, that's the kind of stuff you just don't do,' talking to me like a Dutch uncle. He was one of those few people who have made a real difference to me.

GEORGE GRANT - Hollywood Stars Bat Boy

FRED HUTCHINSON

Hutch was a great athlete. People don't know that. If he hadn't made it as a pitcher, he could have made it as a catcher. He was a good hitter, and he caught in high school and Legion ball. When he went into his senior year in high school he was strictly a pitcher. He couldn't run worth a damn, but he was a good catcher. I used to tell him, 'You clog up the baselines, Fred.'

What I liked about Fred was that if some pitcher knocked me on my ass, he'd come up to me and say, 'I'll get that S.O.B., don't worry.' That's the way the ball game should have been played.

EDO VANNI - Seattle Rainiers

LARRY JANSEN

My American Legion coach in Oregon was helpful to me, and with the Seals the best help came from Larry Woodall during my first season with them. The first time around the league I did pretty well. Then, when we started around again, the hitters all waited for me. Woodall said to me, 'Young man, you're going to have to come up with another pitch of some kind. Let's try this slider.'

I messed with it on the sidelines for six weeks before I decided to try it in a game. That was the difference between my being a pitcher and a has-been. I had adequate speed and good control, but the slider became my 'out' pitch.

Joe Sprinz, Bruce Ogrodowski and Woodall were all older catchers, and they knew the hitters, and they all helped me a lot.

The Seals gave me a $1,500 or $2,000 bonus at the end of the season. With [owner Horace]

Fan favorite Brooks Holder built an excellent seventeen-year PCL career without much fanfare. He broke in with the San Francisco Seals in 1935 and was a regular in the infield and outfield for eight years before being traded to the Hollywood Stars for Frenchy Uhalt. In 1946 Holder purchased his release and signed for a bonus with Oakland, where he was a member of the Oaks' championship "Nine Old Men."

Stoneham, they didn't want to pay me. I think I wanted something like $17,000 and they were going to give me $9,000. So I finally said, 'How about a bonus at the end of the season if I prove I could win?'

So after I win twenty-one, I went up and asked for my bonus. They kept their word to me. Nothing was in the contract.

LARRY JANSEN

JACKIE JENSEN

Jackie Jensen, the Golden Boy, joined us from Cal in 1949. He had a lot of talent, but was always off by himself. He was too good for the rest of us — college hot dog. But he could hit and he could run and throw.

But Jackie didn't know how to play baseball. His talent got him there. Of course, Charlie Dressen had to handle him with kid gloves. But he tried to teach him. He didn't know where to throw the ball or anything else. But he was a fast learner, and he learned and became a good ballplayer.

FRANK KERR - Oakland Oaks

Hall of Famer George L. Kelly, right, welcomed Jackie Jensen after he signed a bonus contract with the Oakland Oaks. This photo was taken at Seals Stadium in 1949.

In 1949, we had just finished a series at Hollywood that we won 4-3, so we're in a pretty good mood as we head home. We're out at the airport, and we get on the plane and taxi out to the runway. Jackie didn't like to fly, and he's nervous anyhow. He's sitting next to me and Artie [Wilson] is right behind us. Jack says, 'I really don't like this. You know I'm a nervous person.' I say, 'Jack, there's nothing to worry about.'

We start to take off, moving down the runway, and all of a sudden the plane stops. A motor gives out, and the pilot comes on the P.A. and says, 'Folks, we've had a little problem.'

I thought Jack and Artie were going to come right out of their seats. They were scared to death. We went back to the gate and they corrected it. We went back out and took off, and Jack said, 'That's it.' I don't know if he flew very often after that.

BILL LAWS - Oaks Radio Broadcaster

JOHN "SWEDE" JENSEN

I made the ball club out of spring training in 1939. In my first year, [Dom] Dallesandro and I alternated in left field against left- and right-handed pitchers. He hit against right-handers, and I hit against left-handers. I think that helped send him to the big leagues the next year. He had a great season.

It was a big adjustment for me. I had never seen pitching like that before. But by 1940, I settled in pretty good. For a

Slugger Smead Jolley.

couple of years I played in left, [Hal] Patchett was in center, and Eddie Stewart was in right field.

The first two weeks of the 1939 season, I think we played at home, and the first road trip, there were some of us that they left at home. They went to L.A. and maybe Frisco. I had played maybe four or five games in that two-week period, against left-handers. We went to the ballpark every day when they were away. The four or five of us took batting practice and everything when they were gone.

After our practice one day, I went in to [general manager] Major Lott and told him that if I wasn't going to go with the team I wanted to be sent somewhere. I wanted to play. So when they put up the list for the next road trip from there on I always went with the team. I may only play one or two games a week, but I did go and I did get to play.

JOHN "SWEDE" JENSEN

CHET JOHNSON

Before Chet Johnson got to the ballpark and after he left the ballpark, he was just an average guy, somebody's dad, an ordinary person. But put a uniform on him and he would go stark-raving crazy.

Tommy Heath liked to pitch Chet in Hollywood and Los Angeles because he often got TV exposure there. One game he started in Los Angeles, Chet promptly walked the bases loaded in the first inning. And here comes Steve Bilko — six-foot-five, 250 pounds, hit the ball out of sight. So Chet calls time out and calls Harry Bright over from third base.

Harry says, 'What do you want?' Chet says, 'Hold out your glove.' Harry does, and Chet drops the ball in Harry's glove and starts running out to center field says, 'You pitch to him.' Harry's standing on the mound with the ball in his glove. He doesn't know what to do with it.

Vinnie Smith was our coach during the Joe Gordon era (1951-52). Chet was having a tough time in another game in L.A. and Gordon sends Vinnie out to get him. So Vinnie goes out to the mound. About the time Vinnie gets to the mound, Chet starts retreating toward second base. Vinnie is following him, demanding, 'Give me the ball, Chester.' Now they're moving towards shortstop, and Vinnie's chasing him, trying to get the ball.

Finally, Vinnie traps him out behind second base, and Chet goes down on bended knees. He reaches into his back pocket, and he's got a big bandana, it must have been four feet by four feet. It's the biggest thing I've ever seen.

And he's pulling this thing out of his back pocket. Now he's crying, pleading for Vinnie not to take him out of the game. And Vinnie's cussing, 'Give me the ball! Give me the ball!' So finally he gave him the ball. And the people went nuts.

BUD WATKINS - Sacramento Solons

Now we had Chesty Johnson. He hit a home run at Wrigley Field and he kissed each base, hugged the first baseman, the second baseman, and so forth. It took him about five minutes to go around the bases. That was quite a sight. We went along with that. We put up with his little book and his antics.

CECE CARLUCCI - Umpire

(Johnson's Little Black Book stunt: When a player came to bat, Johnson also would thumb through a little black book, as if it contained information about how to pitch to the batter.)

One of the really funny guys in the league was Chet Johnson. I was with him with the Seals, and played against him for a few years. He really had pretty good stuff, but he always screwed up the games because he'd have to do something funny. When you're playing behind him, you're waiting for him to do something, and you're thinking that he's probably going to blow the game, and it happened numerous times. The players never said much to him, because they knew he was going to do something.

JACK GRAHAM - San Diego Padres

SMEAD JOLLEY

*S*mead Jolley was one of the finest minor league hitters of all time. He could hit for average while powering the ball. In 1928, "Ol Smead" hit .404 for the San Francisco Seals, having batted .397 the previous season. His lifetime PCL batting percentage was .372. If only he had fielded half as well as he hit ...

I became friendly with Smead Jolley and played with him later in my career. He was such a good guy. As teammates, he wouldn't play catch with anyone but me. He was a good-natured fella.

Late in his career, he didn't play too much, mostly pinch hit. His legs were giving out on him, and he had trouble running. I won the batting championship in 1938 because he didn't have enough at-bats. (Jolley hit .350 with 414 at bats while Uhalt hit .332 with 635 at-bats.)

BERNIE "FRENCHY" UHALT - Oakland Oaks, Hollywood Stars, San Francisco Seals

A superior first baseman for the Sacramento Solons in the 1950s, Vernal "Nippy" Jones also could be counted on to hit at least .300 for the season.

VERNAL "NIPPY" JONES

*N*ippy never talked very much about himself. He was a good roommate, quiet. One year he got over 200 hits (206), and he never even talked about it. He could hit the curve ball. He could hit a breaking pitch as well as anybody alive.

BUD WATKINS - Sacramento Solons

Nippy Jones was a good hitter and a good player. He always hit .300. One time when I was with San Diego, the Solons had just finished batting practice, and as the leadoff batter, I'm first into the batting cage for us. Jones had left his bat in there, and I look at it. It's flat on one side! Another bat, it's flat on one side also. I look at the names. One is Bob Dillinger and the other is Nippy Jones. No wonder those guys hit line drives all over the place!

They honed them down themselves. I told our manager, but we were beating them pretty good, so he didn't say anything.

BUDDY PETERSON - San Diego Padres

I used to get a kick out of Nippy when he hit. These pitchers would throw a couple of fastballs by him, and you could see them think, ' Now I've got him all set up for the breaking ball.' He was laying in wait for the damn thing. Pow! There goes a base hit. He had them set up!

Nippy would flatten his bat out. He would hone one side down, keep the bat with him and not put it in the batting rack. You could never find his bat. We knew it. The rest of the league knew it, but they couldn't find the bat!

JIM WESTLAKE - Sacramento Solons

BOB JOYCE

Longtime Coast League pitcher Bob Joyce threw for the Oakland Oaks and San Francisco Seals. An early proponent of the slider, Joyce won twenty or more games three times and capped off his Seals career with a 31-11 record. Joyce, it was said, could "eat up" a lot of innings.

Bob Joyce was just like Larry Jansen — cool on the mound. It was just like they were pitching batting practice. They weren't killing themselves. Yet of every four guys who come to the plate they get three out. Great control. I think he was the one who taught Jansen how to the throw the slider. He helped a lot of guys with it. Ray Harrell, when he won twenty games in 1944, he had a great fastball and a great curve, but he developed the slider to go with it.

Bob Joyce was more or less at the end of the line when I joined the club. He did go up to the Giants again. He was a good pitcher, just a little short of being a major leaguer.

BILL WERLE - San Francisco Seals

FRANK KELLEHER

Frank Kelleher was a player that I respected a lot, a real family man, an even-tempered man. I don't ever recall seeing him get angry at the plate. He'd be up there, bases loaded, and an umpire would call a third strike on him, and he'd turn around, look at the ump, roll his head a little bit and say, 'Hey, that wasn't too good of a call.' And that was it. He never really got angry.

I talked with him about his ability to keep his cool, and he said, well, he's doing his job, calling it the way he sees it. And that was it. He was the kind of player that you wanted at the plate in a pinch. He was husky, built like a football player. He was a clutch hitter. He had good power and also hit well for average.

GEORGE GRANT - Hollywood Stars Bat Boy

Frank Kelleher used to wear Chet Johnson out. Kelleher could hit him blindfolded. One game in Hollywood, we had the bases loaded with Kelleher coming up, and Johnson walked off the field and into the clubhouse. The ump followed him and demanded, 'What the hell is going on?' Johnson responded, 'I'm not going to pitch to him!'

With the umpire threatening and cajoling, Johnson came back and ended up walking Kelleher, forcing in the winning run. Johnson said, 'I told you so!'

Johnson was a tough pitcher, but not for Frank Kelleher.

CHUCK STEVENS - Hollywood Stars

Frank Kelleher had Popeye's arms. You'd stand out there [on the mound] and look at Kelleher and know what a good hitter he was, and know you had to be careful with him, he hit so well in the clutch.

HERSHEL LYONS - Sacramento Solons

LEO LASSEN —
SEATTLE BROADCASTER

Six of the eight Coast League broadcasters in the late '40s were from Seattle. Leo was one of them, and he must have started in the 1930s. There was Rollie Truitt (in Portland). Bud Foster (Oakland) went to high school in Seattle, Tony Koester in Sacramento, Al Schuss in San Diego and myself.

All the kids listened to Leo Lassen. The thing that intrigued me about it, he could go to a game and get paid for it. I said, 'I've got to get into this racket.'

But I do credit Leo Lassen for indoctrinating me on the finer points of the game. He was a walking tactician of the game. He knew the game, the strategy and all that.

If he had had a better radio voice, he probably wouldn't have remained in Seattle but would have been picked up to work with Red Barber or someone of that level.

DON KLEIN - Seals Radio Broadcaster

Leo also was the official scorer at Seattle. His booth was right next to the press box, and there was a window with a little door opening to the press box. On a close call, we'd look over to see if it was a base hit or an error. He'd open the door, stick his head out and tell us the call, then shut the door before we'd have a chance to question.

BOB STEVENS - San Francisco Chronicle

BILL LAWRENCE

The best outfielder I ever saw was Bill Lawrence. That guy could go get 'em. Nothing got by him. You'd swear you had a double or triple in the gap and he'd glide under it. He was also a very good hitter. He usually hit more triples than he did homers, and he could steal bases.

RUGGER ARDIZOIA - Hollywood Stars, Seattle Rainiers

JOHNNY LINDELL

Johnny Lindell was like a big Airedale dog. The nicest guy, but he was kind of a nuisance. When he wasn't pitching, he'd be in the clubhouse nailing your shoes to the walls. He was always doing something.

He was a knuckleball pitcher, and he always pitched well, except in San Francisco. That wind would pick up that knuckleball and blow it into the next county. Catchers had enough problems when he pitched. They hated it in San Francisco.

CHUCK STEVENS - Hollywood Stars

I took my hat off to Johnny Lindell because he became a great pitcher. He had a good command of his pitches, and even threw that knuckle. And he was smart enough to use that pitch when he had two strikes. Lindell was also able to help himself with that bat occasionally, too.

EDDIE BASINSKI - Portland Beavers

AD LISKA

Ad Liska, who worked wonders with his sidearm pitches.

*A*d Liska was a submarine pitcher who joined the Portland Beavers in 1936 and helped them win pennants in 1936 and 1945. He retired in 1949. During his Coast League career, spent exclusively with Portland, he won 20 or more games three times, winning a total of 198 games.

I had been a sidearm pitcher in high school, and after a couple of years in the minors, I went to Minneapolis. I had hurt my arm a few times going sidearm. Mike Kelly, the manager there, asked, 'Do you think it will hurt your arm if you drop down a little more?'

I said, 'No, I don't think so.' Sammy Bohne, a player-coach, took me under his wing, watching me and instructing the catcher to put his glove on the outside corner. 'When you can hit that spot then you're a pitcher,' he said.

So I start coming down below. It didn't hurt the arm. I always felt that when I shake hands, I do it low. I don't put my hand over my head, so pitching that way is normal. I was at Minneapolis all year — won twenty and lost four. I pitched every four days, had a helluva year.

In l943, '44, '45, I had real good success. Everything I threw seemed to be a strike. Marv Owen actually tried to get me to waste some pitches, but I just couldn't seem to do it. But my feeling was, let the batters hit the ball.

I've actually had the catcher tell batters what pitch he was getting. But he didn't know where it was going or if I was being honest with him.

Jigger Statz used to hit me real good. He used to tell his hitters not to watch my arm, but to watch my knee. 'The ball's going to come out of his knees.' Statz wasn't a home-run hitter, but he was on base a lot, and you don't always have to homer to win games.

The big, hard swingers I used to like because they don't keep their eyes on the ball so good. You move the ball around and it's hard to hit. If you know how you're going to pitch him, you don't have to waste too many pitches.

AD LISKA

Ad Liska had that unusual pitching motion. When he would pitch his fingers would come close to hitting the ground. He couldn't throw a ball overhand, even when he'd throw a ball to the bases or when a ball was hit back to him. He pretty much went underneath.

I saw Ad get on the training bench one time for a rubdown. I'd never seen him get on before. His arm was like a piece of soft rubber. The trainer said, 'Get out of here.' His arm was so flexible and loose.

NINO BONGIOVANNI - Portland Beavers

Ad and I played together at Omaha, before he went to Portland. I had good luck against him. I never strided. If you stride, it will throw you off balance. He had two pitches, a sinker and a slow curve. He'd pitch inside tight, but when he threw the curve, he had to get it outside. If he hung it inside, it would be over the fence.

LOU VEZILICH - San Diego Padres

We had a good matchup going in Sacramento — Ad versus Tony Freitas. They had men on first and third in the ninth inning. Marv Owen was our manager, and he called over to me to play behind the runner because a left-handed batter was at the plate.

Ad was thrown off and balked, and the winning run scored. We get beat, and before we could get into the clubhouse, Liska had put his foot through the door and was gone.

HERM REICH - Portland Beavers

Ad Liska pitched out of the resin bag. The first time I caught him, I said, 'Damn! I never saw the pitch.' He put the resin bag right there (to the left of the mound, where he would release his submarine pitch). It took me a while to overcome that. I had to learn to follow the ball.

Liska's curve ball rose when he threw it. He had one helluva time pitching to left-handers. Right-handers, he jammed. I remember one time he was pitching against Frank Kelleher of Hollywood. He said, 'I'm going to try something,' and he came overhand. Jeez, he threw a sixty-five-mile-an-hour fastball, and Kelleher just stood there and took a called third strike. Well, Ad had found himself a new toy, and he came up with a sore arm.

He also used the pine tar. He was grabbing it all the time. They had all those old-time umpires — Jack Powell and those guys — they let him get away with it: 'Look at old Ad Liska out there. He's been here since '36 ... Strike!'

CHARLIE SILVERA - Portland Beavers

DARIO LODIGIANI

The first base hit I ever got in the Pacific Coast League, we were playing Portland at Oakland and Emil Mailho was on second base, and Oscar Vitt was the manager. Hal Haid, our relief pitcher was due up, and Vitt walks over to our dugout and asks, 'Is there anybody in this dugout that can get a base hit?' And he's looking right at me. I'm a rookie, nineteen years old, so I say, 'I'll hit, Oscar.'

So he says, 'Go up and hit.' So I grab a bat and I walk up to home plate. The closer I get the more my knees are shaking. I'm saying to myself, 'What the hell am I poppin' off about? I should have shut up.'

Roy Joiner is pitching for them, and I stood up against him, and the first pitch he threw — I don't know if it was inside, outside, high, or where — I hit hit it about six or seven inches from my fist, and I hit the prettiest blooper you ever saw over Jack Fenton's head. It bounced down into the right-field corner, and Mailho scored and we won the ball game.

The clubhouses were in center field then, and as we're walking

Infielder Dario Lodigiani was one of Casey Stengel's "Nine Old Men" of 1948. A solid hitter, Lodigiani helped Billy Martin develop his skills around second base. "Lodi" is shown here with the Seals in 1950.

Ernie Lombardi averaged .370 from 1928 through 1930 with the Oakland Oaks.

towards them, Roy Joiner walks by and says, 'You little son of a bugger, stop eating those goddamn hot dogs and start eating steak, will ya!' That was my first hit in the Coast League.

DARIO LODIGIANI

Dario Lodigiani came up to me one time the Oaks were in town and said, 'I hear you can predict the weather up here. Are we going to play today?' I said, 'No, we're not going to play.' He asked, 'How do you do it?' 'I feel it in my bones. We're not going to play.'

So Lodi went into his clubhouse and bet a guy two or three Cokes. 'Tell 'em you got an ache in your ankle, and that's how you know a storm's coming in.' So Lodi got three guys to bet, and here came the rain. Every time he came into Portland, he'd ask, 'Hey, we going to get rained out?' He was betting against his guys, but it was all in good fun. He was a good friend.

AD LISKA - Portland Beavers

ERNIE LOMBARDI

*E*rnie Lombardi broke in to professional baseball with the Oakland Oaks in 1926. After a Hall of Fame major league career, he returned to the Coast League in 1948, signing with Sacramento. He again joined Oakland after he was released by the Solons.

Ernie was the kind of guy you could never get mad at. He was easygoing, good-natured. If he couldn't backhand a pitch, he'd just reach out barehanded and catch the best fastball you could throw.

Ernie couldn't move that fast anymore, but he had been a good defensive catcher. He was a good thrower.

I've seen him hit some pretty long balls. He had awesome power.

MARV GRISSOM - Sacramento Solons

Lombardi had the biggest hands. When he'd swing that bat it made the loudest noise. He could hit so hard and so far. He'd hit balls against the left-field fence for a single.

He led the National League in hitting twice, and the infielders played back on the outfield grass because they knew if they could knock the ball down, they could still throw him out.

In 1948, when he wasn't catching, we had Raimondi and Fernandes. Casey could call on Lombardi to pinch hit.

He created all kinds of problems for the other team. If ever there was a Hall of Famer he was one.

DARIO LODIGIANI - Oakland Oaks

WILLIAM "WEE WILLIE" LUDOLPH

Willie Ludolph and Jack Salveson were my favorites. Willie Ludolph was the best that I caught. He knew how to move the ball around. He had good control. If you asked for high and inside, you got high and inside.

A reporter once asked how he pitched to Mike Hunt of Seattle. He said, 'I pitch him here (pointing to high and inside). I don't pitch him here (showing two inches difference).' And he did it!

He'd throw a curve inside that didn't break much and the batter would foul it off. The next time, he'd throw the curve and keep it out there, and the batter would miss it. It was masterful to watch him pitch.

BILLY RAIMONDI - Oakland Oaks

TONY LUPIEN

Tony Lupien was a real gentleman, a college grad. He was feisty when things got tough but, by the same token he would sit down and talk with you and give you advice.

And always at the end of the season, he would come over and say, 'I'll see you next year.' He'd shake your hand, thank you for taking care of him during the season, and you open your hand up and there is a twenty-dollar bill.

GEORGE GRANT - Hollywood Stars Bat Boy

Tony Lupien, our first baseman, was an individualist. On balls hit wide of first, I'd run over to cover first, and he'd come over so we'd be standing next to each other. Not great range.

Above: William "Wee Willie" Ludolph. Left: Hollywood Stars first baseman Tony Lupien, left, takes a break at Gilmore Stadium to talk with manager Jimmy Dykes. Dykes — who also managed the American League teams in Chicago, Philadelphia, Baltimore, Detroit and Cleveland — was respected and a bit feared by his players. Lupien was Dykes' leader on the field.

He was as bald as a cueball. When he'd be on second and slide into third, Harry Danning, our coach over there, would grab his hat then give it back to him. One night Lupien had a wig on, and when he slid into third and Harry knocked his hat off, he had a full head of hair. You could have heard a pin drop in the stadium, then everyone started laughing.

RUGGER ARDIZOIA - Hollywood Stars

Speedy Emil Mailho earned a PCL batting average of .308 in nine seasons,eight of them with the Oakland Oaks. He was good with his glove, too. When he and Frenchy Uhalt teamed up in the outfield few balls got through to the wall.

JAPHET "RED" LYNN

Red Lynn was funny. We had a lot of luncheons we were asked to attend, and I'd take Red along. Anything you wanted him to talk about, he could do it. He could be a preacher. He could be a railroad man. Anything. He'd talk, and you'd think he had done all this, but he hadn't.

We were in Sacramento, and I rented an airplane to check on some business back home. Red had claimed he was a pilot, too, so I took him along. So we are just over the Buttes, and I pulled the plane up into a power stall and that thing dropped. You could have heard him yell a half a mile away. 'You never flew, you son of a gun!'

But he was a good competitor.

BILL FLEMING - Los Angeles Angels

EMIL MAILHO

When I was a rookie, they wouldn't let me hit. 'Get out and shag.' They were protecting their jobs, afraid you'd take their job.

You had to fight for your job in those days. There were no coaches. You had to know how to do everything when you came up.

I played for some good people in Oakland. Ray Brubaker was a good manager. He liked to do a lot of running. We had Frenchy Uhalt, Leroy Anton, myself. We stole a lot of bases — our club didn't have a lot of power, so we had to. We drove the catchers nuts. Of course, the pitchers had to pay more attention against us.

[Manager] Oscar Vitt antagonized some of the players. He'd tell a player to his face what a great player he was, then he'd turn right around and bad-mouth him. That was a bad trait.

Johnny Vergez was too easy as a manager. Some of the guys took advantage of him. He was a fine person, though. Dolph Camilli was also too easy going. He and Vergez were two of a type ... too calm. They didn't play aggressive baseball.

EMIL MAILHO

JIM MARSHALL

Jim Marshall, our first baseman, was strictly a low-ball hitter. At Vancouver, he went into a slump, and I went out and pitched batting practice to him for about an hour. I was telling him some of the things he was doing wrong. I kept throwing him balls where he couldn't hit 'em. Anything above the belt, he couldn't get.

He was a good fielder and hit for power, but when he slumped, he couldn't hit anything. He never hit well for average.

EDDIE ERAUTT - Vancouver Mounties

BILLY MARTIN

I had known Billy Martin since 1947. We played around together, Billy, Mel Duezabou and myself. We even had a basketball team — Billy, Mel, myself and Lil Arnerich and Babe Van Hewitt, an outfielder in the Cincinnati organization. We were called the "Duezabou Bumpers" in one of the Oakland recreation leagues. We walked through that basketball league, and there were some pretty good teams.

We used to go up skiing in the wintertime. I remember one evening we took the door off of the ski-school office and we carried it up the ski slope. It was Mel, Billy, Lil Arnerich and myself. We got up to top of the hill, and I was going to be the smart one and get on the rear end of this door. I did, and half way down the damn thing turned around! Now we're going backwards. So at the bottom of the hill we hit this big snowbank, and they had to dig me out of it. We did some stupid things.

We also played winter ball together, and I was in Billy's wedding. In fact, the day he got married we had to go out to the Oaks Ball Park to play in the Elks Major-Minor League ball game. Lucky his wife was patient.

CLAUDE CHRISTIE - Seattle Rainiers

Infielder Billy Martin, left, and outfielder Jackie Jensen with the Oakland Oaks in 1949. Casey Stengel made sure the Yankees acquired both players for his New York dynasty of the 1950s.

Charlie Dressen wanted Billy Martin to be a hit-and-run player — move players around. Billy wanted to be a home-run hitter. He'd say, 'I can hit home runs,' and Charlie would say, 'Yes, you can. But that's not your strength.' So they were at each other's throats all the time.

Everybody rubbed Billy the wrong way. Billy was always right, whether he was wrong or right, and he'd fight you on it. But he was a good ballplayer.

FRANK KERR - Oakland Oaks

He was like Eddie Stanky, Leo Durocher and Gene Mauch. Not great on talent, but he'd find some way to beat you. I remember getting in a fight with him once down in Oakland. He came into second with his spikes high, and I can remember being on top of him, pounding him, but it didn't go very far before it was broken up.

He was a very intense ballplayer, loved to play and would do anything to win.

EDDIE BASINSKI - Portland Beavers

The first time I saw Billy Martin, he joined the Oaks up in Portland in 1947. He broke in against Tommy Bridges, and all the Oaks told him, 'Watch out for Bridges' curve ball.' Well, we gave him three straight fastballs, and he's still standing there looking.

He didn't have the great ability, but he could beat you a lot of ways. He was a little brash — upset a few people when he got there — but he played.

CHARLIE SILVERA - Portland Beavers

I was in Oakland the day Billy Martin came to the ballpark for his first time — in a black jacket on a motorcycle. We used to hate them, but only between the lines. After the game was over, they were good guys. But there was no love lost on the diamond.

Billy Martin and I were friends, and one game in 1948 I brought a water pistol to the game and squirted him. He started chasing me, but I was pretty fast. Well, he had to retaliate, so the next day, he comes in with a bigger water pistol. As the season went on, the water guns got bigger. Nobody seemed to mind. In fact, some of the players went out and got their own water pistols.

DON RODE - Seals Clubhouse Boy

LUIS MARQUEZ

Luis and Frankie Austin joined the Beavers in Hollywood and it was a traumatic time for some of the guys. Bill Sweeney was a real redneck, but he was a helluva guy. When Johnny Rucker walked out (to protest blacks joining the team), Sweeney said, 'Baseball is bigger than anybody, and Rucker will either come back or he won't play.'

Luie and Frankie did a helluva job for Portland. One time we were playing in San Diego and Luie slid into second base and Whitey Wietelmann deliberately spiked him.

The next time Whitey came to bat, I wasn't sure if I did it deliberately or I was a little wild, but I knocked him down twice.

After the inning ended, Luie comes up to me and says, 'You my friend, man!'

HAL SALTZMAN - Portland Beavers

I remember when I first saw Luie. We were playing against him and I remember, immediately, you don't like him. He was a real hot-dog guy. But then I got on the club with him, and

some of those things that were irritating are assets now. Not only that, he was a funny guy. I thought, playing against him, he was a hot dog and arrogant, and as an opposing guy you don't like that at all. He was trying to irritate the other club, but he didn't do it in a mean way.

CHARLES "RED" ADAMS - Portland Beavers

Luie Marquez was a great roving center fielder at Portland, and a winning ballplayer. He was Puerto Rican and a helluva guy. You know how the white guys put the black charcoal under their eyes? When I was with Seattle and Portland came to town, Luie came out and was yelling at us, 'Hey! Hey!' We looked, and he had white stuff under his eyes.

He had that infectious personality. The tougher a game got, the more he was a leader in the dugout. He'd go back and forth, 'Come on, you guys. We can do it! We can get these guys.' I loved that about him.

EDDIE BASINSKI - Portland Beavers

Luis Marquez, left, had a reputation as the fastest runner in the league and often was challenged by other players. In this 1950 photo, shot in Portland, he lines up for a (winning) sprint with the Sacramento Solons' Jim Busby.

JOE MARTY

Joe Marty was a slugging, right-handed outfielder with the Sacramento Solons. When he broke in, in 1934 with the San Francisco Seals, some baseball men rated his skills equal to those of Joe DiMaggio. Player intensity made have made the difference. This photograph is dated June, 1949.

I remember when we played the Seals and Joe DiMaggio was just breaking in. Tom Turner, our manager in Portland, said that Joe Marty was the better player.

Joe Marty could still hit when I was in Sacramento. He was near the end of his career, but he was getting out of shape. He owned that bar down the street.

PETE COSCARART - Portland Beavers

Joe Marty was a good hitter. He had pretty good musculature on him — not like Pepper Martin, but he had big arms, as I recall. We had cut-off sleeves in '46, when I played with him, and I remember seeing Marty's arms.

I went back to Sacramento recently and went by the site of the old ballpark. It's now a shopping center, but down the street is Joe Marty's Bar. He was popular with the fans.

HERSHEL LYONS - Sacramento Solons

GENE MAUCH

I had a good rivalry with Gene Mauch. Earlier in the 1956 season, I got into it with him. I had just come down from Pittsburgh with Luis Arroyo when they sent Bill Mazeroski to the Pirates, and I was playing second base.

Mauch was on first, and there was a ground ball hit to Dick Smith, the shortstop. He threw the ball to me, and Gene came in, and he didn't slide. He rolled me at second base, and as I got up, I said, 'Gene, you're playing in a bad spot to be doing something like that.'

He didn't say anything, and I didn't say anything. But in the ninth inning, I was just hoping I could get on first base. I got on first base and I hollered down to Gene, 'I'm taking off!' And as luck would have it, they hit the ball to the shortstop.

Well, I had taken off. It wasn't a hit-and-run or anything. The batter didn't know what I was doing. He hit the ball to the shortstop, and the shortstop threw the ball to Mauch. Well, I was right on top of him by that time, and I pulled a slide that knocked him halfway out into left field. I'll give him credit. He never said a word. But he didn't forget.

FORREST "SPOOK" JACOBS - Hollywood Stars

Gene Mauch was my shortstop in St. Paul in 1946. He wasn't much of a hitter, but in 1956 when they won the pennant with Bilko hitting all those home runs, he's hitting .348! I almost fell off the chair. He was a .240 hitter.

He was a winner. He, Eddie Stanky and Billy Martin were out of the same mold. They were winning ballplayers. They would do anything to win and were just ferocious in their desire to win.

EDDIE BASINSKI - Portland Beavers

GEORGE McDONALD

*G*eorge McDonald was a slick-fielding left-handed first baseman who signed with the Hollywood Stars in 1934 and moved with the club to San Diego in 1936. With the exception of 1945, when he was traded to Seattle, McDonald spent his whole Coast League career with the Padres. He finally requested his release in 1947. McDonald was not a power hitter, but always hit for average.

Bobby Doerr and I broke in with the 1934 Hollywood Stars. Oscar Vitt was our manager. He was all right. We played our games at Wrigley. I don't think there was that much of a rivalry, even though we played in their park.

I didn't play much. Ray Jacobs was our regular first baseman. Jacobs didn't help me at all. I had a pretty good batting streak going, and the next day I come to the ballpark and my bat was sawed in half. In fact, I still think it was him.

That club had Fred Haney at third and Jimmy Levey at shortstop. Willard Hershberger was on that club. Also some good outfielders — Smead Jolley, Cedric Durst and Cleo Carlyle. And Vince DiMaggio, but Vitt didn't like DiMaggio.

Up in Portland one time we drank some sweet gin, and I got sick as a dog. I told my roommate to tell Shellenback I had the flu. We were playing that night and he talked me into going to the park. I had trouble keeping food down, but Les Cook gave me some aspirin. I was still in bad shape during batting practice, and we were going to face Ad Liska, the submarine pitcher. Well, I got a single, a double and a triple. I thought I was going to die running out that triple.

I discharged from the service in the last part of 1944. I had been at Fort Lewis, Washington, and then got traded right back to Seattle. I had a pretty good season in '45. The next season they acquired Earl Torgeson and had to play him. [General manager] Bill Mulligan called me in and said, 'Hey George, you had a good year for us. You can stay here and pinch hit and play a little outfield, or I can trade you.' I told him to try and trade me, not thinking that I might go back to San Diego. God, was that upsetting when I found out I'd been traded back to San Diego. Ripper Collins and I just didn't get along.

I got beaned bad in Seattle in 1945 — Italo Chelini, a left-hander, hit me right over the temple. I was out for awhile. I went out after that and had Joe Demoran throw at me — literally right at me — for a half hour.

We were in Oakland and the dressing rooms were in center field. This was my first game back. So Skip says, 'I'm going to have you lead off and bat just once then leave the game.' As I remember, I batted once, grounded out to second base, then

George McDonald, a solid player who had a reputation as a cutup.

went out to the clubhouse. It went over the wires that I died in the clubhouse. An old friend of mine in San Diego said, ' We stood a minute in silence for you.'

GEORGE McDONALD

I roomed with George McDonald one season. Or I should say, I roomed with George McDonald's bag. He was the best-fielding first baseman I ever saw. He must have saved Mickey Haslin fifty errors over there at third.

JOHN "SWEDE" JENSEN - San Diego Padres

GEORGE "CATFISH" METKOVICH

George Metkovich was terrific. He was fast and he could hit. He came to the Seals through Casey Stengel. He saw him in Los Angeles and told the Seals. He was just a kid, but he had a good arm — oh, what an arm! And he had good speed. He could do everything. He got his chance because of the war.

BERNIE "FRENCHY" UHALT - San Francisco Seals

I pitched most left-handers away with a sinker, then tried to jam them with a cutter, up and in. The first time I pitched against Metkovich, one got away from me and I almost hit him. He was irate with me. But I got him out regularly. I made him hit a sinker. Many times when I got ahead of him, I'd throw the slider, and he'd pull the ball foul. George was a good hitter, but I had decent luck with him, and he didn't hurt me. I respected him as a hitter and treated him as such.

DUANE PILLETTE - Portland Beavers

The 1955 Oakland Oaks power trio, left to right: Jim Marshall, Joe Brovia and George Metkovich. Marshall hit only .239, but thirty of his hits left the park; Brovia hit .325 with nineteen homers; and Metkovich batted .335 with seventeen home runs. The Oaks' pitching was weak in '55, however, and the team finished seventh.

I went to San Diego when George Metkovich was managing. I don't think George was happy as a manager. He didn't seem to manage, it was just like, 'Throw the bats and balls out there and go get 'em.' He relied a lot on Jimmie Reese.

BILL RENNA - San Diego Padres

Metkovich managed at San Diego the last year of Lane Field. I had an attack of appendici-tis and didn't think I was going to pitch any more that season. But George contacted me and asked how I was doing. I said, 'I'm about ready to go again,' so they acquired me from Portland.

He had Earl Averill catching, Bill Glynn at first, Billy Moran at second, Larry Raines at short, Eddie Kazak and Rudy Regalado at third, Dave Pope and Floyd Robinson in the out-field.

Our pitchers were Dick Brodowski, 'Mudcat' Grant, Bill Kennedy, Vic Lombardi. We had to win a double-header the last day to tie for fourth. We had a tremendous club, but George was not equipped to be a manager. It was a crime.

BILL WERLE - San Diego Padres

LENNIE NEAL

Lennie Neal caught me one year. Lennie was a very smart catcher. He would set up — I think they call it framing, giving you a good target. When Lennie gave you a target, he never moved. He was an excellent catcher, not a very good hitter. He was from Scio, Oregon. I said, 'Lennie, nobody is from Scio, Oregon.' He said, 'I am!'

BUD WATKINS - Sacramento Solons

I joined the Oaks in 1951. Don Padgett and Ray Lamanno were the catchers, but they were old-timers. It was the last year for both. In 1952, when Rafael Noble came, they had to play him. I spent most of the time in the bullpen. Still, it was a good team to go to. Johnny Vander Meer and Hal Gregg both pitched no-hitters. I caught both and didn't know Vander Meer's was a no-hitter until the game was over. That's God's truth.

The 1955 season was a frustration. Sometimes you get some good ballplayers, but it just doesn't work. We picked up pitchers Skinny Brown, Brooks Lawrence, Bob Cain and Duane Pillette, and lots of veterans, but the team played poorly.

The 1955 Oaks weren't winning. Attendance just fell off. Brick Laws worked hard to get some good players. I wouldn't blame the bad season on Lefty O'Doul, although I think some players took advantage of him. I never knew Lefty to fine anybody. He always said he would treat players the way he wanted to be treated.

He and Ott were both great ballplayers, and maybe they didn't need much supervision. Maybe they just thought nobody else did either. Maybe in some cases they did.

I was sorry to move from Oakland, but Brick Laws was losing too much money. At Vancouver in 1956, we were really a new team, a different organization — Baltimore. There were a lot of new guys. Pitchers George Bamberger, Charlie Beamon and Fred Besana. George Metkovich, Spider Jorgensen and myself were the only carry-overs from Oakland. The new guys were good guys and good ballplayers, but it took some time to jell.

I never liked managers to say they were going to rest me. I didn't have that problem with Augie Galan in 1953. I never thought much about the record until it was over with, and I was pretty tired after the season. I was injury-free. The next year I got beaned up in Seattle and was out for a while. I was due, I guess. There's a lot of luck involved.

(In 1953, Len Neal caught 174 of the Oaks' 180 games, including 130 consecutive starts. He went 100 games without making an error. Modern-day performances pale by comparison.)

LEN NEAL

The Oakland Oaks' phenom catcher Lennie Neal.

ROY NICELY

Roy Nicely of the San Francisco Seals was the most outstanding shortstop that I have ever seen, absolutely spectacular. He hit only .220, .190. Only had a couple of good years with the bat, but as a defensive shortstop I just marvel at some of the plays that he made. He was teamed up with Hugh Luby, who was also a great second baseman.

EDDIE BASINSKI - Portland Beavers

Roy Nicely worked the double play with Hugh Luby. Luby didn't have a strong arm. I think they still hold the record for double plays. Whenever there was a double-play situation and the ball was hit to Luby, he'd toss over to second, to Nicely, and Nicely, without even looking, would throw the ball to third. It's amazing how many times he caught the runner rounding the base at third, and Jennings could make the tag.

He practiced that a lot, never looking at third. We also had Ferris Fain at first who was known for his ability to throw the runner out at third on an infield hit.

DON RODE - Seals Clubhouse Man

With the 1945 Seals we had Joe Hoover as our shortstop. He was dramatic, but would then throw the ball away. He only lasted about a month. Then Roy Nicely came in.

Nicely took over and became the best shortstop in the league. He was sure-footed. He had a great arm, the quickest I ever saw in baseball. He could throw from [close to the hip] better than anybody I ever saw.

He had one bad feature. He had bad feet and couldn't go to his left. He could go to his right, so he favored that naturally, and anybody who hit the ball to deep short, with that great arm he had, he'd throw him out. He was good on double plays.

BERNIE "FRENCHY" UHALT - San Francisco Seals

IRV NOREN

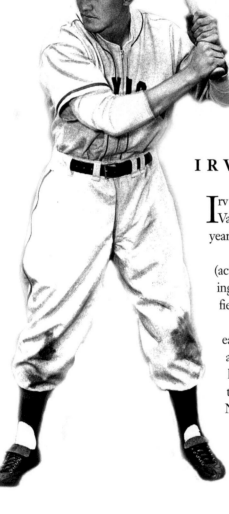

Irv Noren could do it all. He was with the Hollywood Stars in 1949 only, but still managed to win the PCL's Most Valuable Player trophy while batting .330, with twenty-nine homers and 130 RBI.

Irv Noren probably had one of the best years I've seen, in 1949. He won the Most Valuable Player award that year, and was just a youngster. He did everything that year.

I led off and got 200 base hits (actually 202) and must have scored a thousand (actually 121) because he drove in 200 to 300 (actually 130). By September I was wearing suspenders on my ball pants. He ran the buns off of me. He also led the outfielders with assists (thirty).

We were in Seattle for a crucial series, and everyone was supposed to be in bed early, getting their rest. I'm rooming with Gordon Maltzberger. I couldn't sleep. It's about 3:15 in the morning, and I go to the window. From high up in the hotel, I look across at an all-night hamburger joint. There's a big pinball machine, and there's a guy really giving it a ride. Guess who? It was our youngest ball player, Irv Noren.

The next morning I said, 'Hey Irv, you were supposed to be in bed at 11:30 or 12:00, not 3:30 in the morning.' 'Chuck,' he said, 'that machine owed me money, and I wasn't going to let it get away without a fight.'

CHUCK STEVENS - Hollywood Stars

LOU NOVIKOFF

"The Mad Russian," Lou Novikoff, was one of the Coast League's most colorful players. While only in the league for six years, Novikoff's became legendary for free-swinging at the plate and zaniness in the field.

I roomed with Lou Novikoff's clothing. I don't know what he did. I don't know where he went. I know he was often coming in when I was getting up. He was a bad-ball hitter. The best place to pitch him was down the middle.

TONY CRISCOLA- San Diego Padres, Seattle Rainiers

Novikoff — don't waste any balls on him. Pitch straight down the middle, fastballs. If you threw a ball over his head, he'd jump up and hit it. He wasn't the world's best outfielder, but he could sure break up a ball game.

BILL FLEMING - Los Angeles Angels

Lou Novikoff was a wild swinger. He was a good ballplayer, but Lou didn't take care of himself. He joined our ball club later in his career, and I could see why his career ended short.

EDO VANNI - Seattle Rainiers

Lou was looking at that left field wall every time. He had a wild swing. I remember I had him set up for a right hand curve, and I threw it and it was way outside, and damned if he didn't hit it over the right field wall.

PAUL GREGORY - Seattle Rainiers

ALBIE PEARSON

I used to hate it when Albie Pearson or Ted Beard would come to bat. Pearson had great command of the bat. He could hit the ball anywhere, and he was a good little outfielder, too. And he was part of that good ball club down in San Francisco (in 1957).

EDDIE BASINSKI - Portland Beavers

Lou Novikoff was a .300 hitter in the PCL. He broke out in 1940, though, batting .363 with 171 RBI and forty-one homers in 174 games.

CARL "BUDDY" PETERSON

I came out of the service and signed with Portland in 1946 and they sent me to Salem, of the Western International League, in 1947. I grew up alongside the ballpark, Vaughn Street, on the left side. Foul balls were hit over the left-field grandstand, near our house. I was the third house up from the parking lot on 24th street. I lived at the ballpark. I had to be home like at 9 o'clock, but I listened to all the games. I'd lay up there at night and hear all the cheers.

For some reason, I always figured I was going to be a ballplayer. I had the background for it because my father played some pro ball. It was a funny thing: Some of those players who were

Infielder Carl "Buddy" Peterson was a manager's favorite. He played hard (his uniform would go from clean to dirty by the end of every game) and always offered moral support to his teammates.

on the Portland club, like Ad Liska, Roy Helser, Herman Reich, when I was a kid they were with the ball club. Then when I came back from the service and signed with Portland, they were there, the same guys who used to pat me on top of the head.

When I was recalled from Salem, Jim Turner was the manager. When I went to spring training in the Coast League, there were guys who haven't talked to me to this day. They were older. We had to go with the rookies. They didn't even want you to go where they were!

I had a little trouble with that. I happened to be in a beer joint in Riverside. Eddie Fernandes comes up to me and says, 'What are you doing?' I say, 'Having a beer.' He says, 'This is for the older ballplayers.' We had some words, and I said, 'Who in the hell do you think you are?' Now Eddie was a big guy ... well, Frankie Zak stopped us from having a fight. I probably would have been clobbered because I was only about five-feet eight-inches, 150 pounds. He was the only guy I had any trouble with.

Charlie Silvera and Eddie Basinski were a lot of help, and Frankie Zak was a good guy. In those days, the older guys didn't help the younger guys, but Basinski took me under his wing. He helped me turn the double play, position myself. He was friendly to me, and so was Silvera. A lot of those guys wouldn't talk to me. The old timers very seldom helped you out. You weren't in their clique.

When I went to Louisville, I went on option to them. San Diego had a chance to get Alan Richter. Boston was going to send him down, and San Diego thought he was a veteran and that he would fit in well. So they optioned me to go to Louisville.

The American Association is where they sent their younger players for experience. The Coast League had more veterans, so the move made sense. It might have helped me because I had a pretty good year down there, just to play regularly. There were a lot of guys my age, so I fit right in.

BUDDY PETERSON

Buddy Peterson and I got traded for each other. [Manager] Charlie Metro had his fill of Pete, and Pete had his fill of Metro. It's too bad to lose a player over a personality conflict. The best hustle I've seen since Pete Rose.

BUD WATKINS - Sacramento Solons

Buddy was good for the ball club because he was funny in the locker room, kept everybody loose. He would put baseballs inside his shirt where his biceps were, and on his shoulders and stomach. He'd go out there during batting practice with about a dozen baseballs stuffed in his shirt, looking like a big guy. The manager would just shake his head.

EDDIE BASINSKI - Portland Beavers

VIC PICETTI

Vic Picetti was a fabulous prospect out of Mission High School in San Francisco. He chose to sign with Oakland rather than with the home-town Seals or with the New York Yankees because Dolph Camilli, his idol, was managing Oakland. He got into fourteen games as Camilli's mid-season backup, but took over at first in 1945. In 152 games, he batted .282, hitting only one home run but 86 RBI.

Casey Stengel, with his penchant for veterans, farmed Picetti to Spokane for the 1946 season. Everyone who saw him play predicted he would be a star. Tragically, Picetti was one of several Oakland farmhands killed in the bus accident that wiped out the Spokane team of the Western International League.

I was at Vancouver in the Western International League when I heard about the Spokane accident over the radio. I was scared because my brother Babe was playing for Spokane. He had been beat out by the Indian, Levi McCormack, and had been released just prior to the accident at Snoqualmie Pass. But I didn't know that.

I talked to Pete Barisoff (who was in the bus wreck), and he explained to me what happened. He came out of it with a broken back.

It was 2 o'clock in the morning, and he seemed to think the bus driver was blinded by the lights of an oncoming car.

Barisoff said, 'I was awake, drinking beer with some other guys. Most of the guys were asleep. The bus lurched, and I grabbed the bottom of the seat and rode it down.' He said guys went out the window. The bus was catching the top of trees on the way down.

Joe Faria, from Oakland, was in a car following it. He and another player had their wives with them and didn't want to ride the bus because there was sometimes rough language. They were able to flag cars down and get help, but it was a terrible sight.

BOB "SWEDE" JENSEN - San Francisco Seals

MARINO "CHICK" PIERETTI

Chick Pieretti was a diminutive, five-foot seven-inch pitcher with a big heart. He toiled eight seasons, with Portland, Sacramento and Los Angeles, always eating up 250 to 300 innings. His gritty determination made up for his small size.

Chick Pieretti was the only pitcher I knew who didn't run with the pitchers in pregame. But what he would do is take ground balls at third base until he dropped.

I remember one night in Sacramento, Gene Desautels came out to pull him off the mound, and Chick was kind of perturbed. Desautels put his hand out for the ball, and Chick threw it out over the top of the grandstand onto Riverside Boulevard.

He was quite an accordion player, too. He always had lots of work playing for Italian weddings. And he also pitched batting practice for the San Francisco Giants after he quit playing.

BUD WATKINS - Sacramento Solons

Old Chick had those migrane headaches. There were a couple of games over at Multnomah Stadium later in the 1950s he was pitching and they were so bad he had to come out of the game. He was a helluva competitor. Just a little guy, but what a fireball.

EDDIE BASINSKI - Portland Beaver

Right-handed pitcher Marino "Chick" Pieretti was considered an overachiever because he was small. But batters who dug in on him got into big trouble. Pieretti divided his time between the major league and the Coast League, where he often pitched more than 300 innings a season.

FATHER AND SON -
HERM AND DUANE PILLETTE

One of the Pacific Coast League's most remarkable stories is that of Herm "Old Folks" Pillette, a pitcher for twenty-nine years, twenty-three of them in the Coast League. Because rosters were depleted during World War II, Pillette didn't retire until he was three months short of his 50th birthday!

Herm's brother Ted was also a Coast League pitcher, although his career was much shorter. Herm's son Duane, also known as "Dee," followed his dad into the Coast League and into the American League.

I SUPPOSE SAN DIEGO WAS MY PERMANENT HOME. AS A KID I WAS IN EIGHTEEN DIFFERENT SCHOOLS. MY FATHER TRIED TO PUT ME IN PAROCHIAL SCHOOLS WHENEVER HE COULD. HE WAS A HARD-NOSED CATHOLIC. SOMETIMES WE WEREN'T ABLE TO [FIND A CATHOLIC SCHOOL IN THE AREA], SO AFTER A MONTH OR SO, HE WOULD MOVE TO GET ME INTO A GOOD CATHOLIC SCHOOL. THE CATHOLIC SCHOOLS KEPT YOU UP A LITTLE HIGHER, SO I DIDN'T SLIDE BACK THAT FAR. HIS OBJECT WAS TO GET ME INTO COLLEGE BECAUSE HE WASN'T ABLE TO DO THAT HIMSELF.

ALL CATHOLIC SCHOOLS PLAYED ONLY SOFTBALL, SO I NEVER GOT A CHANCE TO PLAY HARDBALL. BUT WHEN I GOT TO SAN DIEGO AND I WENT TO A JUNIOR HIGH SCHOOL, MEMORIAL HIGH, THEY PLAYED BASEBALL. I WAS ECSTATIC. ACTUALLY, I WAS A SHORTSTOP, SO I WENT OUT FOR SHORTSTOP. BUT THERE WERE KIDS QUICKER THAN I, SO I BECAME A PITCHER.

I MADE MY DAD PROMISE ME THAT IF HE GOT TRADED AGAIN, THAT I COULD STAY IN SAN DIEGO AND PLAY BASEBALL AT SAN DIEGO HIGH SCHOOL BECAUSE THEY HAD AN EXCELLENT BASEBALL PROGRAM. AS IT HAPPENED, HE STAYED IN SAN DIEGO AND I WAS THERE FOUR YEARS BEFORE I WENT TO COLLEGE. THAT WAS AS LONG AS I STAYED IN ONE PLACE AT ANY ONE TIME.

DURING THE SUMMER MONTHS I COULD GO TO GAMES AT LANE FIELD, BUT WHEN SCHOOL WAS ON, I COULDN'T GO TO NIGHT GAMES. MY MOTHER WOULDN'T TELL IF I WOULD OCCASIONALLY GO OVER AND SELL PEANUTS, AND THEN CASH IN ABOUT THE SEVENTH INNING SO I'D GET HOME BEFORE MY DAD GOT HOME.

I REALLY WAS A FAN AND TRIED TO MIMIC IN HIGH SCHOOL WHAT I SAW OTHERS PEOPLE DO, NOT JUST MY FATHER. HE WAS MY IDOL, OF COURSE, BUT I'D MIMIC WHAT I SAW OTHER PITCHERS DO, LIKE BACKING UP THE BASE THAT YOU SHOULD AND COVERING FIRST BASE PROPERLY. I DIDN'T SELL A HELLUVA LOT OF PEANUTS, TO BE HONEST.

I DON'T THINK I EVER TOLD MY FATHER ABOUT THE PEANUTS. I WAS MARRIED, IN THE SERVICE AND HAD A CHILD IN THE SERVICE. THEN WHEN I CAME OUT OF THE SERVICE, I WENT RIGHT TO SPRING TRAINING, SO I WASN'T ABLE TO COMPLETE COLLEGE. NOR WAS I ABLE TO GO BACK HOME. I REALLY DIDN'T SEE MUCH OF MY FATHER.

WHEN I WAS SIXTEEN OR SEVENTEEN YEARS OF AGE, THE PADRES USED TO HAVE AN ALL-STAR TEAM OF SERVICE, COLLEGE AND HIGH SCHOOL PLAYERS TO PLAY AGAINST THE PADRE ROOKIES. I MADE THE TEAM, AND SO THEY PITCHED MY FATHER AGAINST ME FOR A FEW INNINGS. THAT WAS REALLY A THRILL.

AFTER HIGH SCHOOL, I WENT UP TO SANTA CLARA, BUT THE WAR INTERVENED. I WAS IN MY JUNIOR YEAR WHEN I ENLISTED, BECAUSE THEY WANTED TO DRAFT ME. SO I ENLISTED IN THE NAVAL AIR CORPS AND SPENT THREE YEARS IN THE SERVICE.

MY DAD AND I JUST MISSED PLAYING TOGETHER. HIS LAST SEASON WAS 1945 AND MY FIRST WAS 1946. WE CAME WITHIN AN EYELASH. HE SAID I COULD SIGN WITH WHOMEVER I WANTED TO PLAY, AND THE YANKEES WERE INTERESTED, BUT I DIDN'T KNOW IF THEY WOULD GIVE ME ENOUGH MONEY. HE SAID, 'THINK OF THE POSSIBILITY THAT IF YOU SIGN WITH ME (IN SACRAMENTO), THAT THEY'LL GIVE YOU A COUPLE OF DOLLARS TO SIGN AND PART OF THE SALE PRICE WHEN THEY SELL YOU TO THE MAJORS.' WELL, I THOUGHT ABOUT IT, BUT THE YANKEES WERE A DETERRENT TO THAT. YOU SIGN WITH THE YANKEES AND YOU SIGN WITH THE BEST CLUB IN BASEBALL. THEN DAD BECAME A SCOUT IN '46.

I SIGNED WITH [YANKEES SCOUT] JOE DEVINE. JOE HAD BEEN INSTRUMENTAL IN GETTING ME A SCHOLARSHIP TO SANTA CLARA. JOE WAS INTERESTED IN ME WHEN I WAS IN HIGH SCHOOL, EVEN THOUGH I WAS IN THE SOUTH.

DAD NEVER REALLY ENTERED INTO BASEBALL TALK

EXCEPT WHEN HE WAS PLAYING. WE USED TO LOVE TO LISTEN TO HIM TALK WITH OTHER BALLPLAYERS IN SAN DIEGO. HE USED TO TALK ABOUT HIS THEORY OF PITCHING AND I'D SIT IN THE DINING ROOM WHILE THEY WERE IN THE FRONT ROOM. I'D PICK UP WHATEVER I COULD. BUT HE DIDN'T TALK MUCH ABOUT BASEBALL AFTER HE RETIRED.

UNCLE TED LOVED BASEBALL, TOO. WE'D TALK BASEBALL WHENEVER WE GOT TOGETHER, BUT HE WAS UP IN OREGON, SO WE DIDN'T SEE HIM THAT MUCH.

DAD SAW ME PITCH ONE BALL GAME IN SACRAMENTO AFTER I CAME BACK FROM THE MAJOR LEAGUES. I WAS WITH PORTLAND. AND HE SAW ME PITCH ONCE ON THE GAME OF THE DAY, ON TELEVISION. THE ONLY HOME RUN I EVER HIT IN BASEBALL, I HIT THAT DAY. I GOT A LETTER FROM HIM. HE SAID, 'WELL, YOU'RE A HELLUVA LOT BETTER HITTER THAN I AM.' THAT WASN'T TRUE. I WASN'T THAT GOOD OF A HITTER.

EVERYBODY WHO PLAYED WITH MY FATHER JUST LOVED HIM. I THOUGHT HE WAS A PRETTY GOOD PITCHER MYSELF. THE YEAR HE LOST THIRTY WAS THE YEAR HE WENT TO THE TIGERS. HE WAS LUCKY ENOUGH TO HAVE A GOOD BALL CLUB BEHIND HIM AT DETROIT, AND HE WON NINETEEN. BEING THAT TYPE OF PITCHER, YOU DON'T HAVE A CHANCE TO SHOW OFF WHAT YOU HAVE UNLESS YOU ARE WITH A PRETTY DECENT TEAM.

AMAZINGLY ENOUGH HE PITCHED UP UNTIL THREE MONTHS SHORT OF HIS FIFTIETH BIRTHDAY.

DUANE PILLETTE - Portland Beavers, San Francisco Seals, Seattle Rainiers

DUANE PILLETTE

In 1947 I started with Newark. Vic Raschi was with Portland and they sent him to the Yankees. They transferred my option to Portland, so I took my family there. Jim Turner was the manager. He was a lot of help. He'd talk theory a lot, but basically they were trying to make the playoffs.

He didn't do much for me or with me in '47, but he wanted to work with me, even to the point that in '48 I requested to stay with the Portland ball club rather than stay with the Yankees, because I knew I would get shipped out again. The Yankees had a really strong pitching staff and I knew my chances were slim. So I stayed with Portland in '48 and I worked real hard.

Tommy Bridges, by the way, was a pitching coach. Tommy's job was to teach me a better curve ball. But he threw his curve overhand, and I was a three-quarter arm pitcher. They didn't think my breaking stuff was that effective, so I was going to pitch overhand with the fastball and the curve and go with my sinker and whatever other breaking stuff I had, three-quarter. So I pitched as they wanted, and went 2-9 or 3-9 till mid-season, and finally Jim Turner said, 'That's enough.'

They worked real hard. They took slow motion pictures of me and monitored my progress, but I just wasn't equipped to throw overhand. My fastball didn't do that much. It moved better at three-quarters. So Turner told me to go to the bullpen and play down there, and we'll get you into some games, then start you again.

I ended up at 14-11. I won twelve games during the second half. I pitched well enough that Casey liked me. When he went up from

Duane Pillette was released by the San Francisco Seals because the team wanted to avoid paying him a bonus. He then signed with Seattle, and ended the season with a 16-8 record.

Oakland to the Yankees, he took Turner along as his pitching coach and he brought me along to learn how to throw a decent change and a curve ball.

They were concerned that the way I was throwing my curve that I would hurt my elbow, and they were right because I ultimately did hurt my elbow. But I felt I was much more effective with my curve throwing it three-quarter than overhand.

In 1949, I came from Portland, making $5,500 for the season. I went to the Yankees and signed for $5,000, and made the ball club. After cut-down time, I went up to see [Yankees general manager] George Weiss. He made me wait for about forty-five minutes. I said to him, ' Mr. Weiss, I've never met you in person, only talked with you by phone, and I thought this would be a good time to meet you.' It was an off-day. He asked, 'What can I do for you?'

I said, 'I am a fifth starter, and I think I've done a pretty good job, and I don't really believe I should have to take a $500 cut in pay to come from the minor leagues and go to the greatest team in baseball.' He sputtered and stammered a few times and arranged his papers. I never sat down — he didn't invite me to sit down. He said, 'Well, what the hell do you want?'

I was going to ask for $6,500, but I felt that I'd get $6,000 if I asked for it, so I upped it to $7,500. And he gave it to me! He was so mad at himself he traded me to the St. Louis Browns. He was tough. Really tough.

DUANE PILLETTE

TONY PONCE

*T*ony Ponce broke in with the San Francisco Seals in September 1953 as a thirty-two-year-old rookie. He had one meteoric run around the league, winning eight, while players found out what he threw. A solid pitcher who threw lots of innings for his team, Ponce was a fan favorite.

I signed out of high school in Whittier, and went to spring training at El Centro with the San Diego Padres. There were a lot of good players there in 1941. Cedric Durst was the manager, Bill Salkeld, Del Ballinger were our catchers. Mickey Haslin, Swede Jensen, Art Garibaldi, George McDonald were all there. It was a good group.

I was sent to Anaheim of the California State League, but then, with the war coming, I had to go into the Army. I served for three years. I rested for a year before returning to baseball after the war.

There were veterans returning from the war, so it was difficult to advance through organized baseball. Casey Stengel signed me for the Oakland Oaks, but they were loaded with veterans.

As far as pitches, I had everything but a great fastball. My fastball was pretty good, and I could change speeds pretty well, and I had good control. I also had a knuckleball, a slider, a fork ball. I could give a batter three balls, then give him three knuckleballs to get him out.

With Ventura, before coming to the Seals in 1953, I went 15-20 — bad ball club. We finished close to sixty games out of first place. Of the twenty games I lost, ten were by one run!

Tommy Heath of the Seals checks to see if Ventura might have some pitching help for the 'big club.' Dario Lodigiani, the Ventura manager, suggests me and also Jose Perez, our catcher and a real good hitter.

We flew up to San Francisco, and got to the ballpark. The Oaks are beating up on the Seals pretty bad, and Tommy asks if I could pitch the last inning. I put them down one-two-three, and Tommy comes up to me and tells me I'm pitching tomorrow!

When San Francisco takes me up, I finish 8-0, so I was 23-20 on the season.

TONY PONCE

Tony Ponce was a control pitcher. He wasn't overpowering, but he had a lot of different pitches and could locate them where he wanted them. He gave you a pretty good game when he went out to pitch. When the game was over and you have gone 0-for-4, you'd wonder how you didn't get at least one hit.

RUSS ROSE - Oakland Oaks

I used to catch Tony Ponce a lot with Ventura before we came up to San Francisco, in September 1953. Tony had an unbelievable month, going 8-0 in ten games.

Tony threw a sinker and a slider. He didn't have great speed, but he had great control. And he threw a knuckler. I would guess he threw about eighty-two miles an hour.

He'd show the slider and the fastball, but he tried to get you out with the knuckleball. And the reason was the air. The air at Seals Stadium was always moving, so Tony had a moving knuckleball.

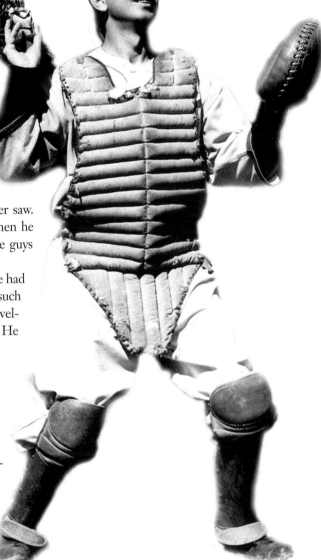

Billy Raimondi in 1940.

When Tony and I went up to San Francisco in September, he was untouchable. The first time around the loop the knuckleball was working real good, and nobody knew him. He was very fortunate.

JOSE PEREZ - San Francisco Seals

RAY PRIM

Ray Prim — old 'Pappy' — he was a real master. He had a smooth delivery with great control, just a little better than anybody thought. He used to be tickled when the clubs would take all their left-handers out of the lineup. He used to say, 'Damn! I just love it when they take all their left-handers out. They don't know I can't get left-handers out.' It used to just tickle him.

He could pitch right-handers in as good as any left-hander I ever saw. He'd had a shot in the big leagues when he was a younger guy. Then he came to the Coast League, like many others did, and some of those guys developed into a real good ballplayers, but never got another shot.

Ray was probably a major league pitcher from his late twenties. He had one of these deliveries where he turns his back to the plate. He had such great flexibility and balance. He was a very smooth guy. He later developed a screwball. There weren't many of those around at that time. He was a true craftsman.

CHARLES "RED" ADAMS - Los Angeles Angels

BILLY RAIMONDI

Billy Meyer was good to me in 1936. I had hurt my arm and Meyer made sure I didn't reinjure it. I was put on the voluntarily retirement list. But that meant I didn't receive any pay, and there were no jobs during the Depression, so I just stayed at home and worked out. If they had released me I would have been out of a job and still received no pay.

I used to keep my mask on with pop-ups so it wouldn't disrupt my glasses. In 1948, a foul pop was hit between third base and home. Merrill Combs and I collided and knocked my mask and glasses off. Ray Hamrick said I should have thrown my mask, but I probably would have lost the ball anyway. Keeping the mask on was safer, and I was used to catching foul pops that way.

Routinely, I'd back up the first baseman on ground balls to the infield. A couple of times I'd get the man at second on the overthrow, but it didn't happen that often. I also got a few runners on overthrows from the right fielder to the first baseman.

I managed a couple of months in 1945. I never wanted to be a manager and I told Devi after the season that I wanted to stay local. Presumably, they got rid of you with a new manager.

I didn't get shaken off too much, and it never bothered me when I did. It's the pitcher's ball game. They should throw what they want. Of course, we'd get together and talk how we'd pitch to certain guys.

I was fortunate. I almost never got hurt. I broke my wrist in '48 and hurt my arm in '35. I did get hit by a ball in the eye — Bernie Uhalt threw a ball from the outfield and it took a bad hop. The eye swelled up pretty good. In 1935, [Oaks trainer] Billy Burke had those leeches. He'd put them on the eye socket. They'd fall off and die, but they'd draw the blood off.

BILLY RAIMONDI

When I signed with the Oakland Club in 1938, Billy Raimondi was the first player I met. He told me what kind of shoes to buy. 'You buy the best. You don't buy second-rate shoes. You buy Feather-Weight shoes. They cost twenty-four dollars.' Wow! Where do you get twenty-four dollars? Which type of bat to use, how to dress — he was my mentor. He steered me right. I roomed with Mel Duezabou. We were both single. Let's leave it at that.

BILL RIGNEY - Oakland Oaks

Billy Raimondi was a good catcher. He didn't have a great arm, but he was quick and accurate, and was good with the pitchers and controlled the game. He had a good feel for the game. He'd hit and run. He couldn't have weighed more than 145, 150 pounds.

CHARLIE SILVERA - Portland Beavers

EARL RAPP

Bill Hall, the Hollywood catcher, was behind the plate when Earl Rapp (of the Oakland Oaks) was batting. He just happens to look up and he catches Earl looking down getting the signs. So [Hall] passes it around the league, and Earl ends up hitting about .270 (.278, and gets sold to Portland). He never hit .300 again. Nobody on our club ever knew it.

BUDDY PETERSON - San Diego Padres

JIMMIE REESE

Jimmie Reese (of the Oakland Oaks, Los Angeles Angels and San Diego Padres) was an exceptional person, and a great guy with a fungo. I saw him pitch batting practice with a fungo. He could do it. They'd put some gloves out in the outfield, and he'd stand at home plate, and he wouldn't miss them by more than three or four feet. He'd hit me about seventy-five ground balls a day. He got me in the big leagues. He could hit them just where he wanted them.

BUDDY PETERSON - San Diego Padres

Jimmie Reese didn't have a bullet arm, but he could get rid of the ball in a hurry.

NINO BONGIOVANNI - Portland Beavers

Jimmie Reese was a great guy. He could pitch with that fungo. I used to catch him in the bullpen. All strikes! Over the plate. It was unbelievable. He managed one year. It liked to give him ulcers. 'No more,' he said, 'No more.' He was helpful to the ballplayers, helping you get in shape, hitting, throwing, anything. He'd come in to pep you up, tell you funny stories.

EDDIE ERAUTT - San Diego Padres

Jimmie Reese was a friend. He's the one who started me on cigars. We were very close. He used to make frames as a hobby. I used to own a liquor store and had lots of photos, all framed by Jimmy.

BOB KERRIGAN - San Diego Padres

HERM REICH

Herm was playing right field for us in a close game against Oakland at Vaughn Street. Herm played that forty-foot fence like he owned it. Anybody who hit a fly ball off that fence and thought he had a double, forget it!

Ad Liska was pitching and we were leading 5-3, with two outs in the ninth, but they had two runners aboard with Earl Rapp batting. It's an overcast night with a heavy mist falling. That's helping to bring some of the soot from the foundry in behind right field to the ground.

I had been watching Rapp in the on-deck circle, swinging and timing Liska's pitches. Now, Liska was a smart pitcher. He had a great sinker ball, and could keep it down. He got a couple by him, but on the third pitch, Earl really got hold of one.

I said, 'Oh my, 6-5 now. We've got to come back in the bottom of the ninth.' After a while, you can tell how far a ball is hit, and this baby was gone!

Well, I turn around and see Reich going back to the wall, jumping up and falling, and tumbling over in front of the fence.

The next thing I know, Reich is getting up, and here comes the ball back at me! He throws the ball in and I say, 'Where the hell did this thing come from?'

And here comes Herm, running by me to the dugout, laughing his butt off. The umpire never called the play. Rapp comes around first. He can't believe it.

So I run in. It's a good thing I took the ball in, because it's dirty! I go into the dugout and I say, 'Herm, that guy hit that ball nine miles.' He said, 'Yeah. It's still going.'

But that's not the end of the story. Three weeks later, we're in Oakland. I see Earl and want to have some fun with him. I said to him, 'Remember three weeks ago when you had a chance to win the ball game at Vaughn Street? I thought you hit that ball pretty good.' He agreed.

I said, 'Since then I've read a lot about that heavy air in Portland. That must have brought your ball down.' He said, 'Yeah, man. Is that air heavy up there!'

EDDIE BASINSKI - Portland Beavers

An agile outfielder known for his unusual accuracy with the fungo bat, Jimmie Reese went to the New York Yankees in 1930 after six seasons with the Oakland Oaks. When he returned to the PCL, in 1933, he joined the Angels in Los Angeles, where he played another six years before becoming a coach with the San Diego Padres.

XAVIER RESCIGNO

Xavier Rescigno was an intense pitcher, very hot-tempered. He had a catcher, Hank Camelli, and they'd argue right in the middle of the game.

Whether somebody got a base hit or he'd walk somebody, he'd stand on the mound, look up at the heavens and say, 'God, where are you? I need you, God. Give me a hand.' He was serious about it. He wasn't kidding around.

BOB KERRIGAN - San Diego Padres

DINO RESTELLI

When I joined the Seals, Lefty O'Doul made me a shortstop. When I was with the San Mateo Blues, a peninsula bush league team, I was playing shortstop. The *San Francisco Chronicle* cartoonist Howard Brodie made a cartoon of Gussie Suhr on a ladder trying to reach my throws from shortstop.

Lefty moved me to third and put John Cavalli at short. He kept telling me that when I fielded a ball, look at the ball, turn it around and read the label, then throw. You have a strong enough arm that you'll make the throw.

Bobby Johnson was our trainer, and he used to umpire our spring training games at Seals Stadium [during World War II]. He would umpire from behind the pitcher, and in one game I picked up a grounder and threw to first, but hit Bobby right in the forehead as he turned to see the play materialize. It knocked him out.

I was shaking as we took him up to the clubhouse. When I hit him, O'Doul said to me, 'Restelli, get out in right field, and get out so far that I don't see you! I don't want to see you!' I wound up playing right field.

DINO RESTELLI

Dino Restelli broke in with the San Francisco Seals in 1944, then was inducted into the Army. Blessed with excellent speed and power, Restelli later divided five seasons among the Hollywood Stars, the Sacramento Solons and the Portland Beavers. His lifetime batting average in the PCL was .308.

BILLY RIGNEY

I don't think I ever saw an infielder that had a better arm than Rig. He could kick a ball and still throw you out. Every once in a while he could show you some power — jack one out of the park.

DARIO LODIGIANI - Oakland Oaks

Billy Rigney had a freshness when he played. Here's where the minors were helpful. The managers would stick with those players. They gave them a chance to play, to prove themselves. You can either play or you can't play.

When Rigney broke in he couldn't hit over .200, but the next year the difference was like day and night. He started hitting the ball hard, batted .288 in 1942. He had a great arm and was always a hustler. And he was smart.

BILLY RAIMONDI - Oakland Oaks

JOHNNY RITCHEY

*I*n 1947, Jimmy Cannon of the New York Post *wrote about Jackie Robinson's integration into the Brooklyn Dodgers clubhouse: "In the clubhouse Robinson is a stranger. The Dodgers are polite and courteous with him, but it is obvious he is isolated by those with whom he plays. I have never heard remarks made against him or detected any rudeness where he was concerned. But the silence is loud and Robinson never is part of the jovial and aimless banter of the locker room. He is the loneliest man I have ever seen in sports."*

In 1948, Johnny Ritchey, a star athlete from the sandlots of San Diego, signed with the San Diego Padres. As Robinson did in the majors, Ritchey broke ground by integrating the Pacific Coast League. Like Robinson, he faced a daunting task.

In 1997, Johnny Ritchey consented to an interview. Because of the lingering effects of a stroke, his charming wife of forty-eight years, Lydia, helped Johnny with the interview. This is their story.

San Diego owner and general manager Bill Starr knew me from when I played at San Diego State. When I came back from playing with the Chicago American Giants of the Negro League, he contacted me about signing with the San Diego Padres. The Padres needed a catcher for 1948.

I signed for a $500 bonus and got $600 a month salary. I also got a $500 bonus from Mr. Starr at the end of the season. He treated me very well. That was good money during those days, and it was about what I had gotten with the Chicago American Giants.

He warned me about the problems I would face. That first year was very lonely for me. I roomed alone and seldom ate with my teammates or did anything with them.

The Oakland Oaks' Billy Rigney is caught in a rundown in a 1942, early-season game against the San Francisco Seals. Don White applies the tag as catcher Joe Sprinz avoids an interference call.

The man who integrated the PCL, Johnny Ritchey, in about 1948. He played with the San Diego Padres, the Portland Beavers, the Sacramento Solons and the San Francisco Seals, usually sharing catching duties with a teammate.

Pitchers threw at me, and I felt runners came into the plate extra hard. Our pitchers didn't retaliate against their hitters. When somebody threw at me, I'd then try to hit the ball right back through the middle. I felt the umpires were fair to me, but I didn't question calls that I felt they missed.

Jim Gleason was a teammate of mine at San Diego State and he was later on the Padres. He was from California. Jim was the kind that would say, 'I have a friend, Johnny Ritchey,' and wouldn't even mention that I was black.

The fans were good to me. I think they were happy to see a player who had grown up in San Diego make it. When he signed me, Mr. Starr told the press he was signing a catcher who could help the Padres, not a black man. I believe he meant it.

The next year, the Padres got Luke Easter, Artie Wilson and Orestes Minoso, but we didn't room together and didn't go out much on the road.

I felt my strength was hitting. I was a pull hitter, but could hit to all fields. I hit good for average, but was a line-drive hitter more than a power hitter. It took lots of work to become a good hitter. I would often bat in the leadoff or the number-two spot. I had good speed, but the Padres didn't steal much when I was there.

JOHNNY RITCHEY

Johnny is a quiet person and he faced the same problems that Jackie Robinson faced. The reason why players like Tony Gwynn can have success today is because of what Johnny went through. Johnny grew up in a multicolored environment in San Diego. He was laid back and was used to dealing with people as people. Now all of a sudden he was thrust into the middle of all of this. We were young and didn't know how to handle it.

In the Negro Leagues, you had so many fantastic players, but you had a lot of talking. Johnny said you would see the players gather around on the ball field as though they were talking strategy, but Johnny said they would be asking, 'Did you see that broad up in the stands?' Those guys kept him in stitches.

The black ballplayers, their sense of humor, it made it hard to play with them. They used to tease him: 'That green-eyed ballplayer from California.' He wasn't really accepted because he was from California.

With the Padres, he couldn't say anything when something happened. He knew that, but he had the right temperament for it. Johnny's presence with the Padres helped encourage black people to go to Lane Field.

The next year Luke Easter and Orestes Minoso joined the Padres. Easter was flamboyant and showed more personality than Johnny could. He had a great year and was very popular with both whites and blacks. Black fans associated more with Luke because he was so open. Johnny had made it easier to accept the other black players.

Minoso was Cuban and didn't speak much English. Johnny and he got along well. Minoso was more sensitive about his color and would react to things against him.

LYDIA RITCHEY

Johnny Ritchey was a very soft-spoken guy, and he was fighting for a job all the time. Everybody accepted him. I never heard any derogatory remarks from anybody, and the fans were behind him also because he was a local guy.

JACK GRAHAM - San Diego Padres

Johnny Ritchey was a good little catcher and a good hitter. I always felt a bit sorry for him when we'd go on the road. He had to stay at a different hotel than we did. He was accepted and appreciated by his teammates.

I read an article that he had some derogatory remarks made towards him by other teams, but I certainly can't remember any incidents. I went down to Atlanta in 1949, and when I got down there, they couldn't even believe that I'd walk on the same field. It was really bad down there at that time.

JOHN "SWEDE" JENSEN - San Diego Padres

JIM RIVERA

There's one man in baseball that I despised — Jim Rivera. I didn't like him as a person and I didn't like him as a ballplayer. He's the only man that I purposely hit. I did it just because of the way he treated me.

DUANE PILLETTE - Portland Beavers

Jim Rivera was a tough ballplayer. He used to steal home and slide head-first into home plate. I can recall once when he stole home and the batter swung at the ball and missed his head by a couple of inches. He was a tough player, but kind of erratic. He didn't treat people very well.

EDDIE BASINSKI - Portland Beavers

JACK SALVESON

Jack Salveson was one of the classic right-hand pitchers in the Pacific Coast League. He was a delightful person, but also a great pitcher to have on your club. If Jack threw over 100 pitches in nine innings, it was a devastating night for him.

He pitched quickly, and everything was for a strike. He believed that the eight people behind him should earn the salary they were being paid. As an infielder, you were liable to have ten to fifteen assists on the day he pitched, and many times Salveson would pitch a game in an hour-fifteen or an hour-twenty minutes

Now think of the consequences of that. Danny Goodman, the concessionaire at Gilmore Field, has 8,000 hot dogs and the game is over in an hour and a half! It doesn't take a rocket scientist to figure that something's got to change. This goes on for two or three games. Now the next start, the game's going quickly. At the end of the fourth inning, the game stops and they start dragging the infield!

That's where it started. That gave Danny Goodman a chance to sell his 8,000 hot dogs.

CHUCK STEVENS - Hollywood Stars

Jack Salveson was with Portland in '47, and he had it all figured out. He'd say, 'I'm going to throw so-many pitches. They're going to hit me or not.' One evening he's pitching in Seattle against Dick Barrett. Barrett lives on one of the outer islands, and he comes up to Jack and says, 'OK, Jack, I've got to catch the 10 o'clock boat to the islands. Let's go.' He'd be out there waiting for the batter. He'd take three warm-ups, and, 'Let's go!' Salveson was the same way. That was their theory: Let's get this game over with.

CHARLIE SILVERA - Portland Beavers

MANNY SALVO

Salvo had pretty good stuff. He was still pretty young. He was tough, could throw hard and he was naturally wild. It made you a little bit leery to face him. He could be a little mean. His fastball had good motion on it.

PETE COSCARART - Portland Beavers

Manny Salvo was a power pitcher. He tipped off his fastball. He'd stop at the top of his windup for a curve, but continue behind his head for a fastball. We tried to tell him, but he wouldn't change.

I liked Manny. I caught him in Sacramento too. When I was traded to Oakland from Sacramento, I hit a home run off him. He took his glove off, put it in his back pocket, and left.

FRANK KERR - San Diego Padres

BILL SARNI

Bill Sarni broke into professional baseball with the Los Angeles Angels at the age of fifteen. Manpower shortages created by World War II prompted the Angels to hire him. Sarni went on to moderate success in the major leagues.

Bill Sarni was a helluva kid, very adult for his age. When I pitched to him, he was only fifteen. I was only twenty-two. He was mature and really a smart catcher. I can recall Ray Prim saying, 'Every time I shake that kid off, they get a base hit off of me. I'm getting to where I just go with him.'

He handled himself very well behind the plate, and everyone thought a lot of him. He was a physically mature kid — a little chunky, but not a fat guy. He looked like he was twenty-one or twenty-two, and that's the way he conducted himself. He was just a very gifted person. That's what had to go on during the war.

CHARLES "RED" ADAMS - Los Angeles Angels

WILLIAM G.H. "SHINE" SCOTT

Shine Scott was the beloved, longtime trainer of the Vernon-Mission-Hollywood franchise. An African American, Scott had no formal instruction as a club trainer. Nevertheless, his players were devoted to him. He also bore the brunt of a continuous flow of jokes, many of them racially tinged.

Everybody loved Shine Scott of the Missions. If you wanted a great rub, just start talking.

Los Angeles Angels catcher Bill Sarni showed great maturity even in his teens, but he lacked the experience and stamina for the long grind of a baseball season. He was with the Angels when the team won pennants in 1943 and '44, but spent most of the time on the bench.

Eventually, he'd realize what he was doing, and he'd say, 'Goddammit, get out of here. I'm giving you a "conversation rub." '

Babe Herman was great at getting on the bench and getting him talking. That's when he first came up with the 'conversation rub' term.

When Shine retired, Wayne Osborne took up a collection for him, and he came out to the ballpark and Wayne gave him the money and said, 'Here's for all the socks that we got off of you and didn't pay for.'

BILL FLEMING - Hollywood Stars

TOM SEATS

Tom Seats worked in the shipyards during the war. He took the train up to Sacramento on Saturday night and pitched both games of a double-header on Sunday. I played in that game. He did quite a job, especially for a man who had hardly any sleep.

He was a strong man. He had arms like an ape, but when he flipped that ball, he had something on it.

Seats became a greater pitcher after he came back from the majors. He went to the St. Louis Cardinals, and was a better pitcher when he returned than when he left the coast.

BERNIE "FRENCHY" UHALT - San Francisco Seals

BARNEY SERRELL

Barney Serrell joined the San Francisco Seals in 1951 after a successful career in the Negro Leagues. Serrell had been with the Kansas City Monarchs from 1942 to 1950. Possibly a bit past his prime, Serrell entered sixty-two games for the 1951 Seals, batting .243.

Barney Serrell was a great player, better than Jackie Robinson. He could do it all. But if The Man threw a black cat on the field, Barney would take the cat and stuff it down The Man's throat.

BUCK O'NEAL - Kansas City Monarchs

Barney had as much or more ability than Jackie [Robinson]. He batted left-handed, and hit left-handers the same as right-handers. He was a smart player. In Mexico, they called him The Professor.

Jackie could stay more more cool around white players. Barney was more hot-headed. I don't think Barney would have taken it.

SAMMIE HAYNES - Kansas City Monarchs

CHARLIE SILVERA

Seals Stadium was like a second home to me, and Charlie Graham tried to sign me. We went up to the [office] tower there in '42. He said, 'I can only give you $125, but we'll keep you close. We can send you to San Jose.' They had a working agreement with them at that time, just that one year, then the league folded.

I always felt that in the American Association, where I played at Kansas City in

1946, they had the younger, hard throwers there. I had to work harder there because they were wilder and with less control.

Then you come to the Coast League. We had Duane Pillette, he had a good sinker, and [Tommy] Bridges with his great curve, and [Ad] Liska, Jake Mooty and Roy Helser. They all knew how to pitch.

Then Turner helped me. He called a lot of pitches, and when I'd come back to the dugout, he'd ask me why he called a certain pitch in a situation. Then he'd explain it to me.

And I hit .247 in 1947. I was hitting against guys like Tony Freitas, Ray Prim — guys who would turn the ball over — and I'm trying to pull the ball.

The next year, Jim Turner tells me, 'You're not going to get a fastball to hit in batting practice. I want you to go up the middle and the other way with the ball.' But I hit .301. What happened, I finally got smart, but Jim Turner was smarter! He was a helluva baseball man.

Turner had pitched to Al Lopez, and he felt Lopez was the best catcher he had ever seen. Turner told me he was going to play me every day. He said, 'I'm going to give you two years of experience in one.' And he did. Turner taught me how to catch the low ball and how to bring a pitch back into the strike zone. You'd be surprised at how many strikes you can get. You can help your pitcher a lot that way.

He taught me how to block the ball in the dirt. He used to say, 'One [missed] ball is one base.' So I became very good at blocking low pitches. He made me a better catcher.

I caught 80 ball games in a row one time. Del Ballinger was one of our other catchers, and he used to take care of me. We roomed together.

I stuck my finger in a fastball one day and it swelled up.

He says, 'Oh, no. I'll be back.' He goes down to a bar and comes back with a lemon. He sticks a hole in the lemon and we put it on my hurt finger. It pulled all the poison blood out of it and I caught the next day.

If that had been in Kansas City, nobody would have thought about that. Everybody out here was just more experienced, knowledgeable, crafty.

CHARLIE SILVERA

ELMER "SMOKEY" SINGLETON

Elmer Singleton's twelve-inning no-hitter was the most disconsolate thing I saw. When he came into the clubhouse, he was really down. In fact, he made the the comment, 'I can see why people jump off bridges.'

Elmer called his own game. Most people don't realize that. He had catchers like Ray Orteig, Roy Jarvis and Ray Partee. He used

Charlie Silvera caught for the Portland Beavers for two years after returning from military service. He learned what he could on his own in 1947, but manager Jim Turner put him on an intensive training regimen in 1948. Casey Stengel later brought Silvera and Turner to the New York Yankees, where they remained for the next eight years. Silvera was used as a replacement for the great Yogi Berra.

to signal with his glove. If he opened the glove up, it was a curve ball, if he kept it closed, it was a fastball, if he held the glove up, it was a change-up. Here the catcher would be calling his signals, and they meant nothing.

DON RODE - Seals Clubhouse Man

When Elmer Singleton was with Sacramento, he was a shell of his former self. He would never make road trips to Phoenix or to Salt Lake City. The air was rarified in both. He was a good pitcher, but the fastball was gone. He dinked you with sliders. He was a smart pitcher.

BUD WATKINS - Sacramento Solons

ARNOLD "JIGGER" STATZ

I can remember Jigger Statz. That's when they decided on the dead ball. Somebody led the league with twenty home runs (Ted Norbert, in 1941). He would play, like, twenty-five feet behind second base, and I'd say, 'Jeez, one of these days he's going to have to run like hell to catch the ball.' But he could do it. He was a smart ballplayer, and he didn't have to do it too often. That was really a dead ball. Boy, did I love it that year.

JOHNNY BABICH - Hollywood Stars

Crafty veteran Elmer Singleton pitched with seven teams in twenty-one seasons. He was a hard-luck pitcher during most of his career: his teammates didn't score a lot of runs, but he still held the game close.

I played against Jigger Statz in 1939. He was like another manager on the field. He played his position well and never had to run too far in Wrigley Field. He had a short right-field fence there. The right fielder played a little over in center, and the power alley in left field was short, so he didn't have too much to roam. But he was just about as good as there ever was in the Coast League. And he wasn't too shabby as a hitter.

RUGGER ARDIZOIA - Hollywood Stars

Jigger Statz was a great outfielder. He was great in going back. He could pick up the the short ones in front of him, and he could go back, in the corner for the balls hit over his head. There were several good center fielders in the league then, but he was the best.

PETE COSCARART - Portland Beavers

Jigger was a real nice gentleman and a tremendous competitor. He was probably forty-four and was still playing center field some. Here he was managing the ball club. I can remember him running in from the outfield to talk to the pitchers.

But Pants Rowland had known Bill Sweeney prior, and I think he had gotten Sweeney over

Infielder Chuck Stevens.

as a coach as part of a long-range plan. Many observers presumed Sweeney was there to take Statz's place. And of course, the 1942 season didn't work out well with the Solons passing the Angels in the last week.

CHARLES "RED" ADAMS - Los Angeles Angels

CHUCK STEVENS

Jim Wilson of the Rainiers owned me, but I owned Allen Gettel. All I had to do was walk out there and I'm four-for-four. When he was pitching, I would expect to end up flat on my butt on the first pitch.

CHUCK STEVENS

Chuck and I were the veterans in the Stars infield. Fred Haney looked to us to visit the pitcher and calm him down. I worked with Johnny O'Neil, Buddy Hicks and George Genovese on the double play. Chuck and I provided maturity for a lot of younger, up-and-coming infielders.

GENE HANDLEY - Hollywood Stars

GUS SUHR

Gussie was a wonderful person, a relaxed sort of fella. Nothing bothered him, just went out and played the game. He gave it his all. He actually came back (out of retirement) and played for the Seals when the war broke out and we lost Ferris Fain.

BERNIE "FRENCHY" UHALT - San Francisco Seals

BERNIE "FRENCHY" UHALT

I chose baseball over football because there was a chance to make a living. In those days, a kid didn't make much money. I was only eighteen years old and getting away on my own. I picked baseball over football scholarships to USC or Cal.

There was a fella named Phil Koerner who came down to Bakersfield to talk with me and try to sign me. He said I could sign a contract with either Oakland or San Francisco. I signed with Oakland because I felt I could play sooner. I met a lot of San Francisco players later and wish I had signed with San Francisco.

I joined the Oaks in 1928. They told me, 'Uhalt, hit the ball to left field because you're not going to hit home runs to right field.' Oaks Park had a high right-field wall and there was a wind that came off the Bay.

They told me to get on base and let Ernie Lombardi and Buzz Arlett drive me in. I would just swing late. But when I got to San Francisco with the large park, I started pulling. I could hit the ball through the hole, all I had to do was get the wrist around.

I was most proud of my defense. As a center fielder, I used to captain the outfield. I used to tell the players, 'If you can't get to the ball, go to the fence. I'll cut across and try to stop it.' I had the speed to get to it. I backhanded a lot of balls and threw out fellows trying to advance a base. They don't practice that today.

After batting practice I never went up and smoked a cigarette like the other players did. I stood out there and saw how the other team hit. I could see if a player was hitting everything to left, for example. I would watch to see where a batter liked the ball and often tell the starting pitcher what I saw. Some pitchers didn't want help, so you talk to those who want to learn.

I wish I had to do it all over again. I wouldn't try to hit everything to left field. I'd put it into play to all fields. If you have confidence, you can hit anybody.

FRENCHY UHALT

Frenchy Uhalt was a great outfielder and an excellent teacher. He would take the younger outfielders in pregame and show them position. On balls between the outfielders, he would tell us to go to the fence. He'd try to cut if off on the way out.

He learned to backhand and throw in one motion — an over-the-top motion — with all he had. He was able to throw runners out at second that way.

DINO RESTELLI - San Francisco Seals

LOU VEZILICH

I broke in during the Depression. I was signed by Justin Fitzgerald for Detroit in 1934. I was signed to a Beaumont contract.

What they would do in those days was finagle the contract: they sign you to one contract then say you don't have the experience, so you end up somewhere else. I ended up at Muskogee. From Muskogee I went to Sioux City. That's where I met Hugh Luby. Also George 'Icehouse' Wilson from, St. Mary's, and 'Cowboy' Smith, from California.

You sign a contract for $200 a month with the Detroit chain. When you get down to spring training, Zellers in the front office comes up and tells you, '[George] Archie, [Roy] Cullenbine, [Benny] McCoy, these players are all going to Houston, but you'll have to take ninety dollars a month.' You know, they probably didn't file the contract. You never got a duplicate.

Detroit had a lot of its players under contract declared free agents by Judge Landis for contract irregularities, so I ended up a free agent. But what are you going to do? You're away from home with no money. When Judge Landis declared me a free agent, I signed with St. Joe and went to Omaha.

That's where Branch Rickey stepped in. At the end of '35, he bought ten of us for the Sacramento Solons. He had bought the Sacramento franchise and needed bodies for the roster. He probably paid $200 apiece. That's how I got to Sacramento.

I had led the Western League in RBI in '35, and get advanced to Sacramento for '36. And what do they give you? Two hundred fifty dollars a month! I hit .296 for Sacramento in '36. I never missed an inning. Then, in '37, I hit .317 and played every inning. Never a pinch hitter or pinch runner. Every inning for two straight years. Whether you had a cold, the flu or whatever, you played. I got a raise to $350, and if I made it to St. Louis, I'd get $400.

Rickey had so much control of the minor leagues. At one time I think he owned nearly all of the Nebraska League until Landis put a clamp on that.

If there was one thing I could do differently, I would have not gotten into Rickey's 'Chain Gang.' I was part of the Chain Gang too long. After having two good years with Sacramento, batting around .300 and playing every inning of every game, I was ready to go to the big leagues, but Rickey wouldn't do anything about it.

After '36 and '37 with Sacramento, in '38 I'm sold to the Cardinals and go three years to spring training with them. I got in at the tail end of the Gas House Gang — Dizzy Dean, Pepper Martin and so forth. In 1938, Rickey took 11 outfielders to spring training to fill four positions! [Joe] Medwick and Terry Moore had positions locked up, and I lost out to Enos Slaughter in the last week. So they shipped me to Rochester. I wasn't good enough for the major leagues, but I had shown I was too good for AAA.

I met with Mr. Rickey three times and never said a word. He would talk for two hours about the problems he had, and wouldn't let me say a thing. I wanted to be traded, but I couldn't tell him. He told me Rochester was a promotion over the Coast.

Finally I wrote Judge Landis and asked to be made a free agent. He wrote back and wouldn't grant it. He said that Sam Breadon, president of the Cardinals, felt he was 'promoting' me by sending me to Rochester, that the International League was a better league than the Coast League.

I had told him that it was not a better league than the Coast League. The pitching in the Coast League was better and that the Coast League was a faster league.

Being in the Chain Gang, he just wouldn't get rid of me. He wanted to keep all of his clubs strong You know, they didn't pay very well anyway. If I could have been traded to another club, I would have gotten more money and I would have had a better chance to reach the big leagues. I was a .300 hitter everywhere I went. I came back to Sacramento for half the season, then was traded to Jersey City.

With the Cardinals, I felt I was in the wrong organization. I never was comfortable there. Too many ballplayers, and they were the lowest-paying organization in baseball. Let's face it, they wanted you for practically nothing.

LOU VEZILICH

BILLY WERLE

I was basically a sinkerball pitcher with good control. I had a good curve ball and change-up. I came in three-quarters or a bit higher. I always had good luck against left handers.

I'm sure that my hitting helped keep me in games. In fact, one game in Portland after we had won the pennant, Lefty O'Doul said, 'Goddang it, you're always griping about your hitting. You're playing first base today.'

BILL WERLE

Billy Werle, a sidewinding lefty, broke in with the San Francisco Seals in 1943, and stayed with them through their 1946 championship season and into 1948. That year, he went 17-7 with a 2.74 ERA in 250 innings, prompting his sale to Pittsburgh. He returned to the PCL in 1955, playing for the Portland Beavers. He later managed in the Coast League. This photo was taken during his stint in San Diego, which lasted from 1958 through '59.

I faced Billy Werle a lot, then played with him. Bill's a real intelligent guy, an entomologist. I really liked him. He was a spot pitcher, didn't overpower you.

I had a great day against him in Portland. I was with Seattle, and hit a three-run homer and a two-run double and a single. Of course, I knew what he was doing. He knew I was a pull hitter, so he just curved the ball, coming from the outside and knick the outside corner. I just laid for that thing and it just kept coming. He became a good manager, too.

EDDIE BASINSKI - Portland Beavers

MAX WEST

I remember Max West with Sacramento in 1935. He was a big strong kid. He was still pretty inexperienced as a hitter, and needed to work with somebody like Lefty O'Doul. But he was speedy and was a good outfielder.

PAUL GREGORY - Sacramento Solons

It was a real pleasure to play with Max West. He was always on me about something, but I didn't pay much attention to him. We were always good friends. I roomed with him the one year, and we got along great.

He was a good outfielder, played well and knew how to run the bases. He used to complain that any ball that was above the waist was a ball, and he'd tell the umpire, 'That was high.' He'd come by me on the way back and ask, 'Where was that second pitch?' I'd say it looked like a strike, right down the middle, and he'd mumble and give me hell for agreeing with the umpire. But that's the way Max was.

I'd swing at all those balls. I was more of a free-swinger, and they'd pitch me up and I'd swing at half of them, and I chased all the curve balls under the plate. But every once in a while, they'd slip up and that's when you'd do a job.

I had him out flying one day. We were in spring training in Ontario. I had flown in from Long Beach, so I said to Max after the workout, 'Why don't you come flying with me? We'll fly around for fifteen or twenty minutes.' So we came back to Ontario and I call the tower and they say, 'You're number three to land, behind the airplane on final and a military aircraft on long final.' I'm trying to find the military airplane to line up behind him. Max is trying to point it out to me, and I can't find it. When we get on the ground, Max says to me, 'I'll never fly with you again. Christ, you can't see!'

JACK GRAHAM - San Diego Padres

Max West was a good hitter. But he was like Eckhardt when he got on base — didn't know what direction to run. But he was young. He was a pretty good outfielder with good power. Seals Stadium didn't bother him. He could pull the ball. They'd throw behind him once in a while. They had to respect him.

JOHNNY BABICH - Mission Reds

Max West, shown here in San Diego Padre livery, was a power-hitting outfielder and a first baseman for the Pads and for the Los Angeles Angels. An average fielder, he took over when he stepped up to the plate. From 1947 to 1952, West clubbed 192 homers and earned 166 RBI.

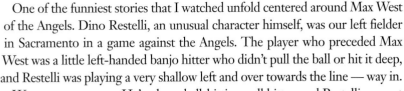

One of the funniest stories that I watched unfold centered around Max West of the Angels. Dino Restelli, an unusual character himself, was our left fielder in Sacramento in a game against the Angels. The player who preceded Max West was a little left-handed banjo hitter who didn't pull the ball or hit it deep, and Restelli was playing a very shallow left and over towards the line — way in.

West comes up next. He's a long-ball-hitting pull hitter, and Restelli was out there counting the clouds, or whatever. He doesn't change to where he should have been against Max, which is way over in left-center and deep.

The pitch to Max was outside and off-speed, and he went out in front of it and squibbed it over third base. And Restelli was standing there and caught it.

It was the third out, and Max stopped halfway down the first-base line and waited for Restelli to come in. When Restelli came by, he stopped him.

Now our team's in the first-base dugout and we don't know what's going on. So Restelli comes in and says, 'What the hell's wrong with him?' We said, 'What happened?' He said, 'Restelli, come over here. My name is Max West. I'm a left-handed batter. I am a long-ball hitter. I am a pull-hitter. You play me, you dumb son of a bitch, in deep left-center.'

ROGER OSENBAUGH - Sacramento Solons

JOYNER "JOJO" WHITE

JoJo White was very positive towards my pitching style. He could see that it made me a more effective pitcher. Of course, JoJo had to face me as a batter before he became my manager in Seattle in 1947.

BUD BEASLEY - Sacramento Solons

JoJo came to the Rainiers in the Fred Hutchinson trade. He was another fast, soft-hitting outfielder. Can you imagine the outfield we had with White in left, Bill Lawrence in center and me in right? Each of us was a legitimate center fielder, and we could all go and get 'em.

Although JoJo was quiet, there is no doubt he was a leader both on the field and in the clubhouse. He helped me a lot.

EDO VANNI - Seattle Rainiers

WILLIAM "WHITEY" WIETELMANN

I played against Whitey Wietelmann in the Eastern League. He was at Hartford. That was a Braves outlet. All of a sudden, he's called up to the Braves, and we're wondering what happened. Why did he get called up? He was the only infielder they could get for $200.

At San Diego, he was a good guy, hard worker, played hard all the time. He'd throw batting

Little got by Joyner "JoJo" White, one of the most intelligent players in the PCL. After his playing days were over he managed the Sacramento Solons and the Seattle Rainiers.

practice, and was always joking. You need a couple of guys like that — take things in stride and not take things too seriously.

JACK GRAHAM - San Diego Padres

Whitey Wietelmann was a good guy, a gung-ho guy. He was a good ballplayer and a good coach. Always had a smile on his face. He stayed on with San Diego when they got the big league club. He had a good major league career before.

BUDDY PETERSON - San Diego Padres

TED WILLIAMS

*T*ed Williams went to Hoover High School in San Diego before signing with the home-town Padres *in 1936. When he signed, he was a skinny kid who loved to hit but didn't care much about mundane outfield chores. He also fancied himself to be a crack pitcher.*

Williams was a reserve outfielder in 1936 and a regular in 1937, before owner Bill Lane sold his contract to the Boston Red Sox. His one mop-up pitching experience in 1936 convinced everyone that Mr. Williams should stick to outfielding.

I signed with the Padres for $150 a month. That was pretty good money, but it wasn't good money for that league. As a matter of fact, if I could have made Binghampton (with the Yankees), I could have made more money than signing with anyone else, but my mother wanted me to stay in San Diego. A year later the Red Sox bought me — the Red Sox got an option on me immediately — then I signed with them and I started getting some money.

I went out one day and talked with Lefty O'Doul. I introduced myself, 'My name is Williams.' 'I know who you are,' he said. I asked him what I always asked a hitter with a little reputation — I said, 'What do I have to do to become a great hitter?'

Seeking an autograph, Dick Dobbins presented a photograph of Ted Williams to the man himself in 1957. Williams signed the picture, and ordered a dozen copies for himself.

He gave me the greatest single boost that I had ever gotten in hitting to that time. He said, 'Kid, don't let anybody change you.' After a while it started to sink in, what he was saying.

I had every advantage a kid could ever have breaking in. I'm on a squad with a lot of older veterans, and they all could give some advice to a kid. I'd get a little hint from them now and then. As the pitchers started to change their style of pitching to me, Herm Pillette — "Old Folks" — said, 'What's he throwing to you, a lot of slow stuff? The next time you're up there, lay back a bit and wait for the slow stuff. Wait for it.' Well, I did what they suggested, and, bang, I hit a drive to left field, then a drive to right field. Those little hints probably did more for my confidence than any other hints I got.

There was no need to send me to a lower league. I was doing pretty good in the league. I hit .271 my first year and .291 my second. Then they sent me to the Minneapolis, a better league than the Coast League at that time, and I won the triple crown. I was really coming fast then.

Everything that was said, I listened and tried them. I was pretty smart in determining what was said to me would pertain to me.

The Yankees felt the American Association was a faster league at that time. They had better players there. The Coast League was a different type of league. The Coast League was a more experienced league. That was a big advantage for me, because I was hearing things there that I wouldn't have heard anywhere else, and I was just coming into my own. I had so many good breaks coming along, I was just very lucky. I was willing to listen. I told every kid to be sure to listen.

Tony Freitas was a little left-hander up in Sacramento — I remember him. I remember Wee Willie Ludolph. I hit him pretty good. The first major league home run was off of [Cotton] Pippen. I didn't hit him well in the minors, but hit pretty well in the majors.

Johnny Babich impressed me pretty much. He could throw it. I hit him pretty good, but he had as good stuff as anyone up there.

TED WILLIAMS

I can recall that we played American Legion ball in San Diego, and Ted Williams was on the team. I'm sure it was at that sports field where they built Lane Field.

The sports writers in Boston looked at Ted Williams as a cocky, know-it-all kid. As a youngster, he'd say, 'Boy, someday people are going to say there goes the greatest hitter in baseball.' They got on him and rode the hell out of him. It wasn't bragging, it was desire.

Ted was an average outfielder. He was more interested in working on his hitting. Ted didn't care much about fielding. He wanted to hit.

And he wanted to pitch also! One day, I think we were playing the Angels. Shellenback let him pitch. Singles, doubles, triples, homers. He finally realized he wasn't a pitcher.

GEORGE McDONALD - San Diego Padres

I played against Ted Williams in sandlot ball on Sundays. He used to play right field. He was a skinny kid. He didn't hit too much then, but he looked powerful and you could see he was going to come around. He was also a pitcher in high school, but what he really wanted to do was hit.

I saw him at a San Diego old-timers game. I hadn't seen him in sixty years. I went up to him and he says, 'Pete Coscarart, I remember you.' We talked about the sandlot days. He asked about some of the people we played with then.

PETE COSCARART - Portland Beavers

Ted Williams and I were good friends. We used to play together during the winter leagues. One time I was playing center field and he came out when he was still in high school. He brought his own uniform. The coach said, 'We're going to put him in the outfield to see what he looks like.' I said, 'Sure. Let him take my place.'

So he went to center field. We had a couple of innings to go, somebody hit a line drive and he charged it, and it went over his head. He looked terrible. But he came up to bat, and he took three swings — real beautiful swings. Somebody on the bench said, 'You know, that kid's got a real terrific swing. If he ever starts connecting, he's going to be a good hitter.' He didn't know what he was saying.

He worked out with us, and what a hitter he became! He never did become a great outfielder, just adequate. He never did have a good arm, but he didn't need anything more but his hitting. When he came into the Coast League the following year, he only played from July on. You could see the improvement by leaps and bounds. It was amazing. He would hit Bill Posedel and some of the others. He hit a couple of home runs and doubles, and just looked great because he had a lot of hitting ability.

STEVE COSCARART - Portland Beavers

I played against Ted Williams in San Diego when he was a rookie. He was a great hitter then. He never swung at a bad ball. The ball would come an inch or two inside or outside and he'd take it. He had great wrists. He hit the ball through to all fields.

We tried to talk about how to pitch him in our clubhouse meetings. He'd do just the opposite. We'd pitch one way and we'd play him that way, and he'd hit the ball to the opposite field.

NINO BONGIOVANNI - Seattle Indians, Portland Beavers

MAURY WILLS

There was one of the most amazing things I ever saw. I pitched against Maury in the Coast League for three years, and he never hit his hat size out here. He couldn't hit you if you ran across the plate. In 1959, I played winter ball with him, and Detroit bought him while we were there. He never gets to put on a Detroit uniform on and ends up in Los Angeles.

Somewhere, he must have been hit by lightning. He's the same guy, he just changes uniforms. In the major leagues, he's a star.

BUD WATKINS - Sacramento Solons

Maury Wills was given a full four-year scholarship to Ohio State University as a quarterback. He had a great arm. He was powerful. He could throw a football sixty yards. But as a shortstop, he really wasn't that sharp when I played with him. He made a lot of errors, and he couldn't turn the double play. He was just an average ballplayer with Seattle.

He was experimenting hitting from the left side, so it was just a so-so year. He was a .267 hitter down here, and for him to do what he did in Los Angeles, I was amazed.

In the Coast League, his production wasn't that good. (He stole twenty-one bases in 1957, and twenty-five each in 1958 and 1959.) Then he steals 104. It's tough for a right-hand hitter to start trying to become a switch-hitter in the middle of his career. I've got to hand it to him.

EDDIE BASINSKI - Seattle Rainiers

Most Pacific Coast League players were amazed at the success Maury Wills had with the Dodgers after he left the Seattle Rainiers. In the PCL, Wills' highest stolen-base total was twenty-five, with Spokane in 1958 and 1959, and his batting average for his three Coast League seasons was .268. The photo above was taken in 1957.

ARTIE WILSON

We were the third team in the Coast League to have a black player on the roster. Artie became the most popular player we ever had. He did it because he performed. He made the plays. The fans just loved to see him come to bat.

He'd lose twenty or twenty-five balls for us every game, fouling off pitches. But you never knew what he was going to do. He was fast, and he hustled and you could hear him hollering out at shortstop on defense. He just had it. And he would sign autographs for the fans. You didn't have to tell him to do it. He enjoyed doing it. He was a great influence on our team.

I must say, [manager] Charlie Dressen didn't know how to handle this. But Charlie didn't mind that the man was black. He had seen it happen in the major leagues with Jackie Robinson. Nobody gave Artie a bad time in Oakland.

BILL LAWS - Oaks Radio Announcer

Artie Wilson supplied the fire department (which was located next to the park) all the balls they needed out at Emeryville. He fouled off more balls over the fence behind third base.

DARIO LODIGIANI - Oakland Oaks

You always have someone that your club just can't get out. Seattle had Artie Wilson. I don't think we got him out ten times all year. No matter what he did, he got a base hit or beat the ball out, or we blew the play. We're playing him up close, because we knew he was just trying to bounce the ball into the ground and beat it out. And, of course, we had to shift around because he hit everything to the off-field.

JACK GRAHAM - San Diego Padres

In 1952, Artie Wilson and Bob Boyd joined the Seattle club. Everybody loved Artie. He spent all his money on clothes. We'd go to Los Angeles, and he'd go out to all the clothes factories. I remember in the clubhouse, he'd be the only guy who had matching undershirts and shorts. They could be peach color or something other.

He'd have parties in his room on the road every night. He'd invite teammates to come over. I remember going to some of them. He was just a great guy.

Bob Boyd was more of a quiet type of guy. He was a nice guy and an excellent first baseman, but he wasn't flamboyant like Artie was.

CLAUDE CHRISTIE - Seattle Rainiers

Artie Wilson was one of the greatest guys I ever played with. He really lent a lot to the ball club. I can't tell you how — just the fact that he was there and played every day. His enthusiasm was catching.

We were playing a twi-night game, and Artie was in the on-deck circle, and somebody wanted to score on a fly ball. The on-deck circle at Sacramento was more behind home plate than in other ballparks. In any case, the throw comes in from left field, and I don't recall whether it was deflected and hit home plate, but the ball bounced and hit Artie right in the eye. I think he temporarily lost the sight in that eye. Now that was 1957, and his last season.

But in 1962, when Artie was forty-two, he was selling automobiles in Portland when Milt Graff, the Beavers second baseman, broke his leg. They asked Artie to come back and fill in at second base for the Beavers, and he did, and finished out the rest of the year.

BUD WATKINS - Sacramento Solons

Artie's great years were with Oakland. He led the league in hitting in 1949. He was a great player with Oakland, not so great when he got to Portland. He wasn't a good double-play man, either. But he could run, steal a lot of bases and score a lot of runs. He made things happen.

He couldn't pull the ball. That drove me crazy at second base. I played him right behind the base, in center field, practically, and he'd still punch that ball through. He could wait on the ball. Because Artie hit the ball the other way, he was looking at that ball a lot longer than guys who pulled the ball. He just sliced the hell out of it. You couldn't strike Artie out. He had a thumb that was severed. Can you imagine playing without a thumb?

Artie loves the game of baseball, possibly more than any-body I've ever met. Even to this day, at his age, at the drop of hat, he will pick up a bat and play pepper or play catch.

EDDIE BASINSKI - Portland Beavers

Artie and Maurie Wills — we never even bothered to go over them in meetings. Artie was going to hit everything to left, and you know Wills is going to bunt twice a game, and the other times he's going to hit to the left side, so you pitch him outside and let him hit over there.

BUD WATKINS - Sacramento Solons

[In 1991 Dick Dobbins interviewed Artie Wilson for Nuggets on the Diamond. *Then seventy-one, Wilson was hoping the Senior Professional League wouldn't fold (it did) because he wanted to go down to Arizona and play in that league. He seemed to have been in good enough shape to do it.]*

GENE WOODLING

G ene Woodling played only one season in the Coast League — *1948— but what a season it was! Not only did he win the bat-ting championship with a new stance devised for him by his mentor, Frank "Lefty" O'Doul, but he broke his ankle and missed six weeks, and he was sold to the Yankees.*

O'Doul saved Woodling. He had a normal, open stance, and he couldn't pull the ball. O'Doul got him to stand up like [Stan] Musial and drop the shoulder towards the pitcher. His hands were in close, so he was forced to pull it. He had to learn to hit off his back foot, and Lefty worked with him on that.

DINO RESTELLI - San Francisco Seals

(In an eight-game series at Portland, Woodling batted .571, with three doubles, three triples, six home runs, fifteen runs batted in and eighteen runs scored. Wow!)

I was a glorified assistant trainer — clubhouse boy. I did work on Gene Woodling on one occasion, and he walked around with a stiff neck for a few days, so they kept me away from him thereafter. The best story about Woodling is, when he came with us, he was a fairly good hit-ter, but not really good. Lefty looked at him once, and said, 'Were going to take care of you.' He tied a rope around his waist, and every time Gene Woodling went to swing, if he was lung-ing, O'Doul would pull the rope

Lefty only had to do it two or three times. What it did was teach him to hit off the back foot. Of course, he went back up with the Yankees and was a star. Lefty rekindled his career.

DON RODE - Seals Clubhouse Man

Gene Woodling was one of Lefty O'Doul's most successful recla-mation projects. Woodling came to the San Francisco Seals from Pittsburgh in a trade for pitcher Bob Chesnes. Unable to turn on an inside fastball, Woodling took coaching from O'Doul and ended up leading the league in hitting with a .385 average.

Seattle Rainiers shortstop Billy Schuster slides safely into home on a steal, tying the score in the eighth inning of the first game of a double-header with the San Francisco Seals in 1940. Looking on are umpire Joe Mazzeo, catcher Wilfred Leonard (late with the tag) and Rainiers center fielder Bill Lawrence. The Seals went on to win, 9-6.

7

A SEPARATE CHAPTER ON BILLY SCHUSTER?

This Los Angeles Railway pass featured a picture of Los Angeles Angels shortstop Billy Schuster, known for his abilities as a player and as a comic.

Yes, Billy Schuster gets his own chapter.

In the annals of Pacific Coast League, probably no one player is more remembered than Billy Schuster. Schuster broke in with the Seattle Rainiers in 1940, was acquired by the Los Angeles Angels, later returned to Seattle, and ended it all with the Hollywood Stars in 1952. In 1940, '44 and '45 he had trials in the National League, falling a mite short each time.

Billy was a true "flake" but he was also a fine player. While there other comics graced the PCL, Schuster was more unpredictable than the rest. Umpires were victimized by him, managers couldn't control him. Players didn't know what to expect from him, and the fans loved him.

That's why a spearate chapter is devoted to him.

For his wife of forty-nine years, Marion, it was love at first sight. But she couldn't control him either.

Billy was always funny. He went to an all-boys school and was very popular in town. He was five years older than me.

Several of us went to the library to study one night. It was a large group and I didn't know everybody, and on the way home, in front of my house, one of the boys said, 'Do you know who this is?' I said, 'No, I don't.' He said, 'This is Bill Schuster.' Actually, they called him 'Dink.'

Schuster during his L.A. days.

I said, 'Dink Schuster. Oh, my.' I had talked about him and told my friends I had known him and here I just met the guy. I ran into the house, I was so embarrassed.

He would borrow one of his teacher's cars and drive around our school with the horn blowing. And I'd say, 'Oh, my god. There goes Bill.' It was always stuff like that.

We used to double-date. One Christmas, Billy and another boy both gave me wristwatches. He said, 'Which one are you going to keep?' I said, 'Yours, of course.'

We got married when I was twenty-one. He had already signed his first contract and had been called up by Pittsburgh the year before. We continued to live in Buffalo in the off-season.

In 1940, I went to spring training in Florida with Bill. He was with Boston, and Casey Stengel was the manager that year. He treated Bill like dirt. He was a mean old son of a gun. At the end of spring training, Bill was sold to Seattle.

We took our car and drove it across country, meeting the club in Sacramento. Bill was at bat thirteen times before he got his first hit. He just bowed and said, 'Thank god for that!' We were in Seattle two years, then he was sold to Los Angeles. I drove the car to Los Angeles by myself.

We returned to Buffalo during the off-season, then moved to Los Angeles permanently after the 1945 World Series was over. The first year we rented Lou Novikoff's house and then we bought a home in Long Beach after the season.

When the Angels were at home, I would load our two girls into the buggy and take them to the ballpark for day games. I'd get a baby-sitter for night games. I seldom missed a game.

Bill was always funny, even way back in high school. I never knew what he was going to do. It was never planned, always spontaneous. He always had something in his mind. Some of the stunts he used over and over, but others just came into his mind when something unusual happened. It would just be an idea, and away he went with it.

He was always one step ahead of everyone else. We never discussed his antics at home after the game. I would read about it in the paper.

At times his actions embarrassed me. 'Oh, god. Here we go again.' But then I'd say, 'Well, it's just Bill.' I can see him now, climbing up the screen and blowing his bubbles. He was the first one to chew bubble gum of any ballplayer.

I had no idea why he did these things or when he was going to do them. Was he out to rattle the pitcher? I imagine. I do know he was always out to win. He would do anything to win. He never thought he was going to lose.

Anything he did, if he played cards with me or even played games with the kids, he had to win. I refused to play cards with him because of his attitude.

I learned not to be embarrassed by his tricks. He was not malicious with any of them. The umpires got tired of him, but he wasn't trying to show them up. Everything he did was clean and in good fun.

He had fans in every city. When he played on the road he'd get fans who would give him a hand everywhere he went. I think Bill wore on manager Bill Kelly's nerves. Bill Kelly was a nervous person, but [manager] Bill Sweeney loved him.

Bill loved to play golf. After the season, he'd take a week off then go look for a job. And he'd get in golf whenever he could. When spring training started, that's when Bill started training. He went 'cold.'

I really didn't have any favorite tricks of his. Everything he did was funny, even around the house, even his winter jobs. He always had funny stories to tell about those. He delivered Kraft cheese and later he worked as a guard at Republic Steel, and he'd come home every night and tell funny stories from work.

And he was a terrific storyteller. We had planned on recording them, but we never got around to it. He had a certain infectiousness to his stories. And he could talk on any topic, non-baseball, anything.

We were married forty-nine years. He passed away (from a heart attack) so quickly, it was such a shock. I never saw another man.

MARION SCHUSTER - Bill Schuster's Wife

He helped coach baseball at our local school, both the boys' and girls' teams. We had asphalt diamonds. My former boyfriend, who I still talk with, says he still remembers my dad and the stories he told them, and how he did coach and teach the philosophy of the game. He is now a scout for the Dodgers, and he recalls so much that my dad taught him.

BARBARA KETTLE - Bill and Marion Schuster's Daughter

Bill Schuster was about as good a clutch ballplayer I've ever seen. He had great hands. You could hit him the roughest hop in the world, and if it was the last out in the game . . . I don't ever remember him screwing up in a jam. He was a better hitter when the chips were down. He was a tough, good ballplayer, but he did some damn crazy things.

He was a battler, and if he didn't come through, it bothered him.

CHARLES "RED" ADAMS - Los Angeles Angels

You know, that dirty rat, when I joined the Portland club and we were in Los Angeles, I was his seventh hidden-ball-trick victim. And this was my friend! We were both from Buffalo. I hit a double, and he's talking to me about Warren Spahn and Frankie Drews and Sibby Sisti and I'm not paying attention.

All the sudden, he's standing next to me and says, 'Hey Ed, look what I've got.' He said, 'Why don't you make a dive for it and we'll make it look good.' I said, 'Like hell.' So he hit me on top of the head. And here's Jim Turner thinking, 'This guy's been in the major leagues?' I could have killed Schuster that day, the dirty rat.

EDDIE BASINSKI - Portland Beavers

I remember one incident in Seattle — I was playing first base, and Billy was with Seattle. He topped the ball to the catcher, and as he ran down the line, he must have been 10 feet inside the first base line. He peeled off, and I caught the ball and said, 'What the

BILL SCHUSTER . . . A real master at the difficult shortstop position, Schuster is a familiar figure in Pacific Coast League parks. Has played with Seattle, Los Angeles, then Seattle once more over the past decade. Had a two-year whirl with the Chicago Cubs in 1944-45 and played with a pennant winner there in 1945.

Delightfully different indeed — it would have been difficult to find a player better suited for the Hage's ice cream slogan.

Variations on a Theme by Schuster

He'd run right out to the pitcher and slide into the mound to be tagged out, or he might run to third.

BOB KERRIGAN - San Diego Padres

We had a pitcher who had just come down from the major leagues, and he had never heard of Schuster before. He was pitching to Schuster in a game at Hollywood, and Schuster hit a ground ball right back to him. He bends down to pick up the ball, and when he straightens up, here's Schuster running right at him, sliding at him. He didn't know what to do. Someone had to yell at him to throw the ball to first base. He finally did, and he came back to the bench and said, 'That man is crazy.' That's something we already knew.

RUGGER ARDIZOIA - Hollywood Stars

In a game at Wrigley Field, I struck out a batter to end an inning while Schuster was in the batting circle. As I'm getting ready to come off the mound, I see this player streaking towards me. It's Schuster.

He came out at a full tilt, got to the pitcher's mound, stopped dead, and said, 'Nice pitch,' and went off to his shortstop position. I didn't know if he was coming out to attack me or what. He was unpredictable.

CON DEMPSEY - San Francisco Seals

'Kewpie' Barrett was a good friend of Schuster's. They had both been at Seattle. When L.A. played Seattle, they'd get together. Kewpie knew all of Bill's tricks. Well, Bill hits one back to the mound, and Kewpie gets the ball and is nonchalant with it. He looks up, and here's old Bill running at him, wide open. Well, Kewpie throws the ball in the direction of first and starts running as fast as he can towards the outfield, with Schuster in pursuit.

CHARLES "RED" ADAMS -
Los Angeles Angels

I saw him get decked one night in Hollywood. Roy Joiner was pitching. It was the first of the ninth, two outs and nobody on. We were leading and Billy Schuster tried to drag-bunt one. Joiner threw him out, and when Billy crossed the mound on the way back to his dugout, Roy was waiting for him. He busted him right in the mouth, laid him out cold!

Schuster was laying on the mound. The groundskeepers were turning out the lights. He was the only guy out there.

EDDIE ERAUTT - Hollywood Stars

I was there when Bill got decked. The game was over, and they turned off the lights right away. I didn't see it. But someone came into the clubhouse and said, 'Schuster's laying out there on the field.' Joiner's walking off, and Schuster ran up to him, I guess, and stopped. Schuster liked to do that. Joiner popped him!

When he came in the clubhouse that night, he looked like a guy who had just seen a ghost. His eyes were that big. He had just come to.

CHARLES "RED" ADAMS

Bill said, 'I woke up and the place was dark.'

MARION SCHUSTER - Bill's Wife

hell is going on?' Of course, he never said anything. Everybody's laughing, the players and the fans.

Well, the next day, we're having hitting practice, and [Rainiers manager] Paul Richards is standing around, and I ask him, 'What the hell is going on with that guy?' He said, 'You've just got to realize, Jack, he's crazy!' So that's all that was said.

He was a good ballplayer. In L.A. he used to run up the screen, act like a monkey. He did all those things to be funny, I guess, to draw attention.

You'll always have somebody on a club who'll do things to draw attention, and you'll think the guy's crazy, but actually, he's working at something. It often helps to keep a club loose.

JACK GRAHAM - San Diego Padres

I remember one time over in San Francisco, it's a clutch situation, and Bill hits a big pop-up, straight up. He starts to run, then realizes it's going foul. Bill runs over behind the catcher with his bat. While the catcher is waiting for the ball to come down, Bill gets over behind him and — whomp . . . whomp . . . whomp — like he's hitting him over the head.

Now the catcher knows Bill's there, and he's got to concentrate on the ball and the wind blowing while all this is going on behind him.

Bill was called out on strikes at a game at Wrigley Field, and he stiffened up, as if he had been shot, and fell straight back. Well, a photographer just happened to catch the picture in mid-fall, so here's this picture of Bill falling dead backwards in the newspapers.

CHARLES "RED" ADAMS - Los Angeles Angels

Schuster was kind of crazy, but a good clutch hitter. We were playing against the Angels one day. Billy had a bunch of free passes that he'd given to his buddies, and they were all along the first-base line. Well, Lenny Ratto was our shortstop, and Billy hit a line shot, one-hopper, headed for left field. The minute he hit the ball, Billy figured he had a single.

Hollywood Stars pitcher Roy "Pappy" Joiner didn't find Billy Schuster particularly funny. During the ninth inning of a game in 1943, Joiner decked Schuster when he ran straight from the batter's box to the pitcher's mound.

Ratto made the greatest play that he ever made in his life: He dove, sliding on his elbow, and in one hop the ball's in his glove.

Schuster's running along, and says, 'Hey guys, I'll meet you at Gate 19 after the game.' He turns around and here's Ratto throwing a bullet to first to get him out. Schuster gets fined fifty dollars for not hustling.

The next day, here's Schuster up at the plate. The story's in the paper — 'SCHUSTER FINED $50 FOR NOT HUSTLING.' He hits a one-hopper to the pitcher. That pitcher is going to throw him out by a mile.

Billy gets into a sprinter's stance, like Jesse Owens. He shot down the first-base line. He didn't stop at first base, ran all the way to the outfield and started climbing the wall. And when he came running back to the dugout he said, 'Now that's hustle!'

EDDIE BASINSKI - Portland Beavers

There was a rail in front of the dugouts at San Diego. He'd cut out and jump the rail in front of the dugout and climb the screen. The umpires made him stop doing that. He was slowing up the game.

BOB KERRIGAN - San Diego Padres

Billy Schuster in August, 1950.

Billy Schuster was classic. First I played against him, then he became a teammate. He later became my manager in the Western International League. Oh man, did we put it on. Whether there was any baseball played or not, we got a crowd.

When I was with the Solons, one night Bill Schuster is batting against me at Wrigley Field. I throw over to first base five times, trying to pick the base runner off. The next thing I realize, Billy is standing next to first base, with bat at the ready, waiting for me to 'pitch' the ball to first base again.

BUD BEASLEY - Sacramento Solons

Bud Beasley is pitching for Seattle, and he's going through all the gyrations that he did. Schuster, no doubt, had been hoping for the moment. Bud starts out with the pumps, working his way up his body. The first time, Bill just leans on his bat.

Beasley starts again, and while Beasley is doing all that stuff Schuster starts doing the hula. He's not going to be out-done.

He hits one back to the mound and runs out there, sticks his hand out, and shakes hands with Beasley.

CHARLES "RED" ADAMS - Los Angeles Angels

We picked him up for pennant insurance in '52. No telling what he was going to do. The first time I ever saw him, he scored a run, but he didn't stop. He kept running and climbed the screen behind home plate at Wrigley Field.

You've got to have guys like that on the ball club. You've got to keep a club loose.

He and I did a TV program at one of the studios in Hollywood on the afternoon before a night game, so I rode to the ballpark with him. We didn't stop at a stop light the whole trip from the studio! He cut across filling stations and everything, scared the hell out of me! He never stopped until we were in the parking lot. He gets out nonchalantly, and as we're walking to the clubhouse, I ask him, 'Do you always drive like this?' He says, 'Every day.'

CHUCK STEVENS - Hollywood Stars

I was told to be careful going into second base because Schuster would step all over you. Once, when I was on first base, I said to myself, 'Well, this is the time to find out.' I didn't like contact in football, but it never bothered me in baseball, so I'm on first base. I go into second base, stealing, and I go in with my cleats up a bit, and he sees it.

After that I went in time and time-again, and I never had any problem. A couple of times after ball games we got together, and we were always friendly.

TONY CRISCOLA - San Diego Padres

I always thought Billy Schuster was underrated. He could make the plays when you needed him. Because of his reputation as a flake, people underestimated his skills. Oh, he *was* a flake.

CHUCK STEVENS - Hollywood Stars

With guys like Schuster and Chesty Johnson, I went along with them all the way. I felt they were good for baseball. As long as they didn't interfere with some technicality of the rules.

I remember one game, Billy Schuster was back behind home plate with a bat, and all of a sudden he's climbing the screen. When he comes to the plate, he points to some fan sitting behind the third-base dugout. He had those great big glasses with those goo-goo eyes, those sparkling prisms. Billy said, 'He's got me in a trance!' The fans loved it and it didn't interfere with the game.

CECE CARLUCCI - Umpire

Billy Schuster was a pretty good ballplayer, and he was funny as hell. He'd be talking to you at second base, trying to pull the hidden-ball trick on you. He'd be talking and walking towards second, trying to pick you off.

He used to eat garlic, then he'd challenge the umpire and, geez, the umpire would retreat, shaking his head, and Billy's laughing like hell.

RUGGER ARDIZOIA - Hollywood Stars

Neill Sheridan put me up to tricking Schuster. We put a plastic bug in a ball box, and Sheridan told me to 'take it over to Schuster — he loves these things.' So I take it over to Schuster. He opens the box up and it's the most god-awful scream you've ever heard. He goes flying up the clubhouse ramp to his locker. We found him sitting on top of his locker. He was deadly afraid of bugs.

DON RODE - Seals Clubhouse Boy

Bill Doran, a longtime umpire for both the Pacific Coast League and the major league, in 1938.

8 THE UMPIRES, GOD LOVE 'EM!

CORNELIUS "JACK" POWELL - Dean of the Umpires

JACK POWELL BEGAN HIS UMPIRING CAREER IN 1921, AFTER THIRTEEN YEARS AS A PLAYER. HE BROKE IN AS A PCL UMPIRE IN 1928 AND BECAME SUPERVISOR OF UMPIRES IN 1950, A POSITION HE HELD TWO YEARS BEFORE RETIRING. AS AN UMPIRE, POWELL WAS BOTH RESPECTED AND FEARED. HE SOMETIMES HAD A SHORT FUSE, AND GENERATED SOME CONTROVERSY, TOO.

ON AUGUST 20, 1937, FOR EXAMPLE, IN THE MIDDLE OF A STIFF PENNANT RACE BETWEEN SACRAMENTO AND SAN FRANCISCO, JACK POWELL SHOWED UP DRUNK AT CARDINAL FIELD FOR A GAME WITH THE PADRES. LOU VEZILICH WAS AT THE CENTER OF THE ACTION.

In 1937, I don't think it has ever happened before. Jack Powell was umpiring, and he was ten minutes late for the game. He was in bad shape when he got there. Everyone was upset. In about the sixth inning, I'm stealing second, and he called me out. The ball hit the shortstop and rolled away. Everybody could see it, still he called me out. Geez, what a commotion.

Phil Bartleme, the Solons president, got a couple of undercover officers and went out on the field and grabbed him under the arms and threw him headlong into the dugout. Lucky they didn't kill the poor guy.

The funny thing about it, several of us — Joe Orengo, Powell, myself — were over at my friend Vince Stanich's house the night before having a couple of beers. Vince was a sports columnist for the *Sacramento Union*. He got to know the players and umpires, so we went over for a couple of beers. But what Powell did after, I don't know.

Powell should have been stopped before he even got on the field. His partner was just a rookie and he was scared of him. Powell was the league's top umpire. It made all the papers — 'UMPIRE GETS KICKED OUT OF GAME!' I understand he took a pledge to never take a drink again.

LOU VEZILICH - Sacramento Solons

(*Jack Powell was put in jail, then released after San Diego Padres coach Jimmie Reese posted his twenty-five dollars bail. Phil Bartleme explained that he feared a riot might follow if Powell wasn't removed.*)

Jack Powell was the dean of Coast League umpires, and he wanted everything done his way. His way often wasn't my way. He wanted force. He demanded respect, whereas I was going to gain it.

I've seen Powell go over to the dugout: 'How many want to go (get thrown out) today?' They'd plead, 'Not today, Jack, please.' That's the way he umpired.

I was in Seattle one night and it was raining. I was behind the dish. It was Lefty O'Doul of San Francisco and Paul Richards of Seattle. They couldn't wait to give me the lineup cards and get the game started. All the fans had umbrellas.

Early in the game, I look up at third base, and Lefty O'Doul's got a little pink umbrella. Some lady gave it to him. Now there are two outs, so I decide to wait and tell him when he walks back to the first-base dugout to get rid of the umbrella. I didn't want to make a scene.

Now we've got Lou Barbour umpiring down at third right next to him and he didn't say anything to him. Well, Jack Powell is in the stands, and he goes over by third base and he's hollering from the stands at Lefty O'Doul. He's giving him hell.

Lefty got rid of the umbrella, and after the third out he comes walking by me and he says, 'Say, Jack Powell just gave me hell, and I guess he's going to get on you. Tell him that you told me to get rid of it after the inning.'

I can't say that. If I'm going to say anything, I should do it right then. I had a great game, and after the game, I go in and Jack's in there waiting for me, and boy, he ripped me from one end to the other.

Well, I said, 'Damn, I wish *I* had an umbrella.' I said the wrong thing, I guess, because when we go into Portland, Jack is there again, sitting in the stands. He tells us, 'Don't let Lefty talk to anyone in the stands.' I thought Lefty was great for baseball. I thought [Hollywood Stars manager] Bobby Bragan was great for baseball.

He said, 'If he talks to anybody in the stands, I want you to knock him.' I thought, 'Geez, this isn't right.' But he's my supervisor.

So here we are, with the National Anthem, and here's some girl, and geez, she's a knockout. She's trying to get Lefty's attention. Lefty keeps saying, 'I can't. The umpires won't let me.'

Well, after the game, Jack got on me again. He said that Lefty kept talking to people in the stands. Jack just wanted it his way.

CECE CARLUCCI - Umpire

BILL ENGELN

Bill Engeln broke into the Coast League as an umpire in 1936 and was one of the most respected and well-liked umpires during his two-decade career.

I respected Bill Engeln very highly, but I couldn't figure this out: Players would call him names — not many of them, because they respected him — but he would call them back and let him stay in the game. Crossing the line might have been kicking dirt or touching him.

Say you're one-on-one, and the guy calls Bill a dirty no-good S.B., and he lets the guy stay in the game. You're going to lose respect for him. But say Bill called him the same name back, and he let him stay in, then the guy can't call him C.S. or anything. That was the difference with Bill.

A young Oakland pitcher named Bob Murphy, a college kid — something happened and Bill called him a name. Murphy writes a letter to the boss, Clarence "Pants" Rowland. So Pants tells Bill to lay off that word. Bill had other warnings, but I guess Murphy was a good Christian boy, and young.

CECE CARLUCCI - Umpire

My uncle, Bill Engeln, umpired for a long time in the Coast League. I was catching one afternoon, and he was having a bad game. I'd turn around and say, 'You stink! You this and you that.' Back in the dugout, my teammates would say, 'How can you talk to him like that? We say boo and we're gone.' They didn't know he was my uncle.

After people found out he was my uncle, he'd tell me, 'I can't call a close pitch on you. Anything close you swing at.' My strike zone was probably three or four inches wider with him. He probably made me a better hitter. You can hit pitches out of the strike zone.

FRANK KERR - Oakland Oaks (and, later, umpire)

CECIL CARLUCCI - "Mr. Ump"

Cecil Carlucci, joined the PCL umpiring staff in 1950 after four years in the California League. "Cece" was always liked and respected for being a straight shooter and for his hustle.

I tried out as a second baseman or outfielder before the war. I was fast and I could go out and catch a fly. I had a chance to go to Bisbee for sixty or seventy-five dollars. Then the war came and I was drafted. I was gone five years. I was with the Combat Engineers in the Aleutian Islands. We built the Alcan Highway.

After I came back, I talked to Buck Fausett of the Hollywood Stars. 'You lost those five years,' he said, 'You know your rules, have you ever thought of going into umpiring?'

I talked to some umpires and they signed me up with the Southern California Umpires Association. I had worked about a dozen games when the Mexican Winter League hired me. That was the winter of 1945-46.

There were fifteen to twenty major leaguers down there getting in shape, and they were having trouble finding anybody who would call strikes. Bob Lemon was there, also Luke Easter and Theolic Smith. Lemon was getting beat up because nobody would call strikes.

They got me down there, and the first game, a Cuban who was in charge of the umpires put me behind the plate. I get my gear strapped up and am ready to walk out, and he says, 'Uno momento, por favor.'

Cecil Carlucci, "Mr. Ump."

He goes back and straps on a gun. I say in Spanish, 'What are you doing with the gun?' He pats me on the shoulder and says, 'Hey, rookie, you don't know too much!' I'm looking for the first bus out of town, and I haven't called a pitch!

So I go to home plate and all I keep saying when I hear they don't call strikes here is, 'You'd better keep swinging that bat!' Well, it was a 3-2 game, and never a peep! Now everyone wants me behind the dish.

When I got back to the States, I get a call from Bill Schroeder of the Cal League, and I spent four years there, making the All-Star team each year, and was rated pretty high.

At the winter meetings in Baltimore, Maryland, I got drafted by the Western International League. That was B ball. I called Jerry Donovan of the Coast League and told him I was through. Well, Donovan called me back and told me to meet with Pants Rowland.

Rowland worked me over for a good two hours. 'Well, what makes you think you're good enough to work AAA?' I kept shooting right back. After two hours, he started smiling, and he opened his desk drawer and pulled out a contract. He had already bought my contract. That was the winter of 1949.

After my first season, I met Jack Powell and he told me I had the best year among the umpires. In the second year, they put me into a two- man crew. The rest of the crews were three-man — we were the only two-man crew. It was to save money.

CECE CARLUCCI

FRANK KERR -
From Player to Umpire

*F*rank Kerr was another player from the Coast League who tried his hand at umpiring. A *catcher during his playing days, Kerr was thoroughly accustomed to standing behind the plate while pitchers hurled fastballs, curves and knuckle balls in his direction.*

I became an umpire on a quirk. In my last year I was a player-coach at Modesto. My knees weren't good, and I complained about the umpiring a lot. The president of the California League said to me one day, 'If you could do better, give it a try.'

Well, I joined the Umpires Association and umpired games in the San Diego area, and was hired by the California League for a year, then on to the Coast League. Balls and strikes came easy. Plays on the bases came easy, but positioning myself on the base, hell, I was all over the place. I thought I could race the ball around the infield.

Once I learned positioning, I was fine. With three-man teams, you are moving a lot. Four-man games today, they get bored. And the umpire at third base, he's standing in one spot for three hours. His back is killing him!

After I became an umpire, my uncle Bill [Engeln] and I would talk rules all the time, and we'd argue about interpretation. The rule book is a small document, but the American League and National League interpretation books are eight-and-a-half by eleven inches and an inch thick! And each league doesn't always interpret the rules the same. We would get down and argue long into the night.

The most trouble an umpire can get into is to have something happen that's not in the rule book.

Up in Seattle in 1957 it is Lefty O'Doul Day and there are 18,000 in the park. The bases are loaded and he's got his pitcher batting. He strikes out, but the ball hits the catcher's knee and rolls over to the ball boy standing by the dugout, not too far away. Well, the ball boy has four balls in his hand. He drops them, catches the live ball, then drops it.

The catcher says, 'Which ball, Frank?' The pitcher's still standing there. I call time and call the managers out to confer. Lefty says, 'So what are you going to do?'

I called the batter out on the ball boy's interference. Lefty accepted that, but when I went to the P.A. and explained the ruling to the crowd, I thought they were going to eat me up. But Lefty just said to his players, 'OK, guys, let's go.' Of course, he was eight runs ahead at the time.

Two years in the Coast League — I went broke doing it. They didn't pay anything.

FRANK KERR

VINNIE SMITH - Chance Umpire

Vinnie Smith and Jim Tabor were with the Sacramento Solons and ran around together. Both were pretty good drinkers. Vinnie saw Tabor die with a delirium tremor, and since that day he never took another drink. He became an umpire and went on to the major leagues.

He got started umpiring in an unusual way. Portland was playing Sacramento in a double-header, and the umpires didn't show up. They got fouled up in their train connections. So the teams picked two ballplayers to umpire the game, and Vinnie did such a good job, both sides agreed for him to umpire the second game. That's how he got started.

BILL FLEMING - Portland Beavers

JACKIE TOBIN

Tobin was another real good ballplayer, but he drank himself out of baseball. After he was finished as a player, he became an umpire. He ended his career by a dangerous mistake in Hawaii.

We had finished a series at home, and the Hawaii Islanders were going to fly from Hawaii to Seattle. We got onto the plane and had taxied out to the runway. Tobin made the comment, 'Well, the plane's probably going to crash and I'm going to be the only one who lives.' The stewardess just happens to be walking by and, bingo, the plane stops, taxis back to the airport and they take Jackie off the airplane.

We had an owner, Nick Morgan — he hated Tobin. And Tobin didn't like Nick Morgan. If it wasn't for Morgan, Tobin would have spent five years in jail. Nick went down to the jail and went to bat for Tobin and got him out of jail.

I remember I was getting a haircut down in Waikiki a week or two after that game, and Jackie comes by. I called him and said, 'Hey, Tob, how's it going?' He was scared to death! You talk about somebody with panic in his eyes. But Nick Morgan got him off. Jackie was slated to go to the majors as an umpire the next year, but that incident cost him the advancement.

BUD WATKINS - Hawaii Islanders

EMMETT ASHFORD

When Emmett Ashford was the first-base umpire, he'd sprint down the line after the umpires' conference at home plate. The fans loved it. He sometimes missed a call because he was playing to the crowd.

BOB KERRIGAN - San Diego Padres

"BALLS AND STRIKES"

I would talk some to the catchers, if they would talk to you. They'd try to influence your calls, but you just call them as they are. You've got to hit the plate, I'm not going to widen it for you.

It's a judgment call, and I don't know two people in this whole world that their judgment is exactly the same. That is part of baseball.

With three-man teams, you go behind the plate once every third day. You can get shell-shocked back there. You call 300 pitches, 150 each pitcher. It's hard to go behind the plate that often and do a good job every day.

You try to visualize a rectangle from about [his stomach] to his knees — not the bottom of his knees, the top of his knees. The rule book says from the armpits to the top of the knees. Well, they never call a pitch at the armpits. The balls get to be belt-high, or maybe a little bit higher, but not up at the letters. That's to the batter's advantage, but you still see guys swinging at balls all over the place.

A lot of guys will call the outside a strike, but they won't give you the inside because they're setting up on the inside. But the most important thing is to be consistent, so the batter knows what to expect. But umpires usually aren't that much different. Their zones are similar.

I've often seen catchers 'lose' strikes. They try to pull balls into the zone, but the umpire has already made up his mind. A catcher catches the ball [back-handed], and pushes the ball out of the zone. Catch the ball like a basket and pull it in.

FRANK KERR - Umpire

I used to talk with the umpires a lot. I felt I worked them like a Stradivarius violin. I had a great rapport with them, and I think I got a lot out of them.

You use the old theory that you don't turn your head. As long as you keep looking out towards the pitcher, you can tell them anything you want to tell them. Once in a while, I'd turn around to them, but not enough to get thrown out, just enough to let them know that if you keep this up, I'm going to be turning around and letting the fans get on you.

CLAUDE CHRISTIE - Seattle Rainiers

Seattle was playing San Francisco in a day game, and I was umpiring the bases. San Francisco had a man on second base with two men out when the man at bat hit a very sharp grounder in the hole between shortstop and third base.

The third baseman from Seattle was a big Italian boy who had just come down from the big leagues that year. He was slow and overweight, and really did not work too hard.

He made a try for the ball, but it hit his glove and went on out into left field. At the time, Bruce Ogrodowski, who was on second base, started toward third.

Cece Carlucci, left, chatted in a hotel restaurant with Portland Beavers owner Bill Sweeney, center, and Seattle Rainiers manager Lefty O'Doul. When O'Doul left the table for a moment, Sweeney suggested it would be a good time for Carlucci to leave the restaurant to avoid the appearance of a conflict of interest. Carlucci later said he was grateful for Sweeney's advice.

After the third baseman missed the ball, he stuck out his arm and tripped the runner, and immediately cried out to me claiming interference on the part of Ogrodowski.

I overruled his complaint, and sent the runner on to third on the play, then on to home for interference by the third baseman. The third baseman gave me a mild beef, and it was just about settled when the Seattle first baseman came over and stuck his nose into the argument.

He said, 'Why don't you punch [umpire] Lee Dempsey right in the nose?' and I said, 'You couldn't whip your own wife. Why don't you punch me in the nose?' He answered, 'I'll do just that as soon as the ball game is over and I'm dressed. I'll meet you across the street from the ballpark at the saloon.'

When the game was over — this was the first time I did not take a shower after a ball game — I hurried over to the saloon to get punched in the nose. Naturally, he was not there.

After arriving back at the hotel, I called him and invited him to my room, telling him I would buy him a couple of drinks and give him the privilege of punching me in the nose. He said all I wanted to do was to get him into an embarrassing position and have him fined by the president of the league, so he refused to meet me.

This is where I made the big mistake. I told him I was working behind home plate next day, and he had better swing at everything close, as I would call it a strike anyhow.

The first ball pitched damn near knocked his head off, and I called it a strike. The second ball practically bounced up there, and I called it a strike. He turned around to me and said, 'I believe you meant what you said,' and I replied, 'I sure did!'

He was a left-handed batter, and the next pitch was at least two feet outside, but he leaned over and hit it right down the third base line to left field, and ended up with a three-base hit! He immediately stood on third base, thumbed his nose at me, and said, 'Call that a strike, you jerk!'

LEE DEMPSEY - Umpire

Left to right, Emmett Ashford, Mickey Hanich and crew chief Cece Carlucci waiting for the start of a game in Hollywood in 1954.

WHAT DO THEY REALLY ARGUE ABOUT?

What do umpires and players discuss when they are arguing? Lefty O'Doul, former big-league baseball star and one of the best managers of the Pacific Coast League, pulled a couple of pretty fast ones on me when I was umpiring in the PCL.

The hitters were having a hard time following the curve ball and I was calling them strikes, which neither the hitter nor the fans cared much about. Finally, Lefty came up to me from the third-base coaching box, pointed his finger right in my face and said, 'If you don't come down to my saloon tonight and have a beer, I'll hate you!' I immediately put my hand close to his face and answered, 'If you don't get back to that third-base coaching box, I'll never come near your joint!' When he went back, everyone clapped and at least a dozen people told me after the game, 'Lefty sure gave you hell when he came up to the plate, didn't he?'

When I first started umpiring in the Pacific Coast League, I decided to try a little psychology on the job. I had always been a problem to umpires when I played, now the shoe was on the other foot. I had my first chance to practice psychology in a game at Hollywood. Butch Moran, a competent first baseman of Hollywood, was up to bat. I called a strike on him and he said, 'You S.O.B., the ball was outside.' I halted the game and said, '*Mister* S.O.B. to you, or get out of here.' 'OK — *Mister* S.O.B.,' Butch said, and the beef was over. Butch and I had no further trouble the rest of the game.

LEE DEMPSEY - Umpire

Gene Mauch, Gene Handley and Billy Raimondi were intelligent ballplayers. You had respect for people like that. And they didn't argue senselessly, so you gave them a little more attention.

CECE CARLUCCI - Umpire

ON FRATERNIZING

The Coast League was first class all the way through and had a wonderful president in Pants Rowland and a great set of umpires under Jack Powell, umpire-in-chief. You paid your own hotel and meals and they gave you a train ticket from one town to another. I was not breaking even as I liked to have a little fun after the games, and that ran into money.

I had an insurance license with Penn Mutual, so I began going over to the different hotels of the ballplayers and selling them retirement policies, a good way for the ballplayers to save some money. I had about fifty ballplayers insured, and this helped the Dempsey Treasury Department a little bit.

But I got a call from Mr. Rowland saying I was not to go over to the ballplayers' hotel anymore to sell them insurance. So I had them come over to mine. This living in a suitcase for short dough did not agree with me very much, so after umpiring the playoff between San Francisco and Seattle, I turned in my case and married a beautiful girl from Sacramento.

LEE DEMPSEY - Umpire

We never tried to stay at the same hotel with the players. I had friends throughout the league. They even started a fan club for me in Portland — a bunch of young girls. I met some people from Oregon City in Palm Springs during spring training. They'd move me out of the hotel when I came into Portland, take me out to the ranch. Rancho Stona had forty-five acres with an acre lake, and I could ride horses. They would give me a car and I could stay there. We stayed at pretty nice places, went pretty first-cabin, and we were always dressed.

One night I went into a nice lounge for a drink and a Seattle pitcher was there with a couple of gals, and he sent over a highball. Every once in a while, you see a guy, but I would never go where the players would hang out. I never wanted to get into some kind of a jam.

One night in Portland, I'm in a hotel that has a restaurant and a little entertainment, and I walk in and Bill Sweeney and Lefty O'Doul are sitting at a table, and they call me over. I wouldn't have done it if there was only one. So I went over and sat down and had a highball with them.

Now, Lefty went to the bathroom, and Sweeney said, 'Cece, it would be a good idea if you leave about now.' I thought about that later and thought that was real sharp. I appreciated it very much.

They could never say about me that I was over-drinking. But I have seen some cases when some umpires had too much to drink and we had to get them out of there.

When I would umpire games in Oakland, I would stay in San Francisco and take the Key System across the Bay to Emeryville. Oakland didn't have the nice hotels like San Francisco did, and it was an easy trip to the ballpark.

CECE CARLUCCI - Umpire

I enjoyed umpiring and I enjoyed the players, but I didn't enjoy that I couldn't fraternize with the players. Here are guys that I roomed with that I couldn't go out to dinner with.

We still talked a lot. Catchers would talk a lot. Ballplayers would come up to talk: 'Hi Frank. How are you?' 'Fine,' I'd respond, 'What are you having for dinner tonight? Can I come over?' 'The hell with you. Let's see how you call it tonight,' they'd say. Stuff like that.

FRANK KERR - Umpire

ON TWO-MAN TEAMS

You try to call the plays fairly and honestly, but you can't help but miss once in a while. One of those misses came for me during a game at Portland.

Having only two umpires and my partner holding a Portland runner on third base, I had the right side of the diamond. I was behind the plate and Larry Barton, their star first baseman, was up to bat. He belted one right down the right-field foul line and over the fence. I called it foul and then the fun began. First I got static from Larry. Then Marv Owen, the Portland manager, put his two cents worth. I stood on my decision and Larry came back up to bat. He belted the next pitch right over the center-field fence, and as he took off for his base circuit trot, I heard, 'Call that one foul, you bum!' It wasn't until the other side came up to bat that I found out I'd really goofed. Their right fielder, JoJo White, the leadoff man, said, 'Nice going, Dempsey. That first ball was fair by two feet. Too bad he had to hit two home runs to score one!'

LEE DEMPSEY - Umpire

When I broke in a lot of the older umpires didn't hustle a lot. They say I brought in a lot of hustle. After my first year, I got a high rating and they put me in a two-man team with Bill Engeln.

In '51, with that two-man team, Pants Rowland told us, 'I'm going to let you fellas fly.' We used to take the trains. So they said that you're going to be the first to fly because you're going to have to work the plate every other night. So we flew. The next year, everybody was flying. A few umpires took the train, but that was their preference.

That's crazy going with two men in the Coast League. You go into a town and you've got three or four games behind the plate in a seven-game series. And if you have a tough game that first night you're there for a long week. You've got to work yourself out of it.

I went five weeks with Engeln then he got a break and they brought in Al Somers. Then Al and I went eight weeks. After that they brought in John Neznevich from Seattle.

Engeln was one of the best umpires I ever worked with. When I first came into the league, he wouldn't let anybody say a word to me. He'd say, 'Lay off that young Italian kid. You guys are going to like him after you've seen him for a while.' That was some of the best umpiring I'd ever seen. Whether you're a ten-man team or two, you do the best you can.

Two-man games could sometimes cause problems. I had a play at home and I called it from fair territory. You could say I was out of position. It was a close game in L.A., with Oakland up 2-1, and it was the tying run. When you have a two-man team there are greater responsibilities to cover.

Gene Baker was on second base for the Angels, and an Angel batter hit a Texas Leaguer not too far out, between first and second. Both the second baseman and the first baseman had a shot at it. Al Somers is drifting towards third, so it's my call.

I thought I could get an angle, so I moved out towards the pitcher's mound. Well, I thought I saw trap so I ruled no catch. Here's Baker coming from second and I'm a good forty to forty-five feet from home plate and I've got to get in to make this call.

It's the most perfect throw you ever want to see into Don Padgett, the Oaks catcher, and Baker makes a great hook slide. Well, I'm in perfect view to see the play — in a slot — but I'm about eight feet out. I stop and they get him by no more than a half-inch to an inch on the outside of the plate, the foul side. Now, that's Wrigley Field and that would have tied the score.

Well, the place erupts and they're saying from the dugout that I'm out of position to call the play. Gene Mauch is on deck and he's going crazy — 'Out of position! Out of position! Why did you call it from fair territory?'

When the writers came down after the game — John B. Olds, Bob Hunter and others — they asked me the same question. I explained my first call was whether there was a catch. If I had stayed at home I would have been in position for the play at the plate, but I couldn't have called the catch. I would do it the same way today.

After that call I had at Wrigley Field, John Neznevich joined Al and me in Seattle and the two-man-team experiment was over.

CECE CARLUCCI - Umpire

ON EJECTIONS

Players had to learn what the limits were. If they talked about your parents, I wouldn't take that in a second. They would have to go. It they called me a wop, I'd call them a krauthead, or whatever. I figured that they had to call me something if they disagreed. But if they called me a dirty so-and-so, that's when they come close to crossing the line. You've got to give them some room.

There is a time to walk away. Definitely a time to walk away. Some guys will come out there and they'll go on and on. If I could get a word in, I'd say, 'Look. I'm going to listen to you.' Well now they figure you're giving in. But you reach a point where you tell them, 'OK, I've heard you. This is the way I saw it and this is the way I'm calling it!' I gave them a chance.

Then I would walk away. If they kept following me and keep going after me, I'm giving them rope. Let 'em hang themselves. Younger guys, you stand your ground more. With the old-timers, I would give them that respect. They want you to listen, even if they are wrong or don't know what they were talking about.

This would normally work — except for [Seattle Rainiers manager] Paul Richards. Nothing would work with him. I think we got him twenty-four times in 1950.

CECE CARLUCCI - Umpire

Portland Beavers manager Jim Turner, right, and outfielder Mayo Smith in a futile attempt to convince umpire Phil Mazzeo to reverse a call.

One game we had Henry Fanning, the one-armed umpire, working home plate. He and Gabby Street got into it, a big argument! I don't know what Street said, but Fanning took off his mask and — pow! — right across the face. In those days you had heavy bars on the mask, and he hit Street right across the face and knocked his teeth out.

RUGGER ARDIZOIA - Hollywood Stars

I was working a game in Sacramento. Pepper Martin was then manager of San Diego. In one of those late innings, he placed himself in the lineup as a pinch runner. He was on second base with two men out. The batter hit a line drive to right field which Joe Marty

Portland Beavers manager Jim Turner argues a call, 1948.

fielded on the first hop. Martin tried to score and made a terrific head-first slide, but missed home plate by two feet.

Marty, who still had a great arm, rifled the ball to Jim Steiner, the catcher. Jim missed Martin as he belly-flopped past the plate. Pepper went over to his bench and Earl Sheely, the Solons manager, yelled out for Steiner to go over and tag Martin. As he did, I called Martin out.

He came running up to the plate, threw his hat down, jumped up and down on it and really gave me hell. I listened a minute and then told him to get back on the bench or out of the ball game. Well, if you knew Pepper Martin, he was booted. Two outs on the same play.

When I first came into the Pacific Coast League, I was umpiring a game in Hollywood on a Saturday night. The first play I had at first base, I called a man safe by a margin of ten feet!

Butch Moran, the Hollywood first baseman, came running up and gave me a terrific argument, so I sent him to the showers quick.

After the game, my partner, Frisco Edwards, who had been in the league a long time, said, 'Lee, I forgot to tell you about Moran. He doesn't like to play Saturday nights and then a double-header on Sunday. That's why he gave you the beef. You fell for it hook, line and sinker!'

LEE DEMPSEY - Umpire

I got kicked out of ball games only three times in ten years. The first time was in Seattle, in 1953. Steve Yuhas was umpiring. Whoever was sitting next to me was on Steve's case all night. Finally, he rips off his mask, comes over to the dugout and throws me out. And I haven't said a word yet! That was the first time.

The second time was when I was with Sacramento. Alex Salerno was absolutely the worst umpire I have ever seen. We were in Vancouver and he blew a call at first base one night. It was so obvious even the Vancouver fans laughed. So I walked to the end of the dugout and said, 'Salerno, you're a bad umpire.' He kicks me out. I didn't cuss him or anything.

So the next night, he's behind the plate, and he calls one of our guys out on a pitch that was damn near over his head. You couldn't have hit it with a tennis racket. So I said, 'You know, I was right last night. You're still a bad umpire.' And he kicks me out again.

BUD WATKINS - Sacramento Solons

In my first year I had to run [Los Angeles Angels manager] Bill Sweeney in Wrigley Field. He was a big name down there, but they also called him 'Tomato Face.' I go to home plate the next night, and I don't want to get anywhere near home plate. I'm off to the side. Bill Sweeney comes up to me and says to me, 'Hey kid, what happened last night was last night. That's forgotten. We have a new game tonight.' Boy, I'll tell you, I changed in one second. I was the rookie, but he got me right out of it.

CECE CARLUCCI - Umpire

One night at Hollywood, I couldn't get anybody out. Even broken-bat hits were falling in. Finally, I took my glove off and threw it over to the first-base umpire, remarking, 'You'd better put this on and shag some of these or we'll be here all night.' Believe it or not, the umpire put on the glove and announced loud and clear, 'Play ball!' It didn't help any.

On one occasion in Los Angeles, I got kicked out of the game for rolling the ball to home plate. The ball was loaded, and the batter asked for the ball. The umpire asked me for the ball, and I rolled the ball to him. So of course, by the time it got to the plate, it was unloaded. So I got fined and kicked out of that one.

I'm pitching a game at Emeryville in 1946 and don't like the feel of the ball, so I ask for a new one. As I'm walking back to the mound with the new ball, I don't like the feel of that one either, so I ask for another. The umpire gives me the original ball, remarking to Lilio Marcucci, my catcher, 'The dumb left-hander has the same ball.'

Well, the dumb left-hander winds-up and throws the ball over the stands and out into the street. So I go up and ask, 'Now may I have a new ball?' The umpire responds, 'Yes, and you can have a bar of soap, too. Go take a shower.'

BUD BEASLEY - Sacramento Solons

PLAYER SUSPENDED FOR SLAPPING UMPIRE

On August 11, 1954, in the heat of a pennant race, the Hollywood Stars' Carlos Bernier slapped an umpire and was suspended for the rest of the season.

The Stars' three-and-a-half-game lead over the San Diego Padres was being threatened by a prodigious Luke Easter home run over the center-field fence, which gave the Padres a commanding lead. In the eighth inning, with Bernier at the plate, umpire Chris Valenti called a third strike. The Stars batter turned and bumped Valenti, and was immediately ejected. Bernier then slapped Valenti sharply across the face.

League president Clarence Rowland was among the 6,159 in attendance, so action was swift and severe. Rowland had suspended Bernier five days earlier for kicking at Bud Hardin of the Angels at Wrigley Field. This second suspension cost Bernier thirty-four games.

The next day, the *Los Angeles Times* ran Rowland's statement on the matter:

"Baseball cannot and will not tolerate umpire assault. Bernier used filthy language and also bumped Valenti after being called out on strikes, then slapped him when ordered out of the game. So I am suspending Bernier for the rest of the 1954 season."

Manager Bobby Bragan's reaction: "It's too bad, for Bernier is the most colorful player in the league. There is no justification, though, for what he did. Carlos is highly emotional and quick-tempered. All of us have talked with him several times this year, Branch Rickey included, and each time he assured us he could keep himself in hand. Then he blew his top anyhow.

"The umpires are partly to blame, though. They have let too many games get out of hand this season. In fact, they seldom have one under control."

Stars owner Bob Cobb said, "It is unfortunate that Bernier's action on the field should endanger his future. Mr. Rowland unquestionably was most considerate in his decision. It is to be hoped that Carlos will appreciate the justice of it and learn his lesson so that next year he can continue playing the game he loves."

Carlos Bernier: "I am not mad at anybody but myself. Mr. Rowland was good to me. I was afraid I might be banned for life. I am not well. I was beaned in 1948 and have been nervous and aching in the head ever since."

Bernier returned to the Stars in 1955 and led the league in stolen bases. He played nine more seasons in the Coast League. A troubled individual, he died by his own hand in 1989.

Tommy Heath would take an occasional drink. In '57 we had a horrible ball club, and we'd get behind 6-0 by the third or fourth inning, and he'd go out there and argue with the umpires with the hopes of getting thrown out. He didn't want to stay around and watch the massacre.

He'd lean out of the dugout and rag at Chris Pelakoudis: 'Hey Greek, is that your nose or a loaf of French bread?' Or: 'You're the only guy who can smoke a cigar in a shower and never get it wet. What a horn you've got!'

One night were down 8-1 in the third inning, and there's a play at first base. It wasn't even close, but Tom goes running out to argue the call so he can get kicked out of the ball game. He's ranting and raving, and Chris is just kind of smiling. Heath is going at it, and finally, Chris says, 'Tom, I know what you're doing. If I've got to be out here for nine innings, you're going to be out here for nine innings.' He wouldn't kick Tom out.

BUD WATKINS - Sacramento Solons

OOPS!

I was working a game before a big audience in Los Angeles. Ray Prim, an excellent pitcher for the Angels was throwing to Johnny Gill, a left-handed hitter from Portland. Prim threw a long, sweeping sidearm curve and, as I bent over on the pitch, I heard a slow ripping 'swoosh' that could only be one thing.

Gingerly, hoping no one in the stands had spotted the mishap, I stretched up and nonchalantly crossed my hands behind my back. My fears were well-grounded. I had about an eight-inch-long gaping hole in the seat of my pants, and we were just in the first inning!

From that point on, I calculated every move with the precision of a ballet-dancing Rockette ... tiptoe to the left ... tiptoe to the left. No wild arm waving. If the fans had gotten wise, they'd have murdered me. My careful, cautious prancing paid off right up until the end of the game.

Fred Haney, who was calling the play-by-play on radio from back of the screen, was the only one who noticed my plight. Fred hissed at me, 'Hey, do you know you've torn your pants?' 'Do I know it?' I said, 'I've been taking cold since the first inning.'

When it ended, Clarence Rowland, the president of the league, came barreling down to the dressing room and demanded, 'Since when did you become a tiptoe umpire, Dempsey?' 'From the first inning of today's game.'

He said, 'Why didn't you take time out and go to your dressing room and change your pants?' I had been waiting for that statement ever since I came into this league. 'What umpire in this league makes enough money to have two pair of pants?' He left abruptly.

LEE DEMPSEY - Umpire

Note: The quotes by Lee Dempsey in this chapter were taken from his memoir Confessions of an Umpire *(Western Printing & Publishing, 1968). Dempsey was a professional football and baseball player, and a Pacific Coast League umpire during the early 1940s.*

ANGEL CITY BASE BALL CLUB
PACIFIC COAST CHAMPIONS — 1934

The winning half of the 1934 Los Angeles Angels/Hollywood Stars rivalry, one of the most intense in PCL history.

9

Ulyses "Tony" Lupien, one of the PCL's few college graduates, was a leader for the Hollywood Stars in 1946 and '47. In '47, he batted .341, with 110 RBI and twenty-one home runs.

THE RIVALRIES

WHEN COMMUNITY LOYALTIES ARE DIVIDED BY TWO OR, POSSIBLY, THREE BASE-BALL TEAMS, SOME CURIOUS RIVALRIES CAN DEVELOP. THEY CAN BE FRIENDLY, AS IN THE CASE OF PORTLAND VS. SEATTLE, OR THEY CAN BECOME HEATED — NO, DOWNRIGHT NASTY — AS IN THE CASE OF LOS ANGELES VS. HOLLYWOOD.

OFTEN IN A RIVALRY, ONE TEAM WILL BE CONSISTENTLY BETTER THAN THE OTHER, SO COMMUNITY BRAGGING RIGHTS ARE LOPSIDED. BUT USUALLY THE IMBALANCE ISN'T PERMANENT. DYNASTIES WANE OR EVEN COLLAPSE. EVEN BAD TEAMS PUT TOGETHER "CAREER SEASONS," SO HOPE REMAINS ETERNAL.

IT'S NO SURPRISE THAT THE MEDIA ARE HAPPY TO STIR THE POT TO INCREASE CIRCULATION, AND TEAM MANAGEMENT IS HAPPY TO PLAY ALONG BECAUSE PUBLICITY ABOUT A RIVALRY HELPS INCREASE ATTENDANCE. PLAYERS OFTEN FEEL IT DEEPLY AND SEEM TO RISE TO THE CHALLENGE.

RIVALRIES ARE WHAT PLAYERS AND FANS REMEMBER. THEY'RE GOOD FOR THE GAME.

THE ANGELS AND THE STARS - NOT YOUR ORDINARY RIVALRY

In the Pacific Coast League, there was no rivalry like that between the Los Angeles Angels and the Hollywood Stars. It developed during the '30s and '40s, and became more intense and, sometimes, ugly during the final decade. This was a West Coast version of the rivalry between the Brooklyn Dodgers and the New York Giants.

The rivalry with the Angels was there from the start. Both parks sold out on the weekends when we were playing each other, especially the Sunday double-headers.

The *Los Angeles Herald* had a reporter, John B. Olds — he was always blasting the Stars, 'the old men.' 'Frenchy Uhalt didn't have it any more, Babe Herman was over the hill,' and all that.

We were in L.A. one time between games of a double-header, and John B. Olds drops by the clubhouse. We'd just lost the first game, and he comes in there. Frenchy speaks his piece, and Olds spoke his, and they're about to go at it. Some us of say, 'Whoa, wait a minute!'

So we got our big travel trunks and put them in a square. 'OK, now go ahead.' So Olds takes off his coat. He was pretty good-sized, and Frenchy isn't so big. Frenchy beat the shit out of him! After that, Olds didn't say so much.

RUGGER ARDIZOIA - Hollywood Stars

We didn't like the Angels, the Angels didn't like us. It was a mutual-admiration society, and we did everything in the world we could to antagonize 'em, and as a result, there were some of the damnedest fights you ever saw. They were knock-down, drag-out, big-time fights, big league all the way.

How did this develop? I've got to think that it was the years the Angels had great ball clubs, and it was sheer dominance. Then the worm turned, and I don't think the Angels players and the Angels fans took kindly to it. And I think the Stars players and the Stars fans figured, 'Well, we're running this thing now.' We didn't rub it in, but we didn't give any ground, either. The media didn't necessarily write anything, but they played up the great rivalry.

I grew up in Long Beach and had a grandfather who was a great ball fan. We'd get on the red car [trolley] to go see the Angels. And now, even after all these years, I still hear from people who really hated us.

The fights — I participated in all of them, and haven't won one yet!

One hectic week began on a Wednesday night. There was a brush-back or something like that. It was not all that uncommon. It was expected that an opposing hitter would get knocked down, and if you didn't, it often cost you later.

We were playing a big series at Los Angeles with a full house. The Angels had a bad ball club, but it was a sunny double-header. Gene Handley's up at the plate and I'm on deck. Ed Runge — he later went to the majors — is umping. He called something against the Angels, and a guy comes out of the stand on the dead run, after Runge. Well, Handley and I tackled the guy and bopped him a few times. If it had been an Angel ball player, we'd been getting the fan off him too. But once the ball game started the least little thing could trigger it.

CHUCK STEVENS - Hollywood Stars

THE FIGHT OF '53

The Angels/Stars rivalry reached its pinnacle (or nadir, depending on your perspective) during an eight-game series, from July 27 through August 2, 1953. This week of hard play and occasional fighting concluded with a huge brawl.

It was quite possibly the biggest fight in Pacific Coast League history. The participants and fans in the stands at Gilmore Field will never forget it. A few of the participants recall the details below.

For me that was the fight of all fights. It was quite a series, the whole eight games. It was a hard-fought series, and a fight broke out on Friday night.

When it came to the double-header on Sunday, they put 5,000 in the outfield for the overflow crowd. I was behind the plate for the first game. Everything was going real good until [the Stars' Frank] Kelleher came up in the first game. He had killed the Angels all week, so it didn't surprise me that they would throw inside on him.

Here comes one in there. I didn't think it was really a very fast pitch. Joe Hatten was the pitcher, and it looked like he might have tried a curve ball way in, but it didn't do much. Well, Kelleher just kind of spun and it nicked him just above the belt line. Naturally, he's going to get first base. Kelleher never said boo to anybody.

Like a dummy, I went and picked up the ball, and I look up and Kelleher is going towards the mound. When he threw that right, I thought it was Marciano! He must have knocked Hatten back twelve feet. He didn't hit him in the face; he hit him in the chest, but he had so much power from running that he knocked him back.

Players came on the field, but we were able to control it. After we got everything settled, I told Kelleher, 'You've got to go.' I didn't put on a big show or anything. The fight was enough.

Then [Stars manager Bobby] Bragan got angry. He wanted Hatten to go. I say, 'No. He didn't throw any punches. And Kelleher went out there.' By then Bragan was furious at me.

So we finally got the game going again, and they got Teddy Beard to run for Kelleher. Bragan was batting. The next pitch, Bragan just swung at it, not trying to make contact, looking like an old lady, and Beard stole second. The next pitch again, same thing. Bragan just swung the bat, a soft little loop, and Beard takes off for third.

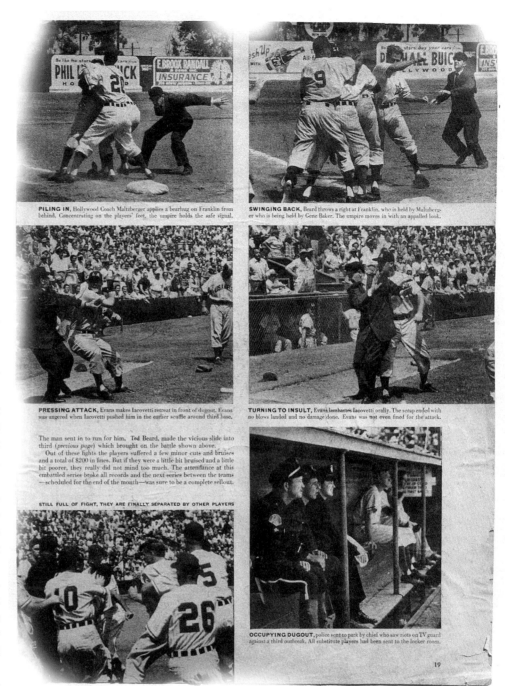

PILING IN, Hollywood Coach Maltzberger applies a bearhug on Franklin from behind. Concentrating on the players' feet, the umpire holds the safe signal.

SWINGING BACK, Beard throws a right at Franklin, who is held by Maltzberger who is being held by Gene Baker. The umpire moves in with an appalled look.

PRESSING ATTACK, Evans makes Iacovetti retreat in front of dugout. Evans was angered when Iacovetti pushed him in the earlier scuffle around third base.

TURNING TO INSULT, Evans lambastes Iacovetti orally. The scrap ended with no blows landed and no damage done. Evans was not even fined for the attack.

The man sent in to run for him, Ted Beard, made the vicious slide into third (*previous page*) which brought on the battle shown above.

Out of these fights the players suffered a few minor cuts and bruises and a total of $200 in fines. But if they were a little bit bruised and a little bit poorer, they really did not mind too much. The attendance at this embattled series broke all records and the next series between the teams — scheduled for the end of the month — was sure to be a complete sellout.

STILL FULL OF FIGHT, THEY ARE FINALLY SEPARATED BY OTHER PLAYERS

OCCUPYING DUGOUT, police sent to park by chief who saw riots on TV guard against a third outbreak. All substitute players had been sent to the locker room.

A Life *magazine report on the "Fight of '53." Note the police officers in the dugout during the second game of that day's double-header.*

The Hollywood Stars had adversaries other than the Los Angeles Angels. In a 1955 game at Hollywood, San Diego Padres catcher Ed Bailey and umpire Pat Orr restrain Stars second baseman Curt Roberts after Eddie Eraut almost dusted Roberts with a pitch.

Well, he's out by ten feet at third, and he comes in with those spikes flying. That's when all hell broke loose. We couldn't stop that fight. We tried everything. I was down three times.

I recall Bobby Bragan next to me saying, 'Hey, Cece, what the hell's going on?' Now that was funny, but then I get up and see [Gene] Baker and Gene Handley boxing — dancing around boxing!

Joe Iacovetti, the umpire at third, grabbed Al Evans, the catcher, from behind, trying to break up the fight. Well, Al thought it was a Hollywood player and started swinging. There he is in *Life* magazine, swinging on Joe. He just barely nicked him across the chin.

They wanted to suspend him for that, but I went to bat for him. He thought it was another player. That day you take your chances. Everybody was on their own, and they weren't really sore at anybody, it was just that darn rivalry.

That's when Chief Bill Parker, of the L.A. Police, comes in. He was driving in his car and heard it over the radio. He sent out word for everybody to get to Gilmore Field, and fifty-five of them came out. What a pretty sight. They were coming from left field, center field, all over. They stopped it for us. We just couldn't do it, not that we didn't try.

Anyway, we get everything pretty well under order, and I cleared all the benches, everybody, put them in the clubhouse. If you wanted a player you sent a bat boy in there to get a player out. It took about twenty-five minutes before we were ready to resume play. We put police in both dugouts, and for the rest of the game everything went perfect.

Now remember, this was the first game of a double-header. We've got another game coming up, and I mentioned to Al Somers, who was the crew chief, 'Al, let's clear the benches before we start the second ball game.' He said, 'No, you're not going to do it.'

I said, 'But we should. There were two fights and emotions are running high.' There's people on the field. I ask [umpire Joe] Iacovetti how he feels, and he agrees that we should clear the field. Still, Al says we're not going to clear the benches.

So I say, 'OK, Al, I'm going to pull the book on you.' The umpire that works the first ball game behind the plate is in charge of starting the second game. 'I'm going to use the fans on the field as reason to keep the police on the field.'

Now that rule existed primarily for ground conditions, rain situations. But I used that rule on him, my own partner and crew chief, because I figure that fights on the field become kind of a field situation.

Al says, 'OK. Then after the first pitch, I'm letting them come out.' Just then there was a knock at the door. It's Chief Parker's aide. He said, 'The Chief doesn't want to tell you how to run the game, but he's offering his police to have them in the dugout and suggesting the dugouts be cleared to start the ball game.' Al had to go with me. The second game ran as smooth as a whistle.

This was probably the biggest fight in Coast League history. It's the biggest fight I've ever heard of. It lasted over twenty minutes. There were guys hurt, guys who were good friends were punching each other, guys just didn't know what was going on.

CECE CARLUCCI - Umpire

During that fight, for some reason I float out to shortstop and I see a grey uniform coming by, so I grab this guy right around the neck. I look down and his biceps look like my thighs. I think, 'Oops, I'm not going to like the outcome of this. I'm going to get the hell beat out of me.' It's Bob Usher. I'm in deep trouble.

He looks up at me and kind of smiles and says, 'Do you want to fight?' I say, 'Hell, no!' So we move out into short left field and watch them go at it.

CHUCK STEVENS - Hollywood Stars

Frank Kelleher was just beating us to death. After his fight with Joe Hatten, Teddy Beard ran for Kelleher and stole second and third, sliding hard into both bases. When he slid into third, Murray Franklin — just acquired from the Stars and playing his first game for us — jumped Beard, and all hell broke out.

I had popped a couple of guys and had hurt my hand when Chuck Stevens grabbed me from behind and asked if I wanted to fight. I said no, so we held onto each other and stayed out of trouble. It's all true.

BOB USHER - Los Angeles Angels

I'm sitting in the clubhouse between games, and a guy in civilian clothes walks into the clubhouse, and I say to Nobe Kawano, our clubhouse guy, and to Bragan, 'Who in the hell is that? Get him out of the clubhouse. This is hardly the time.'

The guy walks directly to my locker, pulls out his badge, and says, 'I'm Captain So-and-So of the L.A. Police Department.' I said, 'Make yourself at home. What the hell are you doing here?'

He said, 'I'm part of the riot squad, Chuck. We're here to get this thing quieted down. These are the ground rules: those who aren't playing in the second game are to stay in the clubhouse. There'll be a runner to come and get you if there's going to be a change. Bragan, you hear that?'

Bragan said, 'Yeah.' And that's how the second game went down. Those who didn't play were in the clubhouse, and there were no problems in the second game.

CHUCK STEVENS - Hollywood Stars

Chuck Stevens, shown here with the Sacramento Solons in 1957, managed to avoid fisticuffs during the Fight of '53.

THE FIGHT OF '57

One of the biggest things I remember about the rivalry between the Hollywood Stars and the Angels occurred in mid-'57. A little left-hander came to join the Angels in mid-season. His name was Tom Lasorda. Lasorda started a game against the Star 'Spook' Jacobs, our second baseman, who led off for us. Nothing was said. He warmed up, the ball was thrown down to second base. Lasorda gets the ball back.

In August, 1957, the Hollywood Stars' Forrest "Spook" Jacobs, center, and Los Angeles Angels pitcher Tommy Lasorda, right, started another fight in the long-simmering rivalry between the Stars and Angels. Jacobs' roundhouse swing, aimed at the ducking second baseman George "Sparky" Anderson, missed completely. Hollywood eventually won the game.

First pitch, he throws the ball in there, and Spook Jacobs bunts the ball down the first-base line. And Lasorda comes busting off the mound, and he didn't even go for the ball. He just body-blocks Spook Jacobs halfway down first base!

I said, 'What the hell is going on here?' Evidently, besides the rivalry between the Angels and Stars, there must have been some bad blood between Lasorda and Spook Jacobs in their careers. But I think the Hollywood Stars and Angels rivalry might have been enough to pop it over the edge.

PAUL PETTIT - Hollywood Stars

Do I remember the Tommy

Lasorda fight? I could never forget it! I'm sure you'll hear different versions, depending on who you talk to. Before talking about the fight, you've got to realize what had happened before.

Fred Waters, a left-handed pitcher, was pitching for us that day, and he had hit a home run. I was leading off — the next batter — so naturally he was going to knock me down. I knew what he was going to do. So he did, and I never said a word.

The next pitch came in and I bunted towards first. Well, he didn't bother to field the ball. I laid back waiting for him to field the ball. He didn't field it, so I said to myself, 'I got a base hit.' So I ran it out, and about two or three feet before first base something hit me from behind. It was Lasorda.

I got up and was thinking Lasorda would be between the pitcher's mound and first base. Johnny Fitzpatrick was coaching first for us and Steve Bilko was playing first base. Well, John tried to grab me, but I got around him. And, of course, I didn't want any part of Bilko, so I bypassed him and got back on the infield.

Well, the three infielders had come running in. One was Bobby Dolan, the shortstop. Sparky Anderson was at second base and Roy Hartsfield was at third. I didn't want anybody getting near me, so I started to swing.

Well, the Associated Press picture of the week was me swinging at Sparky Anderson, and it looked like I knocked the you-know-what out of him, but I had missed him completely, though the picture looked like I decked him. It made a good picture, but I didn't even touch him.

I still didn't get ahold of Lasorda, but Dolan and I got into it, and Hartsfield came in and, of course, I just kept swinging.

The benches cleared. Everybody was on the field. Do you remember Earl Battey, the catcher? We had a second-string catcher by the name of Pete Naton, out of Holy Cross. They were both big, huge. They got into a bear hug. They weren't hurting each other, but they wouldn't let each other go. So they wrestled on the ground. There were different skirmishes. I guess it was thirty to thirty-five minutes before things got straightened out.

And Tommy and I got thrown out of the game.

FORREST "SPOOK" JACOBS - Hollywood Stars

Tommy Lasorda, above, had just given up a home run to Hollywood Stars pitcher Fred Waters. The next batter, Forrest "Spook" Jacobs, below left, bunted towards first. Lasorda ignored the ball and body-checked Jacobs as he ran down the baseline. The Fight of '57 was officially underway.

I think the rivalry had kind of left itself by 1957, and I'll tell you why. Everybody knew the Dodgers were coming to Los Angeles in 1958. The Angels used to belong to the Cubs, and in '57 the Cubs and Dodgers switched and the Cubs took over the Fort Worth franchise, which was the Dodgers, and the Dodgers took over the Coast League '57 club to make room for the Brooklyn Dodgers, who were coming in '58.

So I think it lost its fervor by then. When I was bat boy (in 1949), it was a great

George "SPARKY" Anderson -
Los Angeles Angels

rivalry. I remember the Lasorda-Spook Jacobs affair. It was in Gilmore Field, and Tommy had thrown at Spook. On the next pitch, Spook bunted the ball and was going to run up Tommy's back down along first. Well Tommy ran and threw a body-block on him. Spook didn't expect that. It knocked him clean across the line, and we started fighting.

GEORGE "SPARKY" ANDERSON - Los Angeles Angels

My recollection of some of the rivalry — it seemed that the Stars handled us pretty well then. One of the good things about the rivalry was that we'd fill the ballpark when we'd play.

I had a pretty good rivalry with Carlos Bernier, his speed against my speed. Carlos was a great base stealer, and most people don't realize that the year before we had run a fifty-yard dash and they had called it a dead heat. So when we got out here in the Coast League, they scheduled a big race, and they got everything all set up and got out the publicity. When the day comes, Carlos said he wouldn't run unless he got some dinero, so that race never came off.

BOB TALBOT - Los Angeles Angels

THE PADRES AGAINST OTHER SOUTHLAND FOES

We had a rivalry with the Angels, but the big rivalry was with Hollywood. They always played hard, like the Gas House Gang. They were young and they'd do some goofy things to aggravate you — slide in extra hard or knock you down. In 1950, when we had the real good club, we finished second, behind Oakland, but Hollywood beat us seventeen times.

In 1952, I think we only beat 'em five times (out of twenty-eight). There was always some club that you couldn't beat.

JACK GRAHAM - San Diego Padres

THE OAKS AND THE SEALS VIE FOR BAY AREA BRAGGING RIGHTS

There was a good rivalry between the Oaks and Seals. I've got a headline from the paper: 'OAKLAND-SAN FRANCISCO FEUD REVIVED.' That was in '35. I was hitting good. I usually led off, and Lefty O'Doul had me walked to pitch to Freddie Muller. Freddie hit a double, and I wound up at third base.

I yelled over, 'Nice strategy, O'Doul,' and he went crazy. He yelled, 'Knock that little S.O.B. down the next time he comes up.'

Joe Sprinz was catching, and he said, 'I'm not going to call for a knock-down pitch.' Joe was a good guy. Vince Monzo was just starting as a catcher, so he said, 'I'll go up there.'

So the next inning, Ed Stutz was pitching, and the first pitch is behind me. The next, under my chin. Stutz says, 'So, you won't go down.' He wanted me to hit the ground. The next one was under my chin again, so I threw the bat out at him and we all ended in a rassle at Seals Stadium.

I went out after the pitcher and Vince Monzo came out after me and grabbed me from behind. Seals Stadium was like gravel there. We were rassling on the gravel, but they broke it up fast. Those baseball fights — nobody gets hurt.

I didn't even get suspended. You could do anything those days. I got back up at bat and walked on the next pitch.

In 1944, Brick Laws sold me to the Seals. I had a little squabble with his son, Bill. He was clowning around in the dugout, and I had a bad inning and said, 'Get the hell out of here.'

Oh, geez, it hit the fan! Laws said, 'He can't call my kid names like that and get away with it.' So that was the end of it.

Dolph Camilli was the manager, and he said to Laws, 'Are you going to let a little thing like that get in the way of the best hitter you have?'

When I went to the Seals I killed the Oaks. All the Oakland guys were for me. Frankie Hawkins was playing right field for the Oaks, and one day I hit a triple over his head.

EMIL MAILHO - Oakland Oaks

SEATTLE VS. PORTLAND — THE RIVALRY UP NORTH

The rivalry between the Seattle Indians and the Portland Beavers was a pretty good one. I think we gave a little more when we played them. I remember when I was traded to Portland and we played against Seattle, they couldn't get me out. I was trying to get revenge for them trading me off.

NINO BONGIOVANNI - Seattle Indians & Portland Beavers

There absolutely was a rivalry between Seattle and Portland, and part of the reason was due to Bill Mulligan being canned by Seattle. He just hated them. He hated them with a passion.

When he came to Portland, every time we beat Seattle it meant twenty-five dollars for each player, so that helped our motivation.

When I went to Seattle, they felt the rivalry too. They were games that they wanted to win, and I think they picked up the pace just a little bit.

EDDIE BASINSKI - Seattle Rainiers

In 1934 former Brooklyn Dodgers pitcher Walter "Dutch" Ruether had the pleasure of watching his son, nineteen-year-old Frank, sign with the Seattle Indians. Club owner Bill Klepper showed him the dotted line. Walter was manager of the team at the time.

10

BECOMING A PROFESSIONAL

Before the inaugural game at Los Angeles' Wrigley Field, members of the Angels and the San Francisco Seals carried the flag out to the center-field flagpole.

JOE DEVINE SCOUTS THE WEST COAST — THE YANKEE WAY

J OE DEVINE IS ONE OF THE GREAT BASEBALL SCOUTS OF ALL TIME. A SAN FRANCISCO NATIVE, HE GREW UP PLAYING BALL ON THE SANDLOTS. BY THE EARLY 1920S, HE HAD BECOME A FREELANCE SCOUT, SIGNING PLAYERS AND WORKING OUT DEALS WITH INTEREST-ED TEAMS. HE LATER AFFILIATED WITH PITTSBURGH AND WAS RESPONSIBLE FOR SENDING MANY LOCAL PLAYERS TO THE PIRATES. AMONG THEM WERE DICK BARTELL, JOE CRONIN, AND RAY KREMER. AFTER A BRIEF STINT WITH THE MISSION REDS AS SCOUT AND MANAGER, HE AFFILIATED WITH THE NEW YORK YANKEES, AND NORTHERN CALIFORNIA BECAME "YANKEE COUNTRY." HIS LAST SIGNING FOR THE TEAM WAS ED CEREGHINO, IN 1950.

IN THE 1930S, YANKEE SCOUTING ON THE WEST COAST WAS BETTER ORGANIZED THAN THAT FOR OTHER MAJOR LEAGUE TEAMS. DEVINE HAD JURISDICTION OVER NORTHERN CALIFORNIA, THE PACIFIC NORTHWEST AND SELECTED SOUTHWESTERN STATES. BOBBY COLTRIN, ANOTHER SAN FRANCISCAN, WAS DEVINE'S ASSISTANT. BILL ESSICK, FORMER VERNON TIGER MANAGER, WAS THE YANKEE SCOUT IN SOUTHERN CALIFORNIA, AND DAN CROWLEY ASSISTED HIM.

DEVINE AND ESSICK WORKED TOGETHER CLOSELY AND BOTH REPORTED DIRECTLY TO GEORGE WEISS OF THE YANKEES.

I ACQUIRED THE JOE DEVINE PAPERS — HUNDREDS OF LETTERS AND REPORTS THAT OFFER PERSONAL, IN-DEPTH OBSERVATIONS ABOUT THIS HIGHLY COMPETITIVE, RATHER CUT-THROAT BUSINESS. OTHER PARTICIPANTS IN THE SCOUTING PROCESS ALSO WEIGH IN HERE.

SCOUTING TED WILLIAMS

The following excerpt is from a letter Joe Devine sent to the New York Yankees from San Francisco, California, on September 26, 1937.

Mr. E.G. Barrow, Secretary
New York Yankee Baseball Club
55 West 42nd Street
New York City, N.Y.

Dear Mr. Barrow:

In reply to your telegram regarding outfielder Williams of San Diego and pitcher Tost of the Mission Club ...
Williams, outfielder for San Diego Club: left-handed hitter, right-handed thrower, age 20, 6'1", weight 175 pounds. Williams shows possibilities as a hitter, has good power. This is his second year at San Diego. He originally came out of San Diego High School. We tried to get him, but Lane of the San Diego club had the inside with his mother. She favored the Yankees in a way, but would not let the boy go away from home. Of course Lane sold her on the idea of playing with San Diego and always be home. Boston has the option on the San Diego Ball Club, as they work hand-in-hand.
I am also sure that Ernie Johnson who scouts for the Red Sox out here helped Lane land Williams. Williams is a very slow lad, not a good outfielder now and just an average arm. There is a big doubt whether Williams will ever be fast enough to get by in the majors as an outfielder. His best feature now is that he shows promise as a hitter, but good pitching so far has stopped him cold. I am positive that there isn't one player in the Pacific Coast League that would help the Yankees next year. I am also positive that Walter Judnich, our outfielder with Oakland is the best outfield prospect in the league. I like Judnich better than Williams.

Sincerely,
Joe Devine

WORKING THE BUSHES IN THE BAY AREA

Bobby Coltrin had worked with Joe Devine, and he ran the summer club. I played with the Kenealy Yankees. Bobby ran the club. Bobby then went to work for the Seals, and he had a few of us work out with the Seals.

Joe was closest to us, however, because there were only about three full-time scouts in the area. Jerry Coleman had already signed with the Yankees, and he talked to me about coming over and catching for the Kenealy Yankees. Jerry signed while he was in high school.

Devine lived at 18th and Castro and I lived at 19th and Guerrero [in San Francisco]. I can remember in 1942, when I was a senior, he came by with Ernie Bonham. Ernie was having a great year — he won twenty games — and he came by to see my Irish mother. Of course, he tried to stay close with his people and be able to say, 'Look at what my boy did this past season.' He did stay close to his families, especially if they had some Irish in them.

I got a $2,500 bonus from the Yankees. The Dodgers offered me $2,000. Earl Sheely over at St. Mary's [in Moraga] was working with the Red Sox, and he was ready to offer me the same as the Dodgers, so I went with the Yankees. Mickey Shrader of Cincinnati was going to give me $2,000 and a suitcase to go to Ogden.

I could have gone to college, probably Santa Clara, but my grades weren't the best. The war was on and I wanted to play ball, and $2,500 was a good bonus at that time.

Devine stayed real close to his ballplayers, even after he signed us. He would tell us how far we could go with a contract, and he got us all into the service up at McClellan Field. Dave Kelley, who later ran the Sacramento Solons, was running the recreation program up at McClellan, so a bunch of us — Al Lien, Bill Leonard, Walt Judnich, Dario Lodigiani, Ferris Fain, Rugger Ardizoia, Bob Dillinger, Mike McCormick — went up there. We had a pretty good ball club.

We were playing during the winter, and I guess people got upset, so they shipped us overseas to Hawaii. That's when Joe DiMaggio joined us.

CHARLIE SILVERA - Portland Beavers

Nona Hutchinson and nineteen-year-old son Freddie in 1938. The Detroit Tigers recently had given four players and paid $35,000 for the young pitcher, then a student at the University of Washington.

FRED HUTCHINSON

Frederick Charles Hutchinson jumped from the Seattle preps to the Seattle Rainiers in 1938. On August 12, his 19th birthday, "Hutch" won his 19th game for the Rainiers before an overflow crowd of 17,000 at Sicks' Stadium. He ended the season with a 25-7 record in thirty-five games, twenty-nine of them complete. His ERA was 2.48.

New York Yankees scout Joe Devine followed Hutchinson's progress throughout the 1938 season and reported periodically to Ed Barrow, the Yankee Club Secretary. The following excerpts chronicle the mood of one of the key players in the negotiations. All correspondence is from Devine to Barrow, unless otherwise noted.

June 22, 1938 — Saw Hutchinson work again last night against the San Diego Club. Hutchinson shut out San Diego one to nothing, allowing seven hits and striking out five men, also walking five men. This makes the second straight shutout game for Hutchinson since I have been here. He shut out Portland last Wednesday.

From the looks of the scores it would indicate that Hutchinson has shown real stuff, but to me, he has not shown a good fastball in either game. In fact, he was not as fast last night as he was last week against Portland. He has not shown a real good curve ball in either of these games.

He has had marvelous support, especially by center fielder [Bill] Lawrence, who has cut off at least seven runs in the last two games by marvelous catches. Hutchinson has a pretty good change of pace and appears to have pretty good control.

The big thing for a scout's decision on Hutchinson is to know just how much he thinks Hutchinson will improve over the next couple of years, and to decide whether he will be fast enough for a major league pitcher. Hutchinson will have to show me a better fastball before I would consider recommending him for a large amount of money. I am sure he will go for around $40,000 the way he is going.

August 8, 1938 — My opinion of pitcher Fred Hutchinson after seeing him about a dozen games: HUTCHINSON, age 19, weight 195 lbs. Height 6'1/2," right-handed, left-handed hitter, temperament none too good. His temperament may come from the fact that he hates to lose. I know this boy is a tough loser. Hutchinson's main feature is that he has the "guts."

It is my opinion that Hutchinson is not ready to be a winning pitcher on any club in the major leagues, but we cannot get away from the fact that this boy won 26 ball games and his record is outstanding for his first year in baseball.

Figuring that our pitching material is not outstanding, I am sure that Hutchinson should be given a lot of consideration. He is going to be a strict gamble but taking his age, his size, also his control and change of pace, and as I say the "guts," we can well afford to take a chance on Hutchinson coming up with a curve ball and maybe a better fastball.

August 30, 1938 (to Manager Jack Lelivelt) — Received a wire from Mr. Barrow this morning telling me that the Seattle Club wanted an immediate answer on Hutchinson.

Now, Jack, from what this boy showed me in the games that I have seen him all season I would not be interested in Hutchinson at an outright purchase of $65,000. After thinking it over, and as to leaving him with you next year, as I asked you, and you would want $50,000, I would not be interested in this either.

If you have any proposition where you may want to give us that involves the player for delivery in 1940 — that is to give us an option — you can let me know. The option to be up until September 1, 1939. We may be able to work something out with you satisfactory along these lines.

September 12, 1938 — Regarding Hutchinson they are not going to sell him until the (winter) meeting, and want to deal with us. As Lelivelt says, we have the players he wants. But I told him he had no chance to deal with us on Hutchinson at his asking price of five players outright and $25,000 cash and leave the boy here next year.

September 27, 1938 — Had a talk with Lelivelt Sunday regarding Hutchinson. He definitely told me they would not do anything until the meeting at New Orleans. Said he expected Mr. Emil Sick to talk the matter over with you and Colonel [Jacob] Ruppert in about 10 days.

I asked him if they had come down any in their price and he said, "No," that they had not. We're still asking for five ballplayers outright and $25,000 cash and leave Hutchinson with them next year.

The San Francisco ball club played Seattle in the playoff series at Seattle, and I asked Charlie Graham how Hutchinson looked. He said in the game Hutchinson pitched in Seattle, he showed very little. He thought that maybe from the stuff he showed that he must have been "pitched out" during the season.

A Texas Leaguer dropped in back of short and scored two runs. He then started storming, throwing his glove on the ground and acting like a spoiled kid. Graham told me they beat him up north and he was riding the infielders for making a couple of mistakes. As I said before, we have to be careful of this boy's disposition.

October 24, 1938 — Went down to Los Angeles to see Lelivelt and came to a sort of agreement on pitcher Hutchinson. Our understanding was that I would take up his price on Hutchinson with you and then I would see him again at the Coast League meeting in San Francisco on November 8th.

His asking price to me in Los Angeles was four ballplayers outright and $15,000 cash and the Seattle ball club could keep Hutchinson next year. I told him you did not favor that sort of deal. I told him we would like to have him delivered to us next year, but he said that there was only one club Hutchinson would be of any value to next year and that was Seattle on account of being a drawing card for them. He figured that he needs another year and that he was cutting the price in order to keep him in Seattle.

December 7, 1938 — Seattle submitted two propositions: Purchase Hutchinson for $20,000 and four players; Babich outright and any three; Hartje, Bittner, Kelleher, Salzgaver and Davis on option; or $20,000 and Hartje and Kelleher outright. Also, in either case if Hutchinson doesn't make the club, he will be optioned back to Seattle.

I offered Seattle three players outright and $15,000 for delivery. I feel this offer is $35,000 and as high as I will advise you go on Hutchinson. They refused this offer. Joe Devine

Note: The Rainiers did move Fred Hutchinson at the winter meetings in New Orleans. The bidding war intensified, and the Detroit Tigers gave Seattle $35,000 and four players — pitcher Ed Selway, first baseman George Archie, infielder Tony Piet and outfielder JoJo White — for his contract. In 1939, Hutchinson went east, splitting his time between Toledo and Detroit.

After losing parts of four seasons to military service during the war, Hutch compiled six productive seasons before being appointed Tigers manager during the 1952 season. He was only thirty-one at the time.

George "Bee" Mandish, left, and Joyner "JoJo" White at Edmonds Field in 1946. Mandish was a power hitter, White hit for average.

SIGNING YOUNG PROSPECTS

*T*he West Coast was fertile ground for young baseball prospects. Early in the game, Pacific Coast League teams were unchallenged by the major leagues in their quest for signing prospects. That changed in the early 1930s. With young, enthusiastic kids like these, it was tough to tell if it was a buyer's or a seller's market.

As a scout, they tell you that you should find a pitcher with a real good delivery. To me, a good delivery means you can follow the ball well. The freak delivery, an unorthodox delivery, means he throws a pitch that is tough to follow. But he's got to be in balance or he won't throw strikes.

GENE HANDLEY - Hollywood Stars

I had a tryout with the Oaks in 1927. I was fifteen, and they wanted to sign me right then and send me to the Arizona-Texas League. I said, 'I'm just a kid.'

I had a tryout with the Missions in 1929 and the Seals in 1930, and signed with the Seals. When I signed, no bonus. Not in those days. In 1931, I signed my contract for $225 (a month), but when they shipped me to Arizona, I had to sign a new contract — $165 a month. That wasn't bad. I used to send $100 home to my sister every month.

JOHNNY BABICH - San Francisco Seals

I went to McClymonds High in Oakland and used to work out with the Oaks ball club. I'd go to school half a day, then go out to Emeryville. I got out of school in 1930 and Carl Zamloch signed me in 1931.

We played baseball year-round. I'd take a streetcar to the park with all my catching gear.

BILLY RAIMONDI - Oakland Oaks

I signed right out of Santa Clara High School. Justin Fitzgerald signed me for the Seattle Indians — $150 a month in 1933. That was a lot of money for me, and that was during the Depression.

NINO BONGIOVANNI - Seattle Indians

I broke in in '34. I signed with the Yankees when I was going to Oakland Tech High School and was signed by Joe Devine. He sure controlled the area, and Bill Essick was around too. Also little Bobby Coltrin.

Signing with the Yankees was a mistake. If I had signed with some other club I would have had a better chance. I liked Joe Devine. I played in the winter league in San Francisco because of him. I played with Frankie Hawkins and Chris Hartje. The Yankees signed both.

When I would go to spring training with the Yankees with my brother-in-law, [shortstop] Bill Matheson, he'd see Crosetti and I'd see Lou Gehrig and we'd say, 'What the hell are we doing here?'

I asked [Yankees general manager] George Weiss to trade me out to the West Coast. Weiss made a deal for me, all right. The next thing I know, he works out a deal with Baltimore. I blasted him, really told him off. He said, 'Nobody ever talked to me like that.' I said, 'I have.'

I go over there and boy was I pissed. I had to play for that damned Rogers Hornsby. That's when I went into the front office and told them to get me out to the coast or I was going home. That's how I got to Hollywood in 1939.

I stuck around six years in the Yankee chain and nothing ever happened. I had to get out. I could have gone with the Phillies or I

Nino "Bongy" Bongiovanni in a 1936 Portland Beavers team photo.

could have come back out to the coast and have been with a better team. I'd take the Coast [League] anytime.

LEN GABRIELSON - Oakland Oaks, Seattle Rainiers, Hollywood Stars

I signed in 1935 with the San Francisco Missions because I had grown up playing with teams that the Mission Reds had sponsored. They provided uniforms and equipment, and my team was even called the Mission Reds "A" team. Red Adams, the Missions trainer, was our coach.

This created a real dilemma, however. The truant officer came after me because I wasn't going to school. We finally worked it out that I could finish my education in continuation school. You couldn't ask me to stop playing ball during the Depression. I was bringing home four times the pay that my dad was, and our family needed the money.

EDDIE JOOST - Mission Reds

I signed (in 1936) with the Yankees organization — Bill Essick. Bobby Coltrin came down and signed me to a contract. I went to Akron the first year.

I was with the Yankee organization until 1940. I was at Binghampton, New York, in 1939 and '40. That winter they traded me to Montreal for Bozey Berger. They needed a utility man

My dad had played with Bill Essick in the old Western League. I had other clubs who were interested in me, but it was a foregone conclusion that Bill Essick was going to sign me. That was when everything was wide open. You went to the highest bidder. I got a $300 bonus for signing.

JACK GRAHAM - San Diego Padres

My dad managed a semipro team in San Pedro, E.K Lumber Co., and he used to have a few pro players play for him in the off-season, so he pretty much wanted me to sign. I was playing with men on that team when I was twelve. We also had a great American Legion team — Steve Mesner, Bobby Doerr, Mickey Owen and Dick Conger, who pitched for Detroit.

Bobby Doerr and I were both out of Los Angeles, Fremont High. We played junior high school, I practically lived at his house. Bobby and I quit high school in the eleventh grade and both signed in 1934 with Hollywood. The Depression was part of the reason for quitting. We were offered scholarships to USC, but we wanted to sign. We needed the money.

A worker's average pay in 1934 was about eighteen dollars a week, and we signed for $150 a month! Christ, I used to bring the whole neighborhood kids down to buy them strawberry waffles. I bought a brand new Chevrolet in 1934, a coupe, $625. Twenty some years after that, I went back to the same place where I bought it and the same salesman was there who sold me the car.

The Stars were playing at Wrigley, and we were scouted by George Stovall. He was an old timer then. No bonus. I didn't play much. Ray Jacobs was the first baseman.

GEORGE McDONALD - Hollywood Stars

I signed a contract in 1936. I was still in school, Commerce High, and Joe Baerwold of the Missions signed me on my seventeenth birthday. But I actually had three choices.

When I was at Commerce, we went down to Stanford and I beat the Stanford freshmen. Bobby Grayson was the Stanford coach, and he wanted to give me a scholarship, but I couldn't because I had already signed with the Missions.

And Joe Devine tried to sign me for the Yankees with Bill Essick. But the Yankees, you couldn't get any money from them. I was sold to the Yankees during the 1940 season. That's when Joe Devine finally got me. I didn't have a great record, but I did have sixteen complete games. I pitched pretty good ball, but didn't get much support (14-20, 264 innings pitched).

In my first game, I relieved Johnny Babich down in San Diego — and I pitched five innings of one-hit ball — right out of high school. I remained with the Missions the rest of the season.

RUGGER ARDIZOIA - Mission Reds

I was playing ball in the Valley League in San Francisco, and Oscar Vitt and Vic Devincenzi came out to the ballpark. They watched me play, and after the game Oscar came up and asked, 'Hey, kid, would you be interested in playing pro ball?' I said, 'Yeah.' Well in those days if someone asked you to play ball ... holy cow! If you got a job you were only making about twenty-five dollars a week. I said, 'Sure!' I thought I'd help out the family, so I signed in 1936 with Oakland. I was always a Seals rooter, but Oakland offered me a job, so I took it.

Vic was trying to find a place to play after spring training. He was talking about Springfield and some other leagues in the Midwest. Well, Freddie Muller was the second baseman. He pulls a groin muscle or something, and they took him out of the lineup and I played second base. After his groin muscle got better, they traded him to Seattle, and I stayed there.

DARIO LODIGIANI - Oakland Oaks

I had graduated from Oakland Tech and was playing semipro ball during the winter. Doc Silvey signed me for the Seals and sent me to spring training at Hanford with the Seals in 1937. I had a good spring training. I won a running event, so they could see I could run pretty good, but they were loaded with outfielders and they fully intended on sending me, Larry Powell, Bill Lillard and a few others to Tucson for more experience.

 Before we were sent out, we went on an early road trip to L.A., and I was put in as a pinch hitter. I got a home run in my first at bat in the Coast League. When I hit that home run, I said to myself, 'Well, golly, I'm going to stay with the club for a while.' I was only seventeen, but I felt pretty good about it.

Still, they had already planned their outfield, so I was on a train to Tucson the next day. I was sent to the Tucson Cowboys, and batted .320 in '37. The newspaper ran a clever story about how I slugged my way right off the club. But I did need more experience.

GEORGE "BEE" MANDISH - San Francisco Seals

I played with a C.Y.O. team, and when I was twelve or thirteen, we played in the old Oaks Ball Park. I knew when I was ten years old I wanted to be a baseball player. My grandfather was in the tile business, and he sponsored a semipro team, and every Sunday we'd go out to the ball game.

As I got older, in junior high and high school, my dad would take me down to Bayview Park and drop me at nine o'clock in the morning. I'd play in the 10 o'clock game, hope somebody wouldn't show up for the 12 o'clock game so I could play that one, and the 2:30 game. I would stay all day so I could play.

I didn't make the high school team until I was a senior. I was too small. The coach was afraid I'd get hurt. I grew five or six inches between my junior and senior years.

When I was ready to sign, a Giants scout said to me, 'We would like to sign you, but if you want some advice, I'd sign with an independent club. Now you've got all sixteen clubs interested.'

When I signed with Oakland (in 1938) I got a $500 bonus, then $500 more if I ever made the big club.

BILL RIGNEY - Oakland Oaks

Doc Silvey was the Seals Bay Area Scout. He was enamored with our Roosevelt High School squad. Silvey signed Wil Leonard, Bob Witig and me for the Seals.

When I was a junior in high school, they got me working out with the Seals at San Francisco. In my senior year, they decided to give me an incentive to remember them. Here I am on a fifty-cent allowance and still in high school; they give me $200 a month! Hey, these guys want me! And Lefty O'Doul treated me like a son. All they wanted was for me to come over and work out!

Ferris Fain, signed by the San Francisco Seals in 1939.

Working out with the Seals, my strength was fielding. O'Doul would get me out on the infield and he'd try as hard as he could to hit a ball by me. He'd stand over there with his fungo and he'd rip, and every time I'd catch that ball or block it. Lefty loved it.

Harley Boss was always kidding with me. But when I signed in 1939 with the Seals and took his job, he never talked to me again.

They did impress on me this: We're independently owned. By signing independently, you have a chance of going to any of sixteen clubs instead of being mired in the minors behind some star. We didn't have agents at that time, so we were happy to sign. They didn't give me a bonus, or promise me a percentage when I was sold to a major league team.

Two weeks before I graduate Harley Boss gets hurt, and Charlie Graham and O'Doul got together with school officials and they sign me. My mother had to sign the contract and I join the ball club, on the pretense that I'm going to play. Well, I guess that was their full intention, but prior to me getting into the lineup, they realized that if I played in one game, I would lose one year of eligibility towards the major league draft.

You could play four years before you could be drafted. You could play in September and it wouldn't count. So they held me out until the last two weeks of the season.

FERRIS FAIN - San Francisco Seals

Edo Vanni in 1957.

EDO VANNI - Seattle Rainiers

Hutch and I came out in '38. I used to be clubhouse boy for the visiting teams at Civic Stadium, and when Los Angeles came to town, Jigger Statz was one of my favorites. I'd go out and work with the ball club. That's when [then-Los Angeles Angels manager] Jack Lelivelt took a liking to me. I'd go in and the batting cage and hit with the old-timers. Then when he took over as manager in Seattle, he got ahold of me and asked, 'Well, do you want to play football or baseball?'

I said, 'Well, I guess I'll have to take baseball.' Football was just a secondary thing to me. All I was doing at the University of Washington was kicking field goals and kickoffs, although I had been an all-city quarterback here for two years.

Torchy Torrance signed me to a contract and he really got blasted in the press for it. He was in strong with the university. But they all knew [that I wanted to sign]. Jack knew it. He said, 'I want you to come play ball for me,' and that was it. I was very fortunate to sign with a team under his control.

When I left the University of Washington, my contract was put together by Bobby Morris, who was a football referee in the Pacific Coast Conference. He was like a father to me. I got 4,000 shares of Rainier Beer stock at thrity-five cents a share and a $2,000 signing bonus.

I also had all these incentives in my contract. If I batted .300 I got $250. If I stole forty bases I got another $250. If we won the pennant, I got another bonus. We played a twenty-game schedule, and if I played 180 games I got $250. If I was sold to the majors I got twenty-five percent of my sales price.

So we're going into the last Sunday of the season down in San Diego, and they have to win one game to get into the playoffs. I was hitting .299, and I had to face Tom Seats and Al Olsen. If I hit .300, I got a $250 bonus. I went four for six.

When I got over the .300 mark, Al Strange says, 'Slide into second base and get hurt.' I say, 'Oh, to hell with it.' Lelivelt told me later he was going to give me the bonus anyway.

I wasn't much of a high school player. When I got out of high school, I must have gained pretty close to thirty-five or forty pounds the first year out. I must have grown four inches.

I was actually playing basketball for San Diego State. I really didn't play too much baseball after high school.

I was working for Graybar Electric Company in the afternoons, and they closed up on

Saturday afternoons. One Saturday I stopped by the Northpark playground, and they were having a ball game there. One of the teams was run by Tom Downey of the Brooklyn Dodgers.

They were short a player that day, and one of the kids playing had been a high school teammate, so he said to Downey, 'Why don't you get him to come out and play? He's played some.' I guess I played five or seven games for Downey and, lo and behold, I had about three or four scouts after me.

One day Major Lott, president of the Padres, called me down to the office and said, 'I think you want to play ball, don't you?' I said, 'I certainly would like to try it.'

Lott asked me, 'How bad do you want to play ball?' He didn't get an answer, but he started pulling hundred dollar bills out of his desk, and when he got up to seven or eight hundred, I said, 'I'll sign.' I was out of high school about a year-and-a-half when I signed in 1939.

Downey was very disappointed with me at that time because they offered to send me to New York University, but I didn't think too much of that. I wanted to stay in San Diego, and maybe the fact that Ted [Williams] had played in San Diego before he went to Boston helped encourage me to sign with the Padres.

JOHN "SWEDE" JENSEN - San Diego Padres

I actually signed my first contract with the Red Sox. There was a state semipro tournament here in Oregon, and I signed a contract but asked them to hold it until after the tournament was over with. This was about the same time that a lot of major league teams got in trouble [with the Commissioner's Office] for holding back contracts.

Apparently the Red Sox neglected to file my contract and I'm expecting to go to spring training with the Red Sox and I didn't hear a thing. So I didn't know what to do. I'm a country boy, and there weren't any scouts around to help.

There was a fella out here who was a bird dog for the Seals, and I had worked out with the Seals the year before in Portland. They liked me.

'What do I do now?' I asked him. He said, 'I'd get in touch with Judge [Kenesaw Mountain] Landis.' A semipro umpire in Portland helped me to contact Judge Landis, and Landis wired back, stating that I was a free agent and for me to send him all the details. I then called San Francisco and asked if they were still interested.

I was signed by Eddie Mulligan for the Seals in 1941. He ran the Salt Lake club. I got a $250 bonus for signing.

LARRY JANSEN - San Francisco Seals (signed 1941)

My brother Joe and I grew up in Portland and were clubhouse boys for Rocky Benevento. My brother got the job from Johnny Pesky and I got it from my brother. That was like playing a year of pro ball. We got to work out with the team, and when they went on the road Rocky used to let us use the field. We'd be watering the field and would go out and practice. We'd bring in some kids and play a game, then we'd have to work.

Oscar Vitt managed the Beavers in '41, and he'd have me come out to work out. I was playing American Legion, and he had me come out and throw. Once, the Seals were in town, and everybody stopped and watched all the Seals, even Lefty. The same thing happened with Johnny Pesky and my brother.

Vitt went to Hollywood in '42, and he came to Portland during the winter of '41 to sign me. I got a $5,000 bonus. Brooklyn offered me $15,000, but my dad said, 'I want you to sign with an independent ball club.' That way I got fifty percent of my sales price if I was sold to the big leagues.

So when I got sold to Cincinnati, I got half the price, a check for $10,000. I gave it to my folks. That's why my dad did that deal. That's the chance he took.

EDDIE ERAUTT - Hollywood Stars

I don't think the scouting network was as spread out as it is now. I had a tremendous record down at Stockton. I won some twenty games over four or five months down there, but I don't think anybody ever saw me. In those days they had only Joe Devine and Justin Fitzgerald and maybe one or two others. They didn't comb the bushes because there was such a wealth of talent in the Bay Area that they didn't have to go anywhere else.

BILL WERLE - San Francisco Seals (signed in 1943)

I was still in school when I signed with the Padres in 1945. There were two very active scouts in the San Diego area that were scouting players here. Tom Downey was scouting for the Brooklyn ball club and Herb Benninghoven was scouting for the Cardinals. Both expressed their interest in me and both were offering a contract, but my dad and I decided that it might have been to my benefit to go with an independent club.

The San Diego Padres were independently owned at that time. If I was to be a major league first baseman and I was playing for a team that was independent, then any major league team would have the choice of at least bidding on me.

Pepper Martin had something to do with my signing with the Padres. My dad and I had bickered back and forth with Bill Starr. We're talking cents instead of dollars, and one day my dad and I were in the office with Mr. Starr, and we're talking dollars, and Pepper Martin just happened to be coming into the office and stood at the back of the room, just kind of listening to what was going on.

We were bickering back and forth and Pepper says, 'Mr. Starr, do you want this young man to play for the Padres?' It kind of put Bill on the spot. He said, 'Well, yes, I'd like that.' So Pepper says, 'Well, then, give him the goddamn money.'

It kind of forced Bill's hand. Anyway, I'm sure we would have agreed on something eventually, but that seemed to bring the issue to a head, and I've always appreciated Pepper for being that honest about it.

JACK HARSHMAN - San Diego Padres

I signed in 1946 with Detroit. Bernie DeVivieros signed me for $6,000. At the time I had bonus offers from all sixteen major league teams. The lowest was Cincinnati. George 'High Pockets' Kelly offered me $250. If I had it to do over again, I would have signed with either Oakland or San Francisco.

It was a very bad time to be in a major league organization. We used to joke that major league clubs had three teams: one there, one coming and one going. They didn't know where they stood. Players were coming back after the war, and they didn't know if a particular player was going to come back and be what he was before the war.

And they went out and signed a bunch of other prospects. I always felt I was there at the wrong time. The year after I signed, Detroit went out and signed a catcher named Frank 'Pig' House for $62,000. The big race was on, and big bonuses were being handed out.

I always wanted to play in the Coast League. In the winter of 1950, Detroit sold me to Seattle. I was back home.

CLAUDE CHRISTIE - Seattle Rainiers

You talk about corralling a guy, the Oaks gave me a job in the front office while I was in high school, clipping coupons for Brick Laws. Literally doing nothing. I was pasting. I guess I lost my amateur standing before I signed.

DON FERRARESE - Oakland Oaks (signed in 1948)

I graduated from McClatchy High School and my brother, Wally, graduated from Christian Brothers. Wally initially signed with the Dodgers, and the Dodgers stipulated that if he stayed with their minor league club by July 1, he would get a $500 bonus. They released him. Then he signed with the Oakland Oaks in 1941. In 1942, he played for Oakland and then went into the service and came out in 1946 and played for Oakland again before going to the big leagues with Pittsburgh.

I loved the Seals when I was a kid. Even though I was living in Sacramento, I loved them. I thought Lefty O'Doul was the greatest, and my dream was to sign with the Seals when I was a kid, fourteen or fifteen years old.

I signed in 1948 and went to Salt Lake. In 1949, I was supposed to go back to Salt Lake, but Mickey Rocco, who was supposed to be the first baseman, broke his cheek on a bad hop, so they kept me there for about six weeks. Then I went back to Salt Lake City and hit .344.

Wally was ten years older, just old enough that he didn't help me much. I used to hit right-handed, and he told me to hit left-handed. He told me that when I was ten or eleven. Wally bought me my first first baseman's glove.

JIM WESTLAKE - San Francisco Seals

Slick-fielding first baseman Jim Westlake hit for average but not for power, which hurt his prospects.

Joe Devine signed me for the New York Yankees in 1949. Paddy Cottrell was my coach at Santa Clara University, and he was a bird dog for Joe. I guess everybody knew he was a scout for the Yankees. That possibly cut down the interest in me.

Bernie DeVivieros of Detroit talked to me a couple of times, and Bill Brenzel of the Dodgers talked to me, but they didn't get too serious. I don't remember any offers, only the Yankees. Also, Tom Kelly, who was the co-captain at Santa Clara, also signed with the Yankees. We graduated on a Friday in June and were in the starting lineup at Twin Falls of the Pioneer League on Monday.

BILL RENNA - San Francisco Seals

Pittsburgh flew me down to Hollywood in 1952 for a tryout camp, and I don't think I got anybody out in four days. After three days of getting lit up, Branch Rickey asked me what I wanted to sign for. So I mustered up all my courage and I said, 'Ten thousand dollars.'

It looked like somebody hit him with an axe right in the middle of the forehead. He said, 'What?' I said, 'Ten thousand dollars.' He said, 'We can't give you $10,000. We just gave Dick Groat $45,000.' I said, 'Mr. Rickey, is that the last money that the Pittsburgh organization has?' Well, goodbye.

So I went home and waited for the phone to ring, and it didn't ring very much. Finally, Charlie Graham phoned from Sacramento and said, 'Come on up to Edmonds Field and pitch batting practice and we'll take a look at you.'

Actually I got a better deal from Sacramento because I signed a AAA contract in 1952. I was making $725 a month, and they optioned me to Stockton in the California League, and those guys were making $350 and $400.

If I had signed with the Pirates, I would have been sent to Modesto.

Ernie Broglio, shown here in a 1954 photo, had moderate success with the Oakland Oaks before he was sold to the New York Giants. He later was a twenty-one- and eighteen-game winner with the St. Louis Cardinals.

But Charlie Graham made a lot of sense. These big league clubs would give a player these big bonuses, then, over a period of time, instead of paying them $500 a month as they progressed through the farm system, they'd pay them $300 a month. So over a period of time they'd draw that bonus money right back out of 'em.

BUD WATKINS - Sacramento Solons

I came out of Stanford in 1953. We played in the College World Series, and I visited the Oaks Ball Park after returning from it. Nobody knew who I was. I signed a contract with Brick Laws about 2 o'clock, about the third inning on a Sunday afternoon of the opening game of a double-header with Portland. Brick says, 'Well, why don't you go down to the clubhouse. Augie's expecting you. He'd like to have you in uniform.' Augie Galan was the Oaks manager. So I go down there. I'm the only guy in the clubhouse. Everybody is in the dugout. So I put on a uniform and walk out there.

Augie says, 'Murph, did you sign a contract?' I say, 'Yes.' And he says, 'How'd you like to pitch the second game?'

Holy cow! I had to go back and change my uniform. Lennie Neal was the catcher that day. He didn't catch much. I had pretty good control. They hit rockets at everyone. They hit three at me, and I caught all three of them. Hank Arft, Don Eggert, Fletcher Robbe — boy, they had some good players. We beat 'em 3-2.

Then I lost four in a row, and we went on a road trip, up in Seattle, and I wrote Brick Laws a letter and offered to give the money back. I honest-to-God did.

Brick said, 'You'll be OK,' and then I won three in a row and ended up 4-5. I beat Hollywood on the last day of the season. We ended up going from eighth to seventh that day and we celebrated like we'd won the goddamn pennant.

BOB MURPHY - Oakland Oaks

I signed right out of high school with the Oakland Oaks. I didn't get any bonus. If I had waited six months, after they changed the bonus rule, I would have collected a big bonus. Brick said when I got sold to the majors he would give me a bonus. He said that in front of my mother and father!

When I was sold to the Giants, I asked Brick about that and he said, 'You paid off a debt for me.' I had just finished winning twenty games at Stockton!

In spring training the next year, I went up to Chub Feeney [of the Giants] and asked, 'How much was I sold for?' He said, 'I can't tell you, but why do you ask?'

I told him what had happened, and he took out his checkbook and wrote me a check for $1,000.

ERNIE BROGLIO - Oakland Oaks

STAYING ON THE COAST

There were a lot of guys in the Coast League back then who didn't want to go east. There were guys who said, 'This is the greatest life in the world.' They were getting $600, $800 or $1,000 a month. That was a lot of dough back then. Joe Bowman, who pitched at Portland, was reluctant to go up to the big leagues. He liked it on the coast. He liked the weather, the travel. We traveled on Monday and were in the same town for a week. It was out of this world.

BOBBY LOANE - Los Angeles Angels

Playing in Oakland was great. I lived in Alameda and traveled to the Oaks Ball Park. If I had gone to the majors, I would probably have been the third-string catcher and would have had to pay rent and transportation costs for my family.

Staying with Oakland, I played regularly and was able to live in my own house and have home cooking all the time. For me, it was a no-brainer.

BILLY RAIMONDI - Oakland Oaks

For me, playing on the West Coast was a real break. Playing in the American Association or International League left a lot to be desired. Everybody wants to play in the majors, that's understood, but if you can't make the majors, there's no place to play but on the coast.

BILL RENNA - San Francisco Seals

Bill Renna joined the Boston Red Sox affiliate in San Francisco to get out to the Coast League. the 1957 Seals won the pennant, with Renna supplying much of the power — twenty-nine homers and 105 RBI.

ON BEING A ROOKIE

When I broke in with the Padres, the tradition of veterans not helping rookies held true. We had a third baseman, Mickey Haslin. I can remember spring training at El Centro when I went to get a bat to hit in batting practice, he said, 'Get your you-know-what out to the outfield. We'll do the hitting.'

I played a game up at Portland early in the season of my first year. The umpire Jack Powell was behind the plate, and the pitcher threw one that was about a foot-and-a-half over my head and he called it a strike. I started to say something and he said, 'Stop!' And he says, 'Not only that, the next one's a strike too.' He told me to get myself back in the box and start swinging.

JOHN "SWEDE" JENSEN - San Diego Padres (signed in 1939)

Herb Benninghoven, the old catcher, signed me to a contract with the St. Louis Cardinals and I went to spring training in 1940 with Sacramento. At those times, they carried three catchers. I made the ball club as the third catcher.

We had a fella called Ken Penner, an old-time pitcher. He was going to manage the club at Pocatello, and he talked to me. He said, 'If you come with me to Pocatello, I'll teach you how to become a ballplayer. You can stay here in Sacramento, but you're not going to play. You can come with me and I'll teach you how to become a catcher, the things you should know to succeed.' I said, 'OK.' The best move I ever made.

When he took me, I was as raw as a piece of meat. He taught me how to catch a pop fly. It was different from catching a fly in the outfield. He was probably the best fungo

The San Diego Padres' Whitey Wietelmann beats the throw in a game at Oakland. Oaks catcher Frank Kerr struggles futilely to make the tag while Padres outfielder Dain Clay watches from the on-deck circle and Jimmie Reese gestures from the third-base coach's box.

man I ever met in my life. He was as good as Jimmie Reese!

After a while, he taught me how to work pitchers, how to work different pitchers to different hitters and to remember where the hitter is in the batter's box this series, the next series.

I'd call the game — he didn't call any pitches. But the next day, I'd have to go out to the ballpark — 10 o'clock — and we'd talk baseball until noon. 'What did you throw this guy?' He'd critique me, stuffing a kid's head full of knowledge. I thought you just went out and caught the ball and hit the ball. He made a catcher out of me.

FRANK KERR - Sacramento Solons, San Diego Padres

As a rookie, I never even got to hit batting practice with the pitchers. They'd shove you in a corner. 'Go out there and shag.' They'd nail your shoes to the floor, spit tobacco on your uniform, tie your clothes in knots in the clubhouse. Oh boy, you just had to take it. Just laugh at it and they'd leave you alone.

In my first year, I didn't get to pitch much at all, but I was learning by watching. About halfway through the season, they sent me to Salem in the Western International League. I was happy to go. I wanted to pitch. I got to pitch every four days.

In 1943, when I came back, I got to pitch against Claude Passeau of the Cubs, and after the game, he came up to me and said, 'You're going to be a great pitcher. You've got it.' He said, 'Just be yourself.' I'll never forget that.

EDDIE ERAUTT - Hollywood Stars

Jess Flores gave me the greatest piece of advice from any pitcher. Jess was with the

A solid pitcher, Bud Watkins liked to complete his games. He was stuck with a powerless Sacramento Solons team during most of his career, but he nonetheless denied his opponents enough runs to win many of his games. He was especially effective in Edmonds Field. This photo was taken in 1957.

Solons in 1953, and I asked him for advice to help me become a better pitcher. At that time, players didn't help rookies because they felt they might take their jobs. But Jess told me, 'Hey, Bush, picture this: It's the last of the ninth, bases loaded, two outs and it's 3-2 on the hitter. The batter knows I'm going to throw a fastball. The manager knows I'm going to throw a fastball. Everybody in the park knows I'm going to throw a fastball, but only Old Jess knows what speed I'm going to throw the fastball.'

That was the best piece of advice I ever received in baseball. Tony Freitas put it another way. He asked me, 'What's the secret of hitting?' He said, 'Isn't it timing? So doesn't it make sense that if you screw up the timing, you screw up the hitting?' Neither of those guys could blacken your eye with their best fastball, but they both knew how to pitch.

BUD WATKINS - Sacramento Solons *(signed in 1952)*

In 1942, I was slated to be farmed out, but I started out with the club probably because of my cockiness.

It was funny that I got to pitch at all. The Angels had a good ball club, and they had guys in camp who had good years in higher classifications, and I had just come out of the WI League. I was only nineteen that spring and had played three years, but had the poorest record, win and losses.

I pitched all year and I would wind up winning six and losing fifteen, but I pitched the opener. I remember, I pitched against Damon Hayes, who beat me 1-0 up in Spokane. The second game, Al Lien beat me 3-2, I believe. I pitched four or five games well and didn't win any of 'em. Don Osborn was our manager and, fortunately, he kept pitching me.

In spring training, I went up to Clarence Rowland — that was his first year with the Angels. I was trying to get a few more bucks in my contract, but I couldn't bring up my record. Finally, he said, 'If you sign this contract and if you make a good showing this spring, I'll give you a little more money,'

I pitched one time only all spring. It was understandable. They had Kenny Raffensberger, Ray Prim, Red Lynn, Jess Flores — they were loaded with pitching.

Anyway, I went up to complain a bit to Mr. Rowland. Actually, I thought if I talked to him just right, he'd give me a few more bucks anyway.

He wound up getting mad at me. He said, 'A young kid like you, coming up to complain.' He reminded me of the terrible year I had the year before and that we had a strong pitching staff and here I'm up here complaining because I haven't had a chance to pitch.

He said, 'You are a cocky young kid.' He says, 'You need a couple of more years down in the bus leagues to take some of the arrogance out of you.'

I didn't think of myself that way at all. I was just trying to increase my $150 salary a bit. So I got a bit ticked off myself. So I said, 'I'll tell you what. You told me that if I had a good showing this spring that you might give me a little more money. I'm not up here crying that I'm not on this staff. I can see that I don't belong on this staff. But, I'll tell you what, if you pitch me a little bit and see that I deserve to be on the bus leagues, then that's OK, but if you see that I deserve to be in a higher league, then I want to pitch there.'

Damned if they don't call me in and give me a regular uniform. I start working out with the regular team! I'm sure that Rowland told [Angels Manager] Jigger Statz to 'teach that kid a lesson.' So they pitched me.

When I warmed up, there was somebody warming up right next to me. I don't think they thought I'd get out of the first inning. I went nine and won that game. This was early in the season! The Good Lord was looking out for me.

I hadn't pitched much, just one outing and a lot of batting practice. Well, I breeze through the first five against Portland. I actually got three hits myself, so I'm feeling pretty good. And I see Mr. Rowland sitting up there behind home plate, his hat with the brim up. He gave me inspiration. I was kind of ticked off: 'I'm going to show *you*.'

In the last three or four innings, my legs felt like they weighed a ton, and my stuff wasn't good and they're hitting shots past guys. Ted Norbert hits a two-run home run in the ninth, but we're well ahead. I think we won 7-4.

They kind of had to pitch me again. They couldn't send me out immediately. I was so sore. Jigger asked me to pitch again four or five days later and I had to tell him I wasn't ready. I was too sore. Well, I won six games and lost four before they sent me down.

CHARLES "RED" ADAMS - Los Angeles Angels

The 1944 Sacramento Solon opened at Sicks Seattle Stadium with 12,464 in attendance — a full house. The Solons are lined up on the first-base line.

COAST LEAGUE COMES OF AGE

Tony Lazzeri was one of many players who came out of retirement to fill roster vacancies created by World War II. Lazzeri joined the 1941 San Francisco Seals, played in 102 games and batted .248.

BASEBALL DURING THE HARD TIMES

COOKIE DEVINCENZI WAS AN INDEPENDENT OPERATOR AT OAKLAND. HE NEVER HAD ANY MONEY. HE DIDN'T HAVE A FARM SYSTEM, BUT HE DID SIGN SOME YOUNG GUYS — DARIO LODIGIANI, COOKIE LAVAGETTO, MEL DUEZABOU. DEVINCENZI WAS ALWAYS MAKING DO JUST TO GET A TEAM ON THE FIELD.

When he sold 'Lodi' to the Athletics after 1937, he got some bodies. He made a good deal for himself. He got Hugh Luby and Bill Conroy outright. They got an outfielder named Al Yount. They got George Turbeville, the pitcher, and another player. He got bodies, but the team was old.

In spring training in 1938 we trained in Brawley, just above the Mexican border. We went down by bus and actually picked up one of our catchers along the way. He was just sitting by the side of the road with his bags, waiting to be picked up.

We were in a funky hotel, and a man named Struble was our traveling secretary. He explained the rules to me: 'Let's get this straight. You can have three-dollar breakfasts at the hotel or you can have one dollar and watch what you eat. So it's my first year. I'm having fifty-cent breakfasts.

Devi comes down to Brawley and goes over the books. He comes to me and says, 'You start eating well. Some steaks.' He wanted me fit.

I finally realized, looking at his team, I was the only player that he had that he could sell. I was the youngest player. Everybody else had already been up and back.

BILL RIGNEY - Oakland Oaks

During the Depression, Vic Devincenzi was forced to use young players because he couldn't afford to pay the better, higher-priced players. So we had a lot of kids, then a lot of old pitchers who were hanging on and took lower salaries to keep playing. He was pretty good to us. He treated everyone fairly, but he didn't have any money. We only had one uniform and on the road the uniforms didn't get cleaned.

When times got better, we had sets of three uniforms. We had two at home and one on the road, cleaned all the time. When I used to play a double-header, I'd take a shower, then put a new uniform on for the second game. But in the '30s, your undershirt, they'd be stinking like ever. In the '40s, I'd wear new everything.

BILLY RAIMONDI - Oakland Oaks

Baseball in the '30s — we had to have poise. We had to wear a necktie. You had to have some sort of class or you were gone. If a guy was a star, he'd get taught class real quick.

You only got two dollars a day meal money, but the only time you couldn't afford it was if you started eating steaks on the train. We stayed in good hotels everywhere we went.

The Angels weren't cheap. They went first class. [Angels President] Dave Flemin was a real nice guy. [General manager] Oscar Reichow was all business, like he was trying to get to the major leagues.

BOBBY LOANE - Los Angeles Angels

Seattle Rainiers catcher Al Sueme tags out San Francisco Seals first baseman Gus Suhr in the ninth inning of a 1943 series opener. The Seals went on to win 6-5.

During the Depression, when we went on the road, you traveled by train in those times. We stayed in fair hotels, and you signed your tab at the hotel restaurant. They didn't give us meal money. Some teams did. Sam Gibson of the Seals — they used to call him 'Cornflakes Gibson.' He would save his money and live on cornflakes.

EMIL MAILHO - Oakland Oaks

During the winters early in my career, Steve Mesner and his wife, Charlene, and I and my wife would live good for a couple of months, then run out of money. Steve had a brand new Packard. We'd go in and get two gallons of gas. I can remember when gas was 12.9 cents a gallon. Also, we'd get our eighteen-dollars-a-week unemployment. I remember it was Ken Keltner of the Cleveland Indians who was the first one to do that. They couldn't find a baseball job for us to fill during the winter, so we qualified for unemployment. I hardly ever had to work during the winter.

GEORGE McDONALD - San Diego Padres

During the Depression things didn't cost very much. You could get breakfast for a dollar. That would be bacon and eggs, jam and toast and juice. I smoked cigars — they cost a nickel — and I would drink beer. That was a dime. Other than that, I didn't smoke or drink.

We would get money to take the street car to the ballpark. It would cost a dime. We wouldn't take a cab. It cost too much, except when four of us would share a cab. You could save a lot of money if you'd watch yourself.

I got paid $360 for the season at Sioux City in 1934, and still saved $180. At the end of the season, Hugh Luby and I got jobs in the stockyard tending hogs. We went to work at 6 o'clock in the evening and got off at 2 o'clock in the morning. We got forty cents an hour. But when December came, it got so cold I couldn't hold a pencil. I've got to go home. I came home on a freight train. Coming over Donner Pass was one of the coldest experiences I ever had.

The visiting club usually stayed at a hotel downtown. They were comfortable. You had to get to the ballpark on your own. In L.A., Portland, San Diego you ride the street car. You're going to be there six days. They'll give you carfare. Meal money — they'd give you about three dollars and fifty cents a day. You had to watch your money, but you could eat pretty good for that.

LOU VEZILICH - Sacramento Solons

THE COAST LEAGUE GOES TO WAR

The 1943 season was a difficult year because of the war. Rosters were reduced to eighteen players, and it was hard to find players. That's why Bill Skiff of Seattle contacted me. Skiff asked me to come to spring camp as a favor. He needed a first baseman.

I was running a beer agency and was in the Oakland Fire Department, and that was an essential defense job. I was pretty much out of shape but Skiff knew me and knew I could get back into shape. I did and had a pretty good year.

We only hit fifteen home runs as a team. Nobody in the infield hit a home run that year. The balls got soft because they were overused. The fans had to return any balls hit into the stands because of rationing.

Eddie Carnett actually pitched and played the outfield for us that year. Without war he would have just pitched. Ford Mullen played second base and caught in a pinch. Byron Speece pitched 175 innings for us, and he was forty-six years old! (His record was 13-9 — not bad.) We had to do that.

But after the 1943 season, I went back to the Oakland Fire Department, and then went into the Navy. I did go back to spring training with Seattle in 1946. There were 110 guys in camp, a lot of guys back from the service.

I had a great spring training, but they pretty much had their team already selected from 1945. Once the season opened, we went to San Francisco and I pinch hit. Then we went back to Seattle and they gave 15 of us the old how-do-you-do — they told us goodbye.

Because we were veterans, they had to keep us. Period! A couple of us sued them. So they sent me a telegram telling me to report immediately to Seattle and my back pay will be taken care of. I sent a telegram back telling them to shove it, and I never played pro ball again.

LEN GABRIELSON - Seattle Rainiers

When I was with Oakland we had to get a defense job during the day. We worked at the Hubbell Galvanizing plant while we were at home. We'd work so many hours during the day, then play ball at night. Of course, when we went on the road trip we didn't have to work. Les Scarsella, Cotton Pippen and about five or six of us were there. We all had some sort of defense job.

Some were out at the shipyards in Richmond. I was married. At first, you weren't [given a selective-service draft classification of] 1-A if you were married, but near the end it got so bad I was classified 1-A. But if you got a defense job they forgot about [drafting you into the service].

The worst place to play was San Diego. It was ninety percent servicemen. They'd knock you off the sidewalk. 'You slacker. How come you're not in uniform?'

The ball we hit was like a rock because they couldn't use good rubber in them. It was all synthetic rubbers, so the ball didn't have any life to it. It might have been wrapped looser. I used to get a kick out of poor Billy Raimondi. He'd hit the ball just as far as he could, and the ball would die at the fence and the outfielder would catch it. He just couldn't get against the left field fence.

EMIL MAILHO - Oakland Oaks

I was sold to the Red Sox in '42 but got my draft notice at about the same time, so went right into the service instead. That ended that.

We went to Long Beach at the Army Air Corps Ferry Command, then went over seas. We played a lot of ball overseas, especially in Hawaii.

We later went to Guam, Tinian and Iwo Jima. I was in a support position and was lucky enough to play ball. We had a good club — Red Ruffing, Harry Danning, Chuck Stevens and Nanny Fernandez, also Roy Pitter. He could throw.

John "Pepper" Martin was a St. Louis "Gas House Gang" player who brought the Gas House vitality to Sacramento during the war years.

There was quite a bit of war jitters when I left San Diego. In fact, we had the blackouts here. I don't know why the Japanese didn't come as far as San Diego.

When I returned it didn't take long to readjust. And we were in pretty good shape. Besides, I didn't care too much about spring training for a month. A week or week-and-a-half would have been enough. I actually held out one year so I didn't have to report. I think I got a twenty-five-cent raise, but I was holding out so I didn't have to report.

JOHN "SWEDE" JENSEN - San Diego Padres

After Montreal, I went into the service, in June of 1943. I went in as an air-crew cadet, got washed out and became a physical-training instructor. In '42, I got beaned. I had gotten hit in the cheekbone and it knocked my eye from 20/20 to 20/40. So when I went into the service, it caught up with me. When it came to taking a flight physical, I found out I would be washed out.

The war was winding down by that time and they had so many air crewmen that they were taking people out of the air corps and putting them back in the infantry. I was a voluntary enlistee, so I wasn't included in that. I got to stay in the Air Corps. We had three people from our Kerns club in Utah — Frank Lamanna, Johnny Sturm and Hooks Iott. Those people all went back in the infantry, and in six weeks they were all in China, India, Burma. But the war was over, so they didn't see any action.

Sacramento Solons pitcher Hershel Lyons in 1942.

If you were a professional athlete and if you had a certain number of points, then you could get out to go to spring training, so I was released in February, 1946, to go to Samford, Florida, with the Dodgers. They had about 275 players that were released from the service, and they were all there for evaluation. I had an advantage because I belonged to the big club.

The thing they had to do, they had to waive veterans out of the league after ten days. So I was with the big club ten days after the season started, and the picked me up on waivers. I finished the season with the Giants and didn't hit too much, .219.

I went to spring training with the Giants in '47. That was the first year they trained in Phoenix. I was with them almost to the end of spring training.

We had gone to Hawaii to play exhibitions against the San Francisco Seals, who were training on Maui, but we played the exhibitions in Honolulu. I pinch hit one time in the week we were there, then we played three games in San Francisco, then flew back to Phoenix. The next day I found out they had waived me and I went to Jersey City.

(The San Francisco Seals attempted to acquire Jack Graham for the 1947 season, but failed.)

JACK GRAHAM - San Diego Padres

The war came along after we won our third straight pennant, and I went in. I was the second guy drawn out of a hat. The lady at the draft board gave me a call: 'Edo, you're getting your draft notice in the mail to report to Fort Lewis Monday morning.' So I went down and Told Torchy Torrance and enlisted in the Navy on Saturday. If I've got to go to my battles, I want to ride.

I signed up for two years, but that was a joke. When that came up, the

Gene Handley played on the pennant-winning Sacramento Solons in 1942, and after the war played for the Hollywood Stars under Fred Haney.

war was still on, and I served four. That took all the sting out of me. I wasn't the same. It wasn't the same ball club. It wasn't the same players.

Even the fans were different. New people had come into the area, working in the shipyards and stuff. I came up to the plate one evening, and a guy behind the screen was yelling, 'You dago, you couldn't hit me if I ran by you.' I never had that happen to me before in Seattle.

EDO VANNI - Seattle Rainiers

I lived close to North American Aviation in Southern California. They were making Mustangs, B-25s. I used to walk to work. During spring training, I didn't know whether to leave my defense job or not, so I went to my draft board and told them I was a professional baseball player. 'What will happen to me if I leave the state of California and go back to Pittsburgh?' They told me I'd be in the service within thirty days. That made up my mind right then and there.

EDDIE STEWART - San Diego Padres

The war broke out after I got home in '41. Four or five of us went to work at Kaiser Shipyards in Richmond when the war started. That was Billy Raimondi, Bill Rigney, a left-handed pitcher, George , the trainer, Red Adams, myself. We car-pooled out there. We got eighty-seven cents an hour.

I stayed with Kaiser for six months then went to work at Moore's [Shipyards] and was there until 1945. I actually lost some of my hearing there — the noise. I stayed out of baseball in '42 and '43, and when I went back, in mid-'44, I was sold to San Diego.

I just walked away from the shipyards and started playing again. I had a good year in 1945, led the league in RBI (with 110).

I worked at Rohr Aircraft while I was with San Diego in '45. I would be at work at 7 a.m. and be ready for the night game at Lane Field. I was able to go on the road with the team.

We used to go across the border to Tijuana. They didn't have rationing and we could get steak dinners there. Joe Valenzuela was my roommate and he knew lots of people down there.

It was hard to judge players during the wartime, '44 or '45. How do they stack up against players before the war? It's hard to say. The opposition was weak, too, so how can you tell? All of baseball was a little soft during the war.

LOU VEZILICH - San Diego Padres

I was out of baseball in '43 and '44. It was either the military or stay on the farm. I played semipro ball on the weekends all summer, but I couldn't play professional ball without getting drafted. I think I developed as a pitcher then.

When the war ended San Francisco contacted me and asked me to come down, so I contacted the draft board and told them my situation. They, of course, knew me and they asked if over the last two-and-a-half or three years if I had ever taken a vacation. I said, 'Goodness, no!'

They told me to take a six weeks vacation. That was the length remaining in the 1945 season. I got into seven games, going 4-1.

LARRY JANSEN - San Francisco Seals

I fought the battle of Fort Lewis, Washington. We had a pretty good team up there. The problem is most of the guys went on and fought the Battle of the Bulge in Europe, and half of them never came back. I think the fact that I was playing ball kept me from going overseas. We were used to entertain the troops. We had Tommy Heath at catcher and a lot of other major league and professional players. We won the 29th Service Command championship.

Tommy Heath was funny. We were inducted together. They sent us to Camp Beale, near Yuba City, and Tommy and I would go home on the weekends. He had a wry wit. We'd go into a restaurant or bar, and it wouldn't be long before he had everybody around him.

I missed the 1945 Chicago Cubs World Series, but they sent me a check for $250. That was the best gift a soldier could ask for. Military pay wasn't much.

BILL FLEMING - Los Angeles Angels

When I came to San Diego, I lived in National City. We were still at war and housing was impossible to find, especially in a Navy city like San Diego. Bill Starr had to come up with housing for his players, so the Padres gave away season tickets to anyone who would rent to the ballplayers.

A man had built a new house, and it was empty. All I had to do was pay the monthly rent.

After the 1944 season, I went back home to Walla Walla, Washington, and I was sold by Cincinnati to San Diego. When I got my contract with San Diego, I went to the draft board to see what I should do. They said, 'Tony, whether you go to San Diego or San Antonio, Texas, they're going to take you because you've been out too long.' They said I might just as well go to San Diego and play ball until I am called. So I said thank you and went to San Diego.

So I come down here and am doing real good — leading off, scoring runs, stealing bases — and I get the telegram: Report to Olympia, Washington, in two weeks. So I go to the office and show Bill Starr the telegram and say, 'I'll stay here

The Sacramento Solons' Kemp Wicker in 1942.

one more week then go back home and put my wife some place, then I'll go to Olympia.'

I was to leave on a Monday morning. I go to the park on Sunday, my last day, and [Padres trainer] Les Cook tells me, 'Tony, they want you in the office.'

The girl in the office tells me there's a telegram for me. I open it and it says, 'Disregard induction notice.' I made a whoop, and they said, 'What's the matter with you?' I said, 'I don't have to go!' That's how close it got.

We were in Oakland when they declared peace with Japan. All the restaurants closed, and we couldn't get a meal. So finally someone says, we can get popcorn at the theater. So we went to the theater and got bags of popcorn. The game was canceled, but that was OK.

TONY CRISCOLA - San Diego Padres

THE POSTWAR RENAISSANCE

When I returned from military service there was no place to live. About five of us had to rent cots and we slept in the clubhouse at Gilmore Field. We borrowed the key

Fourth of July, 1948, at Lucky Beaver Stadium, left to right: catcher Charlie Silvera, pitcher Carl DeRose, first baseman Fenton Mole and catcher Del Ballinger.

from the groundskeeper and all went out and had keys made. He'd lock the front door about midnight after night games and you couldn't get back in.

This lasted the whole season. We had roll-away cots. We had to go out and eat. We just slept there. Woody Williams, Bud Sheely — most of them had families back home. They couldn't bring them out.

Frank Kelleher was married and had two kids. He had a trailer under the bleachers in 1946.

EDDIE ERAUTT - Hollywood Stars

After I was mustered out, I went to the L.A. School District. They didn't really have openings because they would be having veterans back from the war, but I managed to get a job with them.

In 1946, I got through teaching in June and I needed money. There was this reserve clause for servicemen, so I applied for reinstatement to the Solons. Sacramento agreed, at the protest of manager Earl Sheely, to sign me for the rest of the season. While I was there with the team and traveled with the team, Mr. Sheely never used me. There was another fella there, Joe Gonzales, from Southern California, who was in the same situation. He got to pitch a little bit in relief.

I got to pitch batting practice and was a member of the team, but I just never got to play. That helped me get over a financial hurdle. They signed me for $600 a month, and that was pretty good pay in those days, especially when I was getting $190 a month as a teacher.

HERSHEL LYONS - Sacramento Solons

I remember, we were probably the first club to come up with those knit tops, the kind that are used as batting-practice tops nowadays. We came up with a set of them, and the first game of a double-header on Sundays we would wear them. Ours were navy blue. They were so close-knit, you'd lose ten pounds wearing them every Sunday. They finally discarded them.

(*Note: These navy blue knits, worn in 1952, were thicker than today's polyester knit uniforms.*)

JACK GRAHAM - San Diego Padres

I can remember enjoying flying throughout the league. Before we flew, we would play a Sunday double-header in San Diego and then catch a bus for L.A. and catch the 7 o'clock train out of L.A. They used to call the game in San Diego at 5 o'clock, and we were on that train for two-and-a-half days to Seattle. When we started flying it was sure great. We'd fly in the day we played and it saved the owners one day of hotel bills. I'm sure they liked that.

JOHN "SWEDE" JENSEN - San Diego Padres

Jack Graham suffered a hitting slump in 1952 with the San Diego Padres, but he started swinging the bat well again the next year, when he was sent to Baltimore of the International League.

The first time I ever flew was the end of the season in 1945. We were in Seattle, and they put us on a DC-3, and that was pretty exciting. It was the first time most of us had ever flown.

LOU VEZILICH - San Diego Padres

In 1948 and 1949, when we would acquire a player, it didn't necessarily have to be from any one team. We could deal with anybody — the Yankees, White Sox, Giants, Red Sox. It depended if one of these major league teams wanted one of our players. We wanted to get the best deal we could.

As it turned out, I think the team that helped us the most was the New York Giants. Horace Stoneham and my dad became great friends, both on the field and off. They had a lot of ballplayers, and Horace wanted to help my dad, and they didn't know where to put them all.

In return, Horace had first call on any young player that he felt might be good for the Giants. Ronnie Mahrt and Bill Taylor were two that the Giants took. Artie Wilson also went up.

BILL LAWS - Oaks Radio Announcer

INTEGRATING THE COAST LEAGUE

*I*n 1948 Johnny Ritchey joined the San Diego Padres, becoming the first African American to play in the Coast League since Jimmy Claxton played for Oakland, in 1916. The following season, Oakland, Los Angeles and Portland integrated their teams. Seattle, the last team to integrate its roster, added Bob Boyd and Artie Wilson in 1952.

While black players encountered a bit less overt hostility on the West Coast, racism was hardly absent from the PCL. It was just more subtle. Most white players said they accepted black players as long as they could hit, pitch and run.

I felt the white players in San Diego reacted well to the coming of black players. After Ritchey we had [Orestes] "Minnie" Minoso, Roy Welmaker, Harry Simpson and a whole raft of other black players. They were all good guys. We only had one black player that was a problem while I was there.

The white players never said anything to him, but the black players got all over him. He was a guy that everything had to be a spectacular catch, and he timed everything in the outfield. If he timed it wrong and didn't get to it, then the black players, they noticed that right away, and they got on him. As far as the whites and blacks getting along, there was no problem.

Minnie Minoso was a great guy. But generally they went their way and we went ours.

JACK GRAHAM - San Diego Padres

I grew up playing with black players in San Diego. It didn't make any difference to me. I knew Johnny Ritchey real well. The people in San Diego didn't know what racism was. We played on teams with blacks all the time.

But when I managed in Macon, Georgia, I couldn't understand it. The 'colored' had to sit out in the left-field bleachers.

We were playing Jacksonville, who had Hank Aaron at the time. Our pitcher hit one of their black players on an inside pitch, and he started for the mound. Well, the left-field section was immediately on their feet. I was catching, and I grabbed the youngster and said, 'Hey, you'll start a riot down here.'

Their first baseman, a tall black man, said to me, 'Mr. Kerr, I'll take care of him. He's

First baseman Luke Easter, left, shortstop Artie Wilson, center, and catcher Johnny Ritchey added major talent to the 1949 San Diego Padres' already powerful lineup.

Luis Marquez, above, and Frankie Austin joined the Portland Beavers in 1949. Austin teamed with second baseman Eddie Basinski and Marquez took over center field. A bit of a hot dog, Marquez was a fan favorite.

from the north. He didn't know any better.' Well, that prevented a riot. We didn't have that out on the West Coast.

FRANK KERR - San Diego Padres

When black players came to San Diego, they stayed at the Douglas Hotel downtown. Their white teammates would stay elsewhere.

Sad Sam Jones was also isolated when he came to San Diego, in 1951. I don't think he liked it. He was a bit wild when he was out here, but he was a great pitcher. He had a curve ball that was amazing against right-handed hitters. They couldn't keep their fannies in the batter's box. It would start out behind them and it would be a strike as they're backing away from it. He had a great fastball, too.

BOB KERRIGAN - San Diego Padres

Ferris Fain used to put together a team of local all-stars to play the Jackie Robinson All Stars or the Larry Doby All Stars, and he was always kind enough to select me to catch. We'd play the teams in San Francisco and Oakland and Modesto, and we actually made some good money doing it.

The white players got used to it quickly out here, and it wasn't a big thing. I was back east, and I know Detroit was one of the last teams to hold out on the color line.

CLAUDE CHRISTIE - Seattle Rainiers

Luis Marquez and Frankie Austin joined us in Hollywood. They were the first black players for Portland, and they were scared to death. I can understand it. The way our dressing area was in Hollywood, rather than facing the rest of the team, they turned their backs to us and put on their uniforms and shoes.

Johnny Rucker refused to suit up for two or three days when we first signed the two players.

Marquez had a little chip on his shoulder, but Austin didn't. It wasn't too long before everyone was talking to Marquez, kidding him. We finally broke the ice. But it was tough on him.

Marquez helped us and went up to Milwaukee. He hurt his leg up there and came back to Portland. He wasn't the same when he came back.

Austin had it easer. As a shortstop, he had to work closely with the second baseman, and he and Eddie Basinski hit it off well.

Later on, Portland acquired Artie Wilson. He was on the downhill side, but he was still a good little ballplayer. He'd holler all the time. The fans loved him.

BILL FLEMING - Portland Beavers

T he following is excerpted from a letter written at the end of the 1952 season to Buzzie Bavasi of the Brooklyn Dodgers. The author is San Francisco Seals chief scout Mickey Shader, whose subjects in the letter included African American outfielder Robert Thurman.

We wish to make a deal for Robert Thurman, outfielder, age 29, bats and throws left, height 6 feet 1 inches, weight 198. In 1951 with San Francisco he hit .274 in 104 games. This season with San Francisco he hit .280 in 116 games. Thurman has good speed afoot, has a good arm and has power. He will help any Triple A club in the country, as he has a world of natural ability. He has been playing winter ball in the Puerto Rico League, where he has starred.

He is a high class Colored player, a hustler and easy to handle. He helps us, but our accent is going to be on youth, as we feel we have some fine young outfield prospects coming along.

Seattle Rainier Joe DeMoran, third from left, admired the game ball from his 3-0 no-hitter against the Los Angeles Angels. He is joined by manager Bill Skiff, left, third baseman Chuck Alleno and catcher Bob Finley.

12

The Sacramento Solons' Harry Bright, a former infielder about to take on duties as a catcher, flings equipment in the air in mock celebration. This photo was taken in March, 1956.

OPEN CLASSIFICATION— COMPETING WITH THE MAJORS

THE OPEN CLASSIFICATION AGREEMENT WITH THE MAJOR LEAGUES ALLOWED PLAYERS UNDER CONTRACT WITH THE PACIFIC COAST LEAGUE TO WAIVE THEIR OPTION OF BEING INCLUDED IN THE MAJOR LEAGUE DRAFT AT THE END OF EACH SEASON. COAST LEAGUE GENERAL MANAGERS WERE WILLING TO GIVE THE PLAYERS A CASH BONUS FOR WAIVING THIS RIGHT. FOR MANY PLAYERS IT WAS AN EASY DECISION TO MAKE.

I signed in 1952 and played most of the year in Stockton. The Solons took me on a road trip the last two weeks of the season. Open Classification was supposed to ultimately result in a third major league, but they didn't have the dollars to back it up.

Players had it written in their contracts: we won't be sold to the major leagues. Players would come down from the big leagues and say, 'I don't want to go back.' Most of them were making more money in the PCL at the time, and playing conditions were as good.

Sacramento did have a couple of farm clubs up north — Idaho Falls, Salem, Lewiston. They had several agreements where they would send some of the players from year to year.

So they were trying to develop their own farm system, but it only lasted two or three years. They didn't have the money to sustain their own farm system. Otherwise, they would have been a third major league, because the talent was there.

BUD WATKINS - Sacramento Solons

When the league had Open Classification, I signed a waiver that I couldn't be drafted. I never had a chance to go to the major leagues until I was pretty well along. If you went to the majors, you were going to play for the minimum no matter what. I was doing better with Brick Laws, so I didn't want to take the chance. If I had been a half-a-dozen years younger, I might not have signed.

LEN NEAL - Oakland Oaks

Oakland Oaks radio announcers Bud Foster, left, and Bill Laws.

Oakland Oaks owner Brick Laws and Paul Fagan of the Seals became good friends. Fagan was pushing the advancement of the whole league to major league status, and

Brick was an ally. I'm sure they met resistance at the Coast League meetings, however. I don't know that Paul Fagan really understood what he was getting into, but he was determined to go ahead and do it. He was sincere about it, it just wasn't a publicity ploy. He honestly felt it could be done and, as it turned out, it was done. It took a few years. They were just a little early.

BILL LAWS - Oaks Radio Announcer

I signed the Open Classification waiver so I couldn't get drafted. They gave me an extra $1,000 to sign it. That was a lot of money in 1954. I had just gotten out of the service and was making $200 a month. I played for San Francisco and got sold to Philadelphia, and they offered me a contract that was worth less than what I had made in San Francisco, although not a lot less.

Infielder Jim Westlake.

I fired it back to Roy Hamey, who was the general manager, so they gave me another $1,000. That's why these guys wanted to stay out in the Coast League and not go to the big leagues. The money was better.

JIM WESTLAKE - San Francisco Seals

Entertainer Joe E. Brown, a frequent visitor at Gilmour
Field, pals it up with Hollywood Stars manager Charlie Root.

13

COAST LEAGUE POTPOURRI

This 1947 Hollywood Stars program featured caricatures of Hollywood's other stars, including, from left, Jack Benny, George Raft, George Burns, Phil Silvers, Leo Durocher and Bing Crosby.

ON SEEING CELEBRITIES AND STARS

WE HAD A LOVABLE GUY OWNING THE CLUB, BOB COBB. BOB ALSO OWNED THE BROWN DERBY NIGHTCLUB. HIS FORMER WIFE, GAIL PATRICK, THE MOVIE STAR, ALSO OWNED STOCK IN THE CLUB. AND FRANK LOVEJOY, A DEAR FRIEND OF MINE, ALSO OWNED STOCK IN THE CLUB, AND BOB TAYLOR. GUYS LIKE THAT.

Every night was a carnival at Gilmore Field, especially 1949 and 1950. We were drawing 500,000. We were winning, and everybody loves a winner. You'd start a ball game and look up in the stands and see George Burns and Gracie Allen, Jack Benny, Cyd Charisse and Tony Martin, George Raft. Every night. It got so tickets were selling at a premium out there.

I can recall a guy yelling at me. It was Phil Silvers. Jimmy Durante, Ziggy Elman — every night was a fun night.

Jimmy Durante sat directly behind first base. We became good friends. One evening I said, 'You know, Jim, that's probably the most precarious seat in the house. There's a guy who plays third base named Jim Baxes who can get a bit wild.' With Baxes, if I saw him take a ground ball and straighten up and zero in on me, I knew the ball was ending up in the stands. Durante giggled a bit, but said he thought he'd be all right.

Well that night, Baxes got a routine hop and winds up and threw the ball about ten feet over my head. I didn't even get a glove on it. It hits a couple of beer cups and a hot dog with mustard. I can still see mustard flying all over the place.

Jimmy got drenched and had to retreat to the men's room for repairs. When he came back after the game, he said, 'You know, I just got a new seating assignment.'

It was very common in the late '40s for Mickey Cohen, the ex-gangster, to walk into Gilmore and sit directly behind the third base dugout with a couple of his muscles. He was a great fan. The theme song on the bench was that if anybody in that box said anything, just smile and wave.

CHUCK STEVENS - Hollywood Stars

When I joined the Hollywood Stars in 1939, I got off to a good start down there. Oscar Reichow, the Stars general manager, called me into the front office one day. I had been hitting pretty well and he asked me if it would be all right to change my name. There was a large Jewish community there and he wanted me to change my name to Manush. I said it would be all right as long as you gave me some more money. He didn't like that, so that was the end of that.

GEORGE "BEE" MANDISH - Hollywood Stars

DRESSING THE HOLLYWOOD WAY

In 1940, the Stars wore a dark blue uniform with a script "Hollywood" across the front on the road. They were very attractive — grabbed a lot of attention — but they were very heavy.

GEORGE "BEE" MANDISH - Hollywood Stars

The Hollywood Stars innovated the shorts. That was 1950, and it was the brainchild of Fred Haney, our manager. Early in the season, the players walked into the clubhouse and there were clothes boxes from the concrete floor to the ceiling. We knew nothing about this in advance. There were four or five people with measuring tapes around their necks.

When the whole club had arrived, Fred Haney suggested to our clubhouse man that he lock the door. Then he opened the boxes, and there were shorts! Wasn't anybody escaping. [Dick] Kewpie Barrett and some of those guys were thinking about it.

Those people in civilian clothes were tailors, and we all had to put on the shorts and have them measured. We all had the worst looking legs you could imagine, but we were a captive audience.

Somebody asked, 'What the hell are we going to do with these things?' Haney responded, 'We're going to wear them!' And we did.

People were worried about sliding in them. Well, there were two types of sliders — knee sliders and hip sliders. Haney had thought it out. You wore a sanitary sock next to your skin. Then on the outer sock he had doubled or tripled the knit, so when you rolled your socks over you had two or three inches to slide on.

The rolled sock gave you a cushion, and you had lots of protection. And there were built in hip pads in the pants.

The first day we wore them, I doubled and didn't have to slide. The next guy hit a ball, and I know that as I rounded third base it's going to be a touch-touch play at home.

Now, Portland had Jim Gladd catching. Jimmy was six feet two inches, 200 pounds.

You talk about a guy running from third to home in mortal fear. All I could see were his shin guards, and I'm bow-legged, little and skinny.

Luckily, I beat the throw, for if I were going to have a collision with him my retirement would have happened years earlier than I had planned.

We filled every park in the Pacific Coast League wearing those things. Any time we wore them the park was sold out. We only wore them on weekends, and after two years they disappeared. I was very surprised that they didn't catch on.

I'm happy to say my shorts are in the Hall of Fame. I happened to have a pair. I probably stole them. The Hall of Fame called and asked if I knew where any of those pants were. I was happy to donate them.

CHUCK STEVENS - Hollywood Stars

I remember when Hollywood played in the shorts. We used to kid them a lot. Jack Salveson didn't like them at all. Bill Sweeney came out to the umpires with the lineup card wearing a dress, and we all waved hankies at them.

BILL FLEMING - Portland Beavers

In 1950, the Hollywood Stars startled their fans — and the rest of base-ball — with these new uniforms. The fashion plates, from left to right: pitcher Lee Anthony, manager Fred Haney, actor Rosey Gilhousen (in traditional garb), infield-er Murray Franklin and outfielder Eddie Sauer.

The Hollywood Stars' Rinaldo "Rugger" Ardizoia was a reliable starting pitcher throughout his career. Born in Italy, Ardizoia was a longtime resident of San Francisco who signed with the San Francisco Missions in 1938, then played for the team after it moved to Hollywood, winning fourteen games for the Stars in their first two seasons. His best season was with the Oakland Oaks in 1946, when he pitched to a 15-7 record and 2.83 ERA, under manager Casey Stengel. Ardizoia finished his career with the Seattle Rainiers.

ON THE ROAD

The 1946 Oaks were a good group of guys. For example, after a Sunday double-header in Portland or Seattle, you'd go right to the train. Raimondi loved to get salami, a loaf and some beer. That was our dinner.

We'd have the first car after the baggage car so nobody could come through. So you'd strip down and relax all day. Some guys would play cards, some guys just read, some did nothing.

We were a team. If you went to breakfast, you looked around for some teammates to eat with. If you went to dinner, the same. If you were going in a cab to the ballpark, you'd ask two or three guys to come along. Or you go to a show, you're always looking for someone to go with. I don't see much of that today.

RUGGER ARDIZOIA - Oakland Oaks

Usually, when we traveled by train, there would be card games. I recall once they banned the card games because some of the players were pretty big losers and that could create friction. I was a pretty big reader. In fact, I'd read late at night, and I would have to go into the bathroom to allow my roomie to sleep.

On the road, Cookie [Les Cook] made the room assignments. I got Dick Aylward as a roomie. He was a terrific guy, but his buddy wouldn't necessarily be his roommate. His buddy was Buddy Peterson. I hung around with Jimmie Reese as much as anybody.

BOB KERRIGAN - San Diego Padres

On the road we used to travel by train, except to San Diego. Those used to be long train rides.

During the war we had all the curtains pulled at night. You'd get tired out spending a couple of nights coming back on the train. We'd often just be in our shorts. But it was a long way back to the dining car.

We never played too much poker on the train, usually pinochle. A lot of the managers wouldn't allow poker.

If you were pitching the next night, you got a lower berth. Otherwise, you got an upper.

BILL FLEMING - Los Angeles Angels

THE FANS

When the Mounties came to town in 1956, we kids were ecstatic. It was as if God has blessed Canada with something. And I know that the adults were also excited about it. It was a big thing for the whole town because growing up in British Columbia, we didn't have major league teams. I identified with the Brooklyn Dodgers and New York Yankees because they were on television so much.

I lived probably less than a half a mile from Capilano Stadium. The kid across the street, an older kid, got a job as a bat boy for the Mounties. That first year, 1956, I hung around the ballpark all summer. That's probably the reason we were put to work the next year.

They had a bat boy and ball boy who were older. I was a relief ball boy. They used to have practices during the mornings for afternoon games and in the afternoons for night games. There was no pay, but we got free food and free entry.

Lefty O'Doul (the Mounties manager in 1956) was a scary guy for me. He was big and seemed gruff. Then we had Charlie Metro (in 1957). He was actually a manager who coached. Charlie Metro was the boss so we didn't talk to him much. I don't recall wanting to talk with him. He always looked like he needed a shave. It didn't seem to me that he was as buddy-buddy with the players as, say, Lefty O'Doul.

Then we had Erv Palica and Spider Jorgenson. They held a special place for me because they played for the Dodgers.

The nicest guy was George Bamberger. Many of the players didn't have a lot of time for the kids, but for some reason Bamberger was always nice to us. He was like a hero for me, always offering us gum. Of course, he was our top pitcher, too.

I can remember Brooks Robinson playing for the Mounties. And we also had Ron Hansen. They weren't there long, but they left an impression on me.

I remember Steve Bilko hitting home runs out of Vancouver. To this day, I can't recall balls hit farther than what he hit. I remember him hitting a rope. It was still rising when it left the stadium. I can recall the players even being amazed at some of the shots he hit.

The Mounties were very important to Vancouver at that time. It seems as the years went on that they diminished a bit, but they were a big event. The scores used to get the headlines in the paper, and the pictures of the ballplayers would be very much on the front page. In some civic event, they would highlight the ballplayer.

Seals Stadium on September 15, 1957, the last afternoon of PCL baseball in San Francisco. This game was meaningless to all but Sacramento Solons pitcher Bud Watkins, who was trying to keep his season ERA below 3.00. Watkins won the game but allowed seven earned runs, bumping his ERA to 3.22 from 2.98.

I had a scrapbook and would paste highlights of games in there. I can remember going around and getting autographs of players to put in the scrapbook. I can remember fans would come down when they got a foul ball and they would pass it to the ball boy to get the player to sign it. It didn't seem to me it was as strict then.

In fact, when they broke bats, people would run down and the player would just hand it over the fence. When they would crack, they'd give them away.

It wasn't uncommon for players to stand around giving autographs before the game. And they had double-headers. Between the games there was a period of time, a half an hour or more. The players wouldn't even change. They would go in and get a drink of water or a bite to eat and they would come out on the field and talk with people in the stands.

MARTIN JOHNSON - Mounties Fan

Billy Raimondi played a remarkable seventeen seasons for the Oakland Oaks before he was traded to Sacramento for Frank Kerr.

I was brought up in Berkeley, and my dad was a real baseball fan. Our weekly family outings were going to the Oaks Ball Park every Sunday when the Oaks were at home. My mother would fix a picnic lunch, and we'd drive to Emeryville for a long afternoon. We would get there in time for batting practice. Mom was never too thrilled with the prospect, especially on Mother's Day.

We always sat in the same area, in the last row of the unreserved seats on the first base side, behind the Oaks dugout. The food stands were right behind us. Peanuts and popcorn and soft drinks were ten cents each. Programs, too. We saw a lot of the same people from week to week.

I saw my first game sometime during the war, but the most exciting year was 1948. Casey came in 1946, and by 1948 he had put together a group of tough veterans. Billy Raimondi and Dario Lodigiani were my favorites, but I also liked Les Scarsella, Brooks Holder and Loyd Christopher.

At night, I would hide under the covers with my little radio, listening to the Oaks games until mom would get mad and make me go to sleep. The Seals-Oaks rivalry was special, and I hated it when Con Dempsey pitched against us.

I remember Vic Picetti, the young first baseman out of San Francisco. Everyone thought he was going to be a big star. He played most of the games at first base in 1945, but when Casey came the next year, he wanted a veteran playing there and Picetti was shipped to the Western International League where he died in a tragic bus crash.

I also remember Jackie Price with the 1946 Oaks. He wasn't a good player but he was a showman. He would perform acrobatic tricks before the game — throwing three balls to three different players at once, hitting upside-down from a rig, and catching fly balls in the outfield in his pants!

Every Monday I would hop on my bike and ride to the local grocery store to get my Remar Bread cards of the Oaks players. If I was too late, my mother would take me down to the factory to get the cards. There was a Smiths Clothing store in town, and they also produced baseball cards. They were free!

When Casey left to manage the Yankees, I wrote a note wishing him well. He responded, wishing the 1949 Oaks success. It was a typewritten letter that was squeezed into the top inch or two of the paper, but it was like gold to me.

JUDY PETERSON - Oakland Oaks Fan

Editor's note: Dick Dobbins used to joke that he married Judy Peterson for her baseball collection. She had a lot of the Oaks cards and some Oaks programs, plus a few magazines. But the Stengel letter was special.
On their twentieth wedding anniversary, she gave Dick the letter. On their fortieth anniversary, he gave it back to her.

I really didn't know much about baseball until I was ten years old. 'The Mutual Game of the Week' was broadcast on Saturdays. My mom would do the wash on Saturdays and I would hang it out and listen to Dizzy Dean. That same summer I went to summer school and some of the kids had baseball cards that I had never seen before — Smiths Clothiers Store and Signal Oil cards. I thought, 'Wow. These are cool.' One of the other boys gave me a large group of them one day. I was thrilled.

I talked my dad into taking me to a baseball game. I don't think my dad had ever been to a baseball game before. We went to see the San Diego Padres play the Oakland Oaks in Emeryville. Along the way, there was a Signal gas station, and he stopped to let me pick up that week's card. They gave me a card of Ray Hamrick.

As we came into the baseball park, it was all wood, with the lights and the color. It was amazing for me. I looked down by the Oaks dugout and Ray Hamrick was signing autographs, so I ran down and got my Hamrick baseball card signed. I was hooked.

In 1949 and 1950, the Remar Bread Company put out Oaks baseball cards. I used to go to the local grocery stores to get the most recent card. The checkout clerk would sometimes just give me one card, so I got more aggressive as I got older and I would meet the bread driver out front, asking for pictures.

This one guy used to give me stacks of them, to the point that I had so many George Bamberger cards that I made decks of playing cards out of the multitude.

When we used to get cards signed, we used the old ink pens. Ballpoint pens had just come out after the war. They were really erratic and made a huge mess sometimes. So we used good fountain pens, and our signatures were cleaner and lasted longer.

My dad was a very good amateur photographer, and I used to fool around taking photos with one of his cameras. Around 1951 they stopped giving Oaks baseball cards away, so a friend and I started taking our cameras to the park so we could make our own cards.

We used to walk right on the field to get the players to pose for their pictures. And a lot of people who were not players were kind to us. Les Cook, the Padres trainer, used to bring group pictures with him when he came to Oakland. Jimmie Reese of the Padres and Eddie Taylor of Seattle and Bill Sweeney, Portland's manager, used to talk with us.

The Emeryville ballpark was wonderful. The grandstand was close to the field, and when you walked in there was the smell of hot dogs boiling. It creaked a lot. It had wooden walkways that gave when you walked on them.

At his first PCL game, in 1948, Oakland Oaks fan Doug McWilliams landed this Signal Oil Company baseball card of shortstop Ray Hamrick — and got Hamrick to sign it.

I recall one game, we looked over and spotted Floyd 'Babe' Herman in the stands. We left the game, ran to the 'F' train station, rode back to Berkeley, got pictures of Herman and went back to the ballpark and got the pictures signed. We really were nuts.

We befriended some of the ballplayers. I really liked Artie Wilson. I just liked his style. He always wore a suit, and he was always smoking a cigar. When he signed your picture, he had you hold his cigar. Now, when I smell a cigar I think of minor league baseball. He was always nice to the kids. He was just a friendly, happy guy, along with being a good ballplayer.

Later on I befriended others, career minor leaguers — Tony Rivas, Tommy Munoz, Bud Watkins. I've maintained a relationship ever since.

My friend and I used to go across the bridge to San Francisco, and when we got older we went up to Sacramento two or three times a year.

Seattle Rainiers general manager Dewey Soriano and manager Lefty O'Doul teamed up in 1957. O'Doul didn't get along well with Soriano and retired after one year with the team.

In the summer of 1956, I didn't have a job, so we decided to go up to the Pacific Northwest and see games in Portland, Seattle and Vancouver. Portland had just moved into Multnomah Stadium, and Vancouver was in its first year of PCL baseball, having received the Oakland franchise.

I remember we left the Bay Area at 6 in the morning and got to Portland at 7 at night. The game was already in progress. I remember the first thing I saw was Ray Shore throwing in the bullpen. He was fifteen feet below us and he was throwing from fifteen feet behind the mound to the catcher. Years later, we took the same trip and got there at 4 in the afternoon. I guess the roads were better.

We saw Portland play Sacramento, then the next night we saw San Diego play at Seattle. I remember a lot of the players being surprised to see us. As we got better with our photography, the players started wanting copies of our work, so they got to know us. That was fun to be recognized and appreciated. That got me started thinking about being a photographer.

The Friday game in Seattle got rained out, so we spent an extra day in Seattle. Luckily the Seattle Seafair was held on Lake Washington on Saturday, so we spent the day watching these speedy hydroplane racing boats.

Seattle had a beautiful ballpark. Artie Wilson was with them in 1956, as was a young Filipino named Bobby Balcena, who was a favorite of mine. I think he got called up to the major leagues for a week or two. That was his whole major league career.

After that we went up to Vancouver to see the old Oakland Oaks and Lefty O'Doul. It was their first year out of Oakland and they had a gorgeous ballpark. It was strange to see guys I knew in pinstripes. They had beautiful uniforms, like the Yankees, but were a bad ball club. Jim Marshall was on first, Spider Jorgensen on third. They had a lot of Baltimore Orioles that I didn't know. Art Houtemann was a favorite of mine, and he was just one of several major leaguers on the way down.

I hardly ever paid to see the Oaks play. In 1950, I worked as a gatekeeper in center field, letting the Knothole Gang kids in. So that year I got in free. We discovered a gate where the television trucks unloaded their equipment very early in the morning. So we used that gate, too. There was hardly ever a game that we had any trouble sneaking in. We'd sit under the bracing of the grandstand, with the dust and the cobwebs, waiting for the gates to open.

I remember a Charles Schulz cartoon showing a kid walking around an old ballpark, and in the last panel, Charlie Brown says, 'My dad would like this ballpark. It's all wood.'

DOUG McWILLIAMS - Oakland Oaks Fan

I got interested in baseball comparatively late. I went through the 'dinosaur stage,' so I probably got hooked at age twelve. But it was like an immediate thing. My dad took me to an Angels-Seattle game early in the 1952 season. I just thought, 'My god, this is just great. Everything about it.'

I remember Gene Baker — so graceful. That was forty-five years ago and I haven't changed since. I probably went to ten games, all with my dad. The next season, 1953, I started going with school chums. We would take the 'V' train to Avalon and walk three blocks to the ballpark. I probably went to thirty games that year.

We would frequently sit in the grandstands, but there was an older man, this great old black guy who said he had played with the Negro Leagues. There was never any reason to challenge him on that. His name was Mr. Robinson, and another friend of mine and I would sit with him. He would show us little subtleties that we didn't understand yet, like three-and-two, two outs, the runner will go. We were amazed. How does he know that? It was a real thrill to just listen to him.

It never occurred to us to sneak in, it was so inexpensive to sit in the bleachers. The 1956 Angels were special to me. I had followed the Angels for five years, and the 1956 Angels put it all together. I had just presumed that the Angels were a .500 team, and every time Elmer Singleton came to town, the Angels would fold. But now it was Singleton who lost.

I remember the intense rivalry with the Stars. I was aware that there was a rivalry by the over-flow crowds at Gilmore, and I was listening to the radio when Teddy Beard bowled Mo Franklin over. I was shocked at what happened. I also remember that the Angels and Stars got tremendous play in the press when they played.

Although I lived closer to Gilmore Field, I became an Angels fan. I think I heard Angels broadcasts first, and I liked the clean, simple lines of the Angels uniforms. I did find my faith shaken once when I met Bobby Bragan at a Stars booster luncheon. I went with a friend who was a Bragan fan.

Bragan would go around to each table and talk to everyone. I was prepared to hate him, but his accessibility was so great that I thought, 'Gee, I was ready to hate him, but he was so friendly.'

The allure of Wrigley Field — the smell of the grass along with its simple beauty, and, of course, the ivy on the walls. The look of the scoreboard and the shadows. We'd sit in the right field bleachers and, especially during a Sunday doubleheader, the shadows would change, creating some of the more unusual scenes. They probably didn't mean anything to me at the time, but later on they helped re-create nostalgic moments.

And also the echos. If there was a small crowd, you could hear people talking, and if someone stomped on a beer cup, there was a large bang that could sound like a rifle shot.

It would be smart to wear a sweater on those Sunday afternoons. It could be cool, and on some days, you could get an inland fog, even in the summer.

When you sat in the bleachers, the scoreboard was behind you, but you always knew when a score was being updated. There was a sound of metal against metal as a new digit was placed in the inning slot for the team in question.

JAY BERMAN - Los Angeles Angels Fan

LUNCH WITH JOE DiMAGGIO

One of the more exciting moments of my life came in May, 1996, when I had lunch and a long talk with Joe DiMaggio. This event was especially momentous for me because Joe requested it — it was a way for him to meet someone who claimed to know a lot about Joe when he was breaking into professional baseball. Joe broke in with the San Francisco Seals in late 1932 and had three distinguished years with the team before joining the New York Yankees in 1936.

Dick Dobbins hit the jackpot at his first major league game, in July, 1949, in Washington, D.C. Joe DiMaggio signed an autograph book for fan Francis Stowe as Dobbins shot a picture of the event. An Associated Press photographer, meanwhile, captured the moment with his camera. That photo went out on the wire and ran in newspapers nationwide. When he returned home to Berkeley, California, Dobbins' buddies treated him like a hero.

This luncheon was set up by a good friend, Jim Basin, whose dad, Sam, had been a teammate of Joe's in his bush-league days and who was a regular companion of Joe's whenever he returned to the Bay Area from his home in Florida.

There were five of us — DiMaggio, Jim, Sam, another collecting buddy of Jim's and mine, Paul Wendler, and me. We sat in a private dining room at Dal Baffo restaurant in Menlo Park, California. For much of the afternoon, my three friends sat back, sometimes amused, I'm sure, as Joe and I conversed.

As we sat down, I handed him a copy of my book *Nuggets on the Diamond*, which was responsible for bringing us together. One chapter in *Nuggets* features three significant Bay Area brothers contingents — the DiMaggios, the Raimondis and the Hafeys.

There are several photos in the book of Joe alone, with his brothers and with others, so the focus is not exclusively on him. Joe thumbed quickly through the pages, then put the book aside. Jim Basin later told me that Joe gave the book a microscopic analysis as they were driving home after lunch, finding at least one small error.

To show him that our paths had crossed before, I pulled out a signed photo of Joe and a slightly starstruck fourteen-year-old Dick Dobbins that was taken in 1949. Actually, I had probably gotten him to sign items for me a dozen times in the past thirty years, but those exchanges don't really count.

The 1949 experience does. My family toured the United States in the summer of that year and I successfully cajoled my mother into letting me go to baseball games along the way. My first was on July 3, in Washington, D.C., and it featured the Yankees!

Yankees manager Casey Stengel had managed the Oakland Oaks to the PCL pennant in 1948, and I just happened to have a baseball card of him that I had been unable to get signed the year before. Can you imagine my having that card with me? Of course you can.

While waiting near the Yankee dugout, an Associated Press photographer came up to me and asked if I would be interested in having my picture taken with Joe DiMaggio. My wildest fantasy became reality. Two images from the photo shoot appeared in newspapers nationwide, including the paper that served my neighborhood, the *San Francisco Chronicle*. Boy, was I big stuff when I returned to junior high in September.

Joe, however, was not impressed with our earlier association, and we set out to order from the menu.

I ordered spaghetti marinara. Joe *was* impressed by that. "Good Italian food," he said, looking on with approval. Actually, I ordered that dish for tactical reasons. I didn't want to order an American-Italian yuppie entree in front of a "real" Italian-American, but I also really like spaghetti marinara.

Well, on to the wars. From the get-go, I felt Joe was testing me. "Who is this upstart?" he must have thought. "Who is he to presume that he knows the innermost feelings of my youth?" Joe, in fact, was charming and affable the whole afternoon. Still, he *was* testing me.

I realized this early in our conversation, when he said, "You of course know my nickname?" What is he looking for — Yankee Clipper? I wondered. Why did he ask me that?

"What, do you mean 'Deadpan?'" I replied.

Correct.

That was too easy, I thought.

But I had an agenda too. There were certain things that I wanted The Master to clarify for me. During my decades of research, I noticed there were things DiMaggio said about certain events that weren't always supported by the evidence.

Foremost in my mind was the question of who was primarily responsible for scouting DiMaggio for the Yankees. Joe had hurt his left knee in 1934, and the "can't miss" label placed on him by every scout in the region melted away. There was doubt that Joe could ever recover from this injury.

DiMaggio stated for the two-volume anthology *The DiMaggio Albums* (Putnam, 1989), "It was about that time the Yankees were seriously looking at me, as were all the other teams in the major leagues. Most of them now thought I was through and quickly lost interest. If it had not been for the persistency of Bill Essick, one of the Yankee scouts, I would never have become a Yankee or maybe even stayed in baseball. He was positive a kid of nineteen could overcome a bad knee, and in the winter he took me to a specialist in Los Angeles for examination and treatments. He was right; I got over it."

This and other comments on the subject that Joe had made over the years never rang clear to me. Bill Essick was an excellent scout, but he was the Yankee scout in Southern California. His equal in the north was Joe Devine — a super scout.

Devine affiliated with the Yankees around 1932. In the late 1920s he was a Pirate scout, responsible for signing Joe Cronin and Dick Bartell, and for scouting Paul and Lloyd Waner, who were on the San Francisco Seals roster. The list goes on.

But in the 1930s and thereafter, the San Francisco Bay Area became Yankee territory. A review of Yankee rosters from the 1930s to the '50s confirms this and shows the extent of Joe Devine's considerable influence.

Essick got to see DiMaggio only when the Seals visited Wrigley Field, in Los Angeles. Devine watched him play in more than half his games. I had been fortunate enough to acquire the Joe Devine papers from his estate, and they make clear Devine had aggressively followed DiMaggio's career both before the accident and after, and had not lost interest because of the injury.

Devine was in regular communication with both George Weiss and Ed Barrow of the Yankees on DiMaggio's progress. One letter stated that Devine had taken DiMaggio to a doctor to have the knee examined, and others outlined the strategy for negotiating with the Seals for his acquisition.

When I asked DiMaggio about Joe Devine's role as a scout, his response was, "Joe didn't like me. He didn't think I'd ever make it, and he pretty much ignored me."

I had planed to give DiMaggio another gift, of sorts — a copy of one of Devine's scouting reports on him. It had not been my intention to make any special point by doing this, but it directly contradicted Joe's perception of Devine. I handed it to him and he gave it only a passing glance. But Sam Basin asked to see it, and after reading it said, "He liked you, Joe."

The letter and scouting report, sent to E.G. Barrow, Secretary of New York Yankees Baseball, is dated August 10, 1935. It read as follows:

> DiMaggio, right handed hitter and thrower. DiMaggio is easily the best prospect in the league. DiMaggio can do everything, run, throw, hit, field and has a very good temperament, as well as plenty of guts and hustle. There is nothing wrong with DiMaggio's leg, am sure you have one of the very best prospects that has been in the minor leagues for years. DiMaggio can play major league ball right from the start. I will see more of DiMaggio when I go to the coast unless Mr. Graham decides to let us have him before the season is over. When I left the Coast, he had just a little soreness left in his arm, that I am sure would be gone by now, but before we close the deal, we should know that DiMaggio is physically fit.

Another curiosity, to me, was that Joe DiMaggio was a right fielder in San Francisco and didn't play center field until after the Yankees purchased him and asked the Seals to shift him to that postition.

I asked him about this. "Nobody is going to convince me that Joe Marty (the incumbent center fielder and a fine prospect in his own right) was faster than you or had a better arm," I said. "If that's the case, why did they play you in right field?"

I then mentioned some possible reasons. "Could it have been that way because Seals Stadium was so deep in right field (385 feet down the foul line) and they needed more speed and a stronger arm out there?"

He looked somewhat enlightened, and responded, "You know, I never thought about it that way."

Another boost for my credibility.

Now it was Joe's turn. Another test question: "Do you remember Jack Fenton?"

"When he was with the Oaks or with the Seals?" I asked, then proceeded to elaborate on both stages of Fenton's career. Fenton was a light-hitting, solid defensive first baseman who started out with the Oaks and was later picked up by the Seals. He was the Seals' first baseman when DiMaggio broke in in 1933.

One evening at Seals Stadium, Joe was hit in the forehead by a line single to right. A large moth flew in front of Joe as the ball skipped on the grass, and he picked up the flight of the moth, not the ball. At the last moment he focused back on the ball, but it glanced off his glove and popped him on the forehead.

Fenton was all over the rookie outfielder, kidding him unmercifully when the inning ended and they returned to the dugout. There wasn't much "Deadpan Joe" could say. But a few innings later, it was Joe's turn to laugh. A high infield pop-up got caught in Seals Stadium's swirling winds, causing Fenton to stagger around the mound to catch it.

As he moved toward third base and the nearby Seals dugout, he stumbled slightly and the ball hit *him* on the forehead. Fenton ran into the dugout, up the ramp and out of the game. Obviously, he didn't bother Joe anymore about the misplay.

Incidentally, of the four or five test questions that DiMaggio asked me, I did blow one. He asked me, in an indirect way, who the center fielder would have been when he broke in. I knew it wasn't Joe Marty, because he was younger than DiMaggio, but I just couldn't pick it up. I guess my excuse was that I wasn't even born when he broke in, but I still couldn't figure it out.

The man's name, it turns out, was Elias Funk — not a household name in San Francisco or major league history.

As the afternoon wore on we enjoyed a steady flow of stories from The Master. They were articulate, fluid and interesting. I later realized he had told each of them a thousand times. This was not the undereducated, shy youngster who joined the Seals. This was a man who had learned how to protect himself by dominating the conversation. He knew what he was ... and what he wasn't.

Jim Basin had brought his camera and offered to take photos of each of us with Joe. Now I would have another DiMaggio photo to put next to the one from 1949.

Joe DiMaggio and Dick Dobbins.

It still is easy to imagine Joe moving like a deer in the outfield or around the bases, which makes that photo — of a man in his eighties, and another in his sixties — a bit of a shock.

As we were leaving our dining room, a party at another table recognized Joe and beckoned him to their table. DiMaggio appeared irritated. You don't order The Master. He declined. Outside, we said our goodbyes.

The lunch, though, has a nice postscript. Eight months later I was working a collector's show when a young man came to my table and said, "I've got to buy a copy of your book." I was, of course, pleased, and told him so.

"I was in Martinez," he continued, "and was talking with Joe DiMaggio, who was born there and still has relatives there. Somehow, we started talking about the old Coast League and Joe said, 'There's a PCL book written by a good friend of mine, Dick Dobbins — *Nuggets on the Diamond*. You should buy his book. He knows his stuff.' "

Needless to say, I was delighted my "good friend" Joe remembered.

DICK DOBBINS - San Francisco Seals Fan

Richard Trowbridge Dobbins

December 9, 1934 - January 3, 1999

Dick Dobbins was one of baseball's — and the San Francisco Bay Area's — best friends. He was born in Berkeley, and his affection for the region and its role in the Pacific Coast League and in major league baseball never diminished.

Dobbins lost his father at an early age, which left his mother, Elinore, to raise him, his older brother Bob and younger sister Elizabeth. Dobbins spent his childhood playing sports and developing what would become a lifelong interest in photography. With his friends in tow, he would sneak into San Francisco Seals and Oakland Oaks games to photograph the players.

Dobbins met his wife Judy in the seventh grade. They attended University of California at Berkeley, married during their college days and eventually moved to Alamo, California, where they spent the next forty-two years. They raised son Peter and daughter Annette, traveled and became avid supporters of the San Francisco Opera.

Dobbins taught at Acalanes High School in nearby Lafayette for thirty-two years, coached Little League and Senior League baseball, football, water polo, swimming and diving. He retired at age fifty-five to finish a pet project, a book about the Pacific Coast League. He also did freelance photography, bought and sold sports memorabilia, and sold uniforms and equipment for various major league teams, including the San Francisco Giants.

Dobbins fulfilled his ambition to write about the Pacific Coast League not once but twice — in 1994, with the publication of the illustrated history *Nuggets on the Diamond*, and in 1999, with the release of this remarkable compilation of Pacific Coast League anecdotes and images. The cancer that eventually took his life didn't dampen his desire to see this book to completion. Even in his last days, he rallied his family, friends and editors to the cause. His perseverance paid off. He enriched us all with his love of baseball and, of course, left us with two truly remarkable books.

BIBLIOGRAPHY

The following sources helped us prepare for interviews and verify information. Taken together, they provide an excellent overall picture of the Pacific Coast League.

Bauer, Carlos. *Pacific Coast League Rosters: 1903 through 1957.* San Diego, 1996

Beverage, Richard E. *Hollywood Stars, 1926-1957.* Deacon Press, 1984

Beverage, Richard E. *The Angels, 1919-1957.* Deacon Press, 1981

The DiMaggio Albums, Putnam, 1989

Dobbins, Dick & Twichell, Jon. *Nuggets on the Diamond.* Woodford Press, 1994

Rogers, Chris. *Schools of Bay Area Baseball Players*, Hercules, CA, 1996

Snelling, Dennis. *The Pacific Coast League: A Statistical History, 1903-1957.* McFarland & Co., 1995

Spalding, John E. Sacramento Senators and Solons, Ag Press, 1995

Swank, William G. & Smith, James D. III. *This Was Paradise: Voices of the P.C.L. Padres 1936-1958.* Journal of San Diego History, 1995

Swank, Bill & Brandes, Ray. *The Pacific Coast League Padres.* San Diego, San Diego Historical Society, 1997. Two volumes: "Lane Field: The Early Years: 1936-1946," and "Lane Field: The Later Years: 1947-1957."

Waddingham, Gary. *The Seattle Rainiers, 1938-1942.* Writers Publishing Service Co., 1987.

INDEX

Page numbers for entries with photographs are printed in *italics*.

Turner, Tom, 88, 198
Turpin, Hal, 70, 92, 94, 96, 116
29th Service Command championship, 291
Twichell, Jon, 6
Uhalt, Bernie "Frenchy," 7, 23, 52, 55, 56, 136, 139, 149, *184*, 187, 194, *194*, 200, 202, 210, 217, 220, 221, 256
uniforms, evolution of, 116, 271, 286, 293, 304, *305*, 310, 311
Usher, Bob, 7, 154, 169, 259
Valenzuela, Joe, 290
Van Hewitt, Babe, 195
Van Robays, Maurice, 61, 63
Vancouver Mounties, 17, 48, 49, 60, 88, 95, *103*, 103-105, 107, 112, 117, *118*, 119, 137, 138, 251, 306, 307, 310
Vandenberg, Hy, 153
Vander Meer, Johnny, 201
Vanni, Edo, 7, 44, 46, 92, 93, 96-97, 116, 144, 173, 178, 184, 203, 224, *274*, 290
Vaughn Street Ball Park (Lucky Beaver Stadium), 29-31, *29*, *30*, 78, 144, 160, 203, 211, 292
Vergez, Johnny, 69, 194
Vernon Tigers, *11*, 13, *13*, 14, 84, 169, 216, 265
Vezilich, Lou, 7, 69-70, 118, 124, 137, 159, 191, 221, 222, 239-240, 287, 290, 294
Vico, George, 99, 101, 131
Vitt, Oscar, 82, *148*, 149, 191, 194, 199, 272, 275
Wade, Ben, 67, 164
Wade, Gale, 86
Waibel, Dick, 131, 132
Walker, Bill, 96
Walls, Lee, 68, 122
Walter, Bucky, 109
Waner, Lloyd, 314
Waner, Paul, 14, 314
Warner, Jackie, 83, 84, 87, 121, *147*
Waters, Fred, 261
Watkins, Bud, 7, 35, 130, 138, 160, 162, 164, 165, 166, 172, 178, 179, 186, 187, 201, 204, 205, 219, 227, 228, 229, 243-244, 251, 252, 278, 282, *282*, 300, *307*, 310
Webb, Del, 113
Webber, Les, 94, 96

Weiss, Bill, 8
Weiss, George, 208, 265, 270, 314
Welmaker, Roy, 294
Wendler, Paul, 313
Werle, Bill, 53, 54-55, 56, 88, 109, 111, 131, 132, 142, 159, 168, 172, 178, 188, 200, 222, *222*, 223, 276
West, Max, 36, 175, *181*, 223, *223*, 224
Western International League, 49, 203, 205, 221, 242, 236, 281, 308
Westgate Park, 38-39, *39*
Westlake, Jim, 7, 44, 88, 129, 131, 142, 159, 172, 188, 277, *277*, 301, *301*
Westlake, Wally, 56
White, Charlie, 104
White, Don, *213*
White, Joyner "JoJo," *10*, 164, 224, *224*, 248, 269, *269*
Wicker, Kemp, 70, 72, *291*
Widmar, Al, 99
Wietelmann, William "Whitey," 119, 196, 224, 225, *280*
Wight, Bill, 78, 79
Wild Horse of the Osage (see John "Pepper" Martin), 70, 137
Wilkie, Aldon, 96
Williams, Dib, 69
Williams, Ted, 8, 15, 70, 75-76, 112, 225, *225*, 226, 227, 266, 275
Williams, Woody, 293
Wilson, Artie, 125, 185, 214, 227, 228, 229, 294, *295*, 296, 310
Wilson, George "Icehouse," 221
Wilson, Jim, 220
Wise, Casey, 86, 87
Witig, Bob, 273
Woodall, Larry, 177, 184
Woodling, Gene, 57, *57*, 58, 61, 229, *229*
Woods, Pinky, 65, 66, 178
World War I, effects on league, 14-15
World War II, effects on league, 14-15, 50, 52, 91, 127, 142, 206, 212, 216, 276, 285, 288, 289, 290, 291, 292, 293, 306, 308
Worthington, Red, 69, *69*

Wrigley Field, 15, 23, 24, *25*, 25-27, *26*, 43, 83, 85, 88, 95, 136, 162, 181, 186, 199, 219, 234, 235, 236, 248, 249, 251, 260, 265, 271, 311, 314
Yankee Clipper, 313
Young, Del, 141
Young, George, *20*
Yount, Al, 285
Yuhas, Steve, 251
Zak, Frankie, 204
Zamloch, Carl, 270
Zernial, Gus, 126